GOD, DREAMS, AND REVELATION

Also by Morton Kelsey

Tongue Speaking
Encounter with God
Healing and Christianity
Myth, History and Faith
The Christian and the Supernatural
The Other Side of Silence
Can Christians Be Educated?
Christianity as Psychology
Sacrament of Sexuality
Psychology, Medicine and Christian Healing
Through Defeat to Victory
Reaching: The Journey to Fulfillment
The Soul and the Redwood Seed
The Cross
Discernment
Dreams
Tales to Tell
The Age of Miracles
Afterlife
Adventure Inward
Reaching for the Real
Caring
Transcend
Prophetic Ministry
Christo-Psychology
Companions on the Inner Way
Resurrection

Revised and Expanded Edition

GOD, DREAMS, and REVELATION

A Christian Interpretation of Dreams

Morton T. Kelsey

Augsburg • *Minneapolis*

To my wife Barbara,
co-worker and co-dreamer
for forty-seven years

GOD, DREAMS, AND REVELATION
A Christian Interpretation of Dreams
Revised and Expanded Edition

Cover design: Hilber Nelson

Library of Congress Cataloging-in-Publication Data

Kelsey, Morton T.
God, dreams, and revelation : a Christian interpretation of dreams / Morton T. Kelsey. — Rev. and expanded ed.
p. cm.
Includes bibliographical references and index.
ISBN 0-8066-2543-0 (alk. paper)
1. Dreams—Religious aspects—Christianity. I. Title.
BF1078.K38 1991
155.6'3'0882—dc20 91-9022
CIP

The paper used in this publication meets the minimum requirements of American National Standard for Information Sciences—Permanence of Paper for Printed Library Materials, ANSI Z329.48-1984. ∞™

Manufactured in the U.S.A. AF 9-2543

05 04 03 02 01 00 99 98 97 3 4 5 6 7 8

Contents

Preface

THIRTY YEARS AGO very little was written on the interpretation of dreams, and I could find no serious modern study of the religious interpretation of dreams. Within the Christian and Jewish communities, the dreams of the Old and New Testaments were ignored or viewed as valueless. In theological circles the subject of dreams and their interpretation was dead and buried. The dreams of Constantine, St. Martin of Tours, Patrick of Ireland, as well as those of the great Greek fathers of the church, were either ignored or ridiculed.

This lack of information presented me with a very real problem. Nearly midway into life I had come into a dark woods, into a blind alley. I found my way out of that stalemate through an understanding of dreams. I worked with a Jungian analyst, a Jew who had escaped from a Nazi concentration camp. He believed that the Holy One still spoke to both sleeping and waking human beings in dreams in the silence of the day and in the night. With his help I discovered that my dreams were wiser than my well-tuned rational mind and that they gave me warnings when I was in danger. They also described in symbols the disastrous situations in which I found myself. These strange messengers of the night also offered suggestions on how to find my way out of my lostness. When I followed these symbolic suggestions, much of the darkness lifted, and my situation no longer seemed hopeless. Many of my psychological and physical symptoms of distress disappeared.

In addition to all this, I found a very personal Being at the heart of reality who cared for me; my theological dry bones were covered with sinew and flesh. And then, as I continued to listen to my dreams, I experienced the risen Christ in a way that I had not thought possible. And last of all, I realized that the Holy One continued to knock on the doorway of my inner being in my dreams even when I paid no attention to them, and he would also be waiting for me when I deliberately opened the door of my soul to the risen Christ. Prayer, contemplation, and meditation, then, became real and necessary aspects of my life as I journeyed toward fulfillment and wholeness.

I wondered why the dream, which had opened up so many avenues for me, had been ignored. Was my experience unique, or did it belong to an important but forgotten Christian tradition? I knew that both the Old and New Testaments were full of dreams, so I read the Bible through again and was surprised at how many dreams I found. Then I began to study the Greek tradition of dream interpretation and discovered much more about dreams and visions than I had realized was there. This led me to study along with a friend, Paisley Roach, the writings of the leaders of the early Christian community. I could hardly believe how central the dream-vision was in early Christianity. About this time I was told by a certified psychological analyst that only certified psychologists had any business trying to interpret dreams. I already knew that religious people had been interpreting dreams for thousands of years. It seemed important to show that this psychological attitude was flawed and arrogant. People had been understanding their dreams long before psychology came on the scene. I started a ten-year study of the use of dreams as a part of religious practice in general and within the Christian community in particular. I was amazed at the amount of data I uncovered. This book presents the evidence that within Christianity the dream has been viewed as one of the most common ways that the Holy One communicates with human beings.

Over the centuries both the Jewish community and the Christian fellowship developed a consistent and sophisticated method of interpreting dreams based on their versions of Scripture. Both of these traditions believed that God was still reaching out to human beings in dreams and visions. Although this view of the dream continued into the eighteenth century, it was almost totally lost after that time as both traditions were first engulfed by a one-sided interpretation of Thomas Aquinas and then by the secular, agnostic scientism of the last two hundred years. When this book first appeared in 1968, it was the first careful historical study of Christian dream interpretation in nearly two hundred years. David Simpson's *Discourse on Dreams and Night Visions*, published in 1791, was the last serious religious discussion of dreams in Western Christianity until we came to modern times.

It is interesting to note that the Eastern Orthodox tradition, however, has never ceased to value the dream as a communication of the spiritual world and of the Divine. The great Russian novels clearly show the veneration in which the dream was held right into the twentieth century. The Orthodox churches were not influenced by Aquinas or Western materialism. In 1990 Joel Covitz's *Visions of the Night: A Study of Jewish Dream Interpretation* was published. It reveals the rich, deep, and wise tradition of the Jewish community—a tradition that was lost to it about the same time Christianity was shorn of a similar part of its heritage.

The tide has turned, in the West, and a veritable flood of books on dream interpretation has been published in the last fifteen years. Many small streams have converged to create a river of interest in dreams. Let us examine some of the smaller tributaries that have come together to create a revival of dream study.

I find a natural, almost instinctive, interest in dreams. Wherever I go I find few subjects that attract more interest. In Singapore I recently addressed a standing-room-only group of over seven hundred people, mostly Chinese Christians, on the subject. The Chinese are still in touch with their unconscious roots and have not been totally brainwashed by Western materialism. When people believe reality consists of nothing more than physical particles moving according to rational and mathematical principles, then the irrational, nonmaterial dream simply makes no sense and is not even worth investigating. Where this view of Western materialism has not become dominant, most people believe that dreams are significant.[1]

Freud's *The Interpretation of Dreams* was published in 1900. Although it did not catch on for many years, finally he and his disciples convinced most modern people that the unconscious was real. He believed that the dream was the royal road to knowing and understanding the unconscious. However, his explanation of how the dream could be interpreted left little place for any religious significance of dreams. He was followed by Carl Jung who had a much wider understanding of the nature of reality. Jung stated that our human psyche was only one part of a vast spiritual universe. He also perceived the effects of a purposeful nonphysical reality that was in touch with human beings. Both a spiritual realm and a purposeful aspect of it are revealed in our dreams according to Jung. A great number of the books listed in the bibliography have been written by Jung or followers of Jung who are interested in the religious implications of his thought. Another large sector have been written by people like me who have found their religious convictions strengthened both by Jung's worldview and his interpretation of dreams.

In the early twentieth century, at the same time that depth psychology emerged, a new kind of religious outpouring was felt simultaneously in many parts of the Christian community. It was often characterized by speaking in tongues and was sometimes related to dreams. The basic conviction common to this movement was that God could be known not only by inference but also by direct experience. When John XXIII asked for a new outpouring of the Holy Spirit as preparation for the Second Vatican Council, this movement became a part of the worldwide Roman Catholic church. It was no longer theologically irresponsible to believe that God touched human lives with many gifts, including dreams and visions. The religious climate was changing and becoming more open to its ancient tradition on the value of dreams. Over the last twenty years Paulist Press has been a leading publisher of significant books on the interpretation of dreams and visions.

Still another group of writers has been interested in the physiological and medical significance of dreams. Dr. William Dement discovered that most dreams are associated with Rapid Eye Movement (REM) sleep and its quite unique brain wave pattern. Even I could quickly identify this particular brain wave on the tracing of the electroencephalogram. An absence of this brain wave pattern and its accompanying dreams could cause severe physical and psychological problems. Sharon Begley summarized the recent development of this research in an article in the August 14, 1989, issue of *Newsweek.* In his book *The Dreaming Brain,* Dr. J. Allan Hobson has written that the brain-mind appears to be a meaning-making or meaning-seeking reality.[2] Another sector of the scientific community has studied a number of scientific discoveries prompted by dreams. R. A. Brown and R. G. Luckcock have reported their findings in *The Journal of Chemical Education.*[3] Charles Panati reviews the scientific evidence for extrasensory perception in his book *Supersenses* and concludes that the dream is the natural altered state of consciousness.

The Encyclopedia of Religion, edited by the late Mircea Eliade, has less information on dreams and visions than Hasting's *Encyclopedia of Religion and Ethics,* which was published nearly eighty years earlier. Few Christian theologians have dealt with the revelatory quality of dreams and visions. A remarkable exception is Henri Nouwen's recent description of a near-death experience in his book *Beyond the Mirror.* Modern men and women seldom take information seriously that is based on authority alone or because of its purely logical rationale. They are looking for experience, and the dream provides an experience of much beyond what is given by the five senses as well as sometimes revealing the structure of the physical world. I was invited to teach at the University of Notre Dame because the head of the Department of Education wanted some empirical evidence of the divine-human contact. He saw just such evidence in the first edition of this book.

Continuing to be interested in dreams and visions, I wrote *Dreams: A Way to Listen to God* as a simple handbook on dream interpretation. I have also included shorter accounts of how we can interpret our dreams in the following books: *Christo-Psychology; Companions on the Inner Way; Adventure Inward: Christian Growth Through Personal Journal Writing;* and *Reaching: The Journey to Fulfillment.* The last chapter of this book has been expanded to provide more detailed suggestions on how we can interpret our dreams. Neglecting the dream can separate us from one of the most significant ways that God reaches out to human beings.

For more than twenty years I have been lecturing on the Christian interpretation of dreams. I have found the same interest in this subject among the Black Zionists of Africa, among the sophisticated students at Notre Dame, among the Chinese in Singapore, among the people of Australia and New Zealand, and among religious communities in this country and abroad. My book *Dreams: A Way to Listen to God* was first published in German from a transcript of lectures that I gave in Germany. When I first preached on the subject of dreams at St. Luke's Episcopal Church, Monrovia, California, in the late 1950s, some twenty-five parishioners sought me out to tell me their significant dreams. Many sophisticated college students at Notre Dame found their agnostic materialism unsatisfactory as they kept a journal record of their dreams. They had no idea that such images, symbols, and stories came unsought into their consciousness as they dreamed. I have also watched many practicing Christians find deeper experiences of God's reality and providence as they have listened to their dreams and visions. When we find that our dreams bring us solutions to problems that our best intelligence could not solve, we often begin to take revelation and the Divine far more seriously. There are few better ways of learning to observe the hand of God in our lives than the persistent Christian practice of listening to these strange messengers of the night.

I call attention to three resources that can aid us in understanding difficult dreams. The *Dictionary of Symbols and Imagery* by Ad de Vries is the most sophisticated and helpful discussion of the many possible meanings conveyed by symbols. The index to the twenty volumes of Jung's *Collected Works* lists every dream symbol that Jung interpreted in his published works. These volumes are a mine of important and helpful interpretive material. *Dreams, Visions and Prophecies of Don Bosco,* for which I wrote a foreword, is the most complete account of the dreams of a significant modern Christian. This saint's educational and humanitarian ministry was directed by his dreams, and he was told by Pope Pius IX to keep a record of them. These dreams and visions occurred in the middle and latter part of the nineteenth century. His record compares with that of Gregory of Nazianzen, the fourth-century saint whom I describe later. The religious dream is still significant in our time.

I can mention only a few of those to whom I am grateful. Max Zeller first introduced me to the wisdom of the dream. Hilde Kirsch's magnificent intuitive grasp of dream symbolism helped me through many difficult places. I have known no one with a wider or deeper understanding of dream symbols than James Kirsch. My work with them was invaluable. When I studied one semester at the Jung Institute in Zürich, Switzerland, I worked with two analysts, Franz Ricklin and Barbara Hannah, at the same time and found that their interpretations of dreams followed the same pattern—a very confirmatory experience.

John Sanford, a friend for more than thirty years, has been one with whom I could discuss my dreams and every aspect of my life. His understanding of religious dream symbols and his knowledge of the unconscious has been a constant source of enlightenment. Three of the best books I know on the meaning of dream symbols are his books, *Dreams, God's Forgotten Language; The Kingdom Within;* and *Dreams and Healing*. Another friend of twenty years, Andrew Canale, has a natural intuitive knowledge of dreams and their meaning that I have found in few others and the compassion that is necessary in dealing with the human soul. His books *Masters of the Heart* and *The Human Jesus* reveal his wisdom. I have kept in touch with both Sanford and Canale regularly over the years, and they have contributed to this book and to others I have written.

This book would never have reached its present form without the research, editing, and typing of Paisley Roach. How does one express adequate gratitude for thirty years of collaboration on more than fifteen books and dozens of articles?

The first edition of this book was written between four and eight in the morning before a busy day at the church. My wife, Barbara, and my children supported a husband and father who was entirely too busy. Each member of my family has experienced times when important meanings have come through dreams.

Cindy Wesley helped me prepare the bibliography, the preface, and the revised portions of this edition.

Whenever I speak on the subject of dreams, people come to me with their dreams. I am again and again startled by the richness, the variety, the religious and Christian significance of the material that these people present to me. I am deeply grateful to those who have shared so much of their lives with me. The human psyche is a mysterious and wonderful creation. I am awed at the range and reach of the soul revealed in the dreams of nearly every human being whom I have come to know deeply.

August 1990
Gualala, California

Acknowledgments

Excerpts from *The Dialogues of Plato,* translated by Benjamin Jowett, copyright © 1953 Oxford University Press. Reprinted by permission of Oxford University Press.

Excerpts reprinted from *Hippocrates: Volume IV. Regimen,* translated by W. H. S. Jones (Cambridge, MA: Harvard University Press, 1931) by permission of the publishers and the Loeb Classical Library.

Excerpts from *The Ante-Nicene Fathers,* edited by Alexander Roberts and James Donaldson, published by the William B. Eerdmans Publishing Company, publisher of the American Reprint of the Edinburgh edition. Reprinted by permission.

Excerpts from *A Select Library of the Nicene and Post-Nicene Fathers,* second series. Reprinted by permission of the William B. Eerdmans Publishing Company.

Excerpts from *The "Summa Theologica"* by St. Thomas Aquinas, translated by the Fathers of the English Dominican Province. Reprinted by permission of Benziger Brothers, Inc.

Excerpts from *Reaching: The Journey to Fulfillment* by Morton Kelsey. Reprinted by permission of HarperCollins Publishers, Inc.

Excerpt from Linda Shimmin reprinted by permission of Linda Shimmin.

GOD, DREAMS, AND REVELATION

Chapter
1

Why Bother with Dreams?

FINDING A CHRISTIAN TODAY who pays religious attention to dreams is unusual; it is even unusual to find a Christian who knows what is meant by this. Modern students of theology do not seem to recognize the existence of a religious point of view on the subject, and ordinary churchgoers, for good reason, are either caught unawares or with a negative attitude by questions about the religious meaning of dreams. In our scientific era they may be quite well informed about the important new research on dreaming. They may even be among the few who pay attention to their own dreams. But in Western Christian society today there is no group, practically no voice at all, that would encourage these people to understand their dreams as a source of religious insight into life. Instead, most twentieth-century Christians simply assume that the idea of finding religious meaning or reality in dreams is a proven fallacy that went out with the Dark Ages, and they see no need to think about it again.

This attitude is strange for several reasons. In the first place, the early Christian church viewed the dream as one of the most significant and most important ways in which God revealed his will to human beings. Dreams were understood to give people access to a reality that was difficult to contact in any other way. Not only do we find this view in the Old Testament, in the New Testament, and in the church fathers up to the time of Aquinas, but it is the attitude of nearly every other major religion of the world. Instead of simply accepting that these people were all off the track, it would be wise to hear what they had to say. Some of the most astute observations about dreams were made by the early Christian thinkers, and this evidence has not been systematically presented to the Christian public in our time.

Then there is the important support for this traditional Christian view which comes from two sections of the healing profession, psychiatry and clinical psychology. In the writings and practice of both of them, the dream has come in for serious consideration. Here it is seen to reveal the autonomous psychic depth of human beings known as the unconscious, and to give hints about attitudes and forgotten contents that, when understood, can heal people of various forms of nervous and mental illness. As this science has developed, more and more medical professionals have come to see the dream as revealing not only the individual psyche, but a collective unconscious, a vast realm of experience that is beyond the individual's ken and which touches realities of a religious and spiritual nature. The work of Dr. C. G. Jung and his followers in particular has revealed the religious implications of the dream, while other medical research, recently reported in the *International Journal of Neuropsychiatry,* is revealing powers of human perception that would have been scoffed at twenty years ago. The influence of these ideas about the dream and the unconscious has also reached far beyond the individual into fields as diverse as modern drama, anthropology, and all kinds of criticism.

Besides this, the current research on sleep and dreaming has shown that dream experience is universal and that it occurs in a regular pattern night after night in spite of most people's total amnesia the next morning. People who are convinced that they never dream are simply not aware of what is going on below the level of consciousness. Studies have demonstrated conclusively that something is going on practically all the time in sleep, while about every ninety minutes a vivid dream occurs, absorbing almost every reaction of the dreamer completely. This work, which we will describe in a later chapter, is in progress at a number of the larger medical schools across the country.[1] It certainly does suggest how limited most Christians have been in their attitude toward dreams and dreaming.

Finally, it must be admitted that human beings are fascinated by dreams. Ever since there have been words to talk about them, these strange happenings in the night have been the subject of wonder and discussion wherever people have gathered to talk about their hopes and fears. Literature is full of dreams. Even in our day when dreams are sophisticatedly rejected, after a few cocktails people begin to talk about the funny dream they had the night before. Whenever I lecture and mention my interest in the serious study of dreams, the questions about them begin to come out, and people invariably show their hunger to talk and to hear more about the meaning of their dreams.

Recently I was visiting the rector of a large and smoothly organized urban parish, a man who admits that he probably has not been bothered by an illogical thought since the first grade. When I mentioned that I was doing some writing on dreams, he could not wait to tell me of the dream that had awakened him a few nights before with the picture of an accident so real that it terrified him. The next day he had learned to his horror of an accident that had claimed the life of a close friend that night. He was still shaken by the experience when I talked with him, and he expressed the hope that someone would write of dreams in religious tradition, for he could find no material relevant to his experience in modern religious writing.

Yet it is easy to forget how many people are concerned with dreams. The person in the street is concerned enough about them to keep a big business going in dream books, which can be found in the paperback racks of almost any newsstand or corner drugstore or in a bookstore's New Age section. There are a dozen or more of them in print at any one time,[2] and they are turned to by millions of people even though the basic idea in them is highly questionable. Most of them try to separate out specific dream images and assign meanings to them in order to foretell the future or to explain certain life situations, and this is quite contrary to the legitimate study of dreams. These books, however, are interesting because they do show how great the popular interest is in the subject and how persistent the popular "common-sense" attitude toward dreams continues to be.

Two Different Attitudes

In fact, it is easy for us in the twentieth Christian century to forget that there can be two very different attitudes about a topic like dreams. The church has been immersed in one point of view for nearly two hundred years, and its teaching and practice show little acquaintance with any other. So before we come to the questions "What is the meaning of the experience of dreaming?" and "What exactly is a dream?" we will explore these two attitudes to see how they differ. According to one attitude, dreaming is an essentially meaningless experience, not worth the time of day (or night). The other sees in dreaming a key to unlocking the secrets of human personality and even to finding meaning beyond the personal.

The most common attitude in our Western culture is the first one. In this way of thinking, the process of dreaming appears to be merely one more way in which the human nervous system reacts automatically to physical stimulus. A dream is "nothing but" the rehash of yesterday's half-forgotten experiences, thrown up mechanically, without any kind of order, before the sleeping consciousness. It is the feedback that occurs as consciousness rewinds itself for another day's activity. Vivid dreams, according to this point of view, result from some immediate stimulus, like dining late on too much pizza or overdoing the apple pie. Or they may be caused by something that happens during sleep, like hearing the siren on a passing fire truck or the creaking of a door, or by letting in too much night air. To be concerned about dreams then is silly; it simply indicates a superstitious mind or else too much interest in pretty poetry.

This attitude was very nearly universal among the intelligentsia of the eighteenth and nineteenth centuries, and it is still held among those influenced by the positivistic science of this period—in other words, by most of us. It was first suggested 2,200 years ago by Aristotle in three little papers on dreaming, although he did not go quite as far as the position I have outlined. It was supported by Cicero a few centuries later, but it had few other exponents in the ancient world.

Then, after centuries of unpopularity, this view was revived to become the accepted point of view. It might well have been correct, but it was accepted without ever being subjected to scientific inquiry. It was considered so obvious and certain that there was no need to spend time and effort verifying it or even to spell it out clearly. In fact, it is hard to find this view fully expressed in written form, although it is assumed in much of the writing in every field of our society. Nevertheless, there is nothing in the present careful research on dreaming that particularly supports this point of view. Instead, studies frequently give both analytical and empirical support to the other point of view, which finds dreams highly significant and meaningful.

The view that dreams are meaningful has been held in practically all other cultures. Indeed, wherever people have not been touched and influenced by our Western worldview with its belief that human beings are limited to sense experience and reason, the dream has been viewed as the chief medium through which nonphysical (or spiritual) powers and realities speak to people. Although some dreams were seen as meaningless or unintelligible, it was important for people to consider their dreams, for through them a person might obtain intimations of things to come or guidance and confrontation from greater than human powers. All of the major religions of humanity have held this view, and as we have shown, it has never been entirely displaced by the skeptical view of the scientific community.

Instead, modern support for the significance of dreams has come from a strange source. Beginning in 1900 with the publication of Freud's carefully documented *Interpretation of Dreams,* the subject has come under serious consideration by the medical profession. Their work, now that it is front-page news in our daily papers, makes it difficult to avoid the significance of dreams.

Freud first saw dreams as the royal road to understanding the submerged personality, that hidden nine-tenths of the human being which we now know as the unconscious. Jung, if his record can be believed, then followed by witnessing dreams that gave hints of the future and that offered suggestions superior to person's conscious knowledge and attitudes. Most recently, the studies of William Dement and others carrying on similar research have demonstrated that dreams are so important to mental health that simply being deprived of them may lead to mental breakdown and even psychosis. These findings, particularly those of Jung, certainly suggest that the dream—

which has been valued and interpreted by all religious groups, Christianity included—is worthy of serious religious consideration and may be one very important access to knowledge. It is true that in the past this understanding has sometimes led to an uncritical and superstitious concern with dreams. Still, their Christian interpretation is an ancient, long-held, and carefully considered religious practice. It deserves to be reviewed and evaluated.

The British writer J. B. Priestley has added a modern voice to this ancient understanding. Commenting on the importance of one early experiment with dreams, Priestly concluded:

> We are not—even though we might prefer to be—the slave of chronological time. We are, in this respect, more elaborate, more powerful, perhaps nobler creatures than we lately have taken ourselves to be. . . . Our lives are not contained within passing time, a single track along which we hurry to oblivion. We may not be immortal beings, but we are something better than creatures carried on that single time track to the slaughter house. We have a larger portion of Time—and more and stranger adventures with it—than conventional or positivist thought allows.[3]

As a matter of fact, when we are perfectly honest, we find that both of these attitudes toward dreams struggle with each other within most of us. Much of the time we are dominated by the attitude of the Enlightenment, which devalued dreams as meaningless, and we ignore them. Then there are times when we awake from a vivid dream strangely moved and troubled, hardly able to shake off its influence throughout the day. Or we read of Lincoln's premonitory dream of his assassination and wonder what it means that dreams sometimes have reality and significance like that. What meaning do dreams actually have? But first, exactly what *is* a dream?

What Is a Dream?

It may hardly seem necessary to define anything so familiar as a dream, but this is just where the fun begins; in defining the familiar we find how little we know. Most commonly the dream is understood as a succession of images present in the mind during sleep. And here, as Dr. Nathaniel Kleitman has shown in his book on *Sleep and Wakefulness*, we are getting into one of the least-understood of human activities. We cannot even say precisely what is meant by sleep except in terms of a certain kind of consciousness. According to Kleitman, it is best described as that period in which there is temporary cessation of the waking state. From time to time in this period anything from a single picture or figure to an elaborate story may be vividly perceived, which is in no sense a direct perception of the outer physical world. Normally this happens four or five times every night, and it can also be "watched" or predicted by keeping track of the sleeper's brain waves, eye movements, and certain other reactions. Indeed, vivid dreams seem to come spontaneously and to be almost as free from our ego control as our perception of the outside physical world.

This is not the only thing that happens in sleep, however. There is a second process closely related to dreaming which can be recalled best between the periods of vivid dreaming. This is a conceptual activity, or simply "thinking," and it is apparently continuous in the parts of the brain that do not go to sleep. Apparently most of the human brain goes right on working whether people are awake or asleep. Whether they are conscious of it or not, vivid dreaming takes over alternately with conceptual activity, which is constantly at work changing perceptions into thoughts and ideas. The psychologists call these processes "primary-process activity" and "secondary-process mentation," and together they produce the underlying psychic life that seems to be basic to conscious thinking and activity. It is no wonder that psychiatrists like Lawrence Kubie have pictured the mind as a magnificent computer, as if designed expressly to the scientist's specifications.[4]

It is from this level of psychic life that the sharp and discrete religious intuition probably comes. These intuitions, which are so valued and prized by religious people for direction and guidance, are in most cases the end product of this kind of secondary-process mentation turned upon religious contents. The religious intuition is therefore of the same nature as the dream (and also the vision) and shares in the same reality.

A third form of dream activity is the spontaneous image or vision that appears to a person in the borderland of wakefulness when a person is not sure whether he or she is awake or asleep. These dreams and visions—they are termed hypnagogic or hypnopompic, depending on whether the dreamer is falling asleep or waking up—are usually flash pictures focused on a single impression, but in some cases whole scenes, even fairly long stories may appear. At times these images coming on the edge of sleep can seem so tangible that dreamers really do not know whether they are awake or asleep, whether the images belong to the outside world or to the figures of the dream. And this leads us to the last and closely related form of dreaming.

This final form is the waking dream or vision, in which the dream images are intruded into the waking consciousness. The images themselves are apparently no different from those that can be experienced during sleep, except that they reach the field of consciousness during periods of wakefulness. They rise as spontaneously and with as little ego control as the dream, and in most cases the visions are involuntary. There are persons, however, who are able to cultivate the ability to look inward and observe this spontaneous rise of dream images because they wish to experience them. This experience, which we shall simply call fantasy, seems to be very similar to dreaming; in it the same kind of images and stories arise within one as in dreams. In other cultures and other times the experience of visions has been far more common than it is among most people today.[5] In fact, as we shall show, the people of other cultures have not distinguished as clearly between the dream and the vision as we do today.

There is an activity, however, that is common in our culture today that is not always so carefully distinguished. This is the daydream, which is different from fantasy. In daydreams the flow of images is not spontaneous but is directed by the conscious center of personality, the ego. The daydream can be created and also changed at will; fantasy, like the true dream or vision, cannot—it must be met with and observed. At times the line between fantasy and daydreams may be a fine one, but unless it is maintained, fantasy loses the spontaneous quality that is characteristic of both dreams and visions.

One other distinction must be kept quite clear because of the popular modern attitude toward visions. Most people are quite suspicious of visions.[6] They probably would not go so far as to find the dream dangerous or pathological. But even though the dream is so closely related to the vision that at times the two cannot be distinguished, visions are feared as a sign of mental disintegration. Most of us automatically assume that any person who experiences a vision must be mentally ill, that any vision must be hallucination. On the contrary, the real visionary experience is quite different from the hallucination in mental illness.

The true visionary experience is seldom mistaken for giving immediate knowledge of the physical world, but only of the "dream" world, or quite indirectly of the physical one. The vision is superimposed on the physical world, or the two may in some way be synchronized, but they can be distinguished just as easily as the dream is usually distinguished from the experience of waking. The hallucination in mental illness, on the other hand, is a definite sign of pathology. Here the same kind of content one finds in dreams arises spontaneously and is attributed directly to the world outside where it does not belong; the "dream" world is mistaken for the physical world of sense experience. People who are subject to this kind of hallucination have lost their ability to distinguish between these two kinds of experience, so they project their inner images directly upon the outer world. Because they cannot distinguish between the two, they are not able to deal adequately with either the outer world or the inner one. Their actions become inappropriate, and they are seen as sick. Such hallucination is a common occurrence in several kinds of mental illness where the ego under stress cannot distinguish between experiences that come to consciousness from psychic reality and those that come from the outer world.

As we shall see, it is not possible to discuss dreams without considering the thought process that goes on in sleep, the true vision, and fantasy as well. The four experiences are basically the same in nature. They are intrusions into consciousness of activities over which we have little if any conscious control.[7]

In the past these spontaneous images and thoughts, distinct from outer physical reality, have been valued as a sign of contact with religious reality. Whether the image was presented in sleep or in wakefulness, whether breaking in unexpectedly or sought and cultivated, it was understood to come from a different world, and nearly all religious groups everywhere have considered that the ability to observe and interpret these images was a religious gift. This was essentially the common Christian tradition from biblical times, through the church fathers, and up into the seventeenth century; in isolated instances it has continued to the present time. In this tradition dreams were significant because they revealed something beyond the human experience that gave purpose and meaning, or warning where spiritual disaster impended. In Jung's terminology dreams can express the reality of the collective unconscious, the objective psyche. In religious terms, they kept the people in touch with the purpose and direction of spiritual reality.

A Neglected Heritage

At the beginning of the twentieth century there was almost no educated person in our culture who seriously considered this way of looking at human experiences. After Freud had broken the ice with *The Interpretation of Dreams,* the reaction to his work showed how deeply men and women were concerned about this area of their lives. But even when the thaw set in and people of all kinds began to show an interest in the study of dreams, there was still one major group in our society with nothing to say about the subject. The Christian clergy, the theologians, are still silent, and this is surprising in itself in a group not noted for silence. It is more surprising when we realize how much there is about dreams in the Christian tradition from the Old Testament on. It is also surprising when we consider the attention given to other aspects of people's inner lives. There are groups in the church interested in spiritual healing, in speaking in tongues, in preparing for the imminent end of the world, and even in the ritual handling of snakes. But there is no significant group that suggests that Christians should listen to their own dreams or make any particular study of the many dreams in the Bible and in subsequent church history.

In fact, I cannot help recalling the consternation I caused in speaking to one group devoted to glossolalia when I said what I meant about dreams. It seemed to them that the idea of taking dreams seriously was much farther out than the practice of speaking in tongues. What does this mean? Is it just dreams that we have neglected, or is it something more?

The trouble is that the dream comes to people neither from the acceptable material world nor from their well-ordered and controllable reason. To value the spontaneously given content of the dream, one must postulate the reality of something in addition to the material world and human reason. Depth psychology calls this reality the unconscious; the early Christian community called it the spiritual world; and these two different terms may well refer to the same reality, as the Catholic theologian Victor White has suggested in *God and the Unconscious*. Unless people believe there is such a realm of reality that can be experienced, they will probably not look very hard for meaning beyond the material world.

Indeed, if there is no meaning beyond the physical world, then what place is there for dreams to come from except the meaningless tag ends of yesterday's sensation? Dreams are then simply the most common example of the human mind or psyche out of commission. They show how irrational its action can be when logical thinking is switched off. Of course, sense experience is also nonrational in the sense that it is not guided or directed by reason; it is just given. But since it is believed that there is a real physical world that is revealed in sense experience, this essential irrationality hardly bothers anyone except a few philosophers. The irrationality of dreams is something else again. So long as we "know" that there is no other world for them to reveal, no world beyond the material one, there is nothing else for dreams to show us but irrationality—our minds at their most irrational, illogical, in fact.

There is no controversy on dreams as there is with glossolalia; the subject hardly ever comes up for consideration. Except for a work by the Spanish Jesuit Pedro Meseguer, *The Secret of Dreams*, published in 1960, and a book published in 1966 in German by a friend, the Reverend John A. Sanford, I have found no serious religious study of the subject since David Simpson's *Discourse on Dreams and Night-Visions* in 1791. It is very difficult for modern people to imagine meaningful psychic reality beyond the grasp of their reason or their physical senses.

Indeed, the greatest thrust of mid-twentieth-century theology is to maintain unequivocally that people have no direct or immediate contact with any nonphysical or "supernatural" realm, and so there is no natural religion. This is the point of view of Bultmann, Bonhoeffer, Barth, Robinson, and a host of lesser lights.[8] These are strange bedfellows, but they all maintain this as almost axiomatic truth. I have more to say about this in the concluding chapter. Interestingly enough, they also all deny the value of depth psychology in human transformation. And this shows as much about the church's real reaction to Freud and Jung as all the furor over Freud's emphasis on sexuality as the prime human motive. Once it is admitted that people are ever changed in the psychologist's office, then the church is faced with a realm of reality that is neither physical nor rational and which is sometimes revealed in dreams. Once the dream is taken seriously, as something given, with religious significance, it is inevitable that there is some direct and "natural" contact with reality other than material or rational. Then the door is open and anything can happen, even transformation. Dreams may well be a doorway to religious significance and a new theology, as well as to the unconscious.

The Author's Point of View

My own belief in the value of dreams did not start from a consideration of their place in religious history. In fact, until my attention was drawn to them by the late Dr. C. G. Jung of Zurich and his followers, I had skipped over the references to dreams in the Bible, hardly recognizing that they were there. But as I worked with some of the followers of Jung, I observed that consideration of dreams was one factor in helping emotionally disturbed people become well. I saw more than one person obtain from his dreams the suggestions he needed to return to health. I then began to study the voluminous work of Jung. In his careful scientific studies, which admittedly are somewhat difficult to read,[9] his accumulated evidence with regard to the value and significance of dreams is overwhelming. I also found support for his evidence in my own experience. It was only after I was convinced from the practical and scientific point of view that dreams had meaning and purpose that I looked back into my Christian heritage. Only then did I find that what seemed so new was not very different from the ancient wisdom of the Christian church. For instance, in the fifth century of our era, Synesius of Cyrene, for one, had anticipated many of Jung's twentieth-century conclusions, and his views have been the basis of Eastern Orthodox interest in dreams ever since.

For the last three decades I have been closely associated with a group of clinical psychologists and psychiatrists. A religiously oriented psychological clinic was established at the church where I was rector. I have seen many people able to return to useful functioning and many others able to deal with their paralyzing religious doubts through a basically Jungian therapeutic practice, which involves an understanding of their dreams. In 1959 I visited Jung in Zurich, and when I told him of what we were doing, he expressed surprise that any present-day church would become so involved with his therapeutic methods. But he went on to say that the nearest approach to his treatment of patients was the classical Christian direction used in France in the nineteenth century by the "directors of conscience" there. During these last thirty years I have observed a mounting mass of evidence regarding the present-day religious value of dreams when they are seriously considered and symbolically understood.

The understanding of Jung also had a surprising effect on my own religious belief. I had been brought up in an environment that was predominantly rationalistic and materialistic, so I had doubted many of the experiences described in the New Testament. Along with the dreams and visions of the New Testament, I had rejected the stories of healing, as well as those of superhuman knowledge and wisdom. Then I discovered that this very careful and highly respected psychiatrist, with a fine record of healing his patients, had encountered many experiences in his patients similar to those described in the New Testament and had made his studies of them available to the public. Reinforced with such reliable current knowledge, I began to reread the New Testament with a greater open-mindedness, and I was surprised by what I found.

I then preached on certain neglected aspects of this New Testament heritage and was amazed to find that my parishioners would come to me, tentatively and half afraid, to tell me of significant dreams and visions and other similar experiences in their own lives. It was almost as if they had been waiting for someone to open up the New Testament so that they could take their own experiences seriously. With this background I began a study of the dreams and visions of our Christian heritage and their possible value for the present-day Christian.

In my own counseling I have used much the same approach. Besides having a regular schedule in the church, for several years I have worked as a licensed marriage, family, and child counselor, and have also served as a management consultant in industry. Particularly with one firm I have found how vitally helpful this Jungian and essentially religious point of view can be in the management process as people become convinced of the value of listening to dreams.

During this time I have been surrounded by some tremendous dreamers who have had some unusual experiences. One man dreamed the name of a publisher interested in my work before even I had access to the information, and he later brought me a dream about the contents of a letter that only I and the distant sender had actually read. In another strange instance a friend found that she had dreamed up the whereabouts of a missing person, a relative whose disappearance had been worrying her family for some time. My study of Jung made it possible to understand experiences like these in a context of religious reality.

Apparently the understanding of dreams formed an essential part of our Christian heritage, and I found that the dream, properly understood, was believed to give religious insight, wisdom, and direction. I began to see that if dreams are accepted as religiously significant, the reality and accessibility of the spiritual, the nonphysical world, is made quite probable. This then necessitates a theology that envisions some direct contact with other than physical reality. Within such a framework the gifts of the Spirit mentioned by Paul in 1 Corinthians 12 no longer appear absurd. Instead, they are one of the crowning evidences of the action of spiritual reality in the life of human beings, and the dream is one of these evidences, a common and natural one. The sheer givenness of the religiously significant dream removes the current doubt that something other than physical reality can invade consciousness directly. If this is true, then the whole charismatic life of the church needs to be considered more seriously from a practical and theological point of view.

I will try to demonstrate this rather novel thesis in several ways. First, I will give a historical survey of the value that has been placed on dreams within the Judeo-Christian heritage, turning first to the Old Testament and Apocrypha and the beliefs of the later Hebrews about dreams and visions. Next I will look at the Greeks, those ancients whom we revere for having so far rid themselves of illusion, to see if their beliefs about dreams were significantly different from those of the Hebrews. With this background, I will take up the dreams and visions of the New Testament. Then, turning to the first centuries of the church's life, I will reveal a surprisingly sophisticated and critical evaluation of dreams by the monumental early Fathers of the church. I will follow this concern of the church, its earnest regard for this aspect of human life, up through the beginnings of our modern scientific era into the present time. Dreams, although intellectually dispossessed from people's lives, are still at work where they live and move.

My interest then leads to the most recent times, to the scientific findings of certain psychological schools and the empirical support that is currently coming from medical research, following the lead of Dr. William Dement. I will then consider the current theological devaluation of dreams, presenting instead an approach in which they have a significant place. From this I will draw my concluding suggestions as to what attitude toward dreams and visions is religiously possible and advisable for modern Christians. A practical list of ways we can use and understand our dreams winds up the discussion.

It is not my intent to present either a treatise on the practical interpretation of dreams or an exhaustive analysis of the dream and visionary material of the Bible or the early church. My purpose is rather to open a door, first by showing how far we have neglected Christian teaching on this subject, and then by making it clear that this teaching is neither as archaic or illusory as most present-day Christians seem to believe. Indeed, this material has important implications for current Christian life and theology.

My purpose is to show how important the dream has been in the Christian view of revelation. In today's changing world, the dream can once again bring home to Christians the reality of a world of spiritual experience that is closer to human beings than most modern people realize. They can find that God still speaks to men and women through this kind of experience.

Once modern Christians admit this possibility and take the trouble to record and consider their dreams, they find new horizons opening up. Others have found direction and guidance in this way—people like Paul, Augustine, and here and there a modern saint or leader. As one learns how such direction was given, he or she begins to discover how dreams can be understood symbolically and acted on. Unsuspected avenues of relation to God and spiritual reality are revealed, which open an exciting new dimension to Christian life and experience. It then takes only persistence and imagination to explore the religious significance of dreams and discover how close God is to our lives. This Christian understanding of revelation even suggests that we may be turning our backs on God when we do not listen to our dreams.

The person who has found this kind of meaning in dreams may wish to study their symbolism in greater depth. An important work on this subject has been written by my friend John Sanford, who is a fellow student of dreams and their Christian meaning. His book *Dreams: God's Forgotten Language* provides an excellent supplement to the material we shall consider. In the preface I have listed several books of my own that give additional information on the religious interpretation of dreams. The ideas presented in these two books can open people to a new realm of Christian living. When grace and providence are experienced through dreams, they become very real indeed. This experience may well be crucial for both Christian theology and Christian life.

Chapter
2

The Dreams of the Hebrews and Other Ancient Peoples

DURING THE LAST CENTURY no book has been studied more carefully or more critically than the Bible. In the process, opinions about its historical accuracy have ranged all the way from literal acceptance of every word to complete rejection of its authenticity. But now that this body of literature, particularly the Hebrew portions, has been analyzed by several generations of scholars, there is general agreement among those working in the field. Today it is concluded essentially without question that the Old Testament contains authoritative traditions that date back to at least 1800 B.C. This book provides a record of the history and travail, religious insights and musings, the moral and ritualistic laws of these people from that time until the first or second century before Christ.

Nearly every aspect of this tradition has been studied exhaustively by competent scholars except for the dreams and visions and associated phenomena of the Old Testament and the New. This is surprising when we consider that visions and dreams, which are often essential to the narrative, are scattered throughout the Old Testament from Genesis to Zechariah. Indeed, the Old Testament presents a clear and consistent theory about the value of dreams and visions as a medium of revelation. It provides, sometimes implicitly, sometimes expressed and examined explicitly, one of the oldest and historically most continuous examples of this belief about dreams that is available to us today.

Yet the dreams of the Old Testament have been largely ignored by the standard biblical studies of the last hundred years. As *The Interpreter's Bible* so casually puts it, "The development of textual criticism . . . not only destroyed belief in verbal inspiration but also opened the way to an empirical investigation" of things like dates and authorship. As historical facts became more and more interesting, the idea that anything important in the Bible could have been revealed in dreams was gradually lost. In Hastings' *Dictionary of the Bible*,[1] for instance, the subject is introduced gingerly and then dismissed as quietly and decently as one wishes one could an embarrassing relative. *The Interpreter's Bible* itself contains no serious consideration of the subject throughout its twelve volumes, while *The Interpreter's Dictionary of the Bible* offers just over one page for both dreams and visions out of nearly four thousand pages of other materials. Other commentaries show the same lack of interest.

Since the modern research into dreams suggests that they may have a far greater significance than has been considered during the past few centuries, it would seem advisable to take a fresh look at this tradition in the Old Testament to see what is actually there. Therefore, in spite of the professional prejudices, let us look first at the theory of dreams and visions which it contains and the Hebrew words it uses to describe these experiences. With this key to understanding the materials that follow, we shall then look at the dream experiences in the historical narrative, the prophetic literature, and the "writings." After following the same ideas as they occur in the Apocrypha and in later Jewish tradition, we shall conclude by showing that this very important aspect of their tradition was far from unique among the Hebrews.

The Hebrew Theory of Dreams

Throughout the Old Testament we find the belief that Yahweh is concerned with human beings and makes direct contact with them in order to give them direction and guidance. Dream and vision experiences were one medium of this communication. Through this means, which was not subject to ego control, God brought people special knowledge of the world around them and also knowledge of the divine reality and will. Dreams and visions were an avenue of revelation that Yahweh continued to use because from time to time they were the best, or even the only way, he could make connection. Because of the importance of dreams, false prophets and charlatans sometimes manufactured false dreams and false interpretations of dreams in order to meet their own needs or the needs of those who hired them. And so the Bible does not express only reverence for dreams; it also offers critical evaluation of them so that people will not be duped by false religions and false religious leaders.

Cruden's *Complete Concordance* also makes this significant statement: "As the belief in dreams was generally connected with consultation of idol-priests, or those pretending to deal in magic, the Israelites were warned against dealing with these. But God revealed his will frequently in dreams, and there were those who could explain them."

Thus there is an open attitude toward dreams in the Old Testament and at the same time a more critical and less superstitious one than is found in any other ancient culture. Dreams and visions are spoken of as actual events, encounters that happen to men and women and make a difference in their lives. But these experiences can also be simulated, and so they must be examined carefully and by the right people.

The way people use language reveals a great deal about the way they look at the world about them. In the same way, the Hebrew expressions for dream experiences reveal much of their attitude toward the value of these nonphysical intrusions into human consciousness.

In the first place, there is no clear-cut distinction between the dream and the vision in the Hebrew language; where moderns see a great gulf of separation, the Hebrews did not. Although the two experiences were sometimes distinguished, more often they were seen as aspects of the same basic perception of reality, different sides of the same encounter from beyond the world of sense experience. The word *dream* (*chalom,* or the verb *chalam*) is related to the Aramaic and Hebrew verb "to be made healthy or strong." The dream is spoken of almost as if this were the form of the experience whose content comes through as a vision. The dream then is the mode or expression of the experience, while the vision is the content, the substance of what is seen or visualized or experienced. Dreams are the normal way to receive such experiences, but the same content can break through in waking moments, and this can happen either out of the blue or as a person turns to this reality for direction. This same overlapping of meaning is also found in the Greek of the New Testament.

We find many examples in which a dream experience is referred to as a vision of the night, as in 1 Samuel 3:15; Job 20:8; Isaiah 29:7; and Daniel 2:19 and 7:2. There are also several places in which dreams and visions are equated through the characteristic parallelism of Hebrew style (Num. 12:6; Job 20:8). On the other hand, the visions of Zechariah are simply introduced by the statement: "In the night I saw . . ." (1:8). When the Old Testament speaks of visions, one cannot be sure by modern standards that this does not signify those that occur in the night and are therefore actually what we would call dreams. And when the Hebrew does speak of a dream, this may carry more the idea of givenness and religious authority that we have come to associate with visions. It is really impossible to discuss the dreams of the Old Testament without describing the visions also. They are of one piece in the Hebrew.

Technically, of course, a vision is simply a visual image, something seen that is not an immediate perception of any outer physical object. The words *chazon, marah,* and their several variations all come from two common Hebrew verbs meaning "to see." But closely associated with visions is the auditory experience that is described as listening to God or speaking with him, in which someone beyond one's ordinary self appears to speak to the individual in his or her own language. Many people know of this experience in dreams when there is a voice and no visual image at all. Sometimes, instead of being the object to which the speaking is directed, the individual becomes the subject through which the speaking is done. This is prophecy if the power speaking is God.

Since it is not too uncommon for people to talk in their sleep or to perform somnambulistic actions, this idea of prophecy is actually strange only because so few of us believe that there is any reality beyond the physical that could make such contact with the individual. In fact, glossolalia in the New Testament is the same experience except that the individual speaks in an unknown language. While our interest will be limited to instances in which voices were heard in dreams or in connection with visual images, it must not be forgotten that the auditory experience alone, when it comes autonomously, is of the same nature as dreams and visions. I will not discuss these auditory experiences here, primarily because there are so many examples that they would require a book in themselves, but also because dreams and visions give a clearer picture of the process by which autonomous materials intrude into our consciousness.

Probably the most common vision described in the Old Testament is the experience of an angel. In spite of the modern fear that the Bible may be talking nonsense when it describes the appearance of angels, they were seldom viewed as concretized "pieces" of spirituality, materializing and then disappearing into thin air. It is true that there are stories in the early chapters of the Old Testament in which angels appear as actual human beings, but these are greatly overshadowed by the passages in which they are not viewed in this way. Later authors left no doubt about their understanding that angelic beings have reality only as characters in visionary experiences. This in no way devalues experiences in which one comes into relationship with these nonphysical entities.

The word for angel, *malak*, or "messenger," can be used either for an ordinary human messenger or to indicate a spiritual messenger of God. There are several dozen passages in which the word is used in this latter sense, and these passages, where the messenger was clearly more than human, show four different ways in which angels were viewed. First, the angel, which is understood to be acting as God's agent, is actually seen in a visionary experience or dream, as in Genesis 22:11; Exodus 3:2; Numbers 22:22; Judges 6:11; and Zechariah 1:9. This meaning is similar to the ancient Greek understanding of dreams in which heroes or gods appeared, which we shall discuss in the next chapter. In other passages the angel is viewed as the impersonal instrument of God, carrying out God's will for weal or woe. In this sense they are more hearkened to than experienced, as in Exodus 14:19; 23:20; 2 Samuel 24:16; 2 Kings 19:35. Third, the angel occasionally appears as a concrete physical being, materializing out of spiritual reality, who drinks and eats and converses with people (Gen. 19:1, 15). These are the passages that embarrass the modern reader. Finally, the idea of an angel dealing with people is used as a substitute for God by those authors who did not speak of God's dealing directly with human beings. In these passages the words for God and angel are practically interchangeable.

The two Hebrew words that are translated by our word *seer* show clearly how highly the Hebrews valued those who could see visions. They are *chozeh* and *roeh*, which are derived from Hebrew words for perceiving, or seeing, the same roots from which the Hebrew words for visions are derived. "The see-er" is an excellent translation for either of these Hebrew words. The see-er is another name for a prophet. That person is the one who perceives more than just the space-time world. Samuel was called a seer (1 Chron. 29:29), and 1 Samuel 9:9 states that a prophet was formerly called a seer. One of the earliest specific references is in 2 Samuel, in which "the word of the LORD came to the prophet Gad, David's seer" (24:11).

In several places in the books of prophecy, as well as in the books of history, the prophet is clearly identified as a seer. Amos is called a seer (7:12), while Isaiah equates the prophet and the seer (29:10), as does Micah in 3:6-7. The latest of these references may well be Isaiah 30:10, which speaks of a rebellious people "who say to the seers, 'Do not see'; and to the prophets, 'Do not prophesy to us what is right. . . .' " Many scholars believe that these words were written very close to the time of Jesus' birth. Here and in other places it is clear that the main task of the seer was to see and understand the visionary realities—to know angels, to hear God's voice, and to see visions.

All of these experiences, then—talking with God, angel, dream, vision, prophecy—express the same basic encounter with some reality that is not physical, and the most common of them is the dream experience. The majority of the Old Testament authors took care to express their belief—as Plato did in later times—that human beings were in contact with two realities, a physical world and a nonphysical one which they called spiritual. The contact they described with this second reality was made directly through these experiences.

As we look at the Old Testament record, we shall not try to distinguish the various strands of Hebrew authorship. It is obvious that certain writers were more concerned with dream experience than others, but the same reverence for the nonphysical breakthrough is found in all of the different strands. It is even more obvious that this reverence was carefully preserved by the later writers. As these people turned to the job of compiling a complete and consecutive story, they approached the earlier records with skill and understanding. Their history, their very approach to life, had been borne out of the visions given to them, and these experiences were not only kept alive in memory; they were expected to continue.

The Great Dreamers—the Patriarchs

The first description of a dream in the Old Testament occurs in the same passage with the first of the references to visions. In Genesis 15:1 Yahweh appeared to Abram in a vision (*machazeh*) to assure him of a great future and to tell him that his own offspring would be the ones to share in it. Abram believed. He made his sacrifice, and then "as the sun was going down, a deep sleep fell upon Abram, and a deep and terrifying darkness descended upon him" (v. 12). God spoke again, this time of the tribulation that would come before the vision was fulfilled, and then there appeared "a smoking fire pot and a flaming torch," which passed between the pieces of the sacrifice (v. 17). This ceremony of covenant which Abram saw in his vision of the night was a ritual used for making agreements between people. In practice the contracting parties sacrificed an animal and cut it in half; then, if they were equals, both walked between the pieces of the carcass, demonstrating their willingness to be bound by the agreement or else to suffer the same treatment. Thus in a numinous and mysterious experience that touched a person to the depth, God turned his promise to Abram into the Covenant, the effective contract between God and human beings.

For Abram this was the verification of the reality of his call from Ur, as genuine an experience of the Holy One as one will find in religious literature. Symbolism like this recurs wherever human beings take note of their religious experiences. Nor was it the only encounter for these people. Hagar, the Egyptian servant, was twice comforted by the angel of God and was helped to bear Abram's child who was to grow up in the wilderness (Gen. 16:7; 21:17). After Hagar's flight three angels appeared to both Abraham and Sarah (whose names were now changed). These were described as angels and also as two men accompanying the Lord himself, who became known only when Sarah's thoughts were read. In spite of Sarah's down-to-earth disbelief, she was to bear a child. Abraham then learned of the angels' terrible errand and was able to intercede for his cousin Lot (Gen. 18, 19). Again, it was through an angel that Abraham's eyes were opened as he was about to sacrifice Isaac. Of that place—where the angel spoke and Abraham looked up to see a ram caught in the thicket and understood the test to which God had put him—it was said, "On Yahweh's mountain there is vision"[2] (22:11-14). Not only was Abraham a seer in the technical sense, but King Abimelech also learned through a clairvoyant dream the true identity of Sarah, whom he had taken for his concubine (20:3).

While Isaac was not recorded as being much of a dreamer, some of the greatest moments in his younger son's life were marked by dreams. As Jacob fled from Esau, whose birthright he had stolen, and stopped for the night to sleep on the rocky ground, he dreamed of a ladder from earth to heaven with angels ascending and descending. The Lord stood above and reiterated the promise given to Abraham in his vision. So deeply moved was Jacob, that he awoke and said, "Surely the LORD is in this place—and I did not know it!" (Gen. 28:11-22). In accordance with the idea of incubation common in these cultures,[3] he felt that the place in which he had dreamed such a dream was the very "gate of heaven" (v. 17). He vowed that if God would remain with him, that place at Bethel would become a sanctuary, and he would give to God a tithe of all he had. To Jacob this experience was no mere dream; it was a religious experience of the most profound kind, one which had the extraordinary result of establishing the idea of tithing, a practice central to the very heart of Judaism.

Jacob spent twenty patient years in his new home with Laban. Then he was given God's help in two dreams to leave his possessive father-in-law peacefully and with wives and wealth. In the first, which Jacob interpreted well, he saw the spotted he-goats mate with the flock and was given God's assurance that he should take the increase and return to the land of his birth (Gen. 31:10-13). The second dream was Laban's, in which God warned him on the night before he overtook the fleeing families not to press matters with Jacob, either for good or bad (v. 24).

The magnificent passage which then follows, the story of Jacob's wrestling through the night with his unknown adversary to win both a blessing and a name, strongly suggests a dream or vision as its origin (Gen. 32:24-32). Jacob had briefly encountered the angels of God after Laban turned back (v. 2), and then he had faced all the practical details of his meeting with Esau. There is a realism about his night in the desert alone, yet not alone, which recalls other descriptions of the dark night of the soul. Later biblical authors referring to this experience held that Jacob wrestled with an angel (Hos. 12:4).

And Jacob, now become Israel, was an old man before another of his dreams was recorded. For at this point his favorite son arose to stand out among all the patriarchs as both dreamer and interpreter of dreams. In good measure it was just this about Joseph that brought on him the hatred of his brothers. Joseph did not dream directly of God, but symbolically of his brothers' sheaves bowing down before his sheaf, and of the sun and moon and eleven stars doing obeisance before him (Gen. 37:5-11). And his naivete in telling his dreams set the scene for the action that followed. Sold into Egypt as a slave, Joseph's similar frankness with Potiphar's wife landed him in an Egyptian prison. Here he was consulted by Pharaoh's erring butler and baker about their own dreams, which they could not interpret. "Do not interpretations belong to God?" Joseph asked, and correctly foretold the future (40:5ff.). Again, when Pharaoh himself was troubled by dreams, the butler remembered the interpreter back in prison. This time Joseph's wise interpretations, explaining the fat and lean cows and the full and thin ears of grain, were rewarded directly, and he was placed in a position of authority over Egypt (41:1ff). These dreams are central to the whole story of Joseph and his brothers.

Finally, when Jacob heard that his son Joseph was alive, he believed it only after God again appeared to him in a vision of the night with reassurance (46:2-4). And Jacob went down to Egypt knowing that God would go with him and in time would bring his people forth. Indeed, if there is any reality in this tradition of the patriarchs, which many modern scholars have come to view with great respect, it is certainly inseparable from the idea that dreams and visions are expressions of human contact with some reality beyond the physical world.

Moses and the Dark Speech of God

While dreams were not emphasized in the account of Moses, this aspect was far from forgotten. The story of the Exodus essentially begins with Moses' visionary experience of the burning bush and the angel, a content that recurs with authority in the dreams of people today (Exod. 3:1-22). Moses was one, however, with whom it was believed that God spoke face to face and so did not use his dark and parabolic speech of dreams and visions with which he communicated to most people. The passage in Numbers that makes this clear (12:6) gives both a deep insight into the Hebrews' reverence for Moses and an understanding of their attitude toward dreams. The Lord was about to become angry with those who questioned Moses, and he said:

> "Hear my words: When there are prophets among you, I the LORD make myself known to them in visions; I speak to them in dreams. Not so with my servant Moses: he is entrusted with all my house. With him I speak face to face—clearly, not in riddles; and he beholds the form of the LORD. Why then were you not afraid to speak against my servant Moses?"

There are many references throughout the time of the Exodus to the angels of the Lord, who drove back the Red Sea and went before the people of Israel as their protection and guide (Exod. 14:19; 23:20; 32:34; 33:2; Num. 20:16). The repeated experience of the pillar of cloud also has a visionary quality, and the appearance of the pillar to Miriam and Aaron was undoubtedly a vision (Num. 12:5).

Perhaps some of us would like to forget that Balaam's ass saw a vision, but this was probably not the first nor the last time an ass has taken the lead. It tallies with the popular belief that animals are sometimes more aware of spiritual realities than their more rationally conscious masters. But the Balaam account is also interesting for the fact that God's message was given directly to a stranger (as it had been to Abimelech) and because it is allowed that he could be conquered by it. When Balaam the seer was approached by the princes of Moab to deliver a curse on Israel, God's word came to him in the night. But Balaam apparently rejected God's message, for he was on his way to Moab when an angel of God appeared first to his ass and then to him. He was shaken, and he set his face toward the wilderness and delivered the truth that he saw instead of a curse (Num. 22:21-40). After this brief contact it is not recorded whether the power of God continued in this way in Balaam's life. The years of conquest followed, and except for the intervening discussion in Deuteronomy which we will take up later, not much consideration was given to dream experiences. Even when the commander of the Lord's army appeared to Joshua, the experience was taken at face value.

But following the account of Joshua's period, we come upon the stories of the book of Judges, which continue the spirit of the earlier biblical narrative. Here angels and signs abound, and the direction of the Lord, which elsewhere had been asked for directly, was sought through them, often in experiences that were clearly visionary. Gideon found his destiny when an angel appeared to him (6:11), while the birth of Samson was announced by the appearance of an angel to both Manoah and his wife (13:2). In Judges 7:13-14 it was a dream that determined Gideon's defeat of the Midianites; in the night the Lord told him to get up and go spy on the enemy camp and he would hear something to strengthen his hand. As Gideon was following these instructions, he overheard an enemy soldier telling his dream of a cake of barley bread that fell on their tent and crushed it. "This is no other than the sword of Gideon," the man's comrade interpreted. Hearing these words, Gideon worshiped, and then he set forth to defeat the enemy.

In the next books we find once again a more careful depiction of the reverence for dreams and visions. The story of Samuel opens with the magnificent description of the child's dream, in which the Lord speaks to him, and the old priest clearly recognizes the action of God (1 Sam. 3:1-18). In this vision of the night, with so many of the signs of the troublesome dreams that come to people today, it is difficult for the child to distinguish between outer reality and the visionary experience. Then he learns that the house of Eli will be overthrown, and he is afraid to tell the dream. Up to this time, we are told, the word of the Lord had been rare in Israel; there was no open vision, or more literally, "no vision breaking through." This vision-dream of Samuel's opened up a new era, and in several places Samuel is described simply as the seer, the one who sees beyond ordinary things.

The Dreams of the Great Kings

In some ways even more striking for us is the casual way in which the statement of Saul in his distress is recorded in the text. Samuel was dead, so Saul could no longer seek his advice. Saul saw his enemies coming upon him, and when he "inquired of the LORD, the LORD did not answer him, not by dreams, or by Urim, or by prophets" (1 Sam. 28:6). Since Saul had lost his guidance, he went to the medium of Endor to ask her to bring forth the spirit of Samuel. Confronting the ghost of Samuel—in itself a visionary experience—Saul asked: "I am in great distress, for the Philistines are warring against me, and God has turned away from me and answers me no more, either by prophets or by dreams; so I have summoned you to tell me what I should do" (v. 15). So desperate was Saul's condition that he broke his own law and consulted with a medium. The distress of Saul at not dreaming is paralleled among some groups of indigenous people who lose their power when they can no longer dream big dreams. It means to them that the gods have left them, and Saul's tragic state is repeated in the adjustment they face.

David was not left in the lurch by his prophets as was Saul. The word of the Lord came to Nathan the prophet in the night with instructions for David that he should not build the temple but should leave it for his heir (2 Sam. 7:4-17; 1 Chron. 17:3-15). In accordance with this vision or dream, Nathan spoke and David obeyed. Later, when the Lord became angry with David's actions and Gad prophesied the people's destruction, David himself saw the angel of the Lord and was given the chance to repent and stay the Lord's hand (2 Sam. 24:16; 1 Chron. 21:15ff.).

As for Solomon, though we might wonder about his dreaming, we find that he was as reverent about it as any of his predecessors. His reputed wisdom stemmed from a dream he had at Gibeon in which the Lord appeared to him by night and said: "Ask what I should give you" (1 Kings 3:5). And in this experience, which sounds very much like incubation, Solomon asked for an understanding mind and received it. Then he went to Jerusalem to make offerings and to hold a feast for all his servants (vv. 6-15). God had come to him and acted; what Solomon did with his wisdom was another part of the story.

After Solomon had finished building the temple, God appeared to him a second time, "as he had appeared to him at Gibeon" (1 Kings 9:2). In the same kind of dream experience he was given the promise of God's protection to his house if he would follow only Yahweh. Solomon saw and listened. Although he evidently forgot what he experienced, for him, as for Saul and David, the dream itself was an experience of contact with more than human knowledge. To be deprived of dreams could be a catastrophe.

But as the kings of Israel got into more and more trouble, the record of their own dreams ceased. Instead, we are told that the word of the Lord came to Elijah and to Elisha, and marvelous things happened. After Elijah had fled from Jezebel's outburst, an angel came and touched him while he was sleeping to show that he was taken care of in the wilderness, and he was comforted (1 Kings 19:5). His experience of earthquake, fire, and still small voice in the cave there at Horeb also had the quality of a numinous vision (vv. 11-18). Again after Ahab's death an angel of the Lord came to Elijah to direct him in his dealings with the new king in Samaria (2 Kings 1:3-4, 15). The wonderful things that Elijah did were told right up to the end of his life. And then in a tremendous visionary experience of the assumption of the prophet, Elisha fell heir to the same spirit and power (2:9-12). As Elijah was taken up by a whirlwind, Elisha saw the horses and chariots of fire, just as they were later seen by the young man who served him (6:17). At that time, when they were surrounded by the forces of the Syrian king, God opened the eyes of Elisha's servant to the same numinous vision of the spiritual power that was available to Elisha. Wonderful things continued to be told about Elisha.

After Elisha's death there was one more vision experience recorded in the biblical books of history: when the angel of the Lord went forth and destroyed Sennacherib's army before Jerusalem (2 Kings 19:35; Isa. 37:36). This incident involved the same destroying aspect of angels that David had once seen turned on his own people. With this, the dream experiences in the historical portion of the Old Testament come to an end. But right up to the end of 2 Chronicles the prophets continued to be seen as seers.[4] These men were important politically and religiously because they were understood to have the power to see beyond the immediate world.

The Prophetic Tradition and Deuteronomy

There are not many religious leaders who have had as much impact on the history and religious life of humankind as the prophets who thrived in Israel from the end of this period (the eighth century B.C.) through the sixth century B.C. These people have been universally admired for their insight into the moral nature of God and their religious endeavor, and it was among them that dreams were first openly valued in the Old Testament. Up to this time dream experiences had been recorded and acted upon, and not analyzed.But now the prophets, who all describe the inspiration of some kind of dreamlike experience, began to voice real concern for distinguishing the true dreamer from the false dreamer, the genuine interpreter from the false interpreter, and the true prophet from the false prophet. They considered it one of the specific tasks of the prophet to be open in dreams and visions to intrusions of another realm of reality and to be able to interpret them correctly.

The writings of these prophets agree in expressing, in one way or another, the basic idea that when the Spirit of God is poured upon people, "your sons and your daughters shall prophesy, your old men shall dream dreams, and your young men shall see visions" (Joel 2:28).

When God poured out his Spirit at Pentecost, the authors of the New Testament pointed back to the significance of this passage. But when God is not with his people, the prophets maintain with Saul that "disaster comes upon disaster, rumor follows rumor; they shall keep seeking a vision from the prophet; instruction shall perish from the priest, and counsel from the elders" (Ezek. 7:26).

The same basic thought is contained in Isaiah 29:10; 32:15; Jeremiah 31:34; Lamentations 2:9; Ezekiel 39:29; and Micah 3:5-8. Thus if life was not to be all bitter, it was essential that there be people who were open to something beyond the physical and that there be those who could distinguish the true vision and true dream from the false, the true prophecy from the false. In these passages, dream, vision, and prophecy are obviously inextricably linked together, as I suggested in the introduction to this chapter.

This concern about the proper understanding of dreams is first expressed in the book of Deuteronomy. Whether this book actually comes from the insights of the seventh- and eighth-century prophets or is an older tradition to which they turned makes no difference in its basic importance and authority among Jews and Christians. Deuteronomy expresses the faith given in the wilderness and says explicitly how it shall be kept. And when it came to the prophet and dreamer of dreams in Deuteronomy 13, a legal problem was tackled that had to be stated conditionally.

According to the Law, prophets or dreamers of dreams are false *if* they say, "Let us go after other gods and let us serve them." Even if they show wonders or correctly foretell the future, they must not be listened to. It is simply accepted as fact that prophets or dreamers of dreams have the power to see beyond the present. But if they use this power to turn Israel away from its God, then their words shall be shunned, and they shall be put to death (Deut. 13:1-5). Yet it never occurred to the author of Deuteronomy to do away with dreams by simply ignoring them or maintaining that they never have value, the simple solution of our time. Instead, this passage implies that the prophetic function of dreaming and interpreting was so important that to pervert it was a heinous offense and had to be punished by death. In a backhanded way, dreamers were thus treated with real reverence.

This whole matter, of course, was complicated by the fact that the Hebrews lived among non-Hebraic people who had their own priests who had dreams and visions and interpreted them; and these priests used other interesting practices for divining the future. There was clearly a will in Israel that their own people stay away from pagan diviners. This is accepted unconditionally in Deuteronomy 18:9-22, which simply directs that there shall not be found among the people anyone who makes his son or daughter pass through the fire or who practices divination, or any soothsayer, augur, sorcerer, charmer, medium, wizard, or necromancer. While this passage, like the same tradition found in Leviticus 19:26-31, is often taken as a prohibition against dream interpretation, dreams are specifically not mentioned in either place, even though the writer practically exhausts the Hebrew words to include all the religious magic of other peoples.

Deuteronomy 18:9-22 is a remarkable passage. Among even the Greeks and the Romans, with their highly developed religious forms and ethical practice, there was no attempt to curb the superstitious practices of the common people. But here it is put in unmistakable terms. The Israelites shall have nothing to do with pagan priests who do liver-reading or call forth the spirits of the dead. Practices like these were rife in the Near East at the time Israel's life and culture were developing, and it was undoubtedly meant that the children of Israel should not take dreams to such priests for interpretation. But the remarkable part is the next section, which tells the people what they *should* do.

The passage goes on to establish in the law the foundation for prophecy and the visionary experience of the prophet. So that the Lord may speak in a direct way to his people, he will raise up a prophet among them who is strong enough to hear the voice of the Lord their God and *see* the fire like that on Sinai. He will put his words in the prophet's mouth. Then it will be up to the prophet to speak what is given. The people must listen, and the Lord will deal with those who will not listen, but for the prophet the penalty again is death if he speaks anything but what is given or if he speaks in the name of other gods. Thus these passages, which are the only part of the law touching on prophecy or dreams, contain no injunction against listening to visions and dreams but only against failure to distinguish the word of the Lord. This placed a real responsibility on those who believed that God could actually approach and speak directly to them. They not only had to speak the word of God which would come to pass, or come true; in effect, the final test for true prophets of the Lord was to see if their prophecies led the people into closer communion with their God.

The Prophets Wrestle with the Problem of Dreams

No wonder Jeremiah wrestled with the problem of the value of dreams (14:14; 23:16-32, 27:9; 29:8-9). He had a responsibility. He also had reason to be skeptical about the way dreams and visions were understood. All around him Jeremiah heard people prophesy soothing words in the face of the disaster he saw brewing, and he tried to picture what made these prophets see only what they wanted to see. Like Ezekiel (chap. 13), he tried to find some method of distinguishing the genuine prophetic dream or vision from those that were self-deluded, "vanities" manufactured out of whole cloth. (And even one's own dreams are hard to check on and easy to forget.) But Jeremiah came to no real solution of the problem, except to suggest that the dream itself be brought into the open for scrutiny (23:28) and that time be allowed to test the interpretation (28:9).

Isaiah took perhaps a more sophisticated view of the problem (28:15; 29:10; 30:9). He too made it clear that judgment waited for those who made a covenant with death and who, to save themselves, told the people just what they wanted to hear. They were "seers of hell" whose "vision with Sheol" would not last (the literal expressions in 28:15, 18). They became blind, unconscious. But then he shifted the burden back upon the people who demanded deceitful things and would not listen to the prophet who told them what he really saw. Indeed, in meeting this problem the Hebrew prophets went deeper than even the rational Greeks in trying to understand the nature of visionary inspiration and its interpretation, and they showed a more critical attitude.

But there was one further step, which had been hinted at in 1 Kings. When Ahab demanded the truth of the prophet Micaiah, the king heard the prophecy of his death. Micaiah then told his vision of a spirit that became a lying spirit in the mouth of all the king's other prophets. At this, one of them stepped up and "slapped him on the cheek, and said, 'Which way did the spirit of the LORD pass from me to speak to you?' Micaiah replied, 'You will find out on that day when you go in to hide in an inner chamber' " (1 Kings 22:24; 2 Chron. 18:23).

This understanding is fully developed in the little-known but deeply significant book of Habakkuk—"the oracle that the prophet Habakkuk *saw*" (1:1, italics mine)—whose words seem almost to be formed in a vision. When the prophet described the way in which it was received, he said, "I will stand at my watchpost, and station myself on the rampart; I will keep watch to *see* what he will say to me" (2:1, italics mine).

It is as if the prophet must go off by himself into his inner watch-tower. In his exegesis of these lines in *The Interpreter's Bible,* Charles Taylor writes that the vision "comes to one whose feet are on the firm foundation of confident expectation, and who rises even a little above the toil and moil to take a look about him. God's revelation, though available for all, is not actually received by all; man must look forth or be on the alert as a watchman stands attentive."

And when the vision comes, it is about visions. The vision takes its own time to form and mature. It comes from a place that has its own time schedule, its own will to break through at the right time.

And the task of the prophet is to put it forth so that all can know. The prophet's words were: "Then the LORD answered me and said: Write the vision; make it plain on tablets, so that a runner may read it. For there is still a vision for the appointed time; it speaks of the end, and does not lie. If it seems to tarry, wait for it; it will surely come, it will not delay. Look at the proud! Their spirit is not right in them, but the righteous live by their faith" (Hab. 2:2-4).

It would be difficult to speak more plainly than this about the autonomy of the vision and its reality. And the advice is excellent: Write it down, for the vision is easily swallowed up in other matters and then forgotten.

All of the great Hebrew prophets seemed to derive their messages from some kind of direct confrontation of God or from some type of visionary experience that had to be interpreted. Either they saw images—as Amos saw the image of a plumb line (7:7), Jeremiah a branch of an almond tree (1:11), Isaiah the Lord upon his throne in full panoply (6:1), or Ezekiel his beautifully specific sequences—or their very being was possessed by God's Spirit and they spoke as the mouthpiece of God. Psychologically there is little difference between having the visual screen possessed by images, and possession of the motor centers, which results in speech. Perhaps in the later prophets there was somewhat more conscious control and awareness during the experience, and perhaps not. They themselves did not distinguish very clearly between the experience of the dream, the vision, the hearing of God's voice, or possession by the Spirit. The important thing was not the actual images but the prophetic ability to see their significance and speak of this. Many people may have seen an almond branch or a plumb line, but it takes the prophetic personality to see the significance and to speak of it.

At the same time, as the prophets agreed, their experience came when the Spirit of God was made available to them and whether they or anyone else liked it or not. Jeremiah complained almost as strongly about his own compulsion to speak as about the evils he had to speak about. Even centuries later the Jews, according to Jerome, forbade people under thirty to read the beginning of the Book of Ezekiel with its marvelous vision of the throne chariot. The most famous of Ezekiel's visions, that of the valley of dry bones (37:1-14), was described as the action of the hand of God upon him which lifted him up and set him down within his insight. This experience has all the qualities of a dream, like many of the other prophetic experiences, even to the being lifted up and set down in another place. The images of Ezekiel, although little studied in recent years, are well known in song and literature. They are genuine productions of what depth psychology would call the collective unconscious, something from beyond the conscious mind and often beyond the limits of personal experience. Comparable dreams and visions are by no means unknown today; in fact, quite recently an experience similar in quality was told to me by a pastor who received it. The specific references to visions in Ezekiel are found in 1:1; 7:26; 8:3; 11:24; 12:22, 27; 13:7, 16; 40:2; and 43:3. These passages, most of them the very ones biblical critics consider likely to be from Ezekiel's own hand, contain the essential message of the prophet.

Isaiah 1:1 speaks of the vision that came to him, while in 6:1 he simply "sees." The inference, however, is clear that he sees something outside of this space-time continuum, something in the form of a vision. Other specific references to visions in Isaiah are 21:2; 22:1; and 29:7, 11. In the last verse Isaiah laments that these visions are to the people as a sealed book, and they wish it so. He also condemns those who turn to some pagan practice of incubation and "sit inside tombs, and spend the night in secret places," instead of waiting for the Lord to speak (65:4).

Among the minor prophets, Hosea received the word of the Lord, and according to his own record, lived out what might be called a vision (12:10) of guilt. The book of Obadiah simply begins with the words: "The vision of Obadiah." The word of the Lord came to Micah, and he "saw" and passed on the warning to false prophets that "therefore it shall be night to you, without vision, and darkness to you, without revelation. . . . for there is no answer from God" (3:6-7).

His meaning may well be that, until they begin to see straight, God will no longer answer the prophets in dreams. Finally, after Nahum's graphic vision of what was to befall Nineveh, there is the Book of Habakkuk, which we have discussed, and then the visions and dreams and angels described by the prophet Zechariah. His experiences, which happened at the time the Hebrews were returning to Jerusalem to rebuild their city and their temple, gave hope and encouragement to this work. The first six chapters are almost entirely taken up with vision after vision, in which the prophet conversed with an angel and saw images in such detail that long analyses would be required to understand them fully. These experiences began with a dream (Moffatt, for instance, translates it so), described in Hebrew simply as what the prophet "saw in the night" (Zech. 1:8), and the following visions may well have come in the same way. In a later chapter the prophet accused the diviners of seeing lies and telling false dreams (10:2), and he followed this charge up by predicting a day of cleansing on which "the prophets will be ashamed, every one, of their visions when they prophesy" (13:4).

Dreams in the Hebrew Poetic Tradition

Alongside of the prophetic understanding of these experiences there was a similar appreciation of the dream developed in the "writings." This last part of the Old Testament for us to look at includes those portions of Scripture that are neither law, history, nor prophecy. Among them, the Book of Psalms and the Book of Job have probably had as great an influence on the devotional life of people as anything written outside of the New Testament. Here we find a great variety of literary references to dreams and visions.

Amid the flood of imagery of the Psalms there are three specific references to visions and dreams and several poetic allusions. Psalm 89:19 sings of God speaking to his holy one in a vision, while Psalm 73 pictures the dream as a nightmare of revelation from which one awakes despising the image of wickedness (v. 20). In Psalm 126:1 the dream is likened to the wish that has been fulfilled.

The psalmist frequently speaks of his communion with God in the night without distinguishing very clearly between sleep or wakeful hours in the darkness. Current studies of the practice of incubation in ancient cultures see vestiges of this practice in several of these passages. André Caquot in his study of the dreams of Canaan and Israel in *Les Songes et Leur Interprétation* refers particularly to Psalms 17, 63, and 91.[5] Showing that to pass the night on the ground was a known rite of lamentation in Israel, he cites the ancient verses of Psalm 91: "Happy the man who stays by the Most High in shelter, who lives under the shadow of Almighty God," protected from "the terrors of the night" (91:1, 5 MOFFATT). Again the psalmist cries out that God tests his soul by night and concludes, "But may our innocent lives enjoy thy favour, may we be satisfied, when we wake to see thy vision" (17:3, 15 MOFFATT). A Norwegian writer, Sigmund Mowinckel, has shown the close connection of this psalm to incubation, and he also suggests that the same thing is seen in Psalm 63: "When I remember thee in bed, and muse on thee by night, my soul clings close to thee, thy right hand holds me fast; for thou hast been my help, and shadowed by thy wings I sing thy praise" (63:6-8 MOFFATT).

While there are other references to disturbing nights, as in 22:2 and 32:4, the psalmist also sings that he can lie down to sleep in safety, which the Lord alone gives (3:5; 4:8). And in the night his song is with the psalmist (42:8), like the maiden in the Song of Solomon (5:2) who tells that she sleeps, but her heart awakes. Certainly in the night season the psalmists found that something came through to them which they knew as the revelation of God.

Throughout the Psalter there are also references to the angels which are messengers of God, destroying the wicked and helping the righteous. The vengeful arm of the Eternal is spoken of in Psalm 35:5-6 and 78:49, but in 34:7; 68:17; 91:11; 103:20; 104:4; and 148:2 the Lord is praised for the protection and power he gives through his angels. These were often-present realities to the psalmist.

In Proverbs there is little concern about dreams, visions, angels, or anything of the sort. It is an intensely "practical" book. The most it says about sleep is that we should not indulge in it too much or too often. The skeptical preacher of Ecclesiastes goes a step further and looks at dreams as another example of vanity (5:3, 7). They mean nothing more than a fool's fears, and their only result is empty words. Throughout the history of the Christian church, whenever a proof text has been needed to support the contention that dreams are of no value, it is this passage to which one is referred, with no reference to the books of Genesis, Numbers, 1 Samuel, or Habakkuk. And yet if we had to weigh each book for its relative value in the Old Testament, Ecclesiastes would certainly show up somewhat on the light side.[6]

Job and Daniel See Dreams and Visions

In the magnificent Book of Job, in some ways the crowning piece of literature of the Old Testament, we find again a great reverence for dreams as communications from God. And as always, where dreams are taken seriously, the same attitude is shown toward visions. Job complained that in addition to all the rest of his difficulties, God frightened him in the night with dreams and visions: "Then you scare me with dreams and terrify me with visions" (7:14). Eliphaz was also terrified by "thoughts from visions of the night, when deep sleep falls on mortals" (4:13). Many moderns in the throes of anxiety and neurosis have felt comradeship with Job in these night fears and have found comfort. In Zophar's speech the parallel was carried further; his understanding told him that the sinner would disappear like the dreams and visions of the night (20:8).

The most important passage about dreams in Job is found in the speech of Elihu, in which he held that God speaks to people in two ways. He speaks once, and then "in a dream, in a vision of the night, when deep sleep falls on mortals, while they slumber on their beds, then he opens their ears, and terrifies them with warnings" (33:15-16).

God's purpose in so treating people is to lead them back to himself and away from the Pit. In this chapter (33:22-24) the destroying and protecting angels are also mentioned, probably as part of the vision. The author of the Book of Job believed that God had some things to say which could be put in unmistakable terms in dreams and visions. It would be difficult to express more clearly a valuation of what can occur in human dreaming. The dream can be an entrance, according to Job, into direct communication with God himself.

A word about Lamentations should be said at this point. This book belongs among the writings in the Hebrew canon of Scripture rather than with the prophets, and indeed the book is a psalm of lamentation. Among the other desolations lamented here—and they are real and terrible ones—is the fact that the vision no longer comes to the prophet. This is as tragic as anything that can happen to the people (2:9).

Those who are not acquainted with the Hebrew Bible may be surprised also to find the Book of Daniel considered at this point. The Hebrew, however, separates it clearly from the prophets, and it is more akin to Job and Esther than to the more mundane and concrete histories. One who is interested in dreams and visions can have a field day in Daniel. Here again the two experiences are constantly equated. Daniel is wise, and his wisdom is manifested largely in his interpretation of dreams and visions (1:17; 5:12). The story has hardly begun before there is a dream, the dream that Nebuchadnezzar had forgotten but which proceeded to trouble him until he could no longer sleep (2:1). He was about to have the wise men (the dream interpreters) of Babylon killed because none of them could tell him his dream, when Daniel heard about the predicament. And God revealed the king's dream to Daniel in a night vision and also its interpretation. He was then able to satisfy Nebuchadnezzar by making known the mysteries of the future that God had tried to show the king. From this point on, Daniel's position in the court was assured.

The rest of the book is filled with dreams. Chapter 4 contains the king's vision predicting his madness, while the entire seventh chapter is devoted to Daniel's dream of the four beasts, and the eighth to his vision of the powerful ram and the interpretation given to him as he slept deeply face downward on the ground. Up to this point the dreams and visions are spoken of almost in the same breath, without distinction, and they certainly cannot be distinguished by content. From here on, the interest seems to shift to the waking vision. Two further visions given to Daniel (9:21-27 and 10:5—12:13) are elaborated in the final chapter. In the midst of his long forecast Daniel remarks that people of violence will lift themselves up to fulfill the vision but will fail (11:14). In addition, the story of the handwriting on the wall (chap. 5) has the unmistakable quality of a group vision, and Daniel is also released by angels from the den of lions, as are Shadrach, Meshach, and Abednego from the fiery furnace (6:22; 3:28). In fact, the Book of Daniel is so much concerned with these experiences that it might well be subtitled "A Romance of the Dream." And this is the note on which we will close the Old Testament.

The Apocrypha

But as we step from the Old Testament into the New, we are not exactly stepping across a gap. The Apocrypha continues the spirit of Job and Daniel, and this was the spirit in which Judaism was bathed at the time of Jesus of Nazareth. This fact was easily forgotten after the Apocrypha was excluded from our Bibles; indeed, it was repressed. The books of the Apocrypha are those found in the Greek translation of the Old Testament, the Septuagint, which are no longer a part of the Hebrew canon of Scriptures. With the rise of Christianity it was necessary to close the list of books in the Hebrew Scripture, and those books that may have been associated with the Christian church, or were known to have been of recent vintage or perhaps were inferior in quality, were dropped from the Hebrew Bible.

The Christian church up until the time of the Reformation, however, looked on these books as having almost the same authority as the other books of the Old Testament. In fact, St. Jerome in the fifth century was the first to explain clearly that there was a difference between the Hebrew and Christian Bibles. But today the average Protestant who is not a student of the Bible hardly knows what the Apocrypha is, and so he or she has no idea how much concern there was with dreams and visions during those centuries just before the birth of Jesus. Six of these neglected books deal in some way with dream experiences, and in three of the major ones dreams are central to the action, as well as in the more complete story of Esther told in the Apocrypha.

In 2 Esdras, Ezra was lying on his bed lamenting the sad fate of his country when the angel Uriel was sent from the Most High to comfort him (4:1-4). Three times the angel came to Ezra, who was then chief priest, to interpret signs and to lay certain visionary images before him. Then he told him, "But tomorrow night you must stay here, and the Most High will show you in dreams those visions of what the Most High is going to do in the last days to those who live on the earth" (10:58-59 GOODSPEED). This apparently was the normal way in which God spoke his message. Ezra began to behold visions in his dreams which go on for pages and pages. They were interpreted to him sometimes by the angel Uriel, sometimes by God. After that he prophesied to the people.

The Book of Tobit is a delightful story in which the angel Raphael directed Tobias on the journey he took to help his father in their exile. At the same time they overcame the demon that afflicted Sarah and destroyed all of her husbands, and so provided a wife for Tobias. But the story does not concretize the angel. Instead, it lets Raphael himself declare that his appearance has been a vision. "All these days," he says, "that I appeared to you, I did not eat or drink, but you beheld a vision. Now give thanks to God, for I must go up to him who sent me, and you must write all that has happened on a scroll" (12:19-20 GOODSPEED).

The Greek version of Esther begins with the dream of Mordecai (11:5),[7] which he saw as a revelation of God's purpose and tried to understand in every detail. As the story then unfolds, with all its political overtones, Mordecai sees his dream fulfilled, and in the end he says, "These things have come from God. For I remember the dream that I had concerning these matters, and none of them has failed to be fulfilled" (10:5).

The Wisdom of Solomon tells of the time when God's all-powerful command brought doom and death that touched even heaven. The author says that apparitions in dreadful dreams then troubled the people, warning them with disturbing fears so that they would not die without knowing why they suffered (18:17-19). In Ecclesiasticus, the wisdom of Sirach, we do find an opposite view expressed about most dreams (34:1-7); they are made for fools, simply to pit this against that, face against face, and shadow against shadow. And when they are divined, all they do is keep the law from being fulfilled. But even so, the writer cannot dismiss all dreams as delusions or deceptions, for he sees that some come as visitations from the Most High and are meant to be taken seriously. The negative comments of Sirach were also quoted throughout the Middle Ages and have been quoted in Roman Catholic circles until this day whenever people have wanted to belittle the value of dreams.

The vision of Heliodorus in 2 Maccabees (3:22-30) reminds one of the vision of Paul on the Damascus road. In both cases the person who received the vision was struck down and later raised up. Where Paul was healed by Ananias, Heliodorus, after his vivid and detailed vision, was restored through the agency of the very angels he had seen, who returned to help him because of the prayers of the high priest. And the narrative ends essentially with the dream of Judas Maccabeus, "a dream that was worthy of belief, a kind of vision," which he told because it gave his men inspiration (15:11 GOODSPEED). In this dream he saw the former high priest Onias with another man, who turned out to be Jeremiah and who presented Judas with a golden sword, a gift from God with which to smite his enemies (15:12-16). And he did. One is reminded of the dreams of Alexander and the high priest Jaddus, which had the opposite result of saving Jerusalem from harm.

As we look over the whole body of these writings, we have to conclude that the authors of the Old Testament and the Apocrypha had a belief about dreams and visions that they considered important. They believed that when people dreamed and saw genuine visions, they were experiencing the breakthrough of another world. This was one way in which God, the Most High, or Yahweh, spoke what needed to be said to men and women. It was the way in which angels appeared and made contact with people. It was an experience that can hardly be distinguished from that of the prophetic inspiration. Indeed, whatever else they have to say about them, the Jewish writings seldom devalued dreams and visions as meaningless. They realized that too much concern with these experiences could lead to superstition or to delusion, but still their inherent value was not negated. They also realized that people could be fooled or could even lie about dreams and visions and that one must be on guard against this deception, whether unconscious or consciously purposed. Indeed these writings leave little doubt about what the Hebrew people believed and taught about the value of dreams and visions and about how basic they were to the revelation found in the Old Testament and Apocrypha. It is difficult to understand this book or the spirit in which it was written unless one clearly understands this belief concerning inspiration, of which its dream theory is an essential part.

Dreams in Later Jewish Literature

The reverence for dreams that is found from Genesis through the Apocrypha continues and even grows in later Jewish literature. In the opening tract of the Babylonian Talmud—which was reduced to written form between A.D. 200 and A.D. 500—there are four chapters (55–58) on dreams. This book, which is second in authority in Judaism only after the Old Testament, consists of the sayings of the famous rabbis and their interpretations of Holy Writ. Many of the famous leaders of Israel during this period spoke of the value of dreams and encouraged the interpretation of them. Rabbi Hisda said that an uninterpreted dream was like an unread letter. Dreams were specifically described here as a breakthrough from the beyond, from the world of the spirit, or from God. There were good dreams and bad dreams, and fasting was one of the best ways to avoid the bad ones. However, the bad ones often were more valuable since they led to repentance and had a more transforming effect.

The *Jewish Encyclopedia* summarizes an excellent article on dreams in these words: ". . . that the most famous teachers frequently discuss dreams and enunciate doctrines regarding them, shows the strong hold dreams had even on the intellectual leaders of Judaism. Belief in dreams was the rule; doubt concerning them the exception."[8] According to this article the dream interpreters were so highly valued that they were nearly always paid for their services.

We find the same reverence for dreams among the Jewish philosophers. Philo, the great Jewish Hellenist of Alexandria, according to Eusebius, was the author of five books on dreams, three of which have been lost. Two of these, which deal with the dreams of Joseph and others around him, are mentioned in other works by Philo. The same feeling persisted in medieval times, as is shown by the work of Maimonides, the theologian who tried to integrate the thinking of Aristotle into later Judaic theology. This man, who was called the second Moses because of his strong influence on the Judaism of that time, believed that dreams were a kind of prophecy, and he expressed this idea carefully in his chief work, *The Guide for the Perplexed.*

> The principal and highest function is performed when the senses are at rest and pause in their action, for then [the imaginative faculty] receives to some extent, divine inspiration in the measure as it is predisposed for

> this influence. This is the nature of those dreams which prove true, and also of prophecy, the difference being one of quantity, not of quality. . . . In a similar manner the action of the imaginative faculty during sleep is the same as at the time when it receives a prophecy, only in the first case it is not fully developed, and has not yet reached its highest degree.[9]

In the Kabbalistic movement, which was once so well known to Christians through the *Zohar* and which played such a part in the development of European scholarship and thought, there is evidence that dreams continued to be seen as communications of the divine. Dreams, it was said in these writings, are the unripe fruit of prophecy. Again, the later fathers of Hasidism showed a similar point of view. These stories of Hasidism have been collected and retold well by Martin Buber. Among them, for instance, is the one about Rabbi Eisik of Cracow, who followed his dreams and was led in the end to a great treasure.

The book *Rosenbaums of Zell* brings the thinking of the first of these movements, the Kabbalah, into the history of our own time. This work tells the story in some detail of a rabbinic family in nineteenth-century Germany. It also sets forth a number of their writings, in which it is clear that one of the chief ways in which these rabbis were given illumination was through dreams. One of those described relates to the integration of the Christ figure (Messiah) into Jewish thinking.[10]

Also described in *Rosenbaums of Zell* are certain dreams that pictured the extinction of the Jewish community in Germany and were dreamed over half a century before Hitler came to power and nearly twenty years before the Zionist movement was suggested as a political reality. These were dreams that came to Reb Hile Wechsler, one of the members of this influential family, about 1880.

> These dreams happened more than once and were of such a compelling nature that he felt the urge to impart them to the Jewish world—the description of his dreams shows the typical cabbalistic ideology. Whenever he awoke after such dreams a verse out of the Scripture was on his lips which gave him the fitting interpretation. Yet he said he was by nature a rational person and not inclined to indulge in fantasies.[11]

The way in which he handled these disturbing dreams also suggests that this was true of the young rabbi. He began by reasoning from the Talmud and from other source works of his faith how much importance he could give to the dreams and how far he could go in seeing them in relation to the practical world. From his dreams and from this strictly rational approach to them, Wechsler was led then to encourage a return of the Jewish community to their homeland of Palestine. Thus, in a time not only of rationalism but of devaluation of dreams, these deeply religious Jewish rabbis were still listening to their dreams for religious enlightenment and prophetic insight. James Kirsch discusses this in-depth in his book *The Reluctant Prophet.*

This attitude of Jewish leaders and scholars was picked up and lived out in popular Jewish thinking. As late as 1902 the famous dream book *Pitron Halomot* was published in translation in New York City; this was a book written by Jacob Almoli during the Turkish occupation of Constantinople. In substance these facts show that the attitude toward dreams which is found imbedded in the Old Testament has lived on in the rabbinic, philosophical, and popular traditions of Israel right up to the present time. Joel Covitz, in *Visions of the Night*, gives a magnificent exposition of Almoli.

Dreams in Other Ancient Cultures

As might be expected, an interest in dreams was by no means unique among the Hebrews. The Old Testament springs out of an ancient and highly developed tradition. Long before the Greeks had put a word on papyrus, the Semitic cultures of Asia Minor and the Tigris and Euphrates valleys were recording an extensive and sophisticated literature. One of the ideas common to these writings was the belief that there are spiritual (as well as physical) realities beyond the control of human beings and that one way to learn what they are like and how they are disposed toward human beings is by listening to dreams and visions. The gods and goddesses, demons and angels—these nonphysical realities with which ancient people found themselves surrounded—revealed themselves in dreams. The Gilgamesh Epic, dating back at least to 2000 B.C., is one of the finest examples of this Sumerian and Babylonian literature. It relates how this earliest prototype of the great hero came to know himself and later overcame the enemy the gods had put in his way. At each step it was through dreams given by beneficent heavenly powers that he was given direction to reach his goal.[12]

Tablets discovered at the eighteenth-century B.C. site of Ugarit tell about a man named Daniel who was blessed by a son after he had slept in the temple and had a dream in which he communicated with his god. This practice of incubation for the purpose of receiving such dreams has been common in many cultures. In the Assyrian Empire, which continued Babylonian civilization, records show the same traditional respect for dreams. The Annals of Assurbanipal tell how the goddess Ishtar, after a prayer from the king, revealed herself to one of his seers in a dream with a message of direction and confidence for the king. Dream books were also used in ancient Assyria, and those that were found in the royal library at Nineveh have been translated in the transactions of the American Philosophical Society. Our own Bible confirms the high regard for dreams among these peoples and also among the Egyptians.

The Egyptian attitude is also learned through much the same kind of sources, rather than in any single document. For instance, among the papyri there are specific instructions for obtaining either a dream or a vision of certain gods. There is a record that King Thutmose IV, while still a prince, encountered one of the great gods in a dream. This was inscribed on a memorial stone found at the foot of the Sphinx, and while some students believe it to be a later restoration, it agrees equally with what we know of Egyptian belief in the time of Joseph and in modern times.

In fact, there is hardly a culture on earth that has not shared this interest in dreams. *The Dream and Human Societies,* published by the University of California Press following an international conference, shows the important place dreams have held from the shamanic culture of Siberia to the Moslem world. Several writers in this volume deal with the reverence throughout Islam for prophetic dreams, those in which the prophet appears.

In *The World of Dreams,* Ralph L. Woods has put together a sizable anthology of similar materials from all over the world. From India we find one of the early Upanishads from nearly a thousand years before Christ, which held that in dreams one lies in an intermediate state between the spirit world (to which he passes in death) and the material world. Thus, the treatise explains, the dreamer is self-illuminated and receives important insights. The Chinese have two chief dream books, the *Meng Shu* and *Meng Chan I Chih,* which were written relatively late. Dating from the seventh and sixteenth centuries A.D., they are less concrete and more philosophical than those of other traditions.

Teutonic people considered the wisest counselor the one who was charged with interpreting dreams; this is pictured in sagas like the Heimskringla, the Nibelungenlied, and the Laxdale Saga, where symbolic dreams are brought for interpretation. The same tradition continued in Iceland, for instance, with the stories of St. Thorlak, who took great pleasure in telling his own dreams.

All of these cultures manifest the belief that, beside the physical world, there is another significant world of reality that breaks in upon the individual, particularly in dreams.[13] As Mircea Eliade has shown so clearly in his *Myths, Dreams and Mysteries,* this idea occurs among peoples everywhere except in modern Western culture, where it is so foreign that people find it difficult to comprehend. It persists among modern primitive peoples, as Woods demonstrates by his collection of dream experiences among Bantus, Ashantis, Navajos, Papuans, and others. Jung found the same thing when he visited the Hopi Indians and certain African tribes to study their dream experiences. I found the same idea among the Senoi of Malaysia in 1991. Laurens van der Post substantiates this with a delightful story of the Bushmen told in *The Heart of the Hunter.* When he pressed these primitive people of the Kalahari to talk about the beginning of meaning in their lives, he was given only one significant answer: "But you see, it is very difficult, for always there is a dream dreaming us." Among peoples who have not been touched by Western positivism, there is an almost universal belief that human beings are in contact through dreams with something more substantial than their own imaginings.

Many Christians fear the suggestion that anyone but a Christian could have contact with more-than-human spiritual realities. This would mean that Christianity does not have a corner on spiritual truth, on religious perception. But the Bible does not suggest that they should. It suggests, instead, that only through the tradition of these Testaments could the Jew, and later the Christian, come into the right kind of contact which would lead them to the center and source of spiritual reality. Christianity does not offer any exclusive contact with the spiritual realm but rather the guidance and power to find one's way through this realm to hope and salvation. It is the universal reality of the spiritual world, in fact, which makes Christianity and its power essential to our lives.

Few people, however, take primitive dream experiences or those of the Assyrians or Egyptians too seriously. But when ancient Greece speaks, our roots are stirred, and we moderns listen. Let us turn now to the thinking of the Greeks on the subject of dreams to see how it tallies with that of other peoples.

Chapter

3

The Greek Attitude toward the Dream

PERHAPS IT SEEMS STRANGE in a study of the Christian interpretation of dreams to devote a whole chapter to the ideas of the Greeks. But there is good reason for doing so. Although the earliest Christian church was born within the Hebrew community, it quickly became a Greek institution, with its main missionary thrust toward the Graeco-Roman world. Its earliest surviving Scripture and liturgy were both in Greek, and from the time of these documents, Greek ideas were penetrating the new church. As it grew, its nascent theology was deeply influenced by Greek philosophy. Thus the Christianity that survived the ancient world was formed by the commingling of the Greek and Hebrew cultures, while that which was exclusively Jewish hardly stayed alive after the second destruction of Jerusalem in A.D. 132.[1] In order to understand the Christian attitude toward dreams in the New Testament and in the Fathers of the church, it is necessary to understand the Greek beliefs about dreams as well as what the Hebrews believed, for their beliefs supported and extended the Hebrew experience and theory.

There is another reason for studying the Greek interest in dreams. Ever since the Renaissance, with its fresh look at ancient cultures, Western people have been rightly astounded at the creativity and intellectual power of the Greek community for several centuries just before the Christian era. During this time, among a relatively small number of people, there flourished a culture that laid the foundation for modern philosophy, art, drama, literature, and scientific thinking. In most Western quarters there is a far greater reverence for Greek things than for Hebrew things, because the philosophic and aesthetic contributions of the Greeks have been more highly valued than the more specifically religious and ethical contributions of the Hebrews. Once it is realized that the Greeks with very few exceptions viewed the dream much as the Hebrews did—as a vehicle for communication from the divine—and with even greater reverence than the Hebrews, modern Western people may be more likely to take seriously the dream tradition of the Old and New Testaments. They may even find reason to listen with open-mindedness to their own modern dream experiences.

It was among the Greeks, as everyone knows, that human beings first learned how to develop and use their reason consciously. Among the Greeks is found the first careful analysis of reason and the first self-conscious philosophy. There is no question that it was the Greek mind that gave the philosophical, theological, rational foundation for Christianity. For the past several centuries many people have been so taken by the magnitude of the Greek discoveries, particularly their understanding of reason and its use, that they believed the Greeks were a "rational" people par excellence. Students have laid so much stress on the rationality of the Greeks that they have failed to see them as living people.

Recent modern scholarship does not uphold this idealistic picture of Greek rationality. As we study the documents of ancient Greece objectively, we find that the Greeks from Homer through Plato and Aristotle, through the poets of the Golden Age, down to the Stoics and Skeptics, were just as concerned with the irrational elements of life as the Hebrews. The Greeks were just as "superstitious," just as moved by the numinous depths of the unknown, as any other early people, the Hebrews included. The fact that they developed rational understanding did not mean that they neglected an interest in the irrational aspects of life, such as dreams, prophecy, oracles, visions, or gods and demons. They were both rational and irrational at the same time. One reason for their greatness was that they avoided no part of the reality of life.[2]

While regius professor of Greek at Oxford, E. R. Dodds wrote a very careful study of these neglected aspects of Greek life in a book entitled *The Greeks and the Irrational.* With painstaking documentation he demonstrates quite clearly and definitively that Greek understanding and culture did not erase or conquer the irrational side of life and that poets and philosophers alike recognized this fact and wrote about it. Jane Harrison, in her equally well-documented study, *Prolegomena to the Study of Greek Religion,* gives extensive evidence of the same fact. The Greeks indeed were quite as irrational as the Hebrews, and their *nonrational* ideas and practices reinforced the direction the developing church was already taking. In discussing the dreams of the Greeks, I shall rely heavily on the material that Dodds and Harrison have so thoroughly brought to light.

It is much more difficult to study the Greek attitude toward a particular subject than the Hebrew. The Greeks never obliged posterity, as did the Jews, by codifying and canonizing their literature in one book. Anyone who can read can discover the ancient Hebrew attitude toward practically anything, and so much critical work has been done on the Old Testament that there is now a generally accepted framework of basic agreement. This is not true of Greek culture. There is a wide variety of Greek literature—some of it discovered only in recent years—and a number of diversified opinions about it. The multiplicity of Greek literary output is often what keeps us from seeing clearly how their thinking on specific matters originated. Where the Old Testament, in most cases, weaves its varying ideas around a few cohesive trends of thought, Greek culture instead presents us with a variety of completely unrelated ideas on nearly every subject, including that of dreams.

In fact, this is especially true of dreams, since this concern of the Greeks represents one of the best examples of their attitude toward the nonrational aspect of life. They manifested the same interest in dreams and the same belief that they were intrusions of a more-than-human world, which we found in the Old Testament, but on the whole without the same caution or critical evaluation we found among the Hebrews. In order to find what pattern there was in the plethora of material, let us look first at the popular attitude toward dreams as revealed in early Greek literature. The importance of dreams in the classical period will then be examined, and we shall finally consider the philosophic and "scientific" attitudes toward dreams as revealed in Plato and Aristotle and later thinkers.

Dreams of the Heroes

Two basically different ideas about dreams can be distinguished in the popular thinking of ancient Greece. The first of these is the archaic point of view, which can be described as an objective view of dreams. According to this idea, which was expressed by the Homeric poets, dreams are supernatural revelations given by the gods or other supernatural figures. Later a second theory was superimposed upon this first one; it was the Orphic idea that during sleep the soul left the body and communed with the gods, returning with important information, either symbolic or direct in nature. These two views became mingled and interwoven in popular thought, which continued to find utmost significance in dreams of both kinds. Both were seen as avenues of contact with "daemonic" reality.

In the poets of Homeric antiquity the references to dreams are many, and almost uniformly they are treated as objective fact. It was a dream figure sent by Zeus to hunt out Agamemnon and stand over him in the form of wise, old Nestor that roused the Greeks to action before Troy (*Iliad* 2.1ff.). In the same way the sad spirit of Patroclus stood over Achilles after Hector was dead (23:65). And in the *Odyssey,* Athene formed an image that came in through the keyhole to bring Penelope a message as she slept (4.795ff.), while the goddess in disguise came to Nausicaa in a dream (6.14ff.).

These dreams, according to Dodds, usually take

> the form of a visit paid to a sleeping man or woman by a single dream-figure (the very word *oneiros* in Homer nearly always means dream-figure, not dream-experience). This dream-figure can be a god, or a ghost, or a pre-existing dream-messenger, or an "image" (*eidolon*) created specially for the occasion; but whichever it is, it exists objectively in space and is independent of the dreamer. It effects an entry by the keyhole (Homeric bedrooms having neither window nor chimney); it plants itself at the head of the bed to deliver its message; and when that is done, it withdraws by the same route. The dreamer, meanwhile, is almost completely passive.[3]

The dreamer knows he or she is in bed asleep and is seeing a dream. In fact, the Greeks of this period did not speak of having a dream, but like the Hebrew experience of seeing an angel, they told of "seeing a dream."

There is no doubt that the Greeks prized these objective dreams with their messages delivered directly to the sleeper. Later on, in the great Periclean age as well as in archaic times, these dreams were considered divine, "god-sent." The bearer of the message might be either a god or a person, even a member of the dreamer's family; it made no difference. Many, many examples in Greek literature show this and also suggest that people generally took such directions seriously and acted upon them. But this was not all. There were also dreams that prescribed some kind of dedication, a plaque, a statue, or even a chapel, which left tangible evidence. Archaeologists have discovered many inscriptions dedicated "in accordance with a dream" or "having seen a dream," and while these do not tell much about the content of the dreams, they leave no questions about the way they were valued. Plato commented on this in the *Laws* (909–10), remarking how frequently such instructions were received in dreams; and the follower of Plato who wrote the *Epinomis* also noted (985) that "many cults of many gods have been founded and will continue to be founded, because of dream-encounters with supernatural beings, omens, oracles, and deathbed visions."

But the Greeks wrote about other dreams besides these objective ones. Even in Homeric times the poets also spoke of symbolic dreams that required interpretation. One of the oldest parts of the *Iliad* (5.149) tells of an interpreter who failed to give his sons the meaning of their dreams when they went off to the Trojan War, while Penelope's dream in Book 19 of the *Odyssey* spoke its own meaning as she slept. In this dream she saw her beautiful geese killed by an eagle, and she was weeping for them when the eagle swooped down and spoke to her in a human voice, assuring her that Odysseus would return and scatter her unwanted suitors like the dead geese. Certainly anxiety dreams were also known to these early Greeks, and there is as good a description in the *Iliad* as any modern psychologist listens to. Four times around the walls Hector fled from Achilles, "*as in a dream* one flees and another cannot pursue him—the one cannot stir to escape, nor the other to pursue him—so Achilles could not overtake Hector in running, nor Hector escape him" (22.199).

Hesiod also wrote of more than one idea about dreams. This eighth-century poet, who probably invented the idea of teaching by poetry, described how the muses spoke to him on lonely Mount Helicon; by his own description Hesiod himself then had the powers of a seer. But later on he wrote that night gives birth, without father, to "hateful Doom and black Fate and Death, and she bare Sleep and the tribe of Dreams" (*Theogony* 22ff., 32, 211ff.).

Although it is often suggested that the objective pattern of dreams in archaic cultures is peculiar to that period, we can legitimately conclude that the early Greeks dreamed much as we do now. The argument, in the first place, that the objective type of dream no longer occurs in our time simply does not hold water. This feeling is probably very common among people who have paid little or no attention to their own dreams, but it is not borne out by the published material, such as the modern dream series found in C. G. Jung's *Psychology and Alchemy.* More likely the fact is simply that all primitive peoples attach greater significance to their objective dreams than to others. Naturally the early Greek heroes would be heroic in their dreaming, as well as in their more conscious activities. But more than this, they undoubtedly remembered the objective dreams, which seemed clear and easy to understand, when the more symbolic dreams, which had to be interpreted, were often forgotten, as they also are today.

The early Greeks also had good reason, like Penelope in the *Odyssey,* to ignore what some dreams were saying. Faced with a houseful of suitors who wanted the place of Odysseus and even threatened to kill her son, Penelope could not trust her dream that the eagle would return. She told the "stranger" who brought her news of her husband that

> in truth dreams, do arise which are perplexing and hard to understand, which in men's experience do not come true. Two gates there are for unsubstantial dreams, one made of horn and one of ivory. The dreams that pass through the carved ivory delude and bring us tales that turn to naught; those that come forth through polished horn accomplish real things, whenever they are seen. Yet through this gate came not I think my own strange dream.[4]

But like Penelope, these early Greeks knew, as far back as we have any record, that there were different kinds of dreams, some of them imperative, and others, just as today, cloudy and uncertain.

Sometime about the fifth or sixth centuries before Christ, however, a new idea was introduced to the popular Greek mind that resembled quite closely the shamanism of the northern peoples of

Europe and Siberia. Whatever its origin—and Dodds makes a good case for the introduction of this new idea from outside of the culture, from the North—this belief was developed by the Pythagoreans and among the followers of Orphism, and it took much the same turn as the similar belief found in early Hindu thinking. This role of the spiritual leader or shaman brought a realization that the power of the dream comes from within the individual, or at any rate from within certain individuals. It was believed that during sleep the soul left the body and communed with other spirits, took trips, or visited with the gods. Thus the body came to be looked upon as the prison house of the soul, the binding element from which the soul waited to be freed; and the state most favorable for this freedom, other than death, was that of sleep. The poet Pindar was one of the first to express this, and it was later found in the writings of Zenophon and Plato.

At the same time in this period of greatness the temples of Aescylapius became important, because here a dream could be sought from the god. It was believed that the sick person who came to be cured and slept within the temple confines could be visited by the god in a dream and so receive a healing touch or an omen.[5] From the fifth century on, incubation became of the greatest importance throughout the Greek-speaking world, down to the latest pagan times and into the modern Christian era. In this way the dream with a direct message or omen continued to be sought by numbers of people, among them the great Sophocles, who offered his home as the first shrine of Aescylapius in Athens, apparently at the bidding of a dream.[6]

Dreams in Classic Greek Literature

Many of the classics of Greek literature contain references to dreams, and this is hardly strange. In the great Greek dramas the authors were creating an essence of life as it really was, a picture that struck at the hearts of those who watched, as these plays still do today. It would be surprising if dreams had not appeared as one of the crises providing dramatic suspense.

In Aeschylus's plays, for instance, we find numerous examples in which dreams occur in this way. In his *Persians,* which was the only Greek tragedy we know of based on actual history, the action begins with the striking scene in which the queen mother is warned through a strange dream of Xerxes' impending death (176–230). One of the most dramatic points in his last play, *Choephoroe,* is the scene in which Orestes learns of his mother's dream of giving birth to an asp that suckles her; this is the scene that lays bare before him the tragic role he is to play (523–52). *Prometheus Bound* was raised entirely to the level of the gods except for the character of Io, and here the fateful quality of dreams is brought into the open. As Prometheus rants at his fate among the gods, he stops to recall what he has done for people. They were huddled phantoms in a dream when he first found them, and one of the greatest gifts he brought them was the ability to understand dreams and to distinguish the true ones from the false (442–506). Later, when Io comes to Prometheus in her half-crazed wanderings and wants to know her fate, he insists that she speak of her sufferings. Io complains of her dreams, the fearful dreams of love that Zeus gave her. She finally had to tell her father about them, and he asked the oracles again and again how the demand of the gods could be met; in the end they learned that, because of her dreams, she was committed to wander the ends of the earth (645–60).

Aeschylus was living in the great age of which Herodotus wrote, when Pheidippides made his 150-mile run before the battle of Marathon. According to Herodotus, the runner was helped by a vision of the god Pan to reach Sparta and bring aid (5.105), while the turncoat Hippias was dreaming of lying in the arms of his mother. Herodotus told that Hippias hoped to regain power by helping the Persians at Marathon and was sure that his dream was a good omen. But as he was directing the operations of the Persians, Hippias sneezed and coughed, and a tooth flew out of his mouth into the sand, and he could not find it. Then he knew that this was the end of his dream: his only share was to be the tiny spot of land of which his tooth had taken possession (5.107). The Persians took the pass and then were defeated on the plain of Marathon. When there was peace again, the Athenians set up a temple to Pan under the Acropolis and established sacrifices in accordance with the vision of Pheidippides.

These were also the years in which the great Pindar was writing his odes. In them Pindar expressed the basic Greek reverence for the dream. "Each man's body," he wrote, "follows the call of overmastering death; yet still there is left alive an image of life, for this alone is from the gods. It sleeps while the limbs are active; but while the man sleeps it often shows in dreams a decision of joy or adversity to come" (Fragment 131, 116B). According to the later writers, Pindar himself had seen a vision of "the Mother of the Gods" in the form of a stone statue and had also seen the establishment of a cult of worship because of his vision.[7]

Sophocles, the man of social position and civic prominence who let the world know of his devotion to the cult of Aescylapius, wrote into his plays both the fateful character of dreams and the need to see them clearly. In *Electra* the queen dreams that Agamemnon lives again and plants his scepter beside the hearth, and it sprouts a tree that overshadows the whole country. The queen reacts one way; she makes a fearful offering to propitiate the dead king. But throughout the rest of the play her dream and the righteous interpretation Electra gives it foreshadow what will actually happen. The chorus sings: "If I am not an erring seer. . . . Justice, that hath sent the presage, will come, triumphant" (470).

In one brief comment in *Oedipus the King,* Sophocles essentially encompassed the whole relationship of the world of dreams to human action and motivation. In this scene Oedipus, who bears the curse that he was destined to slay his father in order to possess his own mother, is talking with Iocasta, his queen. Iocasta has almost persuaded him that no human being can really "see" or divine what is to be, when a messenger comes to tell the king that Polybus, his supposed father, no longer lives. But Oedipus is not relieved of his fear, and the queen almost taunts him with his foolishness. It is better, she says, to live at random; many people have had dreams like this, "but he to whom these things are as nought bears his life most easily" (876–986). Then this woman walks out and kills herself for "nought"—because the king has discovered that she was his mother, wife to his real father, who had died as the seers said he would, by his son's hand.

Euripides also used dreams to set the theme of several of his plays. *Hecuba* begins with the scene in which the former queen of Troy cries out for someone to interpret her tragic symbols, and these dread visions of Hecuba's sleep set the stage for both this play and *The Trojan Women.* The whole story of *Iphigenia among the Tauri* hangs on those "strange visions the past night brought me [Iphigenia], which I will tell to the air, if there is really any help in that" (42–66). Iphigenia is captive of the primitive Tauri and serves them as priestess, sacrificing the Greek warriors who fall into their hands. She has dreamed of the fall of her father's house, with one pillar left standing which sprouts hair and becomes human. To the empty air she says: "The meaning is that my brother Orestes is dead." Then Orestes and his companion, led by the command of the gods, land on the Tauri shore.

As the real meaning of her dream becomes clear (more like Electra's dream), this heroic daughter of Agamemnon throws herself back upon the fates. "Begone, ye lying dreams," she says and bravely helps her brother face the visions of his madness. Finally, as they are escaping from the primitive land, the chorus of captive women relates the reason why dreams are no longer as significant as they used to be. The great earth oracle at Delphi had originally been a dream oracle, guarded by a great serpent. Apollo vanquished the serpent, and then mortals became less concerned with his oracles. When he complained to the father god, Zeus simply stopped Mother Earth from sending dreams to them (1234–83). Without the protection of the serpent, it would seem, the authority of the gods was endangered if mortals could understand dreams.

Throughout his history Herodotus continued the tradition of the divine origin of dreams. A world traveler, he brought back tales and history from all over the known world. He found visions and dreams from as far off as Persia and Egypt that were significant enough to relate. One story he brought back from his African travels was about the variation of incubation found among the Nasamonians in Western Africa. According to Herodotus's description, this nomadic people would return to the graves of their ancestors for divination; after praying, they lay down to sleep there, and dreams came to them which guided their conduct (4.172). In several cases he told how the great figures of history were warned of impending disaster by the dreams that they or those around them received; he also told of omens of great deeds that came in dreams.[8]

By the time of Aristophanes the great age of Greek enlightenment had reached its height and, as Dodds shows so clearly, the reaction had set in. Intellectual leaders in Athens were prosecuted and punished, book burnings took place, and many suffered for their opinions. The comedies of Aristophanes poked fun—none too gentle fun—at some of the most serious matters of Greek life. There was an increasing reliance on dreams, and the diviners, who were always good for a laugh, were mentioned in several of his comedies. For instance, *The Wasps* opens with a discussion between two drowsy slaves who have each had a dream; instead of hiring an interpreter, they decide to save the money and tell them to the audience.

The story of *The Wasps* has to do with an old man who wants to spend all his time standing in the court and judging. Everything has been done to cure him; he has even been taken to sleep the night in Aescylapius's temple. Athens laughed at this first literary notice of incubation in the temples of Aescylapius. But while Athens laughed, the people themselves continued to seek for the divine dream, and the philosophers sought to understand what was going on.

Plato and the Dream

Whatever else we may say about Greek philosophy, it unquestionably reached maturity in the fourth century with the work of Plato. There is hardly a sector of human thought that has not been influenced in some way by his reasoning, for Plato's was one of the greatest minds the world has yet known. While he tried to find a rational way of approaching human experience, he did not attempt to rationalize any part of it out of existence. On the contrary, he placed a high value on people's experiences of the nonrational side of life, including dreams and the way people looked at them.

In the century before Plato there were skeptics who denied the objective value of dreams. Heraclitus, who earned the name "The Weeping Philosopher," saw that in dreams each of us retires to a world of his or her own, and for him this denied what should be the rule—"to follow what we have in common." The poet-philosopher Xenophanes apparently also denied the validity of divine dreams, since he rejected any form of divination. But there was also the great physical philosopher Democritus, who tried to understand an actual physical mechanism by which objective dream experiences could occur. His theory was that there are images—and he even used the Homeric word *eidola*—continually emanating from persons and objects that penetrate the pores of a dreamer's body and cause him to see happenings at a distance, even in another person's mind. This older and respected contemporary of Socrates became known as "The Laughing Philosopher," and it has been suggested that many of his interesting and useful theories were forgotten in modern times simply because he did not seem serious enough to be weighty.

While perhaps Plato did not put the same stress on dreams as some of his contemporaries, he did give attention to their influence on people's actions.[9] In the passages of the *Crito* and the *Phaedo*, when he depicted the last days of Socrates, Plato carefully set down the great master's concern with two of his own dreams. It is not even clear whether Plato was expressing his own opinions or those of his master. The first of these, which has been discussed at length by one Jungian analyst because it is so revealing, occurs in the *Crito* when Socrates was discussing the ship from Delphi whose coming meant death for him:

> SOCRATES: But I do not think that the ship will be here until tomorrow; this I infer from a vision which I had last night, or rather only just now, when you fortunately allowed me to sleep.
> CRITO: And what was the nature of the vision?
> SOCRATES: There appeared to me the likeness of a woman, fair and comely, clothed in bright raiment, who called to me and said: "O Socrates, The third day hence to fertile Phthia shalt thou come."
> CRITO: What a singular dream, Socrates!
> SOCRATES: There can be no doubt about the meaning, Crito, I think.
> CRITO: Yes; the meaning is only too clear. But oh! my beloved Socrates, let me entreat you once more to take my advice and escape.[10]

In the *Phaedo*, Cebes and Socrates were talking about the fact that so many people had noted how Socrates turned poet during his last days in prison. He was turning Aesop's fables into verse and had even composed a hymn in honor of Apollo. The poet Evenus teased Socrates, wondering if the philosopher were trying to equal him. To this Socrates replied:

> Tell him, Cebes, he replied, what is the truth—that I had no idea of rivalling him or his poems; to do so, as I knew, would be no easy task. But I wanted to see whether I could satisfy my conscience on a scruple which I felt about the meaning of certain dreams. In the course of my life I have often had intimations in dreams "that I should make music." The same dream came to me sometimes in one form, and sometimes in another, but always saying the same or nearly the same words: "Set to work and make music," said the dream. And hitherto I had imagined that this was only intended to exhort and encourage me in the study of philosophy, which has been the pursuit of my life, and is the noblest and best of music. The dream was

> bidding me do what I was already doing, in the same way that the competitor in a race is bidden by the spectators to run when he is already running. But I was not certain of this; for the dream might have meant music in the popular sense of the word, and being under sentence of death, and the festival giving me a respite, I thought that it would be safer for me to satisfy the scruple, and, in obedience to the dream, to compose a few verses before I departed. And first I made a hymn in honour of the god of the festival, and then considering that a poet, if he is really to be a poet, should not only put together words, but should invent stories, and that I have no invention, I took some fables of Aesop, which I had ready at hand and knew by heart—the first that occurred to me—and turned them into verse.[11]

In both of these instances it is clear that Socrates takes his dreams quite seriously, and Plato takes Socrates quite seriously. One does not talk of trivia in the last days under sentence of death, at least not this man, and it is certainly with reverence that Plato treats these incidents. Both men saw meaning in dreams. Not only did Socrates take careful note of them, but he took pains to understand and interpret them and tried to live the suggestions that they gave. He wanted to satisfy a certain anxiety, a matter of conscience arising from his dreams, and so he spent part of his last days in an unusual activity that a recurring dream had suggested.

In the *Republic* it is simply accepted that God communicates with people by dreams and waking visions. "He changes not, and does not deceive others, waking or dreaming, either by phantasms or by sign or by word," Plato remarked in Book 2, when he was discussing whether the poets had given an adequate picture of God in their portrayal of certain actions of the gods. He brought up particularly Homer's story of the false dream Zeus sent to Agamemnon, and concluded, "Then, although we are admirers of Homer, we shall not admire the lying dream which Zeus sends to Agamemnon" (*Republic* 2.382). He believed that one should not speak of divine things in this way; when the gods spoke, they spoke the truth, and one of the ways was by dreams and visions.

In the ninth book of the *Republic*, Plato wrote further on dreams. There he showed a clear understanding of the fact that dreams can often reveal the dark, instinctual side of human beings. And as Dodds has pointed out, he no longer saw the clear-cut dialogue between the soul and "the passions of the body" which his earlier works depicted; in the *Republic* this had become an internal dialogue between two parts of the soul itself. Plato knew that dreams could be an expression of the bestial side of human nature, the id of Freud. Yet he also realized that if individuals' lives are in harmony and well balanced, they can approach the timeless unknown and find truth in dreams. By using their reason to keep the "appetites" from simply taking over in sleep, they can leave the other side of their nature free to contemplate the unknown—past, present, and future—and so come most nearly to truth in their dreams. The passage is as follows (italics are mine):

> I do not think that we have adequately determined the nature and number of the appetites, and until this is accomplished our inquiry will always be confused.
>
> Well, he said, it is not too late to supply the omission.
>
> Very true, I said: and observe the point which I want to understand: Certain of the unnecessary pleasures and appetites I conceive to be unlawful; everyone appears to have them, but in some persons they are controlled by the laws and by the better desires with the help of reason, and either they are wholly banished or they become few and weak; while in others they are stronger, and there are more of them.
>
> Which appetites do you mean?
>
> I mean those which wake when the rest of the soul—the reasoning and human and ruling power—is asleep; then the wild beast within us, gorged with meat or drink, starts up and having shaken off sleep goes forth to satisfy his desires; and you know that there is no action which at such a time, when he has parted company with all shame and sense, a man may not be ready to commit; for he does not, in his imagination, shrink from incest with his mother, or from any unnatural union with man, or god, or beast, or from parricide, or the eating of forbidden food. And in a word, no action is too irrational or indecent for him.
>
> Most true, he said.
>
> But when a man's pulse is healthy and temperate, and when before going to sleep he has awakened his rational powers, and fed them on noble thoughts and inquiries, collecting himself in meditation; after having first indulged his appetites neither too much nor too little, but just enough to lay them to sleep, and prevent them and their enjoyments and pains from interfering with the higher principle—which he leaves in the solitude of pure abstraction, *free to contemplate and aspire to the knowledge of the unknown, whether in past, present, or future;* when again he has allayed the passionate element, so that he does not go to sleep with his spirit still excited by anger against anyone—I say, when, after pacifying the two irrational principles, he rouses up the third, in which resides reason, before he takes his rest, then, as you know, he attains truth most nearly, and is least likely to be the sport of fantastic and lawless visions.
>
> I quite agree.
>
> In saying this I have been running into a digression; but the point which I desire to note is that in all of us, even the most highly respectable, there is a lawless wild-beast nature, which peers out in sleep.[12]

Plato gave hints here that he saw something besides a negative or bestial side in human irrationality, and in other passages these suggestions were developed. In much the same way that C. G. Jung came to this realization in the present century, Plato had come to see that some of the highest intuitions and understandings that human beings have arise from their nonrational side, from their dream life. Their greatest gifts are given to them when something more than human breaks through their rationally constructed autonomy and gives them a divine *mania*. "Our greatest blessings come to us by way of *mania*, insofar as *mania* is heaven-sent," Plato wrote in the *Phaedrus* (244),[13] and he went on to show that this mania, or inspiration, is of four kinds. The first of them is prophecy, which was originally called by the name *mania*, and this the ancients testify is "superior to a sane mind, for the one is only of human, but the other of divine origin." The others are catharsis (or healing); poetry, which is inspired by the muses; and the greatest, the inspiration of love.

As Josef Pieper shows in *Love and Inspiration*, his excellent study of the *Phaedrus*,[14] the cathartic or healing mania is sometimes given through dreams. In the tradition of the temples of Aescylapius, he points out, they were the perfect example of being possessed by divine madness, since dreams are something that simply happens to dreamers, in which they are passive. It is not at all dependent upon their conscious rational personality, but in this case was the seed in which dreamers found a new reaction to themselves and to the world around them.

In the *Symposium* (203), Socrates reports what he was told by the prophetess Diotima that

> God mingles not with man; but through Love all the intercourse and converse of gods with men, whether they be awake or *asleep*, is carried on. The wisdom which understands this is spiritual; all other wisdom, such as that of arts and handicrafts, is mean and vulgar. Now these spirits or intermediate powers are many and diverse, and one of them is Love.

It is even more obvious that Plato believed that prophecy was received through dreams and visions. His explanation in the *Phaedrus* was not only confirmed by his reverence for the dreams of Socrates, but it was expanded at length in the *Timaeus*. Here Plato took some pains to demonstrate this belief. Because people might be led night and day only by phantoms and visions, instead of caring for rational consciousness, God contrived to place these images in the lower regions, giving them as reflections on the smooth surface of the liver, which has both a bright and sweet and a bitter quality.[15] Thus the liver is the seat of divination, because at times it is stirred by some gentle inspiration that makes use of its natural sweetness, correcting all things and enabling it to practice divination in sleep.

This, Plato goes on

> is a proof that God has given the art of divination not to the wisdom, but to the foolishness of man. No man, when in his wits, attains prophetic truth and inspiration; but when he receives the inspired word, either his intelligence is enthralled in sleep, or he is demented by some distemper or possession.

If people want to understand what was said in a dream or know the meaning of a vision, they must first recover their wits and be able to judge; but that is not prophecy. There are people customarily appointed interpreters or judges of inspiration, but it is ignorant to call them prophets, for they are "only the expositors of dark sayings and visions . . . [the] interpreters of prophecy" (*Timaeus* 71–72).

One does not take this much trouble to explain something in which he or she does not believe, nor return to it again and again, as, for instance, Plato did in the *Meno* (99–100), in the *Symposium* (203), and in *Ion* (533ff.). Certainly he valued the force of human reason as few people did in that day or any other, but he also believed that, for the highest reaches of life and understanding, something more than human reason is necessary. For prophetic understanding and healing, poetic insight, and even to know love or beauty, there must be intrusions of the divine, the more-than-human realm of reality that sets aside our ordinary, rational consciousness. And these intrusions often take place in dreams, as Pieper shows in his thorough reading of the Greek sources.[16] Plato recognized that dreams also come from the lower, often repressed elements of human nature, which at times he described almost in Freudian terms, save for the explicitness of "the unconscious." Indeed, the greatness of Plato was that he saw human beings as a whole and did not try to fit them or their dream life into one simply understood and easily comprehended point of view.[17]

The New Thinking of Aristotle

Aristotle, however, took a very different approach to the subject of dreams, which he dealt with directly in three little books: *On Sleep and Waking*, *On Dreams*, and *On Prophecy in Sleep*. His thinking on the subject was completely new. Seldom, in fact, do we find such daring originality buttressed by such careful and consistent thinking. Aristotle broke with the time-honored tradition about dreams, which had been nearly universal until his time, and so he gave us a totally different point of view from which the more ancient view can be observed and assessed. Although it had very little popularity in the ancient world, one aspect of his thinking was revived at the end of the Middle Ages, and, fragmented or not, this point of view took over until it became almost unquestioned authority for Western culture in modern times as well as for the entire Moslem world. His thinking is so modern, however, his arguments so commonplace to most of us, that it is difficult not to be swept off our feet when they are brought out into the open again.

According to Aristotle people are in contact only with the world of sense experience, which they come to understand through their reason. Since there is no experienceable nonphysical world from which dreams may emerge, they cannot be seen as anything but residual impressions left upon the soul by the previous day's activities. In the *Metaphysics*, where he uses the dream experience as one example of the category of the nonexistent (Δ.29, 1024b), Aristotle shows clearly that his theory of knowledge is a naive realism that has no place for the reality of psychic phenomena. Therefore, most dreams are nothing more than random reexperiencing—as if something accidentally flips the switch on our mental tape recorder and there are bits of playback. They have practically no significance. But since this, for the most part, was merely Aristotle's way of providing some rational understanding of dreams, we know that it did not occur to him to deny them all significance.

On the contrary, Aristotle believed that the soul was more sensitive during sleep and was, therefore, able to pick up sensations from outside that it would not ordinarily be able to perceive. This quality enabled it to appear prophetic or clairvoyant at times. Likewise, he believed that during sleep the soul was more aware of bodily sensations of which one was unconscious during waking hours, and so dreams might contain hints about the body's functioning that normal conscious thinking could not provide. This kind of prophetic knowledge, however, could be explained by good, natural reasons. He also reasoned that some dreams may bring about their own fulfillment by suggesting a course of action to the dreamer which he or she later pursues, and thus the prophetic result comes about naturally. Other dreams of the future, he concluded, are probably coincidental.

Aristotle's main contention was that dreams are not sent by the gods, that they are natural rather than divine phenomena. He did not come to this conclusion on empirical grounds, however, but by the following reasoning. He believed that the gods are the very epitome of rationality. If the gods sent dreams to people, they would send them only to intelligent and rational people. Instead, the fact is that simple people seem to receive significant and prophetic dreams as often as intelligent individuals. Aristotle was quite sure that the gods would not get their wires so crossed, and he had all the proof he needed in the fact that important dreams are not restricted to the intelligentsia; therefore the gods can have nothing to do with imparting them. His reasoning, of course, was based on the assumption that rationality is the essential quality of the gods and the only aspect of human life that they can appreciate. Jung pointed out quite another possibility in *The Development of Personality,* where he stressed the fact that all gifts are not of the intellect and that the godlike forces of the unconscious are not always intelligent. Still, Aristotle did observe at one point that some dreams have a demonic quality and that in a certain sense nature is demonic. But it is difficult to say exactly what he meant by this. Perhaps he wanted to suggest that there is still something of the unknown and the mysterious in both nature and dreams.

There was no similar rational analysis of dreams and dreaming in ancient literature, and even in the nineteenth century A.D. those who tried their hand at it added little to what Aristotle wrote in the fourth century before Christ. His ideas were gradually accepted during the Renaissance, largely through the church and the efforts of Aquinas, until an exaggerated Aristotelian attitude became the dominant one in Western culture. Yet there is one basic difference between Aristotle and his modern followers. It never occurred to Aristotle to ignore or belittle dreaming or dream interpretation; his idea was rather to bring it under rational scrutiny and analysis.[18] He simply wanted to remove the superstition and quackery that so often surrounds the consideration of dreams. In his time the concern with dreams was already increasing. And whether Aristotle went too far or not, it is our purpose to discover in the rest of these pages.

The Reconciliation in Hippocratic Medicine

It is easy to trace the source of Aristotle's ideas about the relation of dreams to the body. His father was a physician of the Hippocratic tradition at the court of the king of Macedonia. Although Aristotle mentions the great father of Greek medicine, Hippocrates of Kos, only once, he was clearly influenced by this school of medicine and may well have started on his scientific studies as a result of this background. There is a large body of Hippocratic writings that date back to the fourth century B.C. Although it is impossible to determine which, if any, came from the hand of Hippocrates, these writings form the unquestioned base for Greek and Roman medicine. In them we find a far more appreciative view of the value of dreams than is found in Aristotle.

An analysis of dreams is found in the book *On Regimen,* in which the author began his study (in Book 4) by a careful attempt to understand the process of dreaming and relate this to the traditional understanding of its meaning and value. He wrote:

> He who has learnt aright about the signs that come in sleep will find that they have an important influence upon all things. For when the body is awake the soul is its servant, and is never her own mistress, but divides her attention among many things, assigning a part of it to each faculty of the body—to hearing, to sight, to touch, to walking, and to acts of the whole body; but the mind never enjoys independence. But when the body is at rest, the soul, being set in motion and awake, administers her own household, and of herself performs all the acts of the body. For the body when asleep has no perception; but the soul when awake has cognizance of all things—sees what is visible, hears what is audible, walks, touches, feels pain, ponders. In a word, all the functions of body and of soul are performed by the soul during sleep. Whoever, therefore, knows how to interpret these acts aright knows a great part of wisdom.

> Now such dreams as are divine, and foretell to cities or to private persons things evil or things good, have interpreters in those who possess the art of dealing with such things. But all the physical symptoms foretold by the soul, excess, of surfeit or of depletion, of things natural, or change to unaccustomed things, these also the diviners interpret, sometimes with, sometimes without success.

The author then goes on to show how dreams can be interpreted to help in understanding one's physical health. His basic idea is that some dreams, by expressing the outer world simply as it is, show that the dreamer is in good relationship with it and suggest that his or her body is in good health. But when dreams show change contrary to the acts of the day, especially violent change, it is a sign that the soul of the individual is in turmoil and his or her body either is or will be affected. The underlying assumption is that psyche and body are in close harmony and that one greatly influences the other, which is precisely the understanding of modern psychosomatic medicine.

While the direct interpretations do sound funny—for instance, to diagnose circulatory disease from a dream about rivers in flood, or to prescribe purging because a patient dreams of a fiery, hot star—actually they are not so far out compared with the latest thinking in medicine and psychology.[19] This follower of Hippocrates might not sound foolish at all discussing diabetes or arthritis or heart disease with a group of internists and psychiatrists today, trying to picture the interplay of psyche and body that makes for disease or health. At the same time, this Hippocratic physician did not hesitate to mention his belief that some dreams are given directly by the gods.

In fact, on the island of Kos, where medical science had its beginnings, Aescylapius was also present in temple and ritual. As Carl Kerényi has shown in *Asklepios*, his careful study of the mythological origins of Greek medicine, incubation simply represented one side of the healing tradition. On the one hand, the physician studied and knew his patients and told them what to do; on the other, the elements within the patients themselves were given first chance to bring about a cure. In incubation, with its emphasis on dreams, the individual mystery of healing was preserved; although the physician might be called on to administer treatment suggested by a dream, he had no part in the process of incubation itself. For example, one early plaque dedicated by a grateful patient shows him lying on a bed being licked by a serpent, while in the foreground is a picture of the dream he is having of being operated on by the god. As Kerényi suggests, the divine dream undoubtedly played a large part in the amazing development of Greek medicine. And the two approaches continued to live side by side; about 250 B.C. a new temple for incubation was built at Kos, and in the following century it was replaced by an even larger one, serving this original center of Hippocratic medicine. It is not surprising that the same relationship continued as the concern with dreams increased in the later Hellenistic world.

Increasing Concern with Dreams

In these later secular times the growing concern with dreams was part of a generally increasing reliance upon the irrational, the supernatural experience of life. One aspect of this was the spread of Aescylapian healing, which was carried to many places throughout the Greek-speaking world. Pergamum in Asia Minor became one of the chief centers to which people came to be healed by the god. Here the great physician Galen also grew up, and here he studied medicine because Aescylapius had appeared to his father in a dream with instructions for the boy. Galen, who is revered today as the father of modern scientific medicine, was influenced throughout his life by dreams.

His various works describe not only an operation he performed on himself at the bidding of a dream that he apparently had in the temple of Aescylapius, but also his successful treatment of many patients by remedies revealed in dreams and the healing of others in the temple.[20] One of these was Marcus Aurelius, who was the physician's friend; the emperor spent an incubation period in the shrine at Pergamum and later thanked the god for remedies against his blood-spitting and dizziness. During the last half of his life, Galen practiced in Rome, where Aescylapius had long before been established. According to Ovid, the god was brought to Rome with great ceremony, and in the *Metamorphoses* it was described how dreams had made this possible. Traces of the temple carving and the head of the god can still be seen on the walls of the Tiberine Island in Rome.

In other matters dream books were widely used. These works on interpretation grew out of the "tables of correspondences," which Aristophanes undoubtedly refers to in *The Wasps* when the slave asks: "Shan't I give two obols and get us one of those clever interpreters of dreams?" A generation or so later a grandson of Aristides the Just was earning his living by using one of these forerunners of the dream book. After that a long list of men are known to have written on dream interpretation, whose works all have been lost. The only example of this ancient study which has survived to modern times is the *Interpretation of Dreams* by Artemidorus of Daldis, from the second century of our era. Interestingly enough, my search for a copy produced no modern translation from the Greek, but only the one made in 1644 and printed with a commentary in 1690, which is in the rare book room at Harvard.

Artemidorus's work, which is clearly in the Hellenistic tradition, was originally composed of five little handbooks on the meaning of common dream symbols, based on deduction from what he had observed to happen in people's lives. They were meant to be practical, and each one hammered away at the point that dream symbols have different meanings in different situations and for different persons. He followed the older classification of dreams that directly foretell the future and others that, in his estimation, are always symbolic. But Artemidorus was not concerned with arguing whether dreams were sent by the gods or not, since it was his view that all dreams have their fulfillment, each in its own time and manner. Most dreams are simply not to be construed directly, and his purpose was to establish a few rules to help in the complex matter of understanding them and to support this with specific applications.

During these centuries there was scarcely any disagreement with the understanding that dreams are significant. Writers like Vergil, Horace, Lucretius, and others who were greatly influenced by Greece all showed interest in them. Even the philosopher Cratippus, who was otherwise a follower of Aristotle, felt that the divine mind acted directly upon people when their bodies were asleep. Pliny the Elder wrote that, while some dreams are the result of an upset constitution, others are caused by divine intervention. Like the later Dio Cassius (who also wrote an account of the dreams that foretold that Alexander Severus would become emperor), Pliny was inspired to write history because of a dream. Pliny the Younger recorded his consultation with Suetonius about interpreting dreams, while in *The Golden Ass,* with all of its ribald humor, Apuleius presented graphically the Platonic theory of their religious importance.

Cicero, in fact, was the only later writer of any significance who balked at the popular conviction that some dreams might be prophetic. He was so annoyed with the idea that he wrote *On Divinations,* in which he let his brother Quintus argue the facts and the ideas of the great philosophers, including his own friends. The Stoic idea of a natural knowledge of the future, Quintus finally held, gives support to the more primitive theory that dreams of the future are divine gifts. Cicero's reply then tore the theory to shreds, using basically the thinking of Aristotle, and concluding:

> Therefore, let divination by dreams be jeered off the stage, along with the other tricks of the soothsayers. . . .
>
> Now sleep is esteemed a refuge from the anxieties and burdens of life, but actually very many apprehensions and fears are born of it. Dreams, indeed, of themselves, would carry less weight and would be more lightly regarded were it not for the fact that they have been taken under the wing of philosophy, and not by incompetent bunglers, but by men of the highest degree of intellectual power—men who are able to distinguish between consistency and inconsistency and who are looked upon as models of all the philosophical virtues.[21]

Cicero was obviously striking at the common belief in soothsaying and fortune-telling. But his Aristotelian position made it impossible for him to see why human life needed *any* direct contact with spiritual elements, any intrusion of the nonphysical or supernatural that sometimes could bring knowledge of the future. He saw no reason for it. It is interesting that one of his earlier works was to become the basis for most of the medieval interest and belief in dreams.

It is also interesting that when the historians of these ancient times came to Cicero, they set down quite a different picture.

Dreams in the Ancient Histories

Plutarch wrote of Cicero that there had been deep reasons for his support of Caesar:

> For it seems, while Pompey and Caesar were yet alive, Cicero *in his sleep*, had fancied himself engaged in calling some of the sons of the senators into the capitol, Jupiter, according to the dream, being about to declare one of them the chief ruler of Rome. The citizens, running up with curiosity, stood about the temple, and the youths, sitting in their purple-bordered robes, kept silence. On a sudden the doors opened, and the youths, arising one by one in order, passed round the god, who reviewed them all, and, to their sorrow, dismissed them; but when this one was passing by, the god stretched forth his right hand and said, "O ye Romans, this young man, when he shall be lord of Rome, shall put an end to all your civil wars." It is said that Cicero formed from his dream a distinct image of the youth, and retained it afterwards perfectly, but did not know who it was.
>
> The next day, going down into the Campus Martius, he met the boys returning from their gymnastic exercises, and the first was he, just as he had appeared to him in his dream. Being astonished at it, he asked him who were his parents. And it proved to be this young Caesar.[22]

Plutarch did not discuss Cicero's later belittling of dreams, but he did compare the orator with the deeply serious Demosthenes, remarking that Cicero's wit often ran away with his understanding. Unlike Demosthenes, he often used mockery to destroy an adversary. Even when it came to dying, the two were opposites. Cicero met death trying to hide from his murderers, while Demosthenes turned down an offer to negotiate with his enemy, and instead took his own life. He had dreamed the night before that he was acting in a tragedy and acquitted himself as well as he could, but there was a contest in which he was the loser because the props had not been provided for his part on stage.

Indeed, except for Thucydides, none of these ancient historians looked upon dreams the way Aristotle and Cicero did. Thucydides wrote his magnificent account of the Peloponnesian War without making a single reference to a dream; he became not just the "father of history," but of the modern materialistic interpretation of history. Otherwise all the great historians recorded the important dreams that were associated with so many major events. Like Herodotus and

Xenophon before them, Plutarch, Tacitus, Josephus, Philo, Suetonius—all set down these experiences again and again as an essential part of the record.[23] If this seems strange, we must remember that the life of Lincoln furnishes an example of just such a dream before his assassination, which is recorded by the historians who knew him best.

Suetonius, for instance, included the dreams of Nero, which tell so much of the inner life and destiny of this tragic man. It was after the murder of his mother that Nero began to dream. In one recurring vision he saw himself steering a ship, saw the rudder forced from his hand, and then found himself being dragged by his wife into some dark place of torment. Two successive dreams were told by Josephus which were believed to have saved the city of Jerusalem from destruction in 332 B.C. Alexander the Great had taken Gaza, and his armies looked forward to sacking Jerusalem, but Jaddus the high priest was told in a dream to open the city and go out in all his robes to meet the conqueror. When Alexander saw this man robed in purple and gold, he did a thing so strange that his commanders thought he was mad. He went up alone and knelt before Jaddus. Then he revealed that before leaving Macedonia he had had a dream in which this man, in the very same garments, appeared and gave him safe conduct to cross over into Asia. Therefore, when Alexander saw the man of his dream, he had knelt down to worship God.

Plutarch in particular left a record of the way the great people of ancient Greece and Rome regarded their dreams. One of the earliest dreams he related was that of Alcibiades just before he was assassinated. Alcibiades dreamed that he was dressed in the clothes of his mistress, who held him in her arms and painted his face like a woman's. A few days later he died alone in Timandra's arms, and she did indeed take her own garments to wrap and prepare his body for burial.

Many of the experiences Plutarch recounted had to do with war and violence and the direct effect of dreams on history. Jupiter took a hand in one of Aristides' campaigns by appearing in a fascinating dream that told specifically where to prepare for battle and also led to a lasting alliance, as well as the discovery of a very ancient Eleusinian temple. Lucullus once saved the city he was besieging because he dreamed of a man saying to him, "Go a little farther, Lucullus, for Autolycus is coming to see you." The next day, as he was driving the enemy to their boats, he discovered a statue abandoned on the beach. When he was told that it was Autolycus, the founder of the city, then Lucullus remembered the advice of Sulla, that "nothing is to be treated as so certain and worth relying on as an intimation given in dreams." And, instead of leveling the town, he honored Autolycus by turning his city into one of the first urban redevelopment projects in history.

Often these accounts by Plutarch showed how much a dream revealed about a person and what was to happen in his or her life.

Before his final battle Pyrrhus was elated by seeing in his sleep that thunderbolts fell on the city he was about to attack, setting it all on fire; but his adviser interpreted the vision as a warning of the gods not to tread upon the place that has been struck by lightning and so is sacred to them. As it turned out, even the women had trussed up their skirts and pitched in to defend the city, and Pyrrhus and most of his army fell in the battle. Centuries later when Antony dreamed of lightning just before learning of Caesar's plot to kill him, it was his own right hand he saw struck by a thunderbolt. As Plutarch suggested, Antony's downfall was never on this side of the fence; it was his "character to be better in calamities than at any other time." And for Antony, Cleopatra was waiting.

Plutarch also told of Pompey's dream of the theater on the night before his great battle with Caesar. But Pompey dreamed of being a spectator and of hearing the people make a great noise over him as he made his formal entry into the theater. Then he saw himself go forward with his retinue, carrying the many spoils of war, and these he placed as adornments in a temple to Venus the Victorious. When Pompey woke he could not help being encouraged by his vision. But then he remembered that Caesar's family name was derived from the goddess Venus, and he realized in terror that he might be adorning the temple only for Caesar's role on stage. If Caesar won the battle, the temple of Venus the Victorious would be rightfully his, decorated with everything that should have been Pompey's. That day Caesar sliced through Pompey's army like cheese and walked into his camp simply aghast at the splendor—the tables loaded, the wine ready to pour, the garlands and hangings, and rich embroidery underfoot.

Meanwhile Pompey had fled and spent the night in a fisherman's cottage near the coast. But a dream was already making known his presence there. Offshore there was a large merchant vessel waiting for the morning tide. As Pompey seized a rowboat on the river to row out to sea, the captain was telling a vision he had seen in his sleep. Pompey, whom he knew by sight, had appeared—not as he usually appeared in Rome, but as a dejected and miserable man who sat down and talked with the dreamer. Just then one of the crew shouted that they were being hailed by a small boat, and the captain saw the miserable and dejected Pompey of his dream and took him aboard. And so Pompey was started on his journey toward Egypt and death by a dream.

These ancient people revered dreams. Both the classical Greeks and the later Hellenistic people looked to them for messages, sometimes prophetic messages, from a nonhuman source. Only a few of the most skeptical cast doubts upon them as revelations of something beyond human beings, and even these skeptics believed that dreams were, at the least, important indications of the physical state of a person's life. How different this is from the proper attitude of the nineteenth century. The majority of the Greeks did not use their reason and logic to eliminate dreams or other nonrational experiences from life. The Greeks used these faculties, as far as they were able, to develop all their gifts. With this understanding of the attitude of Greek culture, let us now turn to look at the attitude toward dreams found in the Greek New Testament of the Christian church.

Chapter
4

The Dreams and Visions of the New Testament

How much there is in the Bible about dreams. There are, I think, some sixteen chapters in the Old Testament and four or five in the New in which dreams are mentioned; and there are many other passages scattered throughout the book which refer to visions. If we believe the Bible, we must accept the fact that, in the old days, God and his angels came to men in their sleep and made themselves known in dreams.

These words are not the comment of a biblical critic, but of a president of the United States. Abraham Lincoln was discussing a disturbing dream he had had, talking with a group of friends just before his assassination. He went on to say that after the dream, in which he saw his own body lying in state in the White House, he had opened up his Bible, and "strange as it may appear, it was the twenty-eighth chapter of Genesis, which relates the wonderful dream Jacob had. I turned to other passages, and seemed to encounter a dream or a vision wherever I looked. I kept on turning the leaves of the old book, and everywhere my eyes fell upon passages recording matters strangely in keeping with my own thoughts—supernatural visitations, dreams, visions, and so forth."[1] Similar strange events occurred at the time of the assassination of President Kennedy, as I have shown in my book *Myth, History, and Faith.*

These observations of Lincoln about the dreams of the Bible are very much to the point. They are also quite right in associating the dreams so closely with the visions and supernatural visitations, for these are all of one piece. Particularly in the New Testament, they can hardly be separated. In the Greek of the New Testament there were many different ways of describing the fact that one had had a vision or a dream; but the important thing was the content that came before consciousness rather than the exact state in which it came. No hard and fast lines were drawn between the state of dreaming as we understand it and the state of trance or the ecstatic consciousness in which a vision was received. Sometimes two or three quite different names were used to speak of a single experience, and at times it is difficult to be sure which state was signified by the writer. All of them—dream, vision, and trance—were valued to such a degree that there was no urgent need to distinguish one from another. And this basic attitude was shared by later Judaism as well as the Hellenistic world.

"Basic Greek"

Since it is difficult to understand what the Greek New Testament means by these experiences without knowing the words that were used, we shall look carefully at a little basic Greek. There were twelve different words and expressions, each of them a different way of saying that one had come into contact with some reality other than that perceived through the physical senses.

These experiences must all be understood if we are to describe and discuss the dreams and visions of the New Testament, for there is no place to make the break. These authors, instead of defining visions and trances and "appearances" strictly, used now one and then another of these words to picture the occurrence of something real that was like a dream but could happen to some people when they were not exactly asleep. The words all refer to experiences that are alike in this way. They describe how something very real and important which did not originate in the external, physical world and could not have been created by the conscious will, came before the consciousness of one or even several individuals. These people believed that there was a psychic world of nonmaterial reality—a spiritual world—from which these experiences could emerge. Let us look at these expressions and try to see what the New Testament is actually saying.

1. Dream (ὄναρ)

Onar is a common word for *dream* used in much the same sense as we use that noun to mean any content that comes in sleep and is remembered. Precisely, it is a vision seen in sleep as opposed to waking. This word is used in Matthew to tell of the divine visitations to Joseph (1:20; 2:13, 19, 22) and to the wise men (2:12) and to Pilate's wife to warn about harming Jesus (27:19). *Onar* was in common use from the time of Homer on and was frequently used to describe experiences in which the spiritual world spoke.

2. Vision seen in sleep (ἐνύπνιον)

Enypnion signifies a thing or vision seen in sleep. It is derived from the common word for *sleep, hypnos,* and means literally "in sleep," or the events or happenings that occur during sleep. This word was also common in Greek literature, but in the New Testament it is found only in Acts 2:17 and Jude 8. It stresses the givenness, the almost surprise quality, of what is received in sleep.

3. Vision (ὅραμα)

There are three words in Greek that were used in the New Testament for our word *vision.* All of them are related to the verb *horaō,* which can mean either to see or notice in the sense of outer perception, or to see something that is not physical, a vision.

Horama, "vision," is the most common of these words. It occurs twelve times, eleven of them in the Book of Acts (Matt. 17:9; Acts 7:31; 9:10, 12; 10:3, 17, 19; 11:5; 12:9; 16:9, 10; 18:9). It is especially interesting because it can refer to visions of the night or sleeping experiences, as well as to waking visions. Thus it covers both the dream as we know it and the vision. *Horama* is used to translate the Hebrew words for both *dream* and *vision,* and since it can refer to the state in which one receives a vision, it may also refer to the dreaming state. Significantly enough, this word does not make the distinction we so carefully make either between dreams and visions or between physical and nonphysical perceptions.

4. Vision (ὅρασις)

The second of these, *horasis,* can signify the eye as the organ of sight, an appearance of any kind, even a spectacle, but there are also two instances where it means a supernatural vision (Acts 2:17; Rev. 9:17). While the word is related to *horama,* it refers to the supernatural content received rather than to the act or psychological process of seeing it. It has to do with the appearance conferred on things, and here again the distinction between the perception of the physical and the nonphysical is lacking in the Greek. Both "seeings" are genuine perception.

5. Vision (ὀπτασία)

Optasia is still another word for the supernatural vision derived from *horaō,* one that refers almost exclusively to this kind of seeing. Derived from the aorist passive tense of the verb, it has the sense of self-disclosure, of "letting oneself be seen." It is found four times in the New Testament (Luke 1:22; 24:23; Acts 26:19; 2 Cor. 12:1) and can refer either to the content of the visionary experience or to the state of being in which one receives it. Specifically, the idea is a self-revealing of the divine; the Deity permits a human being to see either his own divine being or something else usually hidden from human sight.

6. Trance, ecstatic state (ἔκστασις)

Ekstasis is the word from which the English word *ecstasy* is derived. It means literally standing aside from oneself, being displaced or over against oneself; and ordinarily there is a sense of amazement, confusion, or even of extreme terror. It was used to describe the astonishment of those who saw the mighty works of Jesus (Mark 5:42, Luke 5:26), the awe of the disciples at the empty tomb (Mark 16:8), and the reaction of the crowd to Peter's first healing (Acts 3:10). The meaning is that people have been shaken out of their ordinary attitudes, and thus it can denote a state in which a person's ordinary consciousness has been suspended by God's action so that some new perception will get through to him or her. This was the word for Peter's state when he fell asleep on the rooftop in Joppa and God spoke to him (Acts 10:10; 11:5), as well as Paul's experience when he was praying in the temple and the Lord spoke (Acts 22:17). Thus *ekstasis* may refer to either sleeping or waking experiences, and psychologically both the dreams of sleep and the imagery that occurs on the border of wakefulness, hypnagogic or hypnopompic imagery, fit the condition that *ekstasis* describes. It is misleading to use the word *trance* as a direct translation.

7. To become in the spirit (γίνομαι ἐν πνεύματι)

The whole revelation of John is introduced by the phrase *ginomai en pneumati,* which is quite similar in meaning to *ekstasis* (Rev. 1:10). This expression, "to become in the spirit," signified a state in which one could see visions and be informed or spoken to directly by the spirit. It is translated by Goodspeed as "to fall into a trance," and by Moffatt as "to be rapt in the Spirit." In other places there are related phrases used, as in the Temptation story when Jesus was "led or driven by the Spirit" (Matt. 4:1; Mark 1:12; Luke 4:1), and when Elizabeth was "filled with the Holy Spirit" and suddenly knew that Mary was to bear the Christ (Luke 1:41).

8. To stand by (ἐφίστημι, παρίστημι, ἵστημι)

Sometimes the New Testament refers simply to the fact that some reality stands by (*ephistēmi, paristēmi*) in the night (Acts 23:11; 27:23) or is made to stand (*histēmi*) in the day (Acts 10:30). This may be the Lord, or it may be described as an angel, or even as a human being who appears and commands attention in order to bring some message.

9. Angel (ἄγγελος)

Angelos or *angel,* which occurs so often in the New Testament, can mean either an actual physical envoy, a messenger, or a divine being sent by God. The passages are almost always clear; something very real appears that is seen and usually heard, but the experience is not concretized. The angel is a visionary reality, one of great importance and power. It inspires the emotional reaction of awe and fear that is always present when one comes into contact with the numinous or holy; and the angel's first action is often reassurance, to calm the fear of the person who is having the experience. In many places after a transaction with an angel has been described, the author later refers back to the vision that has been experienced. In fact, there is hardly a reference in the New Testament in which angels can be seen as anything but visionary contents, beings without physical reality who are still powerful and very real and significant.

10. Demons, the devil (δαιμόνια, διάβολος)

Then there are the demons, (*daimonion*) and the devil (*diabolos*). Throughout the New Testament people appear to have direct knowledge of these realities, both as they possess other people and directly in dreams and visions. One reason Paul encourages discerning of spirits is so that the evil ones may be confronted and rejected. But they are no more seen as concrete physical beings than the angels. Demons are nonphysical entities that can be experienced just as one experiences a vision or a dream. Experiences of demons are essentially visions of negative spiritual realities; they were beings without physical aspects who were still real and powerful enough to get hold of a person's physical body or psyche and cause him or her trouble.

11. To see, to perceive (βλέπω, εἴδω, ὁράω)

Twice in Revelation (1:2, 11) the vision is referred to as the action of seeing, using the common Greek verbs *blepō* and *eidō*. Here it is simply stated that John recorded "whatsoever things he saw," as the voice he heard in the Spirit instructed him. Again, in the story of the Transfiguration, the vision was referred to as "what they had seen," using the verbs *eidō* and *horaō* (Mark 9:9; Luke 9:36). These were words with an ordinary range of meaning like our word *see,* which were familiar expressions in the New Testament for the seeing of visions. This usage was also common in Greek literature.[2] Obviously visionary contents were considered just as easy to perceive and observe, just as much given and as valid as the perceptions one has of the outer physical world.

12. Disclosure or revelation (ἀποκάλυψις)

The common Greek word for "disclosure, uncovering, or revealing," *apokalypsis,* was also used for the divine uncovering. Like the English word *reveal,* or *unveil, apo-kalyptō* means simply to uncover. Just as physical things and the secrets of the human heart can be uncovered and brought out of hiding, so can nonphysical things, divine things, be unveiled. What is brought to light is then seen as a revelation.

Throughout the New Testament this word is used to signify things disclosed by God or by the Spirit, either in some direct way, or through dreams and visions or human reasoning and intuition. But there was really little distinction made between revelation that was imparted by

God in thoughts and understanding, and the disclosures that were given in images in dreams and visions. This word *apokalypsis* is not the same as the English word *apocalypse*, with its specialized theological meaning. We have trouble separating revelation from its eschatological meaning, referring only to things to come, the final things in the ultimate divine purpose. The Greek word instead refers simply to any disclosure in the realm of spirit that was formerly hidden. This meaning is found clearly in Romans 16:25; 1 Corinthians 14:6, 26; 2 Corinthians 12:1, 7; and Galatians 2:2. In 2 Corinthians the word is linked closely with visions. Its use throughout the New Testament shows the belief of these writers that people could be given special knowledge of a nonphysical world, that the veil which so often covers this world could be rolled back and one could see what was there. The dream and the vision were two ways in which this revealing took place.

These earliest Christians believed that the meaning and purpose of the outer world originated in this nonphysical, spiritual world and was deeply influenced by it. They believed that God speaks and works through this world, using such nonmaterial media as dreams and trances, visions, and appearances of angels. To them this was one of the regular ways in which God works, one which is complementary to his action through the material world and through history. They saw that through the death and resurrection of Christ there was a spirit of creative power, a new life that was available to people and could come from this invisible world. Christianity, then, offered not a devaluation of the importance of dreams or visions, but a new way of understanding them, and a new, supremely significant content for them to manifest.

It is unfortunate that the visions and trances and even the dreams of the Bible have come to be regarded as purely religious and supernatural. These experiences are still quite common. And while they do sometimes manifest a "more than natural" content, they are still natural experiences that can be observed and analyzed. They come from the world that is natural for human beings to encounter. In fact, the authors of the New Testament had a far more sophisticated view of these experiences than people seem to realize. They had a consistent theory about human beings in which dreams and visions had a definite place. Human beings, they saw, were in contact with both a physical world and a nonphysical one, both of them necessary to them. Neither could be avoided if people were to live with reality as it is. Dreams and visions, then, were important, because this was one way in which the nonphysical world intruded directly into the human psyche. This was basically a Platonic point of view.

Of course, this seems strange to us today. It is difficult to shake ourselves free of the assumption of our culture that human beings have contact with only one kind of reality. But if we are to grasp what they really believed, we must listen to these writers who felt the importance, as well as the difficulty, of describing the various encounters with nonphysical reality. Stripped of all these experiences, the meaning of the New Testament is difficult indeed to grasp. Let us turn to the record itself and see how frequent they are.

Dreams and Visions in the Four Gospels

The account of the life of Jesus of Nazareth begins in Luke with the story of the birth of John the Baptist. His father, Zechariah, was serving as priest in the temple when he saw an angel of the Lord standing by the altar. Zechariah was afraid, but the angel reassured him and then told him that his wife was to have a child, and they were to name him John. When Zechariah left the temple, he was mute, and it was apparent to the people waiting for him that he had had a vision (*optasian*) (Luke 1:11-22).

We have two accounts of the Annunciation. In Luke the angel Gabriel was sent to Mary, and she too had to be told not to fear; she would conceive by the power of the Holy Spirit and was to name her son Jesus. She also learned that her kinswoman Elizabeth had conceived in her old age, and Mary departed to see her. When she arrived, Elizabeth was filled with the Spirit and given knowledge that Mary was to bear the Savior (Luke 1:26-45). What Mary learned through the angel, Elizabeth was taught by being filled with the Holy Spirit (*eplēsthē pneumatos hagiou*). In Matthew, when Joseph found that Mary was pregnant, he was about to dismiss her quietly when an angel of the Lord came to him in a dream (*onar*) to tell him the story and inform him that the child's name was to be Jesus (1:20). Here the Annunciation is given in a dream, and thus far the story of the coming of the Christ child has woven together the different experiences of visions of angels with a dream and information by the Spirit.

In Luke's account the birth of Jesus was literally surrounded by angels. There was first the angel who stood by the shepherds in a great light. They too were afraid. After quieting their fears, the angel gave them the good news that they were to go to Bethlehem and find the child. And then there was a whole army, a multitude of heavenly host praising God (2:9, 13). Certainly the intent of Luke was to convey a tremendous spiritual experience, an experience like the vision (*optasia*) of angels at the tomb in 24:23. These were both visionary experiences, real but not physical, in both cases seen by a group. Matthew's account tells first how the wise men were warned in a dream (*onar*) to avoid Herod and then that an angel appeared in the same way to warn Joseph, and the family fled to Egypt. They remained there until Joseph was informed once more in a dream (*onar*) that Herod was dead. Finally, in a third dream (*onar*), he was instructed not to go into Judea, where Herod's son was ruler (2:12-23). Luke adds that, when Jesus was circumcised on the eighth day, he was called by the name the angel had given before his conception (2:21). Here again dreams and visions that are certainly central to the story are used alternately by Matthew and Luke to describe experiences of nonhuman intervention in the life of Jesus. This, of course, is one of the embarrassments that causes modern scholars to cast doubts upon the historical validity of the whole birth narrative.

While there is no record of dreams as such in the life of Jesus, there were visionary experiences that surrounded all the important events of his life. The first, the experience at Jesus' baptism, is described in the same way by all three Synoptic writers. The Spirit was seen descending upon Jesus in the appearance of a dove, and at the same time a voice was heard from heaven speaking about God's pleasure in Jesus (Matt. 3:16-17; Mark 1:9-11; Luke 3:21-22). Thus the vision was both seen and heard, probably by more than a few people, according to the Gospel of John, where the experience was first reported by John the Baptist (1:29-34). This Gospel later describes what happened when Jesus saw he must reveal himself. "Father, glorify your name," Jesus asked, and when a voice came out of heaven saying, "I have glorified it, and I will glorify it again," some of the crowd heard thunder, and others heard the voice of an angel speaking to Jesus (12:28-29). This experience, so similar to Jesus' baptism, was shared by the whole group, though each person's perception was different.

After his baptism Jesus was led or driven into the wilderness by the Spirit (*pneuma*) to be tempted by the devil (Matt. 4:1; Mark 1:12-13; Luke 4:1-2). This of necessity was a visionary experience. Jesus was guided, not to confront any outer manifestation of evil, but to meet face to face the inner power of evil, to confront its primary source in an experience as real as any physical encounter. After Jesus had withstood the vision of demonic power, the angels came and ministered to him, and he was restored. As Jung has commented in *Psychological Types,* the tremendous significance of the Temptation narrative lies in the fact that it was a vision and not a psychotic error about worldly power. Jung knew what was meant by such an experience; his own encounter with the power of darkness is described in chapter 6 of his *Memories, Dreams, Reflections.*

All through his ministry Jesus dealt with the demons he saw troubling people. He healed many of the sick by casting out demons and all kinds of evil spirits. These stories, telling of people who were released from the power of Satan and made well, occur twenty-seven times in the Gospels.[3] While there are no specific descriptions of seeing the demons or spirits, several times there were auditory visions in which Jesus spoke with them. Once the demons begged to enter a herd of swine and he gave them leave (Matt. 8:31-32; Mark 5:9-13; Luke 8:30-33), and others he rebuked for trying to reveal who he was (Mark 1:25, 34; 3:11-12; Luke 4:33-35, 41). These were clearly realities without physical bodies who were trying to take over and possess a human person and were quite capable of doing so.

In his teaching Jesus showed that he also believed in the reality of nonmaterial beings that were good, or angelic. In John 1:51 he gave Nathanael the expectation of seeing the heavens opened (much as Jacob once dreamed) and seeing the angels of God ascend and descend on the Son of Man. He taught that the angels of children always behold the face of his Father in heaven (Matt. 18:10) and also that the poor man Lazarus was carried to Abraham's bosom by the angels (Luke 16:22). Explaining that people do not marry after death, he showed that in resurrected life they become like the angels (Matt. 22:30; Mark 12:25; Luke 20:36).

Again and again Jesus explained how the Son of Man would come in his glory, and all the angels with him, but he made it clear that not even the angels know when this will be (Matt. 16:27-28; 24:31, 36; Mark 8:38). In both parable and direct statements he taught that angels are reapers who will gather the chosen of God and rejoice in them and acknowledge them (Matt. 13:49; Mark 13:27; Luke 12:9; 15:10). Sometimes he contrasted the angels with the devil or even with the devil and *his* angels, as in the parables of the sower and the sheep and the goats (Matt. 13:39; 25:31-33, 41). When the guard of the high priest came upon Jesus and his disciples in the garden of Gethsemane, Jesus turned to the disciple who had drawn his sword and told him, "Put your sword back. . . . Do you think that I cannot appeal to my Father, and he will at once send me more than twelve legions of angels?" (Matt. 26:52-53). There can be no doubt what this term meant to Jesus; angels were actual entities that did not belong to the physical world but had power to benefit people's lives, to help people in ways that were set against the destructive power of demons and the devil. In Jesus' references to these opposing realities, there is no hint of naïveté, no concretizing of that which is so clearly nonmaterial.

Before Jesus went up to Jerusalem, one of the most amazing experiences occurred, which was shared by the inner circle of disciples. They were on the Mount of Transfiguration when Moses and Elijah appeared to them, and the three disciples saw Jesus filled with radiant light. According to Luke, they stayed awake in spite of being heavy with sleep, undoubtedly experiencing something like a collective *ekstasis*. Coming down from the mountain, Jesus then told them to tell no one of the vision (*horama*, Matt. 17:9; "what they had seen," *eidon*, Mark 9:9; *horaō*, Luke 9:36). Later at Gethsemane, when the disciples had gone to sleep and Jesus was going through the very depth of agony, an angel appeared to him to give him strength (Luke 22:43). After this, one last dream was recorded; as Pilate was sitting to judge Jesus, Pilate's wife sent word to her husband to have nothing to do with that righteous man because she had suffered much in a dream (*onar*) concerning him (Matt. 27:19).

In all the accounts of the Resurrection we hear of angels. Luke describes the two men in dazzling apparel who spoke to the women inside the tomb (24:4) and then tells how the vision (*optasian*) was later described to Jesus by the disciples on the road to Emmaus before the disciples recognized him (24:23). In each of the narratives this appearance of angels in the tomb has an important place (Matt. 28:2; Mark 16:5; John 20:12). Those who were there certainly experienced something more than just an empty tomb; they found something that moved them greatly. These men and women had a vision of *non*-physical reality. Something numinous from the world of spirit appeared to them, and they were ministered to by the Spirit.

The Dreams and Visions of the Apostles in Acts

If this is true of the Gospels, it is even more so with Acts, and here the experiences are even more interrelated. Beginning with what happened at Pentecost, every major event in Acts is marked by a dream, a vision, or the appearance of an angel, and it is usually upon this experience that the coming events are determined.

It was on Pentecost, Acts tells, that the apostles were given the power to pick up the pieces of their lives and begin the organized life of a church with thousands of new converts. As these people were filled with the Spirit and spoke in other tongues ("tongues of ecstasy," according to the translators of the New English Bible), tongues of fire were seen (*horaō*) resting upon each of them, and the crowd who gathered heard words spoken in each of their many different languages (Acts 2:3-11). This was immediately understood by the apostles as a fulfillment of the prophecy of Joel, and Peter quoted the prediction that God would pour out his Spirit and their young men would see visions and their old men dream dreams (Joel 2:28). According to Acts this prophecy was fulfilled on Pentecost, and a vision was lived out. Certainly these men and women, who were a joke to the pagans and treated like criminals by their own people, were empowered by something from beyond the physical world. The experience of tongues was a breakthrough of nonphysical reality; it opened them to new experiences and also to a new understanding of dreams and visions.

Twice when the apostles made their escape from jail it was with the help of an angel (Acts 5:19; 12:6-11). The first time, when the whole group had been arrested after healing great numbers of people, an angel simply opened the prison and told them to go back to the temple and tell more about this way of life; and at daybreak they were doing so. Later, when Peter was arrested alone, an angel appeared in a bright light to take him from where he was chained between two jailers. In this account the apostles showed clearly their understanding that angels were visionary beings who seldom had power to act in the physical sense. When the angel told Peter to get dressed and follow, Peter "did not realize that what was happening with the angel's help was real; he thought he was seeing a vision [*horama*]," which was his usual understanding of angels (12:9). When he reached the house of the apostles, the maid recognized him, but his friends kept him standing outside knocking while they insisted it must be his angel she had seen (12:13-15).

Meanwhile, Stephen, who had been appointed to his ministry by the apostles, was accused before the council. Filled with the Spirit (*pneuma*), he spoke wisdom to them which hit home (Acts 6:10). Stephen told them to look to their own history; it was an angel, he recited, who appeared to Moses at the burning bush, an angel who made Moses their deliverer and gave them the divine law through him (7:30, 35, 38, 53). Stephen all but told them that such powers were still available through the Spirit, and his brief story ends with a theophany. With the heavens open and his eyes full of what he saw (*eidō*), he died asking forgiveness for those who took part in his death, and among them was Saul (7:55—8:1).

In the story of Philip, who was also appointed like Stephen, we see the direct interchangeableness of angels with the Spirit. An angel of the Lord directed Philip to go down toward Gaza, and on the road the Spirit prompted him to join the chariot of an Ethiopian eunuch, a pilgrim to Jerusalem whom he converted right there by the roadside. Later the Spirit caught Philip up so that the eunuch saw him no more, and he went on about his preaching in the towns (Acts 8:26-40). It is clear in this account that Luke considered the experience of an angel essentially the same as prompting by the Spirit. And from this point on the interrelation is unavoidable.

For at this point the unexpected happened. On the way to Damascus Saul was converted, who not only had no expectation of this, but who was going there with the strongest intention of persecuting the Christians. Again the experience is first described objectively, as it was seen to happen and as the group shared in it. A light from heaven struck Paul to the ground blind, and he heard a voice that said to him, "I am Jesus, whom you are persecuting"; those around him heard and were speechless (9:3-7).

When Paul described this to Agrippa in Acts 26:12-23, he spoke of "the heavenly vision [*optasia*]" (v. 19) and outlined to the king the ways in which he had been obedient to it. He also wrote in 2 Corinthians 12:1: "It is necessary to boast; nothing is to be gained by it, but I will go on to visions [*optasias*] and revelations [*apokalypseis*] of the Lord. I know a person in Christ who fourteen years ago was caught up to the third heaven—whether in the body or out of the body I do not know; God knows."[4] For three days Paul was blind, and then the Lord spoke again in a vision (*horama*) and told Ananias to go and lay his hands on a man named Saul so that he would recover his sight. When Ananias objected that he had heard of the evil Saul had done, the Lord convinced him to go (9:10-19), and thus Paul was started on his way as a chosen instrument for the Lord.

In the conversion of Cornelius by Peter there occurred a wonderful mixture of God's speaking through a trance, a dream, a vision, an angel, and by the Spirit (Acts 10). The chain of events began with Cornelius's vision (*horama*) of an angel while he was praying, apparently in the way he had learned from the Jews. The angel let this Gentile know that his charity and devotion had been noticed and that now he was to send to the next town for a man named Peter. Then, knowing very well that Peter was stiff-necked about Jewish law and particularly about eating with Gentiles, the Lord sent him a dream-trance in which he showed him "something like a large sheet" full of unclean animals that he told him to kill and eat. Peter knew that he had dreamed, and he was trying to figure out the wonderful symbolism of his vision (also *horama*) when the men from Cornelius arrived. Before they could knock, Peter was informed by the Spirit that they were outside and that he was to go with them without hesitation. The next day he preached to the whole household of Cornelius, and as the Spirit fell on them, they spoke in tongues, and Peter had them baptized on the spot. There was no avoiding it, for these people had received the Spirit just as he had in the beginning; then they begged him to stay on with them for several days.

Back in Jerusalem, when the circumcision party attacked Peter for this, he told them point by point what had happened. After hearing about his dream-trance and the angel and all the rest, they were convinced that he had done the right thing in bringing Gentiles into the new church, and they glorified God. Thus even the conservatives in Jerusalem were convinced when they knew that there had been dreams and visions and ecstatic gifts of the Spirit (Acts 11:1-18). And because of this they accepted a new turning point—one that was certainly important to us.

The first missionary project was also inspired by the Spirit when a prophet of Jerusalem came to Antioch. He foretold by the Spirit that there was to be a great famine in the land during the time of Claudius, and so the brethren in Antioch determined to send down relief to the Christians in Judea (11:28-30). The church there was also being attacked by Herod, and about this time Peter had his second experience of being taken from prison by an angel (12:6-11). And the next thing told is the rather gruesome way Herod died, which was confirmed by Josephus.[5] Herod had just made a rousing speech and was letting the people glorify him instead of giving the glory to God, when an angel of the Lord smote him and he was eaten by worms and died (12:20-23).

In Antioch, as Paul started out on his travels, the Holy Spirit was giving instructions (13:2), and Paul made several decisions that have been important to history. Probably the most important was his decision to cross from Asia into Europe, taking Christianity there into the heart of the Greek world. Since he was forbidden by the Spirit to speak the word in Asia, and the Spirit of Jesus did not permit his party to go into Bithynia, they passed by Mysia and went down to Troas. Here "a vision (*horama*) appeared to Paul in the night: a man of Macedonia was standing beseeching him and saying, 'Come over to Macedonia and help us' " (16:9). Here the same message is given in experiences of the Spirit, and then in a dream or vision of the night which was exactly like the objective dreams of the Greeks in Homeric times. These were both experiences to which Paul listened with care. Western Christianity, in fact, owes a great deal to this particular dream and to the fact that Paul quickly interpreted it and then acted upon it. It is interesting that at this point the "we" passages begin, and so this story may well be an eyewitness account.

But when Paul came to Corinth, he was discouraged. The agreeable indifference of Athens had left its mark, and now the Jews were attacking him again. Then "one night the Lord said to Paul in a vision, 'Do not be afraid, but speak and do not be silent; for I am with you, and no one will lay a hand on you to harm you, for there are many in this city who are my people.' " Paul obeyed and stayed there to work and preach for a year and a half (Acts 18:9-11). Paul's reverence for this kind of experience has had far-reaching results. The time he spent in Corinth accounts, at the least, for two-thirds of the letters that he left us. Besides the letters to the Corinthians, while he was with these people he wrote his great epistle to the Romans, his epistles to the Thessalonians, and probably his epistle to the Galatians.

Paul's decision to go to Jerusalem is described first as his being resolved in the Spirit (Acts 19:21) and later as being a captive to the Spirit (20:22). But through the Spirit the disciples at Tyre told Paul not to go (21:4). I rather suspect that Paul himself had muddled the Spirit somehow about going to Jerusalem. He told the elders at Miletus that the Holy Spirit kept testifying to him (probably through dreams) that imprisonment and afflictions awaited him (20:23), and after he was arrested in Jerusalem, he recalled how he had once been warned in a trance (*ekstasis*) that the people there would not accept his testimony about the Lord (22:17). Paul might have been wiser to give more consideration to this advice from the Spirit (20:23) and the Lord (22:17). As is the way of the Spirit, however, Paul's mistake was repaired; even though he had failed in Jerusalem, the Lord stood by him again in the night, in a vision or a dream and directed him to go to Rome (23:11).

The last of Paul's recorded dreams occurred once more at a crucial moment. The boat taking him to Rome was adrift before the storm, and the men were frightened and desperate. Then Paul had an experience that gave them all courage. "For last night there stood by me an angel of the God to whom I belong and whom I worship, and he said, 'Do not be afraid, Paul; you must stand before the emperor; and indeed, God has granted safety to all those who are sailing with you.' So keep your courage, men, for I have faith in God that it will be exactly as I have been told" (Acts 27:23-25). Acts ends with the fact that Paul finally arrived at Rome and stayed there for two years, teaching and preaching quite openly. These final, factual chapters again are keyed by a series of experiences, at first described only generically as experiences of the Spirit, which then become as specific as a typical Homeric dream experience.

The Epistles, Revelation, and the Visionary Experience

In much the same way the influence of visionary experiences runs through the rest of the New Testament. While there is only one more mention of dreams as such, all the rest of it is shot through with the idea that the Spirit is directly active in the lives of those who are committed to Christ. There are references to visionary experiences like angels and demons, and many discussions of the inner spiritual person, but it is when Paul comes to his own visions that he is explicit about the nature of these experiences. And then the New Testament closes with an entire book devoted to describing the visions that one man experienced when he was in the Spirit. These books are specifically concerned with demonstrating that the Spirit deeply influences the lives of committed people by the guidance of direct and definite information, as well as by the gradual shaping of their lives.

In addition to the visions and revelation granted to people directly, the New Testament believes that men and women have seen the reality of the nonphysical world incarnated in Jesus Christ, and so they can look to him as their revelation (*apokalypsis*) (Rom. 16:25; Gal. 1:12; 1 Peter 1:13). He is the disclosure of the ultimate nature of nonphysical reality. This, of course, is stressed in the Epistles, but not to the exclusion of other ways of knowing. Unlike some modern theologians, there is little suggestion in the New Testament that the revelation of Jesus Christ has put an end to direct revelation in dreams or visions. Rather, the latter is heightened.

To begin with, Paul told enough about himself in his letters to corroborate the accounts given in Acts of his visions and revelations. In fact, he referred to them several times, twice at some length (2 Cor. 12:1-7; Gal. 1:11-16; also 1 Cor. 9:1; 15:8; and probably Eph. 3:1). Since he was concerned with two things here—first, to make it clear that the knowledge and insight he was discussing could be imparted directly by God, and second, to show that this could make a real difference in one's outer life—he did not need to describe them in detail.

It is from Acts that we know some of the specific content and whether it came in dreams or in broad daylight.

But it is in Paul's letters that we learn his view of these visions and revelations. Some of them he undoubtedly received in dreams, and they gave him insight into the world of the spirit and also guidance and direction in the outer physical world. In three places Paul referred quite definitely to the visionary experience on the Damascus Road. He implied that he could speak much more of such experiences. In them he had been taught by God himself through the Spirit, and not by human beings.

Then in 1 Corinthians 12 Paul enumerated the gifts that are to come to the person who is in the Spirit. The individual who is possessed by the Spirit or in contact with the Spirit is given the wisdom and understanding and power the Spirit possesses. That person has superhuman knowledge and faith; he or she can distinguish spirits, has miraculous powers and the ability to heal and to prophesy, and has the gift of tongues and the power to interpret tongues. The abundant literature on the subject shows that the Spirit was viewed as a *personality* to which the individual could relate or by which he or she could be possessed.[6] Thus the experience of the Spirit was comparable to that of experiencing an angel, and as we have seen, the two were often interchangeable in meaning. In the terms of our Western culture there is simply no other way to describe these experiences except as dreamlike experiences or visions. These people believed that they were in direct contact with a reality that was anything but physical, the Spirit, which saved them from other nonphysical realities that were evil and could destroy them. Nothing else could rescue them from the principalities and powers of that dark world. This is the basic message of Paul and the other New Testament authors.

It is true that the authors of the Epistles were not much more explicit than the authors of the Gospels as to *how* people received this knowledge of nonphysical realities. Aside from Paul's references to his visions, the lone mention of dreams in Jude 8 is about the only indication of the process by which people either became entangled with demonic forces or woke up to the life of the Spirit within them. Here the author warned Christians to beware of the "dreamers" who treat their bodies, as well as the powers above them, dishonorably. The word he used (which is related to *enypnion*) refers to the thing or vision seen in sleep and is translated by Moffatt as "visionaries." While the use may be metaphorical, the passage certainly suggests that these people are being led into evil by their particular dreamings or spurious visions.

Finally, the Book of Revelation, which is also known as the Apocalypse, was written to record the visions that came to John on the island of Patmos. This book is filled with images of angels and other nonphysical realities that have a dreamlike quality and were presented to the author in a trancelike state. He described the fact that he "became" or was "carried away in the Spirit" (*en pneumati*) and then simply saw and heard the visionary beings who spoke and moved before him, as in a dream. Volumes have been written about the symbols and images found in this work, and there will probably be many more before its interpreters run out of meaning.

A great student of apocalyptism, R. H. Charles, has written that the knowledge of both the prophet and the apocalyptic writer "came through visions, trances, and through spiritual, and yet not unconscious communion with God—the highest form of inspiration."[7] It is hard to deny this understanding if we take seriously the belief the early church demonstrated when they canonized the book of Revelation.

Yet *The Interpreter's Bible* insists that

> the claim made in many apocalypses that the predictions came through visionary experiences is a literary device to give greater effectiveness to these writings. That this device is effective is shown by the ready acceptance of the claim by modern students of apocalyptism. . . . Do these purportedly divine visions correctly interpret the past and present and accurately predict the future? Are their depictions of the universe in which we live in conformity with our present astrophysical knowledge? Are their doctrines of God, of Satan, of Christ, of angels and demons, of two ages, of righteousness, and of rewards and punishments in harmony with our best Christian teaching? If our answers are in the negative, then the divine origin of these visions is subject to question.

This introductory study of Revelation then goes on to question the use of literary and traditional sources in this work along with the skill and artistry the author displayed. It even says that, if the author followed the apocalyptic tradition, he probably signed the name of "John" as a pseudonym. It is never once suggested that the book might be the record of one man's inner spiritual journey and that the form of the images is a revelation of his inner spiritual life. As for Paul's visions, *The Interpreter's Bible* quite agrees with what Paul has to say. They just don't discuss it.

The trouble is that Paul and the other New Testament writers are talking about something that seems to be almost entirely foreign to us today. They viewed human beings as beset by a world of dark and evil forces—demons, elemental spirits, Satan, thrones and dominions, and various others—and they believed that people had direct communication with these powers and also with God, his angels, and the Spirit. In my book *Tongue Speaking,* I have made a very careful listing of all these nonphysical realities in the New Testament to show the concern these authors had with these things. Outside of Revelation (which would have extended the list too far) there are hundreds of these references which clearly reveal the belief that people had some kind of direct contact with these realities. As the eminent Dominican scholar Victor White has pointed out with such care in *God and the Unconscious,* these descriptions of a "spiritual world" in Christian tradition are actually very similar to the "complexes" and "archetypes" that have been described in recent times by C. G. Jung and others; the two sets of descriptions, in fact, seem to refer to the same basic reality. As we know, a "complex" can be most clearly seen in the images of dreams and waking fantasies (or visions). And it is probable from the record that this is also the way these realities were seen in New Testament times. I will say more about this in a later chapter.

A Broad Look at the Biblical Record on Dreams

If we look back to the attitude of the entire Bible toward dreams and visions, we find that there are certain similarities and differences between the Old Testament and the New. There was no less reverence for these spontaneous intrusions into human consciousness in one or the other. Neither one made any particular distinction between visions that come in the daytime and visions of the night that come in dreams. Equally, they were the way par excellence by which God speaks to human beings. As Napier says in *The Interpreter's Dictionary of the Bible,* "Among the earlier classical prophets, the vision is a conventional (in prophetism's understanding) means of Yahweh's communication to the prophet of the meaning of immediate events in Israel's immediate history. The vision is at one with the disclosure of the Word of Yahweh." This attitude was accepted as the unquestioned base for the New Testament.

In the Old Testament, however, there was deliberation about the meaning of visions and dreams that did not occur in the New Testament. There was greater fear among the Hebrews as they entered the Near Eastern world of diviners and necromancers and Baal priests than there was on the part of the Christian community. The Old Testament discussed the meaning of dreams and visions and their place in the life of the people, as in Numbers 12 and in Job, Jeremiah, Deuteronomy, and Ecclesiastes. In the New Testament these experiences were simply accepted as one of the ways in which God speaks to his people. The Christian world had to wait for the later church fathers before the same kind of self-conscious deliberation about dreams and visions developed within the church literature. The New Testament simply assumed the general valuation and conclusions of contemporary Judaism, which had gone a step beyond the attitude of the Old Testament and were more closely related to the Hellenistic inheritance from Greek culture and literature. Out of the Old Testament a tradition had developed that ignored some of its more skeptical passages, and on this base the New Testament was founded.

We do not find the push to distinguish true and false dreams in the New Testament, partly because dreams and visions were not discussed and partly because a new solution had been found for this problem. Spiritual reality was seen dualistically. This brilliant Persian solution to the problem of evil had left its impact upon later Judaism. Now in the New Testament the good dreams and visions were attributed to God, the Spirit, or angels, while the lying, negative, or bad ones were seen as the result of demonic activity or infiltration rather than the creation of the false prophet. It is for this reason that the gift of discernment of spirits mentioned by Paul is so important. The individual must now be able to distinguish and differentiate the influences that come to him or her and to others in a nonsensory way. The dream or vision itself is real; but it is now good or bad depending upon which aspect of spiritual reality has given it.

All of this is more or less assumed in the New Testament; it is never clearly or consciously stated in so many words. As we shall see in the next chapters, the church fathers did wrestle with this problem, and as they came to discuss the dream itself as a separate entity, this point of view was stated very clearly. Many of the fathers believed that people were particularly susceptible to demonic influences in sleep and that it was here that these forces had free rein in their lives.

As the church then moved from the apostolic age on, there was no basic change in the attitude of reverence toward dreams and dreamlike experiences. I have found practically no criticism of the New Testament understanding of dreams. Instead, they are finally ignored. I have not even run into a dispensationalist suggestion that God used to speak through dreams and no longer does. The subject is simply not mentioned at all in most biblical criticism.

In summary, we find that the early Christians valued dream experiences as a contact with another realm of reality beyond the physical. This reverent understanding was in no way an isolated tradition but arose from earlier cultures and continued to develop as the new Christian culture developed. It came to these first Christians both from their Jewish heritage and from the tradition of the highly civilized, rational Greeks. It is difficult to eliminate this strand of New Testament belief without striking at the whole belief that there is a nonphysical, spiritual world that exists and influences the lives of people in intuitions, healings, prophetic inspiration, and tongues, as well as in dreams and visions. According to both biblical and Hellenistic traditions, this world is most clearly and widely known in its influence upon people through the agency of the dream or the vision. Let us turn to the understanding of the church fathers about this intrusion of another world of reality into the human conscious mind.

Chapter

5

The Dreams and Visions of the Early Christians

THE LITERARY ACTIVITY that produced the New Testament certainly did not run dry when Christianity began to spread. Instead, those first Christians found they had something to write about, and the range and scope of their writing increased. Soon there was a body of literature that began to fill volumes and that has never stopped growing. There have been changes in its general leanings, however, and in some ways this literature was as important as the New Testament in shaping the foundations of the Christian church. It is nearly impossible to understand later Christianity if one does not know the things these writers considered and discussed. One of the things that mattered to the church fathers was the significance of dreams and visions.

How much the church fathers had to say about dreams and visions, however, is something that cannot even be guessed from any ordinary survey of their works. It is certainly not revealed in what is generally written in the church today. And the English editions of the Fathers that have been used in the church during the past century show some remarkable omissions. There are thirty-eight thick volumes of ante-Nicene, Nicene, and post-Nicene fathers that seem to have been rather carelessly indexed in relation to dreams and similar subjects.

Not only is the indexing of these subjects hit and miss in the English editions, but when there was a choice of materials, the editors often left out those that referred to dream-vision experiences. I first discovered this when I looked for certain works on dreams that had been mentioned by writers of a later period. The very significant writings of Synesius of Cyrene, the early-fifth-century bishop of Ptolemais, have been omitted entirely. Out of John Cassian's twenty-four *Conferences* twenty-two are included in the post-Nicene fathers; only two are missing, the twelfth and the twenty-second *On Nocturnal Illusions*. The theological poems of Gregory of Nazianzen with his dream experiences are not included, nor are many similar passages in Gregory of Nyssa and Jerome. In translating the works of Gregory the Great, the two in which he discussed dreams at some length, *The Dialogues* and *The Morals,* have been omitted without any mention of their content. There is no reference at all to Augustine's *De Genesi ad Litteram,* in which he took the entire Twelfth Book to explain his understanding of dreams and visions. Several of these could not be found in English anywhere, and I had to have them translated from Latin in order to read them.

In fact, there has been no serious study of the thinking of the church fathers on the subject of dreams for at least two centuries, and almost none of the earlier studies have been translated into English. My own study of these materials has occupied me on and off for thirty years. In addition, John Sanford has undertaken the laborious task of reading these volumes one by one with an eye to these and other similar experiences. His list of the references supplements my own, and I am deeply indebted to him for his help.[1]

As we consider these materials, we discuss first the Apostolic Fathers and the New Testament apocrypha that come out of the same period. We then look at a different kind of literature, the apologies that developed around the middle of the second century and forged out the theological foundation of the later church. These writers were followed next by the important school at Alexandria and finally by the Latin fathers, whom we discuss more or less in chronological order, taking up the references to dreams in each of them in the general context of their Christian theory.

The Apostolic Fathers

The first of these Christian authors, the Apostolic Fathers, were men who probably had contact with the apostles themselves. For the most part their works were addressed to the faithful, to strengthen and inspire or to instruct them, and now and then these writings were given the rank of Scripture. Some were even included for a time in the canon of holy books. At the same time, for about the first three centuries of the church's life, there was also a stream of apocryphal gospels and acts and epistles that the church almost uniformly rejected because they were fanciful rather than historical accounts of events surrounding the lives of Jesus and the apostles.

One of the most popular books of this time was the *Shepherd of Hermas,* an inspirational work written to the church in Rome early in the second century. This book, which was regarded as Scripture by many Christians of that time, begins with a vision that the author experiences as he falls asleep and is carried away by the Spirit. This "vision of sleep" is followed by many others like it, and then after certain commandments and parallels are explained, one final dream-vision concludes the work, which is much like *Pilgrim's Progress.* Like Bunyan's masterpiece, its writing has the quality of a genuine visionary experience and is of great value when understood symbolically. In Jung's *Psychological Types* there is a lengthy and brilliant analysis of Hermas as an example of the creative process of individuation taking place in a dream-vision.[2] Jung gives evidence of the authenticity and value of this work that is so strange to the modern world.

It was this unquestionable dream quality that gave the *Shepherd of Hermas* its authority in the long period in which it was so popular; what the author had to say came to him out of a dream-vision experience and so had more value than a consciously conceived writing. The fact that it was read for three centuries in several languages shows the value attributed to dreams in this period.

One particularly important vision was described in the *Martyrdom of Polycarp,* written about the same time. As Polycarp was praying not long before his martyrdom, he was informed through a symbolic vision of what was to happen. He saw the pillow under his head catch fire, and he realized that this image of destruction signified his own impending capture and death.

In both of these works one finds the same feeling about dreams and visions that we have found expressed in Acts, in the Epistles, and also in the Revelation of John.[3]

The New Testament Apocrypha

Among the apocryphal writings that began to appear in this period are some interesting materials based on dreams. These writers were attempting to carry on the tradition of the canonical New Testament, and it is interesting to see how closely these materials are related to those that were accepted as genuine visions of the holy. In the *Acts of the Holy Apostle Thomas,* the Lord came to Thomas in India in a dream to give him instructions as to what he was to do. Later, at the time of his death, a beautiful young man also appeared to Thomas and his friends in a dream to give them comfort and instruction in the last days of the apostle's life; this experience is described in the *Consummation of Thomas, the Apostle.* The Apocalypse of Moses tells a further story of the Garden of Eden, in which Eve was warned in a dream about the murder of Abel by his brother and knew in advance what would happen to her son. And in the *Testament of Abraham,* Isaac dreamed in symbolic images of Abraham's coming death, while at the same time Abraham himself was being prepared by the archangel Michael to understand and interpret the dream that Isaac would tell him.

The *Acts of Xantippe and Polyxena* was written as a religious novel and was the forerunner of the religious romances of the third century of our era. In this romance dreams were used to show the heroine that she should be baptized, and several times there were visions of a beautiful young man who brought important information. This work also described a dream through which Peter was sent on a mission into Greece. In the *Clementine Homilies,* which were probably written late in the second century, there is a delightful passage in which Peter and a certain Simon carry on a lengthy discussion about dreams. There is no doubt, they decide, that God sends dreams that present true visions, and these dreams can come to evil people as well as to good ones; but they feel that to the best of people God will reveal himself through intelligence rather than through dreams. Indeed, the conclusion is that, unless a dream answers the specific questions of people, it has not brought the dreamer into face-to-face contact with God. Finally, the *Clementine Recognitions* describe how demons gain power over people; when people forgo moderation, they are open for demons to strike them in dreams.[4]

For almost three centuries of the church's life, these scattered references are the only apocryphal writings on dreams or visions that have come down to us. In this material the emphasis on dreams did not increase; if anything, it declined, as the apocryphal writers instead saw God speaking and working in more miraculous ways than through the medium of the dream.

Postapostolic Times

About A.D. 150 a new kind of Christian writing appeared. Christianity was faced with two opponents, one from the outside, the other from within. As Christians became the scapegoats of the Roman Empire, it was necessary to show the world how false and ludicrous the opinions of the government and the general populace were. And as divisions and pagan ideas threatened the church from within, it became equally necessary to take a studied and intellectual look at the meaning of Christian experience, to establish and hold what orthodox Christians had found. In this period people came to the fore who were equipped for the job.

Many of the writers at this time had become Christian after thorough training in Greek rhetoric and philosophy, and they took the rational and intellectual approach for which they had been educated. Some of their writings were polemic in nature, others philosophic in the Greek tradition. But whether their aim was to contradict theological error or to give Christianity a place in the cultural heritage of the ancient world, these works on the whole were reasonable, careful, and telling. They were produced by some of the finest minds of those centuries, people who forged out the foundations of Christianity that have stood as the basic faith of Christians from that time until now.

The authors of the New Testament themselves had not been particularly well versed in Greek philosophy, and they probably would have found it difficult to defend their worldview in the academies of the ancient world. The worldview from which they wrote was simply not much discussed by Matthew, Mark, or any of the others, and the same thing was also true of the Apostolic Fathers. But as these new Christian apologists emerged, we find Christians conscious of their place in the ancient world and speaking intelligently to that world. Justin Martyr, Irenaeus, Tertullian, Clement, Origen, Athanasius, Augustine, Gregory of Nyssa, Synesius, and Chrysostom were intellectuals, educated in the world. Although it is possible to look with some condescension on the first Christian writers as philosophically naïve, this attitude is out of place with regard to these later writers. A knowledge of our historic Christian roots makes this fact perfectly apparent.

These church fathers wrote as philosophers who held a worldview quite different from that of the twentieth century. Their view was quite consciously based on the thinking of Plato,[5] which they found compatible with both the biblical tradition and their own Christian experience, and these they merged to produce the first serious Christian theology the world had known. With this consistent point of view, they stood against pagan religion, against the skepticism of the ancient world (of which there was more than we sometimes think), and against the heretical ideas that grew up within the Christian church. Unquestionably, if they had had the chance, they would also have defended this point of view against the Aristotelian thinking that is so basic to our present Christian culture and which leaves little place for the break-through of the divine, or more than human, into human life.

When I began to examine the Fathers to discover their attitude toward dreams, I did not expect to find an attitude very different from our own in the twentieth century. It is true that my own experience was different; through depth psychology I had come to see the value and significance of dreams, but I also knew their importance to the ancient pagan world, which we have discussed at some length in the last chapters. I expected to find these first Christian theologians condemning the pagans for being interested in dreams or, at least, forewarning Christians to be cautious about such dangerous superstition.

Instead I found that when these men spoke of dreams, it was almost always to express a positive view. One essential element of their theological thinking was the belief that God still spoke directly through the medium of dreams and visions. Even the warnings about lying dreams (or demons) were far less frequent than in the Old Testament. As a matter of fact, these great fathers of the church did not have to say a great deal to support the coherent and well-integrated theory they held regarding the place of dreams in human life, for there was no great breach between Christians and sophisticated non-Christians about this.

On the whole, the church fathers accepted the dream theory of the later Greeks and the worldview in which it has meaning very much as these had been expressed by Plato and the Greek dramatists. As I have shown, the Greeks maintained the reality of a world of gods and spirits and strange intimations that existed alongside of the physical world and was revealed in dreams and visions. Like the fathers, they saw the significance of the nonphysical world for human beings and thus believed that dreams are revelations of the greatest consequence for people. In fact, the later Greeks sometimes went overboard about this,[6] while the Fathers were simply more careful and guarded in their statements. Those who are familiar with the writing of Jung will find themselves in a strangely congenial atmosphere here. With slight changes in terminology, it would appear that Jung and the Fathers are talking about the same reality. Of course, they both considered that human beings have an eternal destiny in the world that is revealed by dreams. In the case of the Fathers, it is practically impossible to understand their theory of the spiritual world and revelation unless we understand their theory of dreams and associated experiences.

The Apologists

The first of these men who were able to interpret Christianity to the pagan world was Justin Martyr, who was perhaps the first Christian philosopher. Justin was born a pagan and searched the philosophies of the day until he found in Jesus of Nazareth what he felt Plato had been seeking. He wrote in Rome in the first half of the second century and was martyred for his belief in A.D. 165. Dreams, Justin mentioned in passing, are sent by spirits, and he used this idea to show his belief that souls do not cease after death; in dreams we already have direct spiritual communication with nonphysical realities, and beings who are capable of such communication need not cease with the death of the body. He believed that dreams are sent by evil spirits to hold us in bondage, as well as by God. For Justin Martyr dreams had intrinsic meaning and importance because they give hint of human participation in a more-than-physical world.

Irenaeus, who carried on the tradition of Justin, fought mainly against the gnostic speculation that was so popular among second-century intellectuals. He was a native of Smyrna and became the bishop of Lyons in the last half of the second century. Christianity had spread far from the old centers of Greek culture, and Irenaeus worried about speaking Celtic and letting his Greek become rusty. Like Justin, he assumed that dreams are revelations of a spiritual world. In his principal work, *Against Heresies,* Irenaeus commented appreciatively and intelligently on the dream of Peter in Acts 10; he believed that the dream itself was a proof of the authenticity of Peter's experience. Again, he stressed the authenticity of Paul's dream at Troas, drawing attention like a modern biblical critic to the introduction of the "we" passages at this point. He also inferred from the dreams of Joseph in Matthew that Joseph's dreaming showed how close he was to the real God, and in another context he suggested that the fact that an angel came to Joseph was additional evidence of his close relationship to God.

Irenaeus also used his understanding of dreams to refute the idea of reincarnation or transmigration of souls. Since the soul can receive knowledge directly and communicate it to the body after a dream has occurred, there is no reason that the body should make us forget a former life of the soul if it had one. In still another place he explained that although God is himself invisible to the eye directly, he gives us visions and dreams through which he conveys the likeness of his nature and his glory. Thus God manifests himself not only through mighty works, but through the use of both visual and auditory visions as well. Again, the revelatory nature of dreams is simply assumed. Both Irenaeus and Justin also stated that God only gave visions to people who refused to listen to their dreams.

Another Christian philosopher in this period was Tatian the Assyrian, who was a close follower of Justin for part of his life. In the *Address to the Greeks*, his only complete work that remains, Tatian wrote a long passage on demons in which he explained that the way demons make their presence known to people is through dreams. Since none of these men left works of a more personal nature, we can only guess that their own experience with dreams was probably the same as the experience of Christians who came before and after them.[7]

The School at Alexandria

Two of the keenest minds the early church produced were Clement and Origen in Alexandria. Clement had been pagan; he was probably Greek, and he was certainly widely traveled and highly educated. His bibliography of Greek references in one manuscript took fourteen pages to list. In the Alexandrian school where he settled down at the end of the second century, he probed into the whole subject of reason and faith. Origen, who was his pupil, was even more famous. He was considered one of the greatest minds, pagan or Christian, of the third century; he was a voluminous writer and is credited with establishing theology as a science. Both of these men stated clearly the great significance they saw in dreams.

In discussing the nature and meaning of sleep, Clement urged:

> Let us not, then, who are sons of the true light, close the door against this light; but turning in on ourselves, illumining the eyes of the hidden man, and gazing on the truth itself, and receiving its streams, let us clearly and intelligibly reveal such dreams as are true.

True dreams, Clement believed, come from the depth of the soul, which is always active. He argues that they reveal spiritual reality, the intercourse of the soul with God, and this idea was used by many of the Fathers as evidence for the immortality of the soul. As the following words show, he saw sleep as a time of special receptivity to spiritual reality, a time of special clarity in discovering the soul's destiny:

> Thus also such dreams as are true, in the view of him who reflects rightly, are the thoughts of a sober soul, undistracted for the time by the affections of the body, and counselling with itself in the best manner. . . . Wherefore always contemplating God, and by perpetual converse with Him inoculating the body with wakefulness, it raises man to equality with angelic grace, and from the practice of wakefulness it grasps the eternity of life.

In the *Stromata,* or *Miscellanies,* Clement made two other interesting references to dreams. Since God gives truth symbolically rather than directly, therefore truth should not be communicated to one who has not at least "been purified in a dream." In another section of the same work he described at some length the life of the soul at night in sleep. He believed that "the soul, released from the perceptions of sense, turns in on itself, and has a truer hold of intelligence." Thus are the mysteries celebrated at night. He also believed that we human beings can so purify ourselves that the passions may not even perturb us in dreams.

Almost from the beginning of his writings, which made the Alexandrians famous all over the world, Origen left no doubt about his thinking on dreams. In his great answer to the pagans, *Against Celsus,* he defended the visions of the Bible, saying:

> We, nevertheless, so far as we can, shall support our position, maintaining that, as it is a matter of belief that in a dream impressions have been brought before the minds of many, some relating to divine things, and others to future events of this life, and this either with clearness or in an enigmatic manner—a fact which is manifest to all who accept the doctrine of providence: so how is it absurd to say that the mind which could receive impressions in a *dream* should be impressed also in a waking vision, for the benefit either of him on whom the impressions are made, or of those who are to hear the account of them from him?

Having satisfied his parallel between dreams and visions, Origen then went on to discuss the nature of dreams. He could hardly have introduced his subject with a more concise and adequate statement of the attitude of the ancient world toward dreams.

The discussion that follows has a modern ring to it. Origen saw the dream, not as physical perception, but as the presentation of symbols that reveal the nature of the nonphysical world. He believed that in Jacob's dream of the ladder reaching to heaven, Jacob was presented with a vision of the nature of heaven as valuable and as valid as Plato's discussion of this realm. The image of the ladder, he suggested, was comparable to the degrees of "planets" through which the soul, according to Plato, must pass in going from earth to heaven, and he concluded by referring the reader to Philo's discussion of this vision. Origen clearly was stating here that the understanding of Plato and the vision of Jacob were in agreement with each other.

Writing to the famous Africanus, Origen rejected this friend's doubts as to the value of the story of Susanna in the Apocrypha. Africanus was offended by the idea that Daniel had been "seized by the Spirit," and Origen pointed out that God had seized the spirits of many of the saints and had in so doing "favored [them] with divine dreams and angelic appearances and [direct] inspirations." The opening verses of Hebrews, he went on, support the conclusion that God speaks in these ways by the prophets, just as he spoke to Jacob through a dream and then by the direct appearance of the angel who wrestled with Jacob at Jabbok. Another most emphatic statement occurs in *Contra Celsus,* in which Origen declared that many Christians had been converted from their pagan ways by this kind of direct breakthrough into their lives in waking visions and dreams of the night. He made it clear that many such instances were known of this sort of conversion. Later, in refuting one of Celsus's diatribes against the Jews, Origen remarked, however, that all dreams are not of this quality; some persons may "dream dreams, owing to obscure phantoms presenting themselves." Thus one must distinguish between dreams from God and those originating from phantoms.

When Celsus ridiculed the dreams that occurred in the story of Jesus' birth, Origen countered his statements by saying:

> And that in a dream certain persons may have certain things pointed out to them to do, is an event of frequent occurrence to many individuals,—the impression on the mind being produced either by an angel or by some other thing. Where, then, is the absurdity in believing that He who had once become incarnate, should be led also by human guidance to keep out of the way of dangers?

A few paragraphs later he pointed out that, when Peter had to be broken from his narrow Judaism, he was given a vision that made it possible for him to take the message of Christianity to Cornelius.[8]

Clearly, for Origen, the dream, the waking vision, and divine inspiration were all of one piece. Through these methods God reveals himself to people and gives them a symbolic knowledge of the nature of the spiritual world and of heaven. The dream-vision is an essential part of the method of God's revelation. The content of these revelations put the believer on a par or higher than the best of pagan philosophy when properly understood. Yet at the same time Origen urged caution, for evil spirits can also break through into the lives of people by the same avenue God uses.

Tertullian Offers Evidence about Dreams

The first great Latin apologist was the famed and fiery Tertullian, who flourished at the beginning of the third century and was roughly contemporary with Origen. Few writers of the time turned out more lucid and admirable prose than this controversial church leader, whose background was that of a cultivated North African. His father was a military man and a pagan, and Tertullian was converted to Christianity after studying law in Rome. While his immediate influence on the church was somewhat diminished by his adherence to the Montanist sect, his works were read and studied with great care by later Christians, particularly Cyprian and Augustine, and through them his thinking became one of the foundation stones of our Christian theology.

There are many references to dreams scattered throughout the writings of Tertullian, particularly in his *Apology,* in the *Treatise on the Resurrection of the Flesh,* in the *Defense against Marcion,* in his work on the Trinity entitled *Against Praxeas,* and in his introduction to the *Martyrdom of Saints Perpetua and Felicitas.* We shall not discuss them separately, however, because Tertullian obliged us by writing an excellent and concise statement of his theory of dreams and their relation to the Christian doctrine of revelation in his major work, *On the Soul.* These conclusions of Tertullian expressed the general Christian belief of the third century, which remained the general attitude of thinking Western Christians for the next twelve hundred years, until the thinking of Aquinas began to take over in Western Europe. We shall therefore analyze Tertullian's discussion of dreams at some length, since it is one of the most authoritative discussions in the church's literature. It also compares favorably with modern psychological discussions of the subject.

Tertullian devoted eight chapters of this work (*A Treatise on the Soul,* or *De Anima*) to his study of sleep and dreams. Like modern psychologists who study dreaming, he believed that everyone dreams (as we now know they do), and as evidence of this fact, he called attention to the movements of sleeping infants. What he had to say came from his own observations as well as from the opinions of both the Christian and pagan community. He began by ridiculing the "vulgar" idea that the soul leaves the body in sleep as if it were taking off on a holiday. Rather, he found dreaming an indication that the soul is perpetually active, and this he saw as the best evidence of its immortality. But there is in sleep an *ekstasis*, a standing aside, in which the soul has power to act but is like a gladiator deprived of his arms. This *ekstasis* (the same word is used for Peter's trance in Acts 10, and also for the experience of God in Dionysian religion) is something the soul is given, a givenness that overwhelms it in the same way sense experience does in the waking states. To emphasize this he suggested that we can hardly be crowned for imaginary martyrdom in our dreams any more than we are condemned for visionary acts of sin.

Thus, like Plato, Tertullian saw that dreaming is akin to madness, a madness in which the soul, instead of being given something reasonably sensed, is overwhelmed by something other than sense experience. This is closely related to the idea of some depth psychologists that psychosis is the living out of one's dream life without orientation to the physical world. We might translate Tertullian's meaning into modern terms by saying that in sleep the unconscious makes its autonomous impression on the center of consciousness in the form of the dream.

Tertullian turned his ridicule then on the Epicureans for denying the validity of dreams, and for support he surveyed the whole literature on dream significance and interpretation, citing names like Homer, Herodotus, Heracleides, Strabo, and Callisthenes, as well as the Romans Vitellius and Cicero. He also referred to others whom he did not quote, including five portly volumes written by Hermippus of Berytus. He discussed the use of dreams in divination and also gave the names of the authors who had treated this subject. There is no question that Tertullian was well informed on the extensive literature of dreams that was current in the ancient world. He was making this perfectly evident; he wanted it known that he knew what he was talking about. He mentioned the people of Telmessus, who maintained that dreams are always meaningful (quite like modern analysts) and believed that it was only their own weakness that kept them from understanding a dream. He specifically suggested that dreams have various levels of interpretation, and finally he asked, "Now, who is such a stranger to human experience as not sometimes to have perceived some truth in dreams?"

Proceeding then to analyze the cause of dreams, Tertullian found that they occur from four sources. There are dreams caused by demons; indeed, they inflict most of them, although these dreams "sometimes turn out true and favorable to us." There are also dreams that come from God, and according to Tertullian "almost the greater part of mankind get [*sic*] their knowledge of God from dreams." Third, there are natural dreams that the soul apparently creates for itself from "an intense application to special circumstances." And in the final category are dreams that come from none of these but must be ascribed "to what is purely and simply the ecstatic state and its peculiar conditions"—in other words, the unconscious, the state of standing aside from consciousness. Tertullian called attention to the fact that he was omitting any category based on "ingenious conjecture" about the effect of physical activities, and he criticized Plato and others for holding that the physical body, the liver, fasting, or the like have any particular effect on dreaming. He saw dreams basically as psychic phenomena common to everyone, which can be understood only through careful consideration of people's experiences. Indeed, his total discussion is an example of skillful understanding of the human psyche.

In another passage Tertullian emphatically stated that he was describing not only his own private opinions about dreams, but the body of thinking on the subject accepted by Christians generally. It would appear that dreaming was considered the normal way to receive visions from God. This theology of dreams was stated explicitly by Tertullian in his introduction to the *Martyrdom of Saints Perpetua and Felicitas.* He considered dreams one of the gifts from God, a *charisma.* After he referred to the prophecy of Joel that when God pours out his Spirit, men will dream dreams and see visions, he went on:

> And thus we—who both acknowledge and reverence, even as we do the prophecies, modern visions as equally promised to us, and consider the other powers of the Holy Spirit as an agency of the Church for which also He was sent, administering all gifts in all, even as the Lord distributed to every one as will needfully collect them in writing, and commemorate them in reading to God's glory; that so no weakness or despondency of faith may suppose that the divine grace abode only among the ancients, whether in respect of the condescension that raised up martyrs, or that gave revelations.

Indeed, this was so much accepted that in the narrative that follows it is only the simple statement of St. Perpetua that she awoke which gives away the fact that these visions were received in sleep as dreams. How many other early Christians' visions were received in this way without the acknowledgment of awakening would be difficult to tell.

In any case, the *Martyrdom of Saints Perpetua and Felicitas,* which once had wide circulation, is an example of the practical Christian understanding of dreams. Some critics also ascribe the conclusion of the narrative and its circulation to Tertullian, for these martyrs were fellow North Africans. The dreams, however, were told by Perpetua. After she had been imprisoned, her brother suggested that, since she was there because of her faith, she might ask God for a vision that would show her the outcome. She did ask for such a sign, and she saw the vision of a golden ladder that reached up to heaven. Attached to it were daggers and hooks to slash the careless who did not keep looking up, and at its foot was a dragon. Seeing herself mount the ladder with the others, she then woke, knowing that they must die. She also saw in a dream the figure of a friend who had died, a man who had had cancer of the face. She saw him suffering, but after she had prayed for him, he again appeared to her in another night vision, restored and happy.

In her fourth dream Perpetua saw herself changed into a man in order to fight with the devil and overcome him. She then knew that she would be able to withstand her martyrdom. Because of this dream she also realized that her agony and suffering were caused, not by people, but by the power of Satan. Thus these early Christians were able to hold their persecutors in charity, knowing them to be dominated by Satan and his hosts. These dreams, comprising the central and largest portion of the narrative, reflect directly the popular Christian view of dreams of which Tertullian wrote learnedly.[9]

Theologians Who Wrote of Their Own Dreams

In the years that followed, the tradition set by Tertullian and Origen continued in North Africa with Cyprian, in Alexandria with a succession of church leaders, and in Rome with Hippolytus, and later with Arnobius and Lactantius. Apparently the whole church acted upon the belief that God directs individuals and the destiny of the church by imparting knowledge and wisdom directly through dreams and visions, and this was expressed as it had been in the Book of Acts. In fact, the history of this period by Eusebius reads almost like a sequel to that book. All of these writers accepted the general Christian attitude that Tertullian had so ably presented.

It is difficult for us in the modern Western world to relive those times in which it was important to *know* one's belief. Thascius Cyprian was bishop of Carthage in A.D. 250, when a new wave of Christian persecution began under the emperor Decius. After a period of relative freedom, many Christians looked only for an easy out and recanted, and then the problem arose as to how these lapsed Christians might be received into fellowship again. Many of Cyprian's writings were related to this question, for which he was well prepared by his education as a professional rhetorician. The fire of his words contributed to his own death as a martyr, while his unquestioned orthodoxy made him one of the foundation stones of the Latin church. Even so, the modern editors of his works found it necessary to explain the kind of direct encounter with God that he described in many places. In one letter objecting to some of the most devastating critics of Christianity, he wrote to Florentius Pupianus that he knew the truth of which he spoke because of direct manifestations to him in dreams and visions. Supporting his position by referring to the dreams of the patriarch Joseph, he remarked, "Although I know that to some men dreams seem ridiculous and visions foolish, yet assuredly it is to such as would rather believe in opposition to the priest, than believe the priest." To the church at large he demonstrated that God continued to chide even young people and bring them to their senses in visions of the night, just like Job.

In another letter he wrote that God guides the very councils of the church by "many and manifest visions." He commended Celerinus because his conversion to the church had come through a vision of the night. Cyprian concluded that this gave him greater honor, as Eusebius also testified when he described the good character of this same Celerinus in his *Ecclesiastical History.* In Cyprian's *Treatise on Mortality* he related the vision of a man at the approach of death, a vision that gave certitude to those who were with him and heard the dying man describe "a youth, venerable in honor and majesty, lofty in stature and shining in aspect," who appeared and stood by him. Cyprian's own experience before he was beheaded was described in the restrained and factual *Life and Passion of Cyprian* by Pontius. Told in the martyr's own words, "ere yet I was sunk in the repose of slumber . . . ," he saw a vision of "a young man of unusual stature" who told him what was to happen and so prepared him to go on.

But when the editors of the Fathers came to Cyprian, they could not quite take so much outspoken emphasis on direct encounters with God. They felt the need to support the inclusion of so much detail about dreams and visions that had guided and inspired Cyprian's life, and so they appended the following note to the original discussion of his narrative and letters:

> It is easy to speak with ridicule of such instances as Dean Milman here treats so philosophically. But, lest believers should be charged with exceptional credulity, let us recall what the father of English Deism (Lord Herbert) relates of his own experiences, in the conclusion of his Autobiography: "I had no sooner spoken these words (of prayer to the Deist's deity) but a loud though yet a gentle noise came from the heavens, for it was like nothing on earth, which did so comfort and cheer me, that I took my petition as granted, and that I had the sign I demanded. . . . This, how strange soever it may seem, I protest, before the eternal God, is true. . . ."[10]

In the third century Alexandria was still the seat of Christian learning, and there Gregory Thaumaturgus (or "wonder-worker") and Dionysius continued the traditions of learning that the great school at that city had established. These men were the disciples of Origen who prepared the way for Athanasius and his remarkable formulation of Christian orthodoxy. Both of them were led by dreams. It was told of Gregory, who was born of a wealthy family and studied Roman law, that his declaration of faith came to him in a beautiful dream, as a revelation from the blessed John by the mediation of Mary.[11] In a letter quoted by Eusebius, Dionysius related the vision that had confirmed him in his determination to know both the pagan and heretical

Christian worlds; in it a voice spoke to him, telling him that he need fear nothing, because he stood on secure ground.

Another pupil of the school at Alexandria was Julius Africanus, later the bishop of Emmaus according to some traditions. In his writings there is a story of dreams as fanciful as the nineteenth-century editors thought it was,which therefore leaves little doubt about the attitude of third-century Christians on the subject. Africanus described how, before the birth of Christ, the king of Persia sought wisdom through incubation, and how, sleeping in the holy place, he was given a dream that revealed the coming of the Christ. In Jerusalem, Narcissus, while still bishop, named his own successor because of a night vision that he believed was divine instruction. The man thus selected was Alexander of Cappadocia, who died in A.D. 251 during the Decian persecutions and whose letters remain among the works of the Fathers. In A.D. 300 the bishop of Alexandria was the much-revered Peter, the last to die in the persecution of Maximinus and who was later sainted. In *The Genuine Acts of Peter* the story was told of how his way had been determined by a vision of the night in which a radiant boy of twelve, clothed in a divided tunic, stood before him and told him that he should beware of Arius and his heresy. Later, the next prelate of Alexandria, the Alexander who succeeded to the see in A.D. 312, used this same dream to support his arguments when he was writing against the Arians.[12]

Dreams in Rome

Meanwhile Rome had its first schismatic "pope" when the controversial Hippolytus was made a bishop there in A.D. 215. He believed that Callistus, the regular bishop in Rome, was quite naïve in his theology and also questionable in his life, and some of the most influential Christians followed Hippolytus. In the end the two churches were reconciled after the persecutions of Maximin when both leaders were dead. Although Hippolytus was famous enough to have a statue erected to him in Rome, little was known about him until a century ago. When some of his major writings turned up then, it was discovered that his works as much as any other had given the laws and liturgy of the Eastern church their permanent form.

Hippolytus's works contained various studies, including the last of the apologies written in Greek. In his discussion of evil in the *Treatise on Christ and Anti-Christ,* dealing largely with dreams and visions in the Bible, Hippolytus showed that the prophets had been instructed about the future through visions, some of which were in sleep. "Wherefore," he concluded, "prophets were with good reason called from the very first 'seers.' " There also remain extensive fragments of his commentaries on Daniel, in which he discussed these divine dreams at length, clearly considering them as revelations of the future. In one last work, attributed to Hippolytus but felt by many to be someone else's summary of his genuine writings, we find the same ideas on dreams and visions expressed at even greater length.

In the Latin church the same traditions were continued by Arnobius and his pupil Lactantius. Arnobius was a pagan rhetorician teaching in a Roman colony near Carthage when, according to Jerome, he was led by a dream to seek Christianity. He died a martyr in the Diocletian persecutions in A.D. 303. His only work that has survived, however, was less sanguine about dreams than any of the other ante-Nicene writings. This book was written when Arnobius was a new convert and better informed about pagan ideas than Christian ones. By attacking heathen mythology and the follies of paganism, however, he preserved many choice stories about the gods for future ages. His discussion of the meaning of dreams quoted Plato's *Theaetetus* and warned against diviners and interpreters who devise heathen myths. While the Latin is not clear, he seemed to suggest that Christ would appear directly "to unpolluted minds" rather than in "airy dreams."

We know little about the personal life of Arnobius's pupil Lactantius, who was also a teacher of rhetoric, except that he was close to the imperial family. Constantine the Great selected Lactantius as tutor for his son, and his *Divine Institutes* was written in part to instruct the emperor. In it he referred again and again to dreams from the gods, whom he considered the same as demons. He included a chapter on "The Use of Reason in Religion; and of Dreams, Auguries, Oracles, and Similar Portents," in which he cited examples to show that through dreams a knowledge of the future is occasionally given to pagans as well as to Christians. Interestingly, his example of a logical fallacy is that of a man who has dreamed that he ought not believe in dreams. In both this book and the *Epitome,* Lactantius discussed at length the prophecies that had been fulfilled in the Christ, showing that visions had been brought before the prophets' eyes by the divine Spirit.

In still another work Lactantius suggested that the same Spirit could still instruct people in the same way. This was when he came to Constantine's dream before the battle of the Milvian Bridge. In telling it—somewhat differently from Eusebius's version, which will come to our attention in the next chapter—he added a dream-vision of Constantine's brother-in-law Licinius, in which an angel of the Lord provided him with the prayer that encouraged his men to overcome Daia and so join the emperor. The victory thus won was followed by the Edict of Milan, which freed the Christians from persecution.

Thus, while we encounter two different attitudes in Arnobius and Lactantius, it is clear that these men knew how to receive a divine dream when they encountered it in reality. It would be centuries before rationalism such as Gibbon's influenced our judgment so deeply that we ignored these experiences entirely. Yet there is no more reason to overlook the carefully written account of a dream in Lactantius or Eusebius than to discredit other parts of their story.[13]

Chapter
6

The Dreams of the Victorious Christian Church

NOTHING WAS MORE IMPORTANT to the Christians who survived persecution under Diocletian and Galerius than freedom from these sufferings. It is difficult for most of us to imagine a Christian adherence that involved such risks. Men accused of being Christian could be tortured and killed, their wives and children sold into slavery, and their property given to the informer. But with the victory of Constantine and the Edict of Milan in A.D. 313, persecution of the church almost ceased, and this freedom opened up a new era in the church's life. There was a burst of activity within the church that brought a flow of new literary work. Great Christian leaders arose to solve a host of religious problems. Athanasius laid the foundation for all subsequent Christian thinking, while Augustine in his voluminous writings set the general direction of the Western church for the next thousand years. Under Chrysostom and the great Cappadocians, the mold was also formed for all Eastern Christianity down to the present day. Not one of these great leaders ignored the subject of dreams. Rather, we find each of them taking the trouble to show, often many times, that the dream is one significant way in which God reveals himself to human beings.

Indeed, this new era of Western civilization was opened by the dream-vision that came to Constantine before his battle for Rome. Constantine was not the likeliest candidate to become emperor of the entire Roman world. He had been passed over for the rank of Caesar and probably only saved his life by fleeing the court to join his father's army in Britain. When Constantine's father was dead and Constantine had patiently gained recognition, his chance finally came for the bold, almost desperate move against Maxentius at the Milvian Bridge. The pagan world regarded the outcome of this battle as directed by divine providence. "When the Senate erected a triumphal arch to his honor in A.D. 315, Constantine, in the dedication thereon, ascribed his victory not only to the greatness of his imperial genius, but also to the 'inspiration of the godhead.' "[1] The pagan story of foreboding owls whose appearance on the city walls of Rome announced the doom of Maxentius, along with other current writings, expressed the same general feeling. A few years later the court orator Nazarius added still further that at the Milvian Bridge the dead Caesar Constantius had personally come to his son's assistance at the head of a heavenly army.

The Christian Account

The first account that mentioned the insignia carried by Constantine's army, the Christian sign called the labarum, was written by Lactantius, who was probably closer to Constantine than any other Christian writer. This brief account was included as part of a historical work published soon after the events. In it Lactantius told of the dream of the emperor:

> Constantine was directed in a dream to cause *the heavenly sign* to be delineated on the shields of his soldiers, and so to proceed to battle. He did as he had been commanded, and he marked on their shields the letter X, with a perpendicular line drawn through it and turned round thus at the top, being the cipher of Christ. Having this sign, his troops stood to arms.[2]

Eusebius also told the story of Constantine's victory, in two places. In the *Church History,* which he wrote about A.D. 315, he described only how Constantine had asked in prayer to Jesus Christ for the protection of God before the battle, in which Maxentius was defeated "in a remarkable manner." He added that Constantine ordered a cross placed in the hand of the statue erected to him, with an inscription stating that he owed the victory to this symbol.[3]

Some twenty years later, after Constantine's death, Eusebius added the details that the emperor had told him as a friend. Constantine had affirmed that, before his decision to fight for the liberation of Rome, he had reflected on his need for powerful aid against Maxentius and had meditated on the attitude of his own father toward the one, supreme God. Eusebius then told of the young Caesar's prayer and what happened:

> Accordingly he called on him with earnest prayer and supplications that he would reveal to him who he was, and stretch forth his right hand to help him in his present difficulties. And while he was thus praying with fervent entreaty, a most marvelous sign appeared to him from heaven, the account of which it might have been hard to believe had it been related by any other person. But since the victorious emperor himself long afterwards declared it to the writer of this history, when he was honored with his acquaintance and society, and confirmed his statement by an oath, who could hesitate to accredit the relation especially since the testimony of aftertime has established its truth? He said that about noon, when the day was already beginning to decline, he saw with his own eyes the trophy of a cross of light in the heavens, above the sun, and bearing the inscription,

> CONQUER BY THIS. At this sight he himself was struck with amazement, and his whole army also, which followed him on this expedition, and witnessed the miracle.
>
> He said, moreover, that he doubted within himself what the import of this apparition could be. And while he continued to ponder and reason on its meaning, night suddenly came on; then in his sleep the Christ of God appeared to him with the same sign which he had seen in the heavens, and commanded him to make a likeness of that sign which he had seen in the heavens, and to use it as a safeguard in all engagements with his enemies.
>
> At dawn of day he arose, and communicated the marvel to his friends: and then, calling together the workers in gold and precious stones, he sat in the midst of them, and described to them the figure of the sign he had seen, bidding them represent it in gold and precious stones. And this representation I myself have had an opportunity of seeing.[4]

Eusebius then went on to describe the sign, the labarum, which became the insignia of the Christian emperors, and also told of Constantine's determination to follow the divine vision in his own life.

This story has stuck in the craw of modern rationalistic historians, particularly religious historians. Lietzmann dealt with it merely as an example of legend building. The late nineteenth-century translators of the fathers were scandalized, and the French Catholic church historian Duchesne dismissed the event with these words:

> As to the visions, by day and by night, we have no reason to doubt Eusebius when he tells us that they were related to him by Constantine: but it is difficult for the historian to appreciate the exact value of such testimony, and speaking generally, to investigate with any profit into such personal matters. Leaving, therefore, to mystery the things which belong to mystery, we will confine ourselves here to stating facts known as facts, and to acknowledging that Constantine undertook the war against Maxentius, and in particular the encounter at the Milvian Bridge, in firm conviction that he was under the protection of the Christian God, and from that time he always spoke and acted, in religious matters, as a convinced believer. The monogram of Christ, painted upon the shields of his soldiers, displayed at the top of the military standards, (*labarum*), soon stamped upon coins, and reproduced in a thousand different ways, gave an unmistakable expression of the opinions of the emperor.[5]

Indeed, the eminent religious historians today do not seem to question how Constantine became so conscious of the need for Christian conviction. Perhaps they believe that he understood all the excellent theological reasoning that runs through their own minds.

The Attitude of the Church Historians

While this was certainly not the only dream told in the ecclesiastical histories of the time, these works show almost as much reticence about telling dream experiences as people do today. These experiences were actually relied on very little in presenting the history and activity of the early church. Two others of these historians, Socrates and Sozomen, followed Eusebius's account of Constantine's vision of conversion. Both of them also told how Constantine's mother, St. Helena, visited Jerusalem on the inspiration of a dream and so was led to discover the true cross. Sozomen countered the idea that her information had instead been given by a Jew with these words: "But it seems more accordant with truth to suppose that God revealed the fact by means of signs and dreams; for I do not think that human information is requisite when God thinks it best to make manifest the same."[6] Both writers then described the churches that the emperor ordered built in Jerusalem to commemorate this discovery.

In general these authors were no more concerned with dreams and visions than the secular writers of the period, perhaps even less than the slightly earlier Tacitus and Suetonius. Only two or three further references occur in each of their histories. In one place Eusebius told of a gnostic sect who boasted that certain demons sent them dreams and lent them protection, and in another he recounted briefly the divine vision given to Dionysius of Alexandria, which we have already discussed. The third story was about Natalius, a confessor, who became involved in heresy even though he was warned about it in visions. But when the heretics elected him bishop and gave him a salary of 250 denarii a month, Natalius was so afflicted through the whole night that he went early in the morning to the legitimate bishop to ask forgiveness and to be taken back into the fold—a story very similar to one we shall hear from Jerome's own hand about himself.[7]

Socrates added two stories, one of the Empress Dominica, who was warned in dreams of the death of her child as she and the Emperor Valens withstood Basil the Great. The other was the dream of Justina's father, in which he saw the imperial purple brought forth out of his right side. When he told this dream, the emperor had him assassinated but then married Justina, who bore him a son, the Emperor Valentinian, and a daughter, who married Theodosius the Great. Socrates also mentioned the fact that Ignatius of Antioch had a vision of angels who sang hymns in alternate chants and so introduced the mode of antiphonal singing.[8] In the later writings of Theodoret it was mentioned that John Chrysostom had been shown in a dream where he would be buried and that the Emperor Theodosius, while still only a general, dreamed of being invested with the imperial robe and crown by Bishop Meletius of Antioch.[9]

Sozomen did include several stories about dreams and visions connected with the imperial city of Constantinople. He told how Constantine was directed by God in a dream to abandon the rebuilding of Troy and seek another spot for his capital city; obedient to the dream, the emperor was then led by the hand of God to Byzantium, where he constructed a city whose wonders the historians described.

Sozomen went on to tell that in one of its Christian temples, his own friend Aquilinus received a divine vision in the night, by which he was healed of an illness, and he later was instructed about the power of the cross in another such vision. In telling how Gregory of Nazianzen took over in Constantinople at the end of the Arian controversy, Sozomen added a delightful story about the healing of a pregnant woman in Gregory's church, concluding that in the church of Constantinople "the power of God was there manifested, and was helpful both in waking visions and in dreams, often for the relief of many diseases and for those afflicted by some sudden transmutation in their affairs."[10]

Constantine himself placed an inscription over the gateway of his city, which said "that Christ had helped him on account of his constant and devout reverence for the 'divine'; Christ had quenched the fire of the tyrant, and granted him the rulership of the entire world."[11] Indeed, there is no more reason to discredit the historians who told of God's guidance of Constantine in dreams and visions than there is to discredit Carl Sandburg, who repeats the stories of Lincoln's dreams.There is no reason, that is, unless one is stuck with a theory of reality that denies the possibility of divine knowledge in dreams. As far as Constantine's morals are concerned, those who suggest that what he did to his family precluded anything from God, simply forget that David also ordered the death of Bathsheba's husband, while the fact that Henry VIII ordered the death of his wife did not keep him from having quite a religious influence in the Protestant world.

An Example Today

If these Christian stories about Constantine seem simply incredible, however, let us consider some facts about a more recent Christian warrior, General George Patton, who followed much the same pattern, with the same brilliance and many of the same faults. Patton was a deeply religious man, who half expected and feared a "call" that might send him into the ministry; yet he often abused his position and power. According to the reserved young teacher, Joe Rosevich, who was his personal secretary for over three years, Patton's superb military intuitions often came in sleep, undoubtedly from dreams.

One of these nocturnal inspirations has been described in detail in Ladislas Farago's definitive biography of this great general. It occurred one December night in 1944, during the fateful Battle of the Bulge. Rosevich answered a 4:00 A.M. summons to the office in Luxembourg and arrived to find Patton ready to dictate, still in his rumpled pajamas, with part of his uniform hastily thrown over them. Quickly, point by point, he laid out the order for an attack to be mounted at the very time the Germans themselves were jumping off to attack.

They "were stopped cold in their frozen tracks," Rosevich recalls, and thus Patton avoided a further threat to his beleaguered army.

A few days later, when success was assured, Patton discussed with his secretary the way his inspiration for the operation had come that night. At 3:00 A.M. he had opened his eyes with a start—as on so many other occasions, for no apparent reason. He had not, in fact, known that the German attack was coming; he was simply wide awake, the idea that it was going to happen and that he knew what to do about it fully formed in his mind. It was in this way, he went on, that every one of his inspired ideas had come. It could be "inspiration or insomnia," Patton suggested. But his secretary had so often responded to calls in the night that he knew very well how close the general was to his dreams and how ready to act when inspiration came in them.[12]

Whatever trouble we have in understanding the source of Constantine's uncanny genius, many of us are old enough to remember George Patton and to realize how probable this account is and how much help it offers in understanding the genius of this man in the face of Nazi aggression.

It is interesting to find that similar stories also circulated around the life of another religious emperor, Julian the Apostate. The Roman historian Ammianus Marcellinus recorded that as this last pagan emperor faced his struggle for power, he was visited in a dream by "the genius of the Roman Empire." In this way Julian was prepared, while his opponent Constantius was beset with evil visions and premonitions, even in broad daylight. After Julian's success this spirit came once more to him. This was just before his fatal battle with the Persians. This time his vision left the tent sorrowful, with head veiled. The emperor went out into the night, and a star fell with a streak of light from the sky. The next day Julian was killed, according to Ammianus, whose meticulous accuracy and intimacy with the court at this time made him famed as the reliable historian of this last period of opposition to Christianity.[13]

The Struggle for Orthodoxy and the View of Dreams

As warfare ceased against the Christian church, it began within, in the struggle against heresy, primarily in the great Arian conflict. In this struggle the man who stood almost singlehanded in support of orthodoxy against government interference and dissensions was Athanasius. As bishop of Alexandria from A.D. 328 to 373, he showed a courage and brilliance that laid the foundations of later orthodoxy. Three times he went into exile, and three times he returned. Nearly all historians of this period show admiration for this great man, this monumental figure whose writings are authoritative for the theologians of all churches, Protestant, Catholic, and Orthodox alike.

In an early work, *Against the Heathen,* and in a late work, *The Life of St. Antony,* Athanasius showed that he shared the early Christian attitude toward dreams and visions as revelations of an unseen world. At the same time he was careful, even wary, in interpreting them. In his sermon for Easter in A.D. 341 he admonished his people to beware of those who use dreams and false prophecies to lead people astray, and he referred to the specific statement in Deuteronomy 13. Again, in the *History of the Arians* he referred to the dream-vision of Daniel in which the prophet saw the Antichrist (7:24–25), showing how the interpretation applied specifically to the Emperor Constantius. Because he believed in dreams and supernatural experiences, Athanasius did not hesitate to refer to the dream material of the Bible as authoritative.[14]

The mature genius of Athanasius was already evident in the first part of his great masterpiece of Christian apology, *Against the Heathen,* written when he was only twenty-one. Early in this work he insisted on the importance of the dream as a means of revelation:

> Often when the body is quiet, and at rest and asleep, man moves inwardly, and beholds what is outside himself, travelling to other countries, walking about, meeting his acquaintances, and often by these means divining and forecasting the actions of the day. But to what can this be due save to the rational soul, in which man thinks of and perceives things beyond himself? . . .
>
> For if even when united and coupled with the body it is not shut in or commensurate with the small dimensions of the body, but often, when the body lies in bed, not moving, but in death-like sleep, the soul keeps awake by virtue of its own power, and transcends the natural power of the body, and as though travelling away from the body while remaining in it, imagines and beholds things above the earth, and often even holds converse with the saints and angels who are above earthly and bodily existence, and approaches them in the confidence of the purity of its intelligence; shall it not all the more, when separated from the body at the time appointed by God Who coupled them together, have its knowledge of immortality more clear?[15]

Sometime after Athanasius's exile in the Egyptian desert, in his maturest years, he wrote his *Life of St. Antony,* which reveals his admiration for this charismatic old hermit. It also shows that Athanasius continued to appreciate the human capacity to see more than the physical world. Antony's conversation with angels and demons, his extrasensory knowledge, his healing power, and other gifts are described at length. Thus this work reveals much that does not come out in Athanasius's more polemic writings. Revelation of the spiritual world was one matter upon which Arians and Trinitarians were not divided, and this great theologian's concern with the pressing conflicts of theology and practical church polity kept him from developing his ideas on this subject. Although a later age has looked at his account of Antony's life with raised eyebrows, a careful reading of the document with the insights of depth psychology shows that there is an objective reality to this account.

Athanasius's view of the angelic and demonic betrays little tendency to concretize these beings materialistically. They are seen as psychic in origin but real nonetheless. These encounters with nonphysical reality, which most people have only in dreams, were given to Antony both in direct daytime visions and also in the night, when many of them unquestionably refer to visions in dreams. Athanasius recorded the life of Antony with a mature psychological understanding, showing that the state of a person's soul and that person's fearfulness have a profound effect upon the kind of experience that transpires and the outcome of it. Just as Antony could have conversation with these realities in his waking hours, ordinary people can and do meet them in sleep.

Athanasius quoted with approval Antony's statements:

> And if even once we have a desire to know the future, let us be pure in mind, for I believe that if a soul is perfectly pure and in its natural state, it is able, being clear-sighted, to see more and further than the demons—for it has the Lord who reveals to it—like the soul of Elisha, which saw what was done by Gehazi, and beheld the hosts standing on its side.[16]

One cannot understand the power and vitality of Athanasius if he excises the *Life of St. Antony* from his important works. His interest in Antony shows his own religious aspiration and his belief that the soul can be given direct communication with the nonphysical, the spiritual world, without the mediation of reason or sense experience. Dreams are one form of this communication. This writing, coming from the later part of this great man's life, shows the conviction of his inner life that he had expressed very clearly and simply in one of his earliest writings.

The Same View of Dreams among the Orthodox Leaders

Following Athanasius in the Greek church were four men who established the Trinitarian thinking of the Eastern church once and for all. These four doctors of the Greek church, who forged the structure of orthodox faith, had much in common. The three great Cappadocians—Basil the Great, Gregory of Nazianzen, and Gregory of Nyssa—were the theologians, while Chrysostom was the great preacher who popularized the ideas of these men and made them current in the popular mind. All four men had an ascetic interest. All four have been sainted by the church. All four were from cultured Christian families, had been educated in the best pagan tradition of the time, and were only baptized as adults after an inner conviction of the reality of Christian experience. All four were bishops of the church during the last half of the fourth century; two of them were brothers, and two were close friends. In the writings of all of them one finds the conviction that God speaks through the medium of dream-vision experiences. Since not all of their writings are accessible in English, one must plow through the Latin or Greek of Migne in order to find many of their teachings on this subject.

We turn first of all to Gregory of Nyssa, whose major philosophical work, *On the Making of Man*, deals directly with the meaning and place of sleep and dreams in human life. Since this work was written to supplement the *Hexaemeron* of his brother Basil, it undoubtedly reflects the ideas accepted by all three Cappadocians on the subject of dreams. Tillemont has described this Gregory as "the master, doctor, peacemaker, and arbiter of the churches." He was moved by the brilliant theological tradition of Origen, which Gregory Thaumaturgus had introduced to Asia Minor, and he carried on the best of that tradition.

According to Gregory of Nyssa, when a person is asleep, the senses and the reason rest and the less rational parts of the soul appear to take over. Reason is not, however, extinguished, but smoulders like a fire "heaped with chaff," and then breaks forth with insights that modern dream research calls "secondary mentation." As Plato had previously suggested, and as Jung later confirmed, in the sleeping state the mind has

> by its subtlety of nature . . . some advantage, in ability to behold things, over mere corporeal grossness; yet it cannot make its meaning clear by direct methods, so that the information of the matter in hand should be plain and evident, but its declaration of the future is ambiguous and doubtful,—what those who interpret such things call an "enigma."

Gregory then referred to the dreams around Daniel and the patriarch Joseph, concluding that the interpretation of dreams is indeed a gift from God. He went on:

> As then, while all men are guided by their own minds, there are some few who are deemed worthy of evident Divine communication; so, while the imagination of sleep naturally occurs in a like and equivalent manner for all, some, not all, share by means of their dreams in some more Divine manifestation.

His reasoning was that there is a natural foreknowledge that comes in an unknown way through the nonrational part of the soul—the "unconscious," according to modern depth psychology—and it is through this part of the soul that God communicates directly.

Gregory then enumerated the other meanings that dreams can have, offering quite a complete outline of the subject. He suggested that dreams can provide mere reminiscences of daily occupations and events. Or they can reflect the condition of the body, its hunger or thirst, or the emotional condition of the personality. Dreams can also be understood in medical practice as giving clues to the sickness of the body. Again anticipating depth psychology, he wrote:

> Moreover, most men's dreams are conformed to the state of their character: the brave man's fancies are of one kind, the coward's of another; the wanton man's dreams of one kind, the continent man's of another; the liberal man and the avaricious man are subject to different fancies; while these fancies are nowhere framed by the intellect, but by the less rational disposition of the soul, which forms even in dreams the semblances of those things to which each is accustomed by the practice of his waking hours.[17]

Indeed, far from stating a superstitious belief, Gregory laid out quite well the principle upon which today's analytical study of dreams is based.

In addition to these philosophical reflections on the religious and secular meaning of dreams, Gregory also told, in a sermon entitled "In Praise of the Forty Martyrs," of a dream that occurred while he was attending a celebration in honor of the soldiers who had withstood a last, brief outburst of persecution. In the dream these men of Licinius's army, Christians who had died in the freezing waters of a pond rather than deny their faith, came upon him with rods and lashes for his Christian lethargy. When Gregory awoke, he was shaken to the depth by his lack of Christian devotion. Thus, he told, he was started on the serious practice of his Christian way. In the same sermon he also told of a soldier attending the memorial celebration who was healed by the appearance in a dream of one of these martyrs.[18] Again, in his *Life of St. Gregory Thaumaturgus* he told of the dream-vision in which the earlier Gregory had beheld the Virgin Mary and John, who discoursed before him, answered his questions on the Trinity, and gave him thoughts which he then put forth in his well-known creed, *A Declaration of Faith.*[19]

It is clear that philosophically, practically, and personally Gregory of Nyssa believed the dream could be a revelation of depths beyond the human ego. Interestingly enough, however, like many of the Latin fathers, he did not mention the relation of false dreams and demons, although this matter was discussed by his brother Basil.

Basil the Great left as great an impact on the church as any of the Eastern fathers. Because of his outstanding mind, he was able to stand against the best of the Aristotelian, Arian thinkers. His personal courage in confronting the Arian emperor Valens and his willingness to suffer for orthodoxy gave conviction to those under his banner. His personal asceticism and his writings on this subject deeply moved his own age and laid the foundations for later Greek monasticism. Here he showed the influence of another great theologian, Origen.

In his commentary on Isaiah, Basil indicated that the Scriptures were intended by God to be somewhat difficult to comprehend. First, they were meant to exercise our minds and keep them occupied and away from lower things; and second, they were designed to take longer to understand because the things we have to work over longer stay with us longer. For much the same reason, therefore, dreams are obscure and involved so that they require our sagacity and mental agility in no slight degree. He concluded:

> The enigmas in dreams have a close affinity to those things which are signified in an allegoric or hidden sense in the Scriptures. Thus both Joseph and Daniel, through the gift of prophecy, used to interpret dreams, since the force of reason by itself is not powerful enough for getting at truth.[20]

That Basil believed in continuing to consider dreams is indicated by the letter he wrote to a woman in which he interpreted the dream she had sent him. He suggested to her that her dream meant she was to spend more time in "spiritual contemplation and cultivating that mental vision by which God is wont to be seen." In introducing *The Hexaemeron,* his exposition on cosmology based on the opening chapters of Genesis, he referred with approval to "the testimony of God Himself" in Numbers 12:6-8 that only Moses came to know the Lord face to face, while he spoke to all others in a vision or a dream. Twice in his treatise *On the Spirit* he referred to the fact that the Spirit spoke through dreams to the patriarchs Joseph and Jacob.[21]

In spite of his theoretical agreement that dreams are sources of revelation, Basil found them a cause of embarrassment. In his early asceticism he learned that they spoke of levels of the human psyche that he could not control by his rational mind, and so he warned Gregory of Nazianzen that it is better not to sleep too hard, because this opens the mind to wild fancies. It was hard for Basil to bear the fact—now commonly accepted by modern psychology—that dreams do compensate for one's conscious attitude. Even worse was Basil's experience with his former friend Eustathius. This turncoat ascetic and his friends told dreams and interpretations against Basil that put him in a very bad light. In making his reply, Basil had to admit that some dreams do come from God, but he warned that every dream is not a prophecy. They can be false and demonic, he added, and "bring strife and division and destruction of love." He complained about the gossipy nature of the non-Christian dream interpreters and warned Christians to stay away from them. He concluded the defense of his reputation from Eustathius's attack with these words: "Let them therefore not give occasion to the devil to attack their souls in sleep; nor make their imaginations of more authority than the instruction of salvation."[22] It is surprising that this is the first time we come upon an expression of such negative feelings about the misuse of dreams, that up to Basil there had not been this concern about pagan or unorthodox interpreters in the writings of the fathers.

Gregory of Nazianzen was one of the most attractive of these fourth-century figures. Willing to give himself to the doctrines laid down by Origen and Athanasius and to use all his energy and eloquence to support them, he was able to put Christian love first. His letters reveal the depth of his personal relationships, and in the orations his honest understanding and teaching have been preserved, summing up the thinking of the orthodox leaders in its clearest and most palatable form. Alone among the Greek fathers Gregory shared the title of "Divine" or "Theologian" with John of the Gospels. He was a close friend of Basil the Great and spent much time in ascetic practice at Basil's retreat. Against his own wishes, he first took the small see of Sasima to help his friend. Later he was asked to come to Constantinople, where he rallied the orthodox forces with his educated mind and his personal purity. The building of the great center of orthodoxy, the Church of the Resurrection in the Eastern capital, was the work of Gregory. But when his person caused embarrassment as president of the Second Ecumenical Council in A.D. 381, he resigned both as patriarch of Constantinople and as president of the council and went into retirement from the world until his death.

Had not Gregory left us his theological poems, we would not realize the important part that dreams played in his life. Since these poems tell about Gregory himself, they tell things that did not have a place in his arguments against heretics. They reveal a theory and practice on dreams that was integrated in one consistent theological pattern. He told in the second book of these poems: "And God summoned me from boyhood in my nocturnal dreams, and I arrived at the very goals of wisdom."[23] The major themes of Gregory's life, his purity and his devotion to the Trinity, were given and reinforced by his dreams. In the story of one of them he told how chastity embraced him as two maidens who came to him with warmth and affection. When he asked who they were, they replied: Temperance and Virginity. Then they asked him to mix his mind with theirs, his torch with their torch, so that they might place him near the light of the immortal Trinity. This vision of the night led him to renounce the "severe yoke of marriage" and give himself to the ascetic way.[24] In another place he told that this nocturnal vision was the hidden spark that set his whole life aflame for God.[25]

Again, Gregory told of a dream in which he saw himself sitting on a throne in humble fashion. He was speaking, and people came from all sides to hear his words. Then they began to argue what he should say, "But from my mouth there poured forth / That the Trinity alone ought to be adored."[26] In other places he referred again to the fact that Chastity embraced him through his dreams[27] and that he was promised by his mother to God, to whom he was bound by "the dangers and the favors of the night."[28]

In one place in his poems he counseled caution in interpreting dreams, in these words: "Devote not your trust too much to the mockery of dreams, / Nor let yourself be terrified by everything; / Do not become inflated by joyful visions, / For frequently a demon prepares these snares for you."[29] Yet in his funeral oration on Basil, Gregory praised the visions of Jacob and Joseph to show that his friend had been greater than these dreamers.[30]

The records of this attractive life, which was crucial for Christian orthodoxy, leave no doubt that one very important fount of his religious conviction was his experience of God through dreams, and there is nothing in his theoretical writings to suggest that it should not be so with other people.

During the period of these great Fathers there were many lesser lights in the Greek church. While it is impossible to discuss them all, Cyril of Jerusalem was one who produced some of the standard fourth-century expositions of the faith. In a letter he wrote to the Emperor Constantius, Cyril described a public vision that occurred in Jerusalem in A.D. 351. On the morning of Whitsunday, the seventh of May, about 9:00 A.M., people flocked out to see the bright cross that hung in the sky, brighter than the sun, stretching from Golgotha to Mount Olivet and remaining there for several hours. He regarded this sign as a good occasion for announcing the beginning of his episcopate to the Emperor.[31] Here was an experience as objective and powerful to that time as the experiences of the unidentified flying object today, one similar to that attested by Constantine.

John the Golden-mouth

To the Greek church the writings of John Chrysostom, John the Golden-mouth, have authority approaching that of the Scriptures themselves. The great Cappadocians were primarily concerned with establishing the Nicene faith. Chrysostom went on from there and preached in his inimitable fashion on every subject, bringing the implications of this faith to bear on every aspect of the life in Constantinople of the late fourth and early fifth century. Chrysostom lived what he spoke and imposed a Christian discipline on his clergy and the court. This brought out the enmity of the emperor's wife Eudoxia. He was banished and recalled and then banished again.

Even in exile the banished bishop continued as a power. The empress finally sent him on foot to one of the farthest and most inhospitable spots in the empire, and as he neared the end of his journey he died. In all this he maintained the finest Christian perspective. No wonder the people of his time revered him as a saint and brought his body back to Constantinople to rest with the emperors and patriarchs. His works were balanced, careful, and irenic. His liturgy and his homilies became the model of later Greek piety and religion. His commentaries on Scripture anticipated modern methods of exegesis; they were far more historical and critical than allegorical.

While there is no systematic treatment of dreams in the works of Chrysostom, he had enough to say about them, and in enough different ways, to indicate that he shared the current sophisticated attitude toward dreams as a source of revelation. Perhaps even more significant, he made no suggestion at any point that Christians should not take their dreams seriously. There is not even a reference anywhere in his writings to the biblical passages that urged caution in the use of dreams. He simply expressed his ideas about their value when the issue presented itself in one of his homilies. For instance, in the discussion of Pentecost in the homilies on Acts he stated specifically: "To some the grace was imparted through dreams, to others it was openly poured forth. For indeed by dreams the prophets saw, and received revelations."[32] According to Chrysostom, dreams are sent to those whose wills are compliant to God, for they do not need visions or the more startling divine manifestations, and he mentioned Joseph, the father of Jesus, and Peter and Paul as examples of this truth.[33]

A dream is no small thing, he concluded. Rather, it can be a revelation and sure sign from God, as we know not only from the New Testament, but from the dreams of Abimelech and Joseph as well. And like those of Daniel, dreams can be given for the common good, as well as for personal direction. To show this he discussed at length the dreams surrounding the birth of Jesus.[34] In other discussions he also mentioned twice the consolation that Paul had received from God in dreams and how these experiences encouraged him to go on.[35]

Chrysostom took care to explain that we are not responsible for our dreams; we are not disgraced by the things we may see in them, or guilty for what we may do there. These images are given, and do not reveal an external physical reality. They do, however, reveal spiritual reality for people, who can even be buffeted so much by angels in dreams that they are as terrified as if a hostile human being were coming at them. Dreams may also reveal the state of people's souls, their bad conscience and bad character. Dreams can even deter them from acting on their immoral desires.[36]

As Chrysostom came to each dream experience in the parts of the Bible he commented on, he took them up one by one, trying to understand them directly. He wrote page after page on the way in which God revealed himself to Abraham and then to Joseph in dreams and visions of the night.[37] He took particular pains to understand the nature of the *ekstasis* of Peter's dream on the rooftop in Joppa, which he considered was one way of perceiving spiritual reality.[38] In all of the discussions of Paul's experiences and the dreams around the life of Jesus, there is no hint that these experiences did not happen in the present, just as they did in those times. Only once, in talking about Jesus' baptism, did he suggest that such visions did not occur as often in his own time. He concluded that God gives them when they are needed—"evermore at the beginnings of all wonderful and spiritual transactions"—but that faith could take the place of these more obvious break-throughs of the divine into human life.[39]

Sir Thomas Browne once mentioned how often Chrysostom himself dreamed of Paul, remarking that it was no wonder, since Paul was so much on the saint's mind,[40] but I have not been able to locate these personal references. Yet in other places Chrysostom left no doubt how these great fathers of orthodoxy viewed the tantalizing phenomena of sleep; dreams were one possible and often used means of revelation from the world of spirit.

An Original Thinker

About the same time in the early fifth century, Synesius of Cyrene, with his Neo-Platonic education under the famous Hypatia, came into the church. He also brought a wife, because of whom he had become Christian at about the age of thirty-five. Soon after, he was asked to become bishop of Ptolemais. He agreed on the condition that he might continue to hold certain of his heterodox opinions; his conditions were accepted, and Synesius became one of the most noticed bishops of his time. It was no wonder; he was a handsome man, whom one church historian called "as original as he was attractive."[41] Brought up in North Africa with great wealth, Synesius's cultivated interests ranged over everything from geometry and astronomy to farming. The book he wrote on dreams represents the culmination of early Christian thinking on the subject.

In many ways this work of Synesius's is the most thoughtful and sophisticated consideration of dreams to be found until we come to the modern studies of Freud and Jung. Although almost forgotten in the West, it was highly valued throughout the centuries in the Eastern Empire, and as late as the fourteenth century it was the subject of a detailed and careful commentary written by Nicephorus Gregoras, one of the intellectual leaders of his time. He remarked on its difficulty and obscurity, which he was trying to clarify for ordinary people.

The real difficulty (aside from the ancient terminology) was that Synesius wrote a very complex study of dreams. He was not trying to simplify the subject; instead, he was laying the foundation both philosophically and psychologically for the value of dreams. Augustine Fitzgerald, who has provided a very scholarly translation of this and some of Synesius's shorter works, remarks that no one in the ancient world made a finer attempt to understand the nature of the human psyche.

Synesius believed that the entire universe was a unity, and therefore the dream expressed its meaning as well as, and for certain reasons better than, any other experience of it. The dream, according to Synesius, arises from the faculty of the imagination that lies halfway between reason and the world around us (or rational consciousness and sense experience). It participates in both of these entities but is not tied down to space and time as is the experience of our senses. Synesius's description of the imagination is quite close to Jung's empirical description of the collective unconscious. In sleep the imagination is free; untrammeled by space and time, it can converse with the gods, explore unknown universes, and discover the stars. He concluded:

> One man learns . . . while awake, another while asleep. But in the waking state man is the teacher, whereas it is God who makes the dreamer fruitful with His own courage, so that learning and attaining are one and the same. Now to make fruitful is even more than to teach.[42]

Having laid out a sound reason for discussing dreams, Synesius then enumerated the blessings to be gained from studying them. For the pure soul who receives impressions clearly, a proper study of dreams gives knowledge of the future with all that this implies. Important information is also provided about bodily malfunction and how it can be corrected. Far more important, this undertaking brings the soul to consider immaterial things, and so, even though it was begun merely to provide knowledge of the future, it turns the soul to God and develops a love of him. Synesius also told how dreams had helped him in his writings and in his other endeavors and how they often gave hope to people who had been oppressed by the difficulties of life.

Synesius made fun of people who relied on the popular dream books, insisting that only by constantly comparing dreams with experience could they be understood. Their essential nature is personal, and they must be understood by the dreamer in terms of his or her own life. Some of them seem to be direct revelations of God, but there are also many dreams that are obscure and difficult to interpret. Synesius suggested that those who are serious in studying them should keep a record so that they know their sleeping life as well as their waking one. He even saw the connection between mythology and dreams and explained his belief that the myth is based upon the dream; a true interest in mythology helps people find the more vital meaning in their own dreams. Finally, Synesius showed the reason for his belief that dreams give hints about eternal life. As the sleeping state is to the waking one, so the life of the soul after death is to the dream life, and thus this state gives some idea of the kind of life that is led by the soul after death.

I have spent several pages describing Synesius's work because it is such an important summary of the church's thinking. Synesius's importance is recognized and commented on by psychologists of the Jungian school. His enthusiasm for his subject is clear, as in the following:

> For whatsoever things of use and of sweetness those hopes, which nourish the race of men, hold out to him, and as many things as fear controls—

> things ominous and withal gainful—all these things are found in dreams, nor by any other thing are we so enticed towards hope. And the element of hope is so abundant and so salutary in its nature that, as acute thinkers maintain, men would not even be willing to continue life, if it were only to be such as they had at the beginning . . . these hopes have such force that he who is bound in fetters, whenever he permits the will of his heart to hope, is straightway unbound. . . . And when it spontaneously presents hope to us, as happens in our sleeping state, then we have in the promise of our dreams a pledge from the divinity.[43]

This was the same thinking that was expressed by the great doctors of orthodoxy.

The Doctors in the West

The four men who became recognized as the doctors of the Western church were Ambrose, Augustine, Jerome, and Gregory the Great, each of whom was quite different from the others. Ambrose and Gregory, who came from wealthy and influential families, were in high civil positions when they turned to the church, while Augustine and Jerome were the scholars, with an interest in classical literature. Each of these men taught that dreams and visions were one of God's methods of revelation to human beings, and we shall find this expressed in both personal and theological terms in their writing. We shall also consider three other writers in this period who touched significantly on the same subject—Macrobius, Sulpicius Severus, and John Cassian.

There have been few personalities in Western Christianity as attractive as Ambrose, the bishop of Milan in the last part of the fourth century. Born about A.D. 340, he was educated for a civil career and rose rapidly to become governor of Northern Italy in the time when Milan was the seat of Western imperial power. He was still being instructed for baptism when the people of Milan chose him for their bishop by popular outcry. Believing that this was a call from God, he submitted, gave his wealth to the poor and to the church, and studied theology, interpreting the conclusions of Eastern orthodox thinking for the West. He stood firm against the encroachments of civil authority and once even called the Emperor Theodosius to public repentance for what he had done. Through actions like this Ambrose set the pattern for Western church-state relationship. His works on ethics, theology, and asceticism became standard for the Latin church, and many of his hymns are still sung.

Ambrose's own experience left no question of the depth of his belief about dreams. In his most famous letter, the letter to Theodosius calling for his repentance, he declared that God in a dream forbade him to celebrate communion before the emperor unless he repented. These are his dramatic words:

> I am writing with my own hand that which you alone may read. . . . I have been warned, not by man, nor through man, but plainly by Himself that this is forbidden me. For when I was anxious, in the very night in which I was preparing to set out, you appeared to me in a dream to have come into the Church, and I was not permitted to offer the sacrifice. . . . Our God gives warnings in many ways, by heavenly signs, by the precepts of the prophets; by the visions even of sinners He wills that we should understand, that we should entreat Him to take away all disturbances . . . that the faith and peace of the Church . . . may continue.[44]

Ambrose was deeply moved by the death of his brother Satyrus, who had also resigned an official post in order to be with Ambrose and relieve him of his secular affairs. Out of his grief Ambrose wrote the two exquisite books in which he contemplated his brother's death and then his own belief in the resurrection. At the close of Book 1 he compared the former nights of painful separation with his present joy in dreams that brought him the reality of his brother's presence. He wrote:

> I grasp thee whether in the gloomy night or in the clear light, when thou vouchsafest to revisit and console me sorrowing. And now the very nights which used to seem irksome in thy lifetime, because they denied us the power of looking on each other; and sleep itself, lately, the odious interrupter of our converse, have commenced to be sweet, because they restore thee to me. They, then, are not wretched, but blessed, whose mutual presence fails not, whose care for each other is not lessened, whose mutual esteem is increased. For sleep is a likeness and image of death.
>
> But if, in the quiet of night, our souls still cleaving to the chains of the body, and as it were bound within the prison bars of the limbs, yet are able to see higher and separate things, how much more do they see these, when in their pure and heavenly senses they suffer from no hindrances of bodily weakness. And so when, as a certain evening was drawing on, I was complaining that thou didst not revisit me when at rest, thou wast wholly present always. So that, as I lay with my limbs bathed in sleep, while I was (in mind) awake for thee, thou wast alive to me, I could say, "What is death, my brother?"[45]

In another famous letter Ambrose described how the bodies of the two martyred saints Gervasius and Protasius were discovered and brought to the place he consecrated to them in his new church. This event made a great stir in Milan, and a man long blind was healed during the dedication. Ambrose, however, played down the part his own experience had played; he mentioned only that before the discovery a prophetic spirit had entered his heart. It was Augustine, describing the period after his baptism in Milan, who told that the place where the saints' bodies had been hidden was revealed to Ambrose in a dream.[46]

In his more theological writings Ambrose supported the idea that the Holy Spirit speaks through dreams. He showed that an angel who speaks through a dream is functioning at the direction of the Holy Spirit, since angelic powers are subject to and moved by the Spirit. The Holy Spirit not only confirmed his presence to Joseph in a dream, but directed Paul through visions and intuitions, and spoke particularly clearly to Peter in his dream-trance experience on the rooftop in Joppa. Ambrose discussed at length the experiences in Acts 10, saying, "How clearly did the Holy Spirit express His own power!" Not long before his death he also wrote a letter of instruction to a certain group of Christians who had been without a bishop for a long time, recommending to them the way Peter had prayed for his revelation in Joppa.[47] In all these discussions he treated the dream and the vision as being of equal authority.

In a book on the duties of the clergy, Ambrose referred to the wisdom and prudence of Solomon, Joseph, and Daniel as exemplified by their ability to interpret dreams. Inferring that his own clergy might do the same, he remarked that "confidence was put in [Daniel] in all things, because he had frequently interpreted things, and had shown that he had declared the truth."[48] Ambrose's long discussion of the dreams in his commentary on Joseph begins with the words "Finally divine grace bloomed forth in the body. Since he dreamed. . . ." The prophetic nature of Joseph's dreams was revealed not only in the events of the patriarch's own life, but also in certain events in the life of Jesus. Thus, Ambrose showed, these dreams represented the fact that the life of Joseph in the Old Testament was symbolic of the Christ to come. The eleven sheaves, for instance, symbolized not only the eleven brothers, but also the eleven disciples who adored Jesus. In the second book of *On the Decease of Satyrus* he followed much the same thinking in considering Jacob's dream at Bethel and his encounter with the angel at Jabbok.[49] In none of his works was any reference made to the biblical passages that are critical of dreams.

Ambrose believed that dreams and visions were one means that people had of contact with those who had died and of knowing and experiencing things beyond the ordinary senses. He also believed that the Holy Spirit used dreams to instruct and warn people when they needed such admonition and that a part of wisdom was the prudent interpretation of these experiences from God.

Between Two Worlds

If any one man stands between this era and the modern world, it is Augustine. There is good reason for his influence, not only on Western Catholicism, but perhaps even more on Luther, Calvin, and the entire Protestant world. Within his own experience, Augustine was able to stand between several pairs of worlds, particularly the spiritual and the worldly. His youth was spent carelessly, or sometimes almost carefully, doing what he should not and absorbing gnostic Manicheism. At the same time he became an excellent teacher of rhetoric, and so came to Milan, where Ambrose was bishop. Here he was touched by Neo-Platonism and, turning toward Christianity, he sought out personal contact with Ambrose.

It was then that Augustine had his great religious experience, which brought him to baptism. And in the next half century Augustine went on, almost singlehandedly, to prepare the intellectual foundation for Western Christian thinking for another thousand years. Until Aquinas became accepted, Augustine was *the* Western theologian.

Not only do we find in Augustine a deeply religious, mystical longing and experience, but here was one of the most inquiring minds of the time. His philosophical ability and the penetrating psychological insight his studies show would make him important entirely apart from his Christian connections. The study of dreams is for Augustine a significant tool in understanding both the psychology of humans and their relations with God and the spiritual world.

Augustine's psychology and epistemology were based upon a sophisticated psychophysical dualism in which he saw two essentially different kinds of reality—the purely corporeal or physical, and the noncorporeal or "mental," which is spiritual in nature. This is essentially the theory that Lovejoy supports in his classical study of modern epistemology, *The Revolt Against Dualism.* It is again essentially the theory of the objective psyche proposed by C. G. Jung and his followers to explain the experiences of their medical and psychological practice.

Augustine's study of perception was as sophisticated as any in the ancient world. He saw reality as consisting of outer physical objects to which we react with our bodies, and then of the impressions of this sense experience, impressions that are "mental" in nature. We then have the inner perception of this sense experience, and finally the mental image in its remembered form. It is the action of the ego (called the will by Augustine) that unites these perceptions to the object. In one place he calls the faculty of imagination the bridge that mediates the object to consciousness, thus presenting almost the same thinking as that worked out by Synesius of Cyrene. Augustine saw a human being as possessing an outward eye that receives and mediates sense impressions and an inward eye that observes and deals with these collected and stored "mental" realities called memory.

In addition to the realities that come from outer perception and from inner perception of "memories," autonomous spiritual realities (angels and demons) can present themselves directly to the inner eye. These are of the same nature as the stored "mental" or psychic realities that are perceived inwardly. Augustine writes that people in sleep or trance can experience contents that come from memory "or by some other hidden force through certain spiritual commixtures of a similarly spiritual substance."[50] These autonomous realities are nonphysical, yet they can either assume a corporeal appearance and be experienced through the outward eye or be presented directly to consciousness through the inner eye in dreams, visions, and trances. Thus, through dreams, people are presented with a whole storehouse of unconscious memories and spontaneous contents; they are given access to a world that the Fathers called the realm of the spirit, which Jung has seen as the "objective psyche." Human beings have no control over this world; the contents of a dream or vision are as objective, as much "given" to the inner eye, as sense experience is to the outer eye.[51]

Augustine admitted that it was easier to describe what the angels and demons do than to explain what they are. In discussing the dreams that people have of the dead, he stated that it is not the dead people themselves who appear (just as one does not expect the living person to know when one dreams of him or her), but "by angelical operations, then, I should think it is effected, whether permitted from above, or commanded, that they seem in dreams to say something."[52] Just as angels have direct contact with the human psyche and present their messages before the inner eye, so also do demons.

> They persuade [men], however, in marvelous and unseen ways, entering by means of that subtlety of their own bodies into the bodies of men who are unaware, and through certain imaginary visions mingling themselves with men's thoughts whether they are awake or asleep.[53]

Augustine, as we can see, considered these experiences equally important whether they came in a waking vision or a dream.

When asked by his lifelong friend, the bishop Evodius, how human beings can have such strange experiences of telepathy and clairvoyance, or precognition, Augustine replied that ordinary experience is strange and difficult enough to explain and such things as this happen, but they are beyond human power to explain. It should also be noted that, although Augustine believed that these visionary experiences are important sources of knowledge, the highest experience of God transcends even these means. Dreams and visions do not reveal the nature of God, but they are given by him. They are examples of his providential care, his gifts. Referring to a dream that had brought conviction about life after death, he wrote of this vision: "By whom was he taught this but by the merciful, providential care of God?" It is also clear that Augustine found the operation of the inner eye and its lack of dependence upon the physical body to be excellent grounds for belief in the persistence of the human psyche after death.[54]

In addition to presenting a theory of dreams and visions, Augustine also discussed many examples of providential dreams in the course of his writings. One of the most important of them was the famous dream of his mother, Monica, in which she saw herself standing on a measuring device while a young man whose face shone with a smile approached her. She was crying, and when he asked why, she told of her sorrow that her son turned away from Christ. He told her to look, and suddenly she saw Augustine standing on the same rule with her and she was comforted. Realizing the significance of the symbolism, she was able to go on praying for him with patience and hope; her dreams and visions are also mentioned in several other places in *The Confessions.*[55]

Fascinating stories of a number of parapsychological dreams, as well as stories and discussions of other influential dreams, are found in various places in Augustine's writings. Particularly in the correspondence with Evodius there are accounts of dream experiences as uncanny as any in the modern literature on psychical research, or even in the Bible. Some of this material is included in the appendix, and there are other references in a letter to Alypius and in *The City of God,*[56] as well as in material already referred to. It is no wonder Augustine was led to study these experiences so thoroughly and with such faith in his Christian calling.

Jerome, the Scholar

While Jerome was not the most charming of the Fathers, he certainly made his talents known, and his influence on the church was great. An irascible disposition and a caustic pen kept him in trouble with both friends and enemies. But at the same time he spared no effort on his writings, which gave real support to orthodox Christianity against the threat of Arianism and did much to popularize asceticism and monasticism. His monumental gift to the church was his translation of the Bible into the Latin Vulgate.

Born into a wealthy Christian family about the same time as Augustine, in the last great age of the Western Empire, Jerome grew up in the great port of Aquileia at the head of the Adriatic Sea. There he studied the pagan masters and began his own literary work. He studied in Rome, traveled, collected a library, and gathered a congenial group of friends who were interested in becoming monks. It was then that his life was completely altered by a dream. Jerome had been torn between the classics and the Bible, which seemed to him rough and crude in comparison with Cicero and Plautus. He would fast and keep vigil, but only to read the masters. In Antioch he became very sick, and this experience happened, as he wrote dramatically in one of his most famous letters:

> Suddenly I was caught up in the spirit and dragged before the judgment seat of the Judge; and here the light was so bright, and those who stood around were so radiant, that I cast myself upon the ground and did not

> dare to look up. Asked who and what I was I replied: "I am a Christian." But he who presided said: "Thou liest, thou art a follower of Cicero and not of Christ. For 'where thy treasure is, there will thy heart be also.' " Instantly I became dumb, and amid the strokes of the lash—for He had ordered me to be scourged—I was tortured more severely still by the fire of conscience, considering with myself that verse, "In the grave who shall give thee thanks?" Yet for all that I began to cry and to bewail myself, saying: "Have mercy upon me, O Lord: have mercy upon me." Amid the sound of the scourges this cry still made itself heard. At last the bystanders, falling down before the knees of Him who presided, prayed that He would have pity on my youth, and that He would give me space to repent of my error. He might still, they urged, inflict torture on me, should I ever again read the works of the Gentiles. . . .
>
> Accordingly I made an oath and called upon His name, saying: "Lord, if ever again I possess worldly books, or if ever again I read such, I have denied Thee." Dismissed, then, on taking this oath, I returned to the upper world, and, to the surprise of all, I opened upon them eyes so drenched with tears that my distress served to convince even the credulous. And that this was no sleep nor idle dream, such as those by which we are often mocked, I call to witness the tribunal before which I lay, and the terrible judgment which I feared. . . . I profess that my shoulders were black and blue, that I felt the bruises long after I awoke from my sleep, and that thenceforth I read the books of God with a zeal greater than I had previously given to the books of men.[57]

Soon after this Jerome went into the desert as a hermit. He continued to study, and after a few years, he went to Constantinople under Gregory of Nazianzen. Then began his varied career as scholar, biblical consultant in Rome, and, until his death, head of his monastic community in Bethlehem.

Jerome's studies also gave him good reason to value dreams and visions. In commenting on Jeremiah 23:25-32, he shared Jeremiah's concern, indicating that dreaming is a kind of prophesying that God can use as one vehicle of revelation to a soul. It can be a valuable revelation from God if a person's life is turned toward him. But dreams can become idolatrous (like prophecy in the name of Baal) when they are sought and interpreted for their own sake by those who are serving their own self-interest instead of God. The value of the dream depends upon the person who seeks it and the person who interprets it. Sometimes God sends dreams to the unrighteous, like those of Pharaoh and Nebuchadnezzar, so that the servants of God may manifest their wisdom. Thus it is the duty of those who have the word of the Lord to explain dreams.[58]

This word could not be sought, however, by pagan practices like incubation. In commenting on Isaiah 65:4, Jerome went along with the prophet and condemned people who "sit in the graves and the temples of idols where they are accustomed to stretch out on the skins of sacrificial animals in order to know the future by dreams, abominations which are still practised today in the temples of Aescylapius."[59]

Later, however, in the discussion of Galatians, he brought up specifically the dream in Acts 16 in which Paul "was given the true light (*lucam vero*)."[60]

Jerome made no distinction at all between the vision and the dream. In his discussions of the dream of Joseph about Mary's conception, one would not know whether the vision had been received awake or asleep. God speaks through sleep as well as through visions. He also referred to Peter's dream in Joppa as a revelation of God with symbolic meaning, and in another place he called attention to the prophecy of Joel as proof that the Spirit had been poured out upon humanity. He discussed again and again what Ezekiel had to say about visions. For instance, Ezekiel 8:2 shows that "the visions make it possible to know the sacred things," while the next verse reveals that the prophet, because he was "brought in visions of God to Jerusalem," was carried there "not in the body, but in the spirit." Thus the dream-vision is seen as transcending time and space. There are also pages and pages about the dreams in Daniel.[61]

In *The Life of St. Hilarion*, Jerome gave a picture very similar to that of St. Antony by Athanasius. He wrote of the same concern with demons that come in the night, and although he did not use the word "dream," the whole character of the book suggests that this was what he was speaking of.[62] But when he got into his sharpest conflict, the controversy with his former friend Rufinus, Jerome revealed a great deal more about the attention these men paid to dreams.

In the heat of this fight, involving subtle charges of heresy, Rufinus questioned Jerome's sincerity by suggesting that he had not been faithful to the oath given in his great conversion dream; he must have reverted to secular reading to remember so much. Jerome came back with a defense of his religious calling and also of his memory, and then he attacked Rufinus for letting himself be misled by someone else's dream. This was a reference to the dream of one of Rufinus's friends, who had dreamed of him as a ship crossing the seas to Rome with answers to many puzzling questions. Rufinus had introduced his own *Apology* by telling this vision and how it had compelled him to begin the book to which Jerome objected so much. Jerome then told more of his own dreams, which would make an interesting study for an analyst. He told of dreaming of himself as a young man in a toga about to make a speech before his teacher of rhetoric and of waking up happy that it was not so. He also told about dreams of his own death and of "flying over lands, and sailing through the air, and crossing over mountains and seas!"[63] Indeed, Jerome, in his anger, revealed almost as much about the way these great Christians regarded their own dreams and the depth of their own experience as others who wrote out of love.

Yet in the end he fixed the ground firmly that would justify a growing fear of these experiences. In translating Leviticus 19:26 and

Deuteronomy 18:10 with one word different from other passages, a direct mistranslation, as we shall show, Jerome turned the law: "You shall not practice augury or witchcraft [i.e., soothsaying]" into the prohibition: "You shall not practice augury nor observe dreams." Thus by the authority of the Vulgate, dreams were classed with soothsaying, the practice of listening to them with other superstitious ideas.

A Contrast to Jerome

During these years another Westerner was writing who was to have an increasing influence on Western thinking for centuries. This was Macrobius, whose *Commentary on the Dream of Scipio* became one of the main philosophical handbooks of the Middle Ages and also the most important and best-known dream book in medieval Europe. We know next to nothing about this man, except that he lived when Jerome did and that, although he may even have been a Christian, he based three popular works entirely on Cicero and the wisdom of classical Greece and Rome. He was one of the first of a group of summarizers who tried to gather together this wisdom for the people of the fourth, fifth, and sixth centuries. In his influence on medieval thought he stands right up with Boethius and Isidore of Seville.

Macrobius's *Commentary* presented a very simplified version of Platonism, in many ways inaccurate and far from the mark; yet it evidently made people who read it think they understood Plato. In fact, most of the Middle Ages got its knowledge of Plato and Platonic thought either from Chalcidius, who is practically forgotten today, or from the writing of this fourth-century summarizer. There are hundreds of manuscript copies of his *Commentary* still in existence, and it had run through thirty-seven printed editions before 1700.[64] No wonder the thought of Plato carried so little weight in the Renaissance; what Plato Macrobius offered was made into an understandable, oversimplified, and otherworldly base for medieval philosophy in the West. In it philosophy and a rather rigid dream interpretation were bound to one another.

The *Commentary* opened with several chapters in which Macrobius expounded and reiterated, in clear and concise Latin, the popular dream theory of his time, thus preserving for later ages what was essentially the theory of Artemidorus. He classified dreams as of five types. The first type is the enigmatic dream (*oneiros* or *somnium*), which conveys its message in strange shapes, veiled with ambiguity. This is the common dream, with many varieties. Next is the dream that foretells the future in a true way, the prophetic vision within a dream (*horama* or *visio*). Slightly different from this is the oracular dream (*chrematismos* or *oraculum*) "in which a parent, or a pious or revered man, or a priest, or even a god clearly reveals what will or will not transpire, and what action to take or to avoid." The fourth type of dream is the nightmare (*enypnion* or *insomnium*), which "may be caused by mental or physical distress, or anxiety about the future." These dreams arise from the conditions of the day before. Finally, there is the apparition (*phantasma* or *visum*), which "comes upon one in the moment between wakefulness and slumber. . . . [One] imagines he sees specters rushing at him or wandering vaguely about . . . either delightful or disturbing." To this class belongs the incubus with its sense of weight. The last two types, according to Macrobius, were "not worth interpreting, since they have no prophetic significance."[65]

This classification tells a great deal about the dream theory of the secular fourth century. It is interesting to see how much agreement there was between this theory and that of later church fathers. Macrobius also considered that the soul, when asleep and disengaged from bodily functions, was better able to perceive truth, but he discussed this only in Homer's symbolism about "the gates of horn and of ivory." Until the medieval Platonism was challenged in the twelfth century, this dream theory was treated by most civilized Westerners as simply accepted and common knowledge.

St. Martin of Tours was also contemporary with Jerome, and the man who wrote his biography was a good friend of both Jerome and Augustine. This was Sulpicius Severus, a Christian who was a highly educated lawyer. He practiced this profession until his wife's premature death about A.D. 392, when he entered the priesthood. While he had already gained a wide reputation, Sulpicius is remembered today mainly for his close friendship with Martin. Like his other work, his famous life of the saint was written in such polished and carefully styled Latin that he has been called "the Christian Sallust."

In this book he told about two dreams that were important in the life of this famed ascetic who had so much to do with spreading both Christianity and education in Gaul. Once when the weather became extreme Martin gave away his clothing until he had only his cloak, which he cut in two and gave half to cover a naked beggar. That night in his sleep Martin had a vision of Christ dressed in the part of the cloak he had given the poor man, and he heard Jesus saying to the angels, "Martin, who is still but a catechumen, clothed me with this robe." Later Martin was warned in a dream to visit his parents, who were still pagans. Obedient to the instruction, he set out to visit them, was able to convert his mother, and this was the last time he was to see his parents.[66]

In one of Sulpicius's undisputed letters, he also told of his own vision experience about the time Martin was dying. He spoke of the "light and uncertain" morning sleep—the kind of sleep when visions do occur—in which Martin appeared, clearly recognizable and "in the character of a bishop, clothed in a white robe, with a countenance as of fire." Martin then ascended into the air, followed by one of his disciples who had died not long before. Sulpicius then described with awe how he was still rejoicing over the vision when two monks brought the news of Martin's death and how he was moved both by grief and by the knowledge that God shares the numinous depth of reality and his deepest mysteries in this way.[67]

John Cassian also wrote an interesting discussion of dreams about this time, in relation to nocturnal emissions. This section is available only in Latin, however; the nineteenth century was too prudish to translate and publish it. Since nocturnal emissions were considered polluting, the question arose as to whether the voluptuous dreams that often accompanied them would make a monk unworthy to receive the Eucharist. The monk with whom Cassian discussed this concluded that if a person's life is exemplary, then these dreams are sent by the enemy, the devil, and do not affect the moral quality of the dreamer. Even the best of men may be invaded with this kind of dream. They are nocturnal illusions sent by the Evil One.[68] Within two hundred years the last great doctor of the church, Gregory the Great, would find even more to fear in dreams than this.

The Beginning of Darkness

Between the time of Augustine, Ambrose, and Jerome and that of Gregory, a great deal had happened in Italy. Rome had fallen, the Western Empire no longer existed as such, and the church had forgotten persecution. Italy had been overrun by Goths and Lombards and then partly conquered again by the emperor at Constantinople, whose regent resided in Ravenna. Education and culture had declined, and the Dark Ages were beginning. The influence of these conditions was quite apparent in Gregory the Great, who belongs more to the Middle Ages than to classical times.

Gregory, who was born in A.D. 540, was an educated Roman gentleman but no more. He knew only his own language and had little philosophical or literary background. He came from a senatorial family and was an excellent and conscientious administrator in trying times but without intellectual sophistication in any sense. Around him were the growing ignorance and superstition of a dying culture, and so Gregory was both more superstitious about dreams and more fearful of these experiences that held such interest for the ordinary person. He admitted their validity on one hand and warned in strong words of their danger on the other. For the first time in the writings of the church fathers, the warning passages of Leviticus 19 (in Jerome's Vulgate translation), Ecclesiastes 5, and Ecclesiasticus 34 were emphasized again and again. Jerome's anger and unconscious fear had done their work.

In two places Gregory described the six sources of dreams in almost identical words. The first was in the *Morals*, his discussion of the Book of Job, and then in the *Dialogues*, where he was so concise and to the point that we quote him in full:

> It is important to realize, Peter, that dreams come to the soul in six ways. They are generated either by a full stomach or by an empty one, or by illusions, or by our thoughts combined with illusions, or by revelations, or by our thoughts combined with revelations. The first two ways we all know from personal experience. The other four we find mentioned in the Bible. If dreams did not frequently come from the illusions of the Devil, the wise man surely would not have said, "For dreams have led many astray, and those who believed in them have perished," (Ecclesiasticus 34:7, Douay), or "You shall not divine nor observe dreams" (Leviticus 19:26, Douay[69]). From these words we can readily gather how detestible dreams are, seeing that they are put into a class with divination. And if, at times, dreams did not proceed from our thoughts as well as from diabolical illusions, the wise man would not have said dreams come with many cares (Ecclesiastes 5:2). And if dreams did not arise at times from the mystery of a revelation, Joseph would not have seen himself in a dream preferred to his brethren, nor would the angel have warned the spouse of Mary to take the child and flee into Egypt. Again, if at times dreams did not proceed from the thoughts in our minds as well as from revelation, the Prophet Daniel, in interpreting the dream of Nabuchodonosor, would not have started on the basis of a thought, saying, "Thou, O king, didst begin to think in thy bed what should come to pass hereafter: and he that reveals mysteries showed thee what shall come to pass." And a little later, "Thou O king, sawest, and behold there was as it were a great statue: this statue, which was great and high, tall of stature, stood before thee," and so on (Daniel 2:29, 31). Daniel, therefore, in reverently indicating that the dream was to be fulfilled and in telling from what thoughts it arose, shows clearly that dreams often rise from our thoughts and from revelation.
>
> Seeing, then, that dreams may arise from such a variety of causes, one ought to be very reluctant to put one's faith in them, since it is hard to tell from what source they come. The saints, however, can distinguish true revelations from the voices and images of illusions through an inner sensitivity. They can always recognize when they receive communications from the good Spirit and when they are face to face with illusions. If the mind is not on its guard against these, it will be entangled in countless vanities by the master of deceit, who is clever enough to foretell many things that are true in order finally to capture the soul by but one falsehood.[70]

In the *Dialogues* Gregory had already shown how "God strengthens timid souls with timely revelations in order to keep them from all fear at the moment of death." He gave several examples of people who were given warning of their death and reception into heaven by the revelation of dreams. He also told how Benedict, the abbot, once agreed to come on a certain day to lay out the site for a new monastery and, instead, came to one of his followers in a dream to give the instructions. In one instance he told how a very holy monk had all physical temptation taken away in a vision, and there were other examples of external events associated with dreams, quite different from the more nonphysical understanding of such happenings among the earlier Fathers. Flowers were seen in a dream, and their actual odor later appeared about the man's grave; after a dream of fire before the altar the very spot in the floor was found charred. In other stories a recalcitrant monk saw "with his own eyes the invisible dragon that had been leading him astray," while still another died and was found lying outside the grave several times until the abbot forgave him by placing the consecrated Host on his breast.[71]

On the other hand, Gregory's letters to Theoctista, the emperor's sister, reveal how he tried to get rid of "all phantasms of the body" and to find God through faith rather than in visions of him. It is hard to blame Gregory for wanting to forget the "legion of demons" and "tumults of thoughts" that pestered him. But in his *Pastoral Rule* he took a vision like Jacob's dream of the ladder to heaven to mean that those of high estate must be related to "the bed of the carnal." And in the same work he emphasized that Balaam's ass saw "an angel which the human mind sees not." He was also careful to point out to Theoctista how little Peter relied on the power of his vision in Joppa. To one of his bishops he inveighed against soothsayers and diviners of any kind, showing clearly his fear of pagan culture.[72]

Gregory was torn between two attitudes and experiences, and as "teacher of the Middle Ages," he passed on the same split. For six centuries the value of dreams was accepted with increasing credulity, and then with Aquinas, as we shall see in the next chapter, dreams were placed in an Aristotelian context and so nearly filed away that their value is ignored and even forgotten by most of the Western Christian church.

The Dreams of Islam

Shortly after the death of Gregory, the dream as a medium of revelation was given great emphasis in the new religion of Islam. This new spirituality, with roots in Christianity and Greek culture as well as in the Arab world, placed the dream in as central a position as any other culture. That same influence still exists in Islam today. But until Western scholars realized how much fascinating material this tradition had produced and began to pore over its texts, most of us knew very little about the influence the dream has had in Islamic society. At a recent scholarly and scientific meeting on the dream, held in France, six of the twenty-five papers chosen for publication in book form pertained to the dream lore of Islam. It is significant that none of the studies in this volume, *The Dream and Human Societies,* related to the specific place of dreams in the Christian tradition.

Islam begins with the dream, for much of the Koran was delivered to the prophet Mohammed in dreams or in a trancelike state. The prophet's function was simply to record whatever was given. The first of Mohammed's revelations came to him at the cave on Hira, a hill not far from Mecca. There in the month of Ramadan, toward the end of the month, he fell asleep and heard a voice telling him to read, and he replied that he could not. He awoke from the dream and went outside the cave, where he saw a vision of the angel Gabriel, who told him that he had been selected as Allah's messenger. Later, after he returned home, his wife took him to a wise old man who taught him that the heavenly messenger he had seen was the same who had brought God's message to Moses. From this time until his death the prophet's dreams formed one of the most important avenues of his inspiration.[73]

After the time of the prophet, major revelation through the dream or any other method was closed in Islam, but still anyone who dreamed of the prophet was to view his dream as a true one. In addition the emphasis laid upon dreams by the prophet led to a flowering of dream study in the popular culture and a proliferation of dream books such as is found in practically no other culture. This study was considered a scientific endeavor rather than a religious one, and it expanded and adapted the ideas of Artemidorus, whose book was soon translated into Arabic. Besides the catalogues of thousands and thousands of dream images, detailed methods of interpreting dreams were developed. These were careful and supposedly rational methods, rather than the prophetic interpretation found in the Old and New Testaments and the church fathers. This distinction, which is so fundamental to the understanding of dreams, also marks the real difference between the approach to dreams in Islam and the way they were valued in classical Christianity.[74]

Some of the most recent studies in this field, however, deal with the religious use of dreams among the Shiites and Sufis. In these sects of Islam, where prophecy was regarded as continuous rather than ceasing with the prophet, the dream was considered the way par excellence through which the individual found entrance into *'ālam al-mithāl,* that stage of ontological reality lying between physical reality and the "world of intelligibles." Some of the great Arab thinkers were followers of these sects and left records of their own initiatory dreams, working out whole philosophies about the dream-vision and its relation to this realm. The closest Christian material is found in the dream analysis of Synesius of Cyrene and the visions of Swedenborg. This material becomes all the more significant and interesting as the parallels are seen in the studies of Freud, Jung, and other depth psychologists, concerning the reality of an objective psyche and its manifestation in dreams and in free or active fantasy. The mystical Sufi tradition, far from being an archaeological curiosity, is still very much alive in modern Islam. A similar tradition was also alive in Christianity through the Middle Ages, and there was far more intercourse between the two than we have usually realized. Let us turn now to this period in Western Christianity.

Chapter
7

Modern Christianity and the Dream

THERE IS A LONG JUMP between the understanding of the Fathers and the modern attitude toward dreams and visions, so long that it is hard to believe they have both been attitudes held by Christians. Yet, by the end of the Middle Ages, Thomas Aquinas was already putting into words a new thinking about God that would make it easy for the church to avoid most of these experiences. Later on, when skepticism about supernatural dreams and visions began to grow, the lack of a religious approach left only superstition to oppose the growing doubt. The attitude of the skeptic became so generally accepted in Western culture that sensible people were embarrassed to hold any other belief. This attitude has not developed, however, as the careful decision of rational people; instead, it has grown more like an unconscious split in Western personality.

Indeed, it is surprising how little is known of what lies behind our modern ideas about the dream. Even the most specialized encyclopedias fail to list the people who wrote in this area of medieval thinking, and it has been almost by accident that I discovered the materials that show what was happening. Leads about the church's thinking have turned up in scholarly works on Chaucer and on ancient Greece, in one of Jung's careful footnotes, in fact almost anywhere but in writings about the church. Gradually a picture began to form.

On one hand was the speculative thinking that was so important in the church in this period, and here dreams were actually considered seriously up into the eighteenth century. Still, what was there to say about them that had not already been said? These writers were bound by the traditions of the church; and since the ancients, without scientific methods, had pretty well exhausted the speculative possibilities of dream evaluation, one had only to select the correct classifications and the theory that was right.

But then the church had to deal with both the experiences described in the Bible and the prohibition against observing dreams which Jerome had written into the Old Testament law. The actual visions and dreams experienced by people raised problems. Most of the time the church took care to let people know that these came from any place but God and that there was little need for them. Individuals like Joan of Arc were led to amazing efforts by the visions they had, and everyone knows what happened to her as a result. There were also the saints like Francis of Assisi, who had a vision at the very time the miracle of his stigmata was occurring, and St. Francis came near to condemnation before he was beatified. Even Luther often fought it out with the devil before tackling a problem in the outside world; in fact, Luther's famous inkwell was thrown at a vision of the devil. Many others, from St. Teresa to Jakob Boehme and John Bunyan, found their lives directed and changed by dreams and visions.

These experiences were hard for the church to accept unless they simply reinforced accepted doctrine. If, instead, the authority of the church seemed to be questioned, they were looked at with real suspicion. The medieval church feared any questioning of its authority, and confidence in a direct contact with God through dreams was just such a threat. The church thus gradually came to a position about such experiences that made it unnecessary (even unseemly) for most of us to take notice of them at all. All necessary truth about God had been laid down, and people did not need direct contact with God anymore. As we look at this period, let us see how this way of thinking happened to come about in the church and also how different it was from classical Christianity and how far it has influenced our own thinking and attitudes.

Let us look first at the medieval theory of dreams, considering two important works on this theory and also some bits of evidence showing how universal it was. We then turn to the influence of Aristotle through Aquinas, whose formulations led the church in the end to abandon any emphasis on the value of dream experience. Finally, following briefly the seesaw of opinion that occurred after that, let us consider some examples of significant dreams right down to modern times, which show that although the dream has been rejected in theory, it has remained important in practice.

Medieval Speculation

For several centuries after the time of the Fathers there is almost no record of the thinking in the West about dreams and visions. These were the "Dark Ages" in Western Europe, when records of any kind were few and most people had not been either Christian or literate for very long. In the Eastern half of the Roman Empire, where Greek culture continued to flourish, there was no interruption in the traditions of the Fathers. The same kind of dream experience the Fathers had spoken of continued to be described by the spiritual leaders of the Eastern church, and the same thinking persisted.[1] In the fourteenth century, for instance, one learned Greek commentary was written on the theories of Synesius. In the West in the fifteenth and sixteenth centuries a new interest in the literature and culture of Greece and Rome developed, as material on those subjects became available. Manuscripts that Greek scholars had brought with them when they fled to the West after the seige and fall of Constantinople were eagerly received. During this renaissance of learning, the serious study of dreams once again emerged. Two excellent studies, one Catholic and the other Protestant, were written toward the end of the sixteenth century. Both authors exhibit a wide knowledge of pagan and Christian classic studies on dreams. Jewish rabbis at this time were also writing on the religious significance of dreams. Joel Covitz, a Jewish rabbi and a Jungian analyst, reveals the depth and wisdom of that tradition in his recent, groundbreaking book *Visions of the Night: A Study of Jewish Dream Interpretation.*

This period saw the West develop a rational and materialistic view of reality as Aristotle's theories began to dominate its thinking. The rich tradition of the late Middle Ages was lost because Aristotle's views found wide acceptance—and he had seen little value in dreams. Indeed, students must dig deep into the history and records of the sixteenth and seventeenth centuries to find this material. My search for some of this material started from an important footnote in Jung's *Psychology and Religion: West and East,*[2] in which he quoted two writers who had summarized the thinking of the Middle Ages on dreams. One was a Jesuit priest, Benedict Pererius; and the other, Gaspar Peucer, was the son-in-law of the Protestant reformer Melanchthon. Jung had cited a passage from each of their works in order to support his point that, while the medieval writings did not deny the possibility of God's Spirit being poured out in dreams, neither did they encourage this idea, because it was a practical threat to church authority.

Both of these men were writing on the subject of divination about the end of the sixteenth century. The theology of Thomas Aquinas had been formulated long before, but the full meaning of his neglect of the dream did not catch on very quickly. Until it did, there was quite a different Christian attitude at work in most of the medieval church, and it would seem that the actual biblical and patristic tradition on dreams played a greater part in the growth of our modern culture than we are accustomed to believing. This possibility is rather interesting, and the discovery of Pererius's book shows that it is quite likely the fact.

Pererius's book, written in medieval Latin in 1598, bears this title: *De Magia: Concerning the Investigation of Dreams and Concerning Astrological Divination. Three Books. Against the False and Superstitious Arts.* A copy can be found in the rare book room at Harvard University. Since this work had apparently never been translated before, I am grateful to Elizabeth Shedd of Palo Alto, an expert in medieval Latin, who translated the work for me. In the following paragraphs I will try to summarize the most important of Pererius's ideas.

Pererius, who was concerned with the possibility of God's speaking to human beings through dreams, was also down to earth. His purpose was to establish that Christians had something to gain from considering their dreams, but he saw that certain people were too careful about examining every dream "anxiously and superstitiously." Nor could any one explanation account for all dreams, especially when some of them seemed to give such clear and sensible direction to life while others were so cloudy and obscure. And so he began his inquiry by asking: "Can one have any faith in dreams?"

For his answer Pererius turned to the authorities. He carefully considered the teachings of the Stoics and Epicureans and then of the Bible and the Fathers. He quoted Gregory I, Synesius, Augustine, Cassian, and Justin Martyr as his authorities. He discussed learnedly the theories of Plato, Aristotle, Porphyry, and Hippocrates, citing passages from Homer and Vergil and reciting the experiences of famous people. On this evidence he then determined that there were four causes of dreams. They were caused first of all by the body and its physical condition. Second, they were caused by the emotional life of the soul, its anger, its fear, its affections. They were also caused by the craft and cunning of the devil and his evil spirits, and these dreams, which were often obscene and impure, could sometimes foretell the future without any good reason. And finally there were divine dreams, which posed the important question of how to recognize them.

> As it occurs to me now [Pererius pointed out], one can determine whether a dream has been sent by God in two ways. First, certainly, the excellence of the thing signified in the dream: if things, of which certain knowledge can only reach man by the will and grant of God, become known to a man through a dream, they are of such kinds as are called "future contingencies" in the schools of theologians. Indeed they are the heart's secrets which, enclosed within the soul's deepest recesses, completely conceal themselves from all intellectual perception of mortals; and, finally they are the principal mysteries of our faith, made manifest to no one except by the instruction of God. A dream, therefore, which contains this sort of knowledge and revelation may be considered divine.
>
> Second, the divinely inspired dream is powerfully conveyed by a certain interior illumination and stirring of souls whereby God thus enlightens the mind, influences the will and convinces man of the trustworthiness and validity of this dream in order that he may clearly recognize that God is its author and freely decide that without any doubt he both wants and ought to believe in it.

At this point Pererius quoted Gregory, and then added:

> Thus, just as the natural light of the mind makes us clearly perceive the truth of first principles and embrace it with our approval immediately before

> the introduction of any proof, so indeed, when dreams have been given by God, the divine light flooding into our souls has effect with the result that we recognize these dreams as being both true and divine and are confirmed in our faith.

Pererius then went on in scholastic style to discuss why God should use dreams, why he gives them to the uneducated, why they are obscure, and who should inquire into and interpret dreams. He concluded that the Bible is full of examples of divine dreams and that God reveals himself in this way because the soul is freer and less analytic when it is withdrawn from the body and thus released from sense experience. In addition, God uses dreams to demonstrate his ability to reach people when no other force can and to give evidence of the soul's immortality. Pererius believed, contrary to the ideas of Aristotle, that God does give revelations to the uneducated just to show that the learning of worldly people can cut them off from the higher pursuits and to show that piety is superior to knowledge.

Although people should not base the whole of their lives upon a study of dreams, those sent by God can awaken a person to the direction and purpose, even the dangers of his or her life. Most important is finding the proper interpreter, and here Pererius held that

> the shrewdest appraiser of human dreams, the most apt and accurate interpreter, will be naturally he who is most thoroughly versed in human affairs and likewise one who, as an extremely experienced man, has attained to a complete and perfect knowledge, confirmed by many tests of human character, interests, customs and persuasions, which also assume great variety in different men; one who, as it were, grasps the very pulse of man's social and individual activity.
>
> Yet again, it is up to him to explicate divine dreams who stands in readiness to apprehend them, since it is clear that no one can interpret them unless he be divinely inspired and instructed. "For no one has known," says Paul . . . "what is of God except the spirit of God." But this is especially so since the symbols of divine dreams are ordained through the plan and will of God alone and for this reason can be made known to men only through the revelation of God.

For a good interpreter of dreams, then, find a person who has had plenty of experience and is also open to the voice of God, and that person probably has the makings of either a good psychologist or religious counselor in depth. Whatever else one may say of this scholastic Jesuit, one certainly cannot call him naïve or unlearned. While he was not as original or as consistent as Synesius or Augustine, his approach to dreams was certainly more sophisticated than that of Gregory the Great, or, for that matter, of most moderns, except for Freud and Jung. It is an interesting commentary on our current valuation of the dream that only in our times has Pererius's book been translated from medieval Latin.

A Protestant Takes the Same Approach

Gasper Peucer's work, written a few years earlier, was also in Latin, but a French edition was published in 1584. It is called *Les Devins, ou commentaire des principales sortes de divination.* While Peucer wrote from a Calvinistic and humanistic background, he covered much the same ground as Pererius, so as to suggest that both men followed a generally accepted and well-known body of opinions about dreams.

Peucer included a more specific consideration of Macrobius's theories of dreams, and his discussion of the various kinds—*fantasme, somme, songe, vision,* and *oracle*[3]—probably came directly from Macrobius, who classified dreams as apparitions, nightmares or "mere" dreams, enigmatic dreams, prophetic visions, and oracular dreams. Peucer then went on to the causes of dreams, holding that there are natural causes that come from the body and the emotions, and spiritual causes from God, the holy angels, and demons. He made an unsatisfactory attempt to relate dreams to the physiology of the brain, whose function had recently become the subject of serious attention, and there was also an attempt to understand sleep in terms of the medical doctrine of humors. But the more Peucer tried to be knowledgeable about the science of his time and to relate dreams to these findings, the more absurd he seems. He believed, like Pererius, that dreams that come from natural causes should be studied by the physician.

He also believed that demons were responsible for many deceiving dreams, such as those that occurred in ancient pagan temples during incubation and "*telles sont en tous temps les visions des anabaptistes, Enthousiastes & semblables frénétiques, bodillans en cachette après leurs nouvelles révélations* ['such are in our times the visions of the Anabaptists, those fanatics who act as if they were deranged, always stalking stealthily after their new revelations']." He too discussed the dreams of the famous men of antiquity at some length. In addition he discussed visions, which he considered of the same category as dreams, drawing attention to some interesting group visions that occurred in his time. These he believed occurred most often in the air around fighting armies.

Peucer was more restrictive in his conclusions than Pererius, and he found that except for particularly holy people, investigation of dreams is dangerous. He based this on the understanding that

> those dreams are of God which the sacred scriptures affirm to be sent from on high, not to everyone promiscuously, nor to those who strive after and expect revelations of their own opinion, but to the Holy Patriarchs and Prophets by the will and judgment of God. . . . [Such dreams are concerned] not with light matters, or with trifles and ephemeral things, but with Christ, the governance of the Church, with empires and their well ordering, and other remarkable events; and to these God always adds sure testimonies, such as the gift of interpretation and other things, by which it is clear that they are not rashly to be objected to, nor are they of natural origin, but are divinely inspired.

Here in effect is the intellectual snobbery of Aristotle, although not yet backed by the careful thinking necessary to support Aristotle's position. There was still a place for God to communicate with people, if they were saints at any rate, through divine dreams and visions.

Confirmation from Many Sources

These works by Pererius and Peucer give an idea of the attitude toward dreams that came out of the Middle Ages, and here and there we find bits of confirmation like pieces of the puzzle. In the eighth century the Venerable Bede wrote in his ecclesiastical history of England about the monk Caedmon, who, like Solomon, was given a gift from God in a dream. Unlike Solomon, Caedmon had been tongue-tied in company, and during his dream he received the ability to write and to sing poetry.[4] All through the Middle Ages the delightful story of Theophilus of Adana and the salvation he received in a dream was kept alive. This saint had been tempted and had promised his soul in writing to the devil. But he repented, and when the Virgin appeared to him in a vision, he saw that he wanted no part of the deal. His prayers were answered that night; he received back his bond in a dream and awoke to find the paper lying on his breast. This story circulated in one Latin translation after another until it was set down in final form by the Bollandist fathers in the *Acta Sanctorum*.[5]

Some time about the twelfth century an anonymous work, *On the Spirit and the Soul*,[6] became so popular that it was included in the works of various saints; it elaborated at length on the different ways divine visions were received. Using Macrobius's classification of dreams, this writer concluded that prophetic *visions* (L. *visione*, or class of dreams) could be either corporeal, spiritual, or intellectual, depending on whether they came through the senses, the imagination, or direct intuition. In the same period John of Salisbury followed much the same classification in discussing dreams in the *Polycraticus*, while the great Jewish theologian Maimonides also dealt with them as a source of prophecy in his chief work, *The Guide for the Perplexed*.[7] Even the remarkably secular *Roman de la Rose*, which was still enormously popular in the sixteenth century, admitted that the dream was a way in which God could give revelation to people. Besides a careful account of dream theory, the entire story of this poem was conceived as a dream.

The obscure cleric who captured the imagination of fourteenth-century England in *Piers the Ploughman* also used dreams again and again to get his message across. This poet, William Langland, shared the ideas that were to be summarized so well by Pererius and Peucer, and he wrote on the assumption that they were true. His story showed that for him the vision of a dream was a significant religious truth that could be seen and interpreted. In the next century the writings of Chaucer gave a popular yet detailed and knowledgeable picture of the clerical interest and reverence for dreams. In the *Canterbury Tales,* dream material contributed to many of the stories, and here the influence of Macrobius in Christian thinking was quite apparent. In fact, we do not find a clear separation at this time between secular and religious writing.[8] Meanwhile, inside the church something else was happening.

A New Teaching

Thomas Aquinas was one of the greatest thinkers of all times. The philosophy of Aristotle formed the basis of the brilliant Arab civilization of the ninth, tenth, and eleventh centuries. It was the creative thinking of that time. Through Moorish Spain these ideas percolated into Europe and became the accepted point of view. Could Christian theology be accommodated to this new philosophy? Aquinas made a synthesis of biblical tradition and the philosophy of Aristotle and produced the *Summa Theologica,*[9] one of the most comprehensive theological and philosophical systems the world has seen. He found himself with two masters, and they had very different things to say about our knowledge of the spiritual dimensions of reality and about dreams. We have already discussed Aristotle's view of dreams; for him they had no divine significance. The Bible described the dream as one channel through which revelation was received. Aquinas looked at this subject from every side but came to no final conclusion on either the natural human experience of the Divine and the supernatural or on the subject of dreams. One can find statements from Aquinas that lean both ways. He certainly did not suggest that one should study dreams as a way of finding the direction of the Holy Spirit. Those who followed Aquinas were not as open minded and careful as Aquinas and followed Aristotle and his idea that dreams had no divine significance. Thus dreams were no longer considered significant in the theological circles of Western Europe, both Catholic and Protestant, from the fourteenth century to today. Let us look at what Aquinas writes about dreams and revelation.

In his long section on prophecy and revelation in the *Summa* (2.2.Q–171–74), he carefully discussed the dreams and visions of the Old Testament prophets and the kinds of images that came to them. He examined the relation of dreams to knowledge of the future, to angels and demons, to the beatific vision, and to ecstasy. Yet the closest he came to a conclusion about dreams and revelation was to say that:

> abstraction from the senses takes place in the prophets without subverting the order of nature, as is the case with those who are possessed or out of their senses; but is due to some well-ordered cause . . . for instance, sleep. (2.2.Q–173.3)

He suggested that dreams were a lower form of prophecy (2.2.Q–174.3). The reason he did not come to any conclusion on the subject was that dreams did not really fit into his system, and so he put them back into the hopper.

This is quite clear in other places where Aquinas discussed dreams from the Old Testament. In the section on divination he considered the references in Genesis, Job, and Daniel that show that it is all right to practice divination by dreams. But then he explained that this was only lawful when the dream came from divine revelation or natural causes but not if it came from demons or false opinion, and so the whole question boiled down to determining the causes of dreams.

One of Aquinas's most comprehensive statements on dreams needs to be read in its entirety. While recognizing that some dreams may come from God, he gave no directions on how we can be sure that they are from God. He also gave no encouragement to the ordinary people to look at their dreams. The general attitude is that dreams are dangerous and rarely give us an experience of the Divine.

> Accordingly it is to be observed that the cause of dreams is sometimes in us and sometimes outside us. The inward cause of dreams is twofold: one regards the soul, in so far as those things which have occupied a man's thoughts and affections while awake recur to his imagination while asleep. A such like cause of dreams is not a cause of future occurrences, so that dreams of this kind are related accidentally to future occurrences, and if at any time they concur it will be by chance. But sometimes the inward cause of dreams regards the body: because the inward disposition of the body leads to the formation of a movement in the imagination consistent with that disposition; thus a man in whom there is abundance of cold humors dreams that he is in the water or snow: and for this reason physicians say that we should take note of dreams in order to discover internal dispositions.
>
> In like manner the outward cause of dreams is twofold, corporal and spiritual. It is corporal in so far as the sleeper's imagination is affected either by the surrounding air, or through an impression of a heavenly body, so that certain images appear to the sleeper, in keeping with the disposition of the heavenly bodies. The spiritual cause is sometimes referrable to God, Who reveals certain things to men in their dreams by the ministry of the angels, according to Num. xii. 6, *If there be among you a prophet of the Lord, I will appear to him in a vision, or I will speak to him in a dream.* Sometimes, however, it is due to the action of the demons that certain images appear to persons in their sleep, and by this means they, at times, reveal certain future things to those who have entered into an unlawful compact with them.
>
> Accordingly we must say that there is no unlawful divination in making use of dreams for the foreknowledge of the future, so long as those dreams are due to divine revelation, or to some natural cause inward or outward, and so far as the efficacy of that cause extends. But it will be an unlawful and superstitious divination if it be caused by a revelation of the demons, with whom a compact has been made, whether explicit, through their being

invoked for the purpose, or implicit, through the divination extending beyond its possible limits.

This suffices for the *Replies* to the *Objections*, 11, 11.9–95.6

Twice more Aquinas struggled to make sense of Numbers 12:6. But Aquinas could not fit this into the philosophical system of Aristotle, and so in the end "the Philosopher" won and the Bible lost. In the end Aquinas actually went contrary to the Bible and the fathers in this matter of revelation (2.1.Q–113.3; 3.Q–7.8).

At the outset it was undoubtedly Aquinas's purpose simply to open the storehouse of Greek thought to Western Christians. But the Islamic medicine and astronomy and philosophy that were beginning to flood Europe were couched in Aristotle's terms rather than in the original Greek thought. There seemed to be no choice but to translate Christianity and the Bible point by point into the language of Aristotle. It did not seem to bother Aquinas that this created a theology based upon only half of the Christian story or that a large part of the New Testament was played down. He simply ignored not only the dreams, but the experiences of angels and demons, the healings, tongue speaking, and miracles in general in most of the New Testament, particularly in the Book of Acts.

Indeed, there is no place for dreams either in the philosophic system of Aristotle or in the theology of Aquinas. According to both of these men we receive knowledge only through sense experience, and the only thing peculiar about dreams is that we become more sensitive to sense experience at night. To settle this Aquinas quoted Aristotle:

> Impressions made by day are evanescent. The night air is calmer, when silence reigns, hence bodily impressions are made in sleep, when slight internal movements are felt more than in wakefulness, and such movements produce in the imagination images from which the future may be foreseen. (1.Q–86.4)

Because of his philosophic background, it was impossible for Aquinas to believe that the human psyche could communicate directly with any reality that was not physical, such as an angelic or demonic abstraction, a "thinking thought."

He criticized his predecessor Augustine just because he did believe in dreams and in the ability of the soul to experience spiritual reality directly:

> As Augustine says (Confessions xii), the soul has a certain power of forecasting, so that by its very nature it can know the future; hence when withdrawn from corporeal sense, [as in dreams] and, as it were, concentrated on itself, it shares in the knowledge of the future. Such an opinion would be reasonable if we were to admit that the soul receives knowledge by participating [in] the ideas as the Platonists maintained, because in that case the soul by its nature would know the universal causes of all effects,

> and would only be impeded in its knowledge by the body; and hence when withdrawn from the corporeal senses it would know the future. But since it is connatural to our intellect to know things, not thus, but by receiving its knowledge from the senses, it is not natural for the soul to know the future when withdrawn from the senses. (1.Q–86.4)

Aquinas then concluded that dreams were really not significant or sure, because he believed that we have no direct, immediate contact with spiritual reality. This is a rather important conclusion with all sorts of implications for modern theology.

It is just at this point that the theologians today find it so difficult to accept what Jung is saying. It is precisely Jung's contention that in dreams and visions we do have direct participation in nonphysical reality and that dreams demonstrate this fact if one will observe them carefully. To follow Jung's understanding one must break with Aquinas at this point, for Jung accepts dreams as a direct participation in the collective unconscious or the objective psyche—a world of spiritual reality. Aquinas, on the other hand, put the matter very clearly: there is no direct participation in whatever reality lies beyond the physical, and so dreams cannot have any special religious significance.

Aquinas was very consistent. Whenever he discussed dreams or divination, the same basic approach was apparent. In discussing whether human beings can know God directly, he stated the same conclusions and criticized Augustine once more:

> But our soul, as long as we live in this life, has its being in corporeal matter; hence naturally it knows only what has a form in matter, or what can be known by such a form. Now it is evident that the divine essence cannot be known through the nature of material things. . . . This can be seen in the fact that the more our soul is abstracted from corporeal things, the more it is capable of receiving abstract intelligible things. Hence in dreams and alienations of the bodily senses divine revelations and foresight of future events are perceived the more clearly. It is not possible, therefore, that the soul in this mortal life should be raised up to the supreme of intelligible objects, that is, to the divine essence. (1.Q–12.11)

> We cannot know of God *what He is,* and thus are united to Him as one unknown. (1.Q–12.13)

What is "divine revelation" then? In his discussion of prophetic dreams Aquinas carefully completed his clarification. It is the same as that which comes in the natural order by which images are represented to the mind, first to the senses, then the imagination, and finally to the passive intellect. He concluded that "prophetic revelation is conveyed sometimes by the mere infusion of light, sometimes by imprinting species anew, or by a new co-ordination of species" (2.2.Q–173.2). But nothing new can be added. The only difference from everyday worldly experience was one of degree and the addition of divine light by which any matter could be judged.

In another place Aquinas followed Aristotle's explanation of dreams on the basis of the vapors that arise from the body (1.Q-84.8). And finally, in the supplement, those who completed the *Summa* made it clear that dreams are an inferior kind of experience because sleep is only half life, as Aristotle said in the *Ethics* (Supplement to 3.Q–82.3).

For both Aristotle and Aquinas there was an ethical reason for avoiding dreams and other direct intrusions into the human psyche. Both men believed that if there were such happenings it would cast doubt upon the free will of human beings and so on the possibility of ethical behavior. They did not believe in freedom as a many-point scale, but saw it only as an either-or proposition. Modern psychological study points out that people can be free and yet not be as free as they think they are. Neurosis is a perfect example of a partial loss of freedom, and psychosis exhibits a very nearly total loss. People's psyche and intellect may not, in fact, be as free as they wish. Their task may well be to seek freedom through greater consciousness, but none of this would abrogate ethical responsibility.[10]

In the end, Aquinas's life contradicted what he had written. He did come into direct relationship with God and ceased to write and dictate. When he was urged to go on, he replied: "I can do no more; such things have been revealed to me that all I have written seems as straw, and I now await the end of my life."[11] But this is not what the Western world knows of Aquinas. Our view of dreams might well be different today if the church had paid attention to his experience.[12] Instead, Catholics and Protestants alike have taken only one aspect of Aquinas's treatment of dreams seriously. The influence of this one-sided view has grown in the entire Western Christian community until, as a practical matter, there is no room for any other view. However, this did not happen overnight.

Seesaw of Opinions

It took many years, in fact, before Aquinas's views were revered as they were before Vatican II. All through these centuries in which modern culture was developing, the opinions and experiences of thoughtful people seesawed back and forth, until the nineteenth century, when Aquinas became the basic theologian of the Roman Catholic church.[13] By then his teaching was also the *de facto* view of practically the entire body of Protestant believers. Students like Pererius and Peucer were forgotten as if they had never written, for there was really no need to get behind the view Aquinas presented, which was so congenial to the developing rationalism and materialism of our time. As we look at the writings of this next period, we see how well his views were tailored to fit the thinking that was being shaped.

Among those who sided with Aquinas was John Calvin, that most rationalistic of Protestant theologians. In the *Institutes* Calvin made no room for revelation of God through images of any kind, which certainly excludes dreams, since they are usually imagery. Yet Calvin also shared the ideas of his time about the value of dreams. In his *Commentaries on the Book of Daniel,* written about the same time that Peucer and Pererius were writing, he defended the idea that God speaks in dreams as carefully as if he had no question about it.[14] In this work his explanation about the relation of people's beliefs to their understanding of divine symbolism in dreams was as careful and lucid as one expects from Calvin. There were two inconsistent ideas in him, one of the intellectual scholar, the other of the man and the Christian. The trouble is that most of us know the basic ideas of the *Institutes,* but hardly anyone remembers what Calvin wrote about the dreams in Daniel. Few people realize the deeply spiritual side of Calvin so beautifully described by Howard Rice in his recent book, *Reformed Spirituality.*

Fifty years later, Jeremy Taylor, whose writings had such popular influence in seventeenth-century England, preached at some length about dreams. Among other things he told his congregation that

> dreams follow the temper of the body, and commonly proceed from trouble or disease, business or care, an active head and a restless mind, from fear or hope, from wine or passion, from fullness or emptiness, from fantastic remembrances, or from some common demon, good or bad: they are without rule and without reason, they are as contingent, as if a man should study to make a prophecy, and by saying ten thousand things may hit upon one true, which was therefore not foreknown, though it was forespoken, and they have no certainty, because they have no natural causality nor proportion to those effects, which many times they are said to fore signify.[15]

In short, he concluded, do not expect anything from dreams, and it is interesting that the good divine, in reaching this conclusion, quoted Artemidorus rather than the Bible or any of the Fathers.

About the same time, one of England's great physicians was reaching quite a different conclusion. Although Sir Thomas Browne was not a clergyman, his writing on personal religion places him more on the side of religion than otherwise. In his delightful and mature essay on dreams, he discussed much of the material we have been over, concluding that Aristotle did not know what he was talking about and that there are dreams that come directly from angels and demons.

> If there bee Guardian spirits, they may not bee unactively about us in sleepe, but may sometimes order our dreams, and many strange hints, instigations, or discoveries, which are so amazing unto us, may arise from such foundations.

As a physician Browne saw that dreams may well reveal the inner person, and in the following remarkable passage he suggested the insight that would one day come to Freud and Jung and be developed:

> However dreames may bee fallacious concerning outward events, yet may they bee truly significant at home, and whereby wee may more sensibly understand ourselves. Men act in sleepe with some conformity unto their awaked senses, and consolations and discouragements may be drawne from dreames, which intimately tell us ourselves. . . .

Thus the author of the *Religio Medici* counseled the individual not to ignore his dreams, adding a most modern note: "That some have never dreamed is as improbable, as that some have never laughed."[16]

John Wesley, the founder of Methodism, was another Englishman who saw that dreams have a value that defies rational explanation. In one of his sermons preached about the middle of the eighteenth century, Wesley called attention in several ways to their mysterious nature and to the fact that God does sometimes reveal himself "in dreams and visions of the night." He also outlined their causes in much the same way that they have been discussed ever since Tertullian. While he did not directly tell his people to pay attention to dreams, his thinking clearly suggests that he was open to his own dream experiences. Wesley concluded that dreams are like digressions or parenthetical expressions, which need no proof of being related to the rest of life.[17]

An even more positive view was expressed by one other English clergyman before the nineteenth century began. In 1791 David Simpson, who was Wesley's close friend, published the work that he called *Discourse on Dreams and Night Visions;* in it he wrote:

> Dreams are of great consequence in the government of the world, of equal authority with the Bible. . . . And has not the experience that many men have of significant dreams and night visions a more powerful effect on their minds than the most pure and refined concepts?[18]

Yet how many of us have ever heard of Simpson's work? The eminent philosophic writer L. L. Whyte, who calls attention to it, also notes that Simpson was not alone in holding the ideas he developed. At the time, they were shared by the physicist G. C. Lichtenberg in Germany, by the physician von Herder, and by others, and from that time on more and more scientists began to take an interest in the world of the dream. But within the church there seemed to be nothing to say about it. Simpson's work is the last serious religious discussion of dreams until we get to modern times. Indeed, he even feared this would happen.

God's Forgotten Speech

With the Freudian explosion of interest in dreams, one might think that the church would take a fresh look at its rich tradition on the subject. Instead, in the last half century there has been almost no serious attempt to consider the dream religiously. Only four works by orthodox clergy which even touch on this subject came to my attention when I first gathered this material, and only one of these was actually an effort to search out the Christian point of view on dreams.

The earliest of them was Canon Burnett Streeter's work *Reality,* published in 1927, which set out to prove that religion was scientifically acceptable and, as a corollary, that biblical dreams were Freudianly acceptable. His thought was that normal persons may become so preoccupied with a religious challenge that they find it represented symbolically in their dreams. According to his theory, this was what happened to Peter at Joppa (Acts 10). Peter's dream-trance was merely his primitive way of dealing with his conflict over having to eat with Gentiles. The condescension in Canon Streeter's conclusion is apparent; it is interesting how easily he looks down on people like Augustine and Origen and Athanasius as he says:

> In the modern world the mental balance of a seer of visions is suspect and, in general, not without good reason. The primitive mind thinks in pictures, and in pictures it reasons and resolves, but the intellectual tradition of Europe for the last four centuries has trained the race in conceptual thinking. In the half-waking life of dreams symbolic thinking is still universal; but in the full waking consciousness it is usually only the less vigorous minds, or vigorous minds when temporarily unstrung, that reach important conclusions along this route. But at earlier states of human culture, this rule did not hold; visions were often moments of supreme illumination for the most vigorous intellects and most creative wills.[19]

I had hoped for something better in John Baillie's recent discussion of the theology of sleep, but this eminent Scotch divine, too, fell for only the narrowest of modern depth psychology. He took as his example the passage from *Pilgrim's Progress* in which Christiana listens to Mercy's dreams and shows her that it is true and that "God speaks once, yea twice, yet man perceiveth it not, in a dream, in a vision of the night. . . . We need not when a-bed, lie awake to talk with God; He can visit us while we sleep, and cause us to hear His voice." To this Baillie replied, "Of course, the great change that has overtaken the theology of sleep is that the ancients believed dreams to be premonitory of the unborn future, whereas we moderns regard them rather as uprisings from the half-buried past."[20] Then his discussion turned to ways of controlling our dreams, of getting only good dreams by thinking proper thoughts before retiring. In Baillie's theology there was simply no way for God to break into people's lives in dreams. It was not a question of whether they were meaningless or the products of pure chance; he simply did not believe that God could speak the unexpected, anything that people could not anticipate, in a dream.

A change had indeed overtaken the church since the time of Peucer and Pererius. A change in Baillie's thinking came at the end of his life when he had a religious experience similar to that of Aquinas.

This was also apparent in a work written about 1960 by the Spanish Jesuit Pedro Meseguer and published in English as *The Secret of Dreams*. This is an excellent little book, which covers the subject as it had not been approached in the church for many, many years. It provides scientific and psychological information that are needed, but the religious conclusions are strictly limited by Father Meseguer's Thomistic background. For instance, he holds that "the prospective function [in dreams] . . . is nothing but an aspect of all the functions. . . . The unconscious, when it looks into the future, is only continuing the work of the conscious."[21] In his book it is simply not "done" to look for the supernatural or direct contact with God in dreams. These are questions that Meseguer discusses only in the context of established theology.[22]

One work has been written, however, that recognizes in dreams the striving of the individual soul to find God. This is a book by John Sanford, an Episcopal priest in this country who wrote for American readers in terms of the experience of people like you and me. His book was first published in this country in 1968, after being translated and brought out in German[23] by the Jung Foundation in Zürich, Switzerland. It demonstrates, both theoretically and through experiences, that dreams do speak out of a realm that is different from the ordinary world but in a way that helps individuals relate to their everyday lives. It was written to describe the mysterious power that dreams can have in our lives, and it develops theological and psychological understandings similar to those set forth in these pages. Sanford's book, *Dreams: God's Forgotten Language,* opens up a new understanding of dreaming for religious people, and it deserves far more consideration than can be given to it here.

Modern Christian Dreams

Modern Christians do still dream. And when they are aware of the deeper springs of life, they occasionally take their dreams seriously. The best way to be sure of this is to produce the dreams of Christians, the experience, in fact, of three ministers and one Roman Catholic saint from different parts of this period that has been so hostile to dreams and dreamers.

The first of these was John Newton, one of the most revered and unusual men in the English church, who lived at the beginning of the nineteenth century. He was a man to whom other ministers came for guidance, and he also wrote a number of the hymns we sing today, among them "Amazing Grace." John Newton did not grow up like this, but as a seaman and slave trader. Early in his autobiography he told the story of a dream that had warned him of the danger of this way and had given him a sense of God's providence. Twenty years later, when he was about to enter the ministry, he wrote:

> The most remarkable check and alarm I received (and, for what I know, the last) was by a dream. Those who acknowledge Scripture will allow that there have been monitory and supernatural dreams, evident communications from heaven, either directing or foretelling future events: and those who are acquainted with the history and experience of the people of God, are well assured that such intimations have not been totally withheld in any period down to the present times. . . .
>
> For my own part, I can say, without scruple, "The dream is certain, and the interpretation thereof sure." I am sure I dreamed to the following effect; and I cannot doubt, from what I have seen since, that it had a direct and easy application to my own circumstances, to the dangers in which I was about to plunge myself, and to the unmerited deliverance and mercy which God would be pleased to afford me in the time of my distress.

His account, which he had told and retold, continued as fresh as if it had happened yesterday:

> The scene presented to my imagination was the harbor of Venice, where we had lately been. I thought it was night, and my watch upon the deck; and that, as I was walking to and fro by myself, a person came to me, (I do not remember from whence,) and brought me a ring, with an express charge to keep it carefully: assuring me, that while I preserved that ring I should be happy and successful; but if I lost or parted with it, I must expect nothing but trouble and misery. I accepted the present and the terms willingly, not in the least doubting my own care to preserve it, and highly satisfied to have my happiness in my own keeping.
>
> I was engaged in these thoughts, when a second person came to me, and observing the ring on my finger, took occasion to ask me some questions concerning it. I readily told him its virtues; and his answer expressed a surprise at my weakness, in expecting such effects from a ring. I think he reasoned with me some time upon the impossibility of the thing; and at length urged me, in direct terms, to throw it away. At first I was shocked at the proposal; but his insinuations prevailed. I began to reason and doubt myself.
>
> At last I plucked it off my finger, and dropped it over the ship's side into the water; which it had no sooner touched, than I saw, the same instant, a terrible fire burst out from a range of the mountains, (a part of the Alps), which appeared at some distance behind the city of Venice. I saw the hills as distinct as if awake, and they were all in flames. I perceived, too late, my folly; and my tempter with an air of insult, informed me, that all the mercy God had in reserve for me was comprised in that ring which I had wilfully thrown away. I understood that I must now go with him to the burning mountains, and that all the flames I saw were kindled upon my account. I trembled, and was in a great agony; so that it was surprising I did not then awake: but my dream continued.
>
> And when I thought myself upon the point of a constrained departure, and stood, self-condemned, without plea or hope, suddenly, either a third

person, or the same who brought the ring at first, came to me (I am not certain which) and demanded the cause of my grief. I told him the plain case, confessing that I had ruined myself wilfully, and deserved no pity. He blamed my rashness, and asked if I should be wiser supposing I had my ring again?

I could hardly answer to this; for I thought it was gone beyond recall. I believe, indeed, I had not time to answer, before I saw this unexpected friend go down under the water, just in the spot where I had dropped it; and he soon returned, bringing the ring with him. The moment he came on board the flames in the mountains were extinguished, and my seducer left me. Then was "the prey taken from the hand of the mighty, and the lawful captive delivered." My fears were at an end, and with joy and gratitude I approached my kind deliverer to receive the ring again; but he refused to return it, and spoke to this effect:

"If you should be intrusted with this ring again, you would very soon bring yourself into the same distress: you are not able to keep it; but I will preserve it for you, and, whenever it is needful, will produce it in your behalf."

Upon this I awoke, in a state of mind not easy to be described: I could hardly eat or sleep, or transact my necessary business for two or three days. But the impression soon wore off, and in a little time I totally forgot it; and I think it hardly occurred to my mind again till several years afterward. It will appear, in the course of these papers, that a time came when I found myself in circumstances very nearly resembling those suggested by this extraordinary dream, when I stood helpless and hopeless upon the brink of an awful eternity; and I doubt not that, had the eyes of my mind been then opened, I should have seen my grand enemy, who had seduced me wilfully to renounce and cast away my religious profession, and to involve myself in the most complicated crimes, pleased with my agonies, and waiting for a permission to seize and bear away my soul to his place of torment. I should, perhaps, have seen likewise, that Jesus, whom I had persecuted and defied rebuking the adversary, challenging me for his own, as a brand plucked out of the fire, and saying, "Deliver him from going down to the pit: I have found a ransom."

However, though I saw not these things, I found the benefit: I obtained mercy. The Lord answered for me in my day of distress; and blessed be his name, He who restored the ring, (or what was signified by it,) vouchsafes to keep it. O what an unspeakable comfort is this, that I am not in my own keeping!—"The Lord is my Shepherd." I have been enabled to trust my all in his hands; and I know in whom I have believed. . . . But for this, many a time and often (if possible) I should have ruined myself since my first deliverance; nay, I should fall, and stumble, and perish still.[24]

Amazing grace! Newton gave up slave trading, entered the ministry, and subsequently wrote his great hymns.

How Christ Came to Church

The second of these dreamers was the great Baptist minister in Boston at the end of the nineteenth century, Dr. A. J. Gordon, and the dream he described was an experience that affected his entire ministry and life. The spiritual autobiography he wrote revolved around the dream and described what had happened since that day "when the truth of the in-residence of the Spirit and of his presiding in the church of God became a living conviction."[25] His story began with these words:

> It was Saturday night, when wearied from the work of preparing Sunday's sermon, that I fell asleep and the dream came. I was in the pulpit before a full congregation, just ready to begin my sermon, when a stranger entered and passed slowly up the left aisle of the church looking first to the one side and then to the other as though silently asking with his eyes that some one would give him a seat. He had proceeded nearly half-way up the aisle when a gentleman stepped out and offered him a place in his pew, which was quietly accepted. Excepting the face and features of the stranger everything in the scene is distinctly remembered—the number of the pew, the Christian man who offered its hospitality, the exact seat which was occupied. Only the countenance of the visitor could never be recalled.
>
> That his face wore a peculiarly serious look, as of one who had known some great sorrow, is clearly impressed on my mind. His bearing too was exceeding humble, his dress poor and plain, and from the beginning to the end of the service he gave the most respectful attention to the preacher. Immediately as I began my sermon my attention became riveted on this hearer. If I would avert my eyes from him for a moment they would instinctively return to him, so that he held my attention rather than I held his till the discourse was ended.
>
> To myself I said constantly, "Who can that stranger be?" and then I mentally resolved to find out by going to him and making his acquaintance as soon as the service should be over. But after the benediction had been given, the departing congregation filed into the aisles and, before I could reach him, the visitor had left the house.
>
> The gentleman with whom he had sat remained behind however; and approaching him with great eagerness I asked: "Can you tell me who that stranger was who sat in your pew this morning?"
>
> In the most matter-of-course way he replied: "Why, do you not know that man? It was Jesus of Nazareth."
>
> With a sense of the keenest disappointment I said: "My dear sir, why did you let him go without introducing me to him? I was so desirous to speak with him."
>
> And with the same nonchalant air the gentleman replied: "Oh, do not be troubled. He has been here to-day, and no doubt he will come again."
>
> And now came an indescribable rush of emotion. As when a strong current is suddenly checked, the stream rolls back upon itself and is choked in its own foam, so the intense curiosity which had been going out toward the mysterious hearer now returned upon the preacher: and the Lord himself "whose I am and whom I serve" had been listening to me to-day. What was I saying? Was I preaching on some popular theme in order to catch the ear of the public? Well, thank God it was of himself I was speaking. However imperfectly done, it was Christ and him crucified whom I was holding up this morning. But in what spirit did I preach? Was it "Christ crucified preached in a crucified style?" or did the preacher magnify himself

while exalting Christ? So anxious and painful did these questionings become that I was about to ask the brother with whom he had sat if the Lord had said anything to him concerning the sermon, but a sense of propriety and self-respect at once checked the suggestion.

Then immediately other questions began with equal vehemence to crowd into the mind. "What did he think of our sanctuary, its gothic arches, its stained windows, its costly and powerful organ? How was he impressed with the music and the order of the worship?" It did not seem at that moment as though I could ever again care or have the smallest curiosity as to what men might say of preaching, worship, or church, if I could only know that he had not been displeased, that he would not withhold his feet from coming again because he had been grieved at what he might have seen or heard.

We speak of "a momentous occasion." This, though in sleep, was recognized as such by the dreamer—a lifetime, almost an eternity of interest crowded into a single solemn moment. One present for an hour who could tell me all I have so longed to know; who could point out to me the imperfections of my service; who could reveal to me my real self, to whom, perhaps, I am most a stranger; who could correct the errors in our worship to which long usage and accepted tradition may have rendered us insensible. While I had been preaching for a half-hour he had been here and listening who could have told me all this and infinitely more—and my eyes had been holden that I knew him not; and now he had gone. "Yet a little while I am with you and then I go unto him that sent me."

One thought, however, lingered in my mind with something of comfort and more of awe. *"He has been here to-day, and no doubt he will come again"*; and mentally repeating these words as one regretfully meditating on a vanished vision, "I awoke, and it was a dream." No, it was not a dream. It was a vision of the deepest reality, a miniature of an actual ministry, verifying the statement often repeated that sometimes we are most awake toward God when we are asleep toward the world.[26]

A Saint Receives Certainty

Thérèse of Lisieux was canonized in 1925. She died in 1897, at the age of twenty-four, and she had the dream that I quote just a year before her death. Her own story was written, as a letter of obedience, to Sister Marie of the Sacred Heart. As she tells, when she awoke from the dream, the effect was immediate; her life had become serene, her belief a certainty. Since the dream was understood to come from Jesus, the part of her letter that follows was addressed directly to him:

> Jesus, my well-beloved, how considerate you are in your treatment of my worthless soul; storms all around me, and suddenly the sunshine of your grace peeps out! Easter Day had come and gone, the day of your splendid triumph, and it was a Saturday in May; my soul was still storm-tossed. I remember thinking about the wonderful dreams which certain souls have been privileged to experience, and how consoling an experience it would be; but I didn't pray for anything of the kind. When I went to bed, my sky

was still overcast, and I told myself that dreams weren't for unimportant souls like mine; it was a storm that rocked me to sleep. Next day was Sunday, the second Sunday of May, and I'm not sure it wasn't actually the anniversary of the day when our Lady did me the grace to smile on me. As the first rays of dawn came, I went to sleep again, and dreamed.

I was standing in a sort of gallery where several other people were present, but our Mother was the only person near me. Suddenly, without seeing how they got there, I was conscious of the presence of three Carmelite sisters in their mantles and big veils. I had the impression that they'd come there to see our Mother; what was borne in upon me with certainty was that they came from heaven. I found myself crying out (but of course it was only in the silence of my heart): "O, how I would love to see the face of one of these Carmelites!" Upon which, as if granting my request, the tallest of the three saintly figures moved towards me, and, as I sank to my knees, lifted her veil, lifted it right up, I mean, and threw it over me. I recognized her without the slightest difficulty; the face was that of our Venerable Mother Anne of Jesus, who brought the reformed Carmelite order into France. There was a kind of ethereal beauty about her features, which were not radiant but transfused with light—the light seemed to come from her without being communicated to her, so that the heavenly face was fully visible to me in spite of the veil which surrounded both of us. I can't describe what elation filled my heart; an experience like that can't be put down on paper. Months have passed by now since I had this reassuring dream, but the memory of it is as fresh as ever, as delightful as ever. I can still see the look on Mother Anne's face, her loving smile; I can still feel the touch of the kisses she gave me. And now, treated with all this tenderness, I plucked up my courage: "Please, Mother," I said, "tell me whether God means to leave me much longer on earth? Or will he come and fetch me soon?" And, she, with a most gracious smile, answered: "Yes, soon; very soon, I promise you." Then I added: "Mother, answer me one other question; does God really ask no more of me than these unimportant little sacrifices I offer him, these desires to do something better? Is he really content with me as I am?" That brought into the Saint's face an expression far more loving than I'd seen there yet; and the embrace she gave me was all the answer I needed. But she did speak too: "God asks no more," she said. "He is content with you, well content." And so she embraced me as lovingly as ever a mother embraced her child, and then I saw her withdraw. In the midst of all that happiness, I remembered my sisters, and some favours I wanted to ask for them; but it was too late, I'd woken up. And now the storm no longer raged, all my sky was calm and serene. I didn't merely believe, I felt certain that there was a heaven, and that the souls who were its citizens looked after me, thought of me as their child. What gave more strength to this impression was the fact that, up till then, Mother Anne of Jesus meant nothing to me; I'd never asked for her prayers or even thought about her except on the rare occasions when her name came up in conversation. So when I realized how she loved me, and how much I meant to her, my heart melted towards her in love and gratitude; and for that matter towards all the Blessed in heaven.

Jesus, my Beloved, this was only a prelude to greater graces still with which you'd determined to enrich me.[27]

All three of these were persons who were still close to their spiritual roots. They listened and found that God still speaks in dreams. They had a sure conviction, and because they knew their dreams to be of the same substance and significance as the deepest religious experience, they were able to find meaning that the rationalism and materialism of our time denies. Why, we may well ask, are we so little able to ignore the worldview that surrounds us? In our time is there no context of religious experience into which the dream might fit?

Dreams that Convinced the Author

The dream that started my serious study of these mysterious messengers of the night was an unpleasant one. I had come to a new parish as pastor. I had tried to do everything I could to revive an unhappy congregation. I had an intellectual faith but little experiential knowledge of the Divine. I was working too hard and for the wrong reasons. I became more and more anxious, and one night I had the following dream:

> I came to the church to start the Sunday morning services. Instead of going into the large, poured concrete, north Italian Gothic edifice in which we worshiped, I went into the little old wooden church that was now in reality used as a meeting hall. As I prepared for the service there, the dream turned into a minister's nightmare. First of all I could not find my vestments, and for an Anglican priest this was like going naked before the congregation. I looked for my sermon notes and could not find them. Then I went into the altar to start the service and could not find my place in the prayer book. I decided to start the service nonetheless and turned around to begin. I saw that a dead tree had fallen through the main body of the church, and I was struck with horror as I did not see any way that I could have the *collection* taken up through the branches of the dead tree. I awoke in a cold sweat.

I realized how deep my anxiety was. On a Sunday not long after that dream I actually made the mistake of skipping over the entire consecration prayer in the Communion service of that time and did not discover what I had done until I found the bread lying unbroken on the patten. I then added the consecration prayer and concluded the service. Even the bishop's executive secretary, who was a part of the congregation, failed to make mention of my confused liturgy. About the same time I found myself dreaming of hostile human and inhuman figures who were pursuing me and trying to destroy me.

The anxieties became so severe that I began working with a Jungian analyst. I could find no one within the church qualified to deal with my problems and was unhappy that I had to look for help outside the Christian community. The psychologist helped me see how my dreams were trying to show me the nature of my problems and how

I might deal with them. As I continued to listen to my dreams and deal with my doubts and uncertainty, my dreams became more positive. The thugs and gangsters were no longer pursuing me. My prayer life and my ministry became more real and vital. And strangest of all, I found people coming to me for spiritual guidance. I had certainly not advertised my way of finding Christian growth. When I told Jung of this experience, he replied: "When your unconscious is ready to help, the unconscious depths of others will know."

Two dream experiences confirmed that I was moving toward a new depth of religious conviction and practice:

> This time I dreamed that I was driving in the country in my car when I found that I was being pursued again by a witch. Suddenly the demonic thing was astride the hood of my car, and I saw that it was no use trying to escape. I stopped the car and faced the creature. She was still coming at me when it suddenly occurred to me that I did not have to be destroyed by a creature like that. I got out, bent on tearing her to pieces. But there beside the road was a bucket of water, and I picked it up and threw it. Three times I doused the witch, "In the name of the Father, and of the Son, and of the Holy Ghost." As I did this she began to shrink, and then she dissolved and disappeared.
>
> A few days later I dreamed that I was in the church. It was Whitsunday, and I was celebrating the Communion service with great joy, wearing a gloriously beautiful red chasuble. The church was filled, and there was a sense of an unearthly presence surrounding me.

The dreams did not eliminate all my anxieties or doubts, but they put an end to religious hopelessness and brought me out of a dead-end street. I think that I finally got the message that God was there, that the services of the church carried real power, and that my religious journey was going in the right direction. I knew the presence of a loving, caring God who wished to draw me closer to eternal life both in this world and hereafter. I only wished that the Christian community had been prepared to guide me on this inner journey.

Let us look now at how some psychologists and psychiatrists have found not only psychological meaning in dreams but religious meaning as well.

Chapter

8

Psychologists Explore the Dream

SIGMUND FREUD PUBLISHED in 1900 *The Interpretation of Dreams,* which mapped out a way of exploring the relation of the dream to the unconscious side of the mental life of human beings. It is difficult to stress enough the great importance of this contribution, although Freud himself recognized it and more than once remarked that the publication of his book had been timed to coincide with the beginning of a new era. Of course he was neither the first to discover the unconscious nor the first to see the significance of dreams from a scientific point of view. But he was the first modern scientist to connect the two; he was the first to make an empirical study of any length on the subject and the first to write about it with clarity, indeed with such convincing power that his opinions could not be ignored.

This is an impressive list of firsts, and interestingly enough, the literary world was quick to perceive his significance. In his own profession, however, Freud met with little but contempt. It took eight years to sell out the first six-hundred-copy edition of his book. While it was difficult to ignore him, the ideas he offered could be laughed at, and for a long time laughter would be a good defense against the contribution he offered.

Even so, there had been medical professionals who valued dreams in almost every age from Hippocrates down. People like Daniel Tuke, Wilhelm Wundt, Bernheim, and many others whose names are hardly remembered[1] had been seeking to explain the dream because they saw that it was significant from a medical point of view. But they failed to see that dreams had any particular relation to consciousness. They often failed to see the dream as a psychic reality and instead tried to tie it to the physical functioning of the brain. This was a good idea, but it was still only an idea that has yet to be demonstrated.

There were also thinkers in other fields who had discovered the unconscious, and some of them had written clearly about this. Literature from its inception seemed to understand that human personality has deeper levels of being and a deeper purposiveness than is revealed in our conscious awareness. Shakespeare and Goethe both reveal a knowledge of this deeper level of personality, as do other literary figures. Indeed, it appears that the greater the stature of the author, the greater his or her understanding and knowledge of this realm of being. From the philosophical side, during the nineteenth century, C. G. Carus and Eduard von Hartmann had both written extensively about the unconscious, the former in a work he called simply *Psyche,* and the latter in his massive *Philosophy of the Unconscious.* There was no lack of thinking about this shadowy side of human personality, but it remained entirely speculative until a definite relation began to be established between dreams and the unconscious. Those who are interested in this period of growing curiosity about the structure of the human psyche will find an excellent study in the work by L. L. Whyte, *The Unconscious Before Freud.*[2]

Freud Makes Contact with the Unconscious

Freud above all was the first to show a practical, psychological application for delving into unconscious material and the meaning of dreams. For Freud, before anything else, was a physician whose interest was in making sick people well. He had received his training in neurology under Charcot in Paris, and following the lead of the French school, he had made use of hypnotism but was disappointed in its lasting effect in healing mental disturbances. He searched instead for some other means of making an impact upon the personalities of his patients that would enable them to come to terms with what disturbed them and to get well. He found this tool in dream analysis. What he found, in essence, was that understanding the elements of dreams enabled people to see what was going on in the part of themselves, of which they were not aware, to come to terms with themselves, and so recover from neurosis. To Freud dreams were interesting not only theoretically, but from a practical point of view as well.

Writing with a clarity, simplicity, and logical force that few philosophers or literary people share, Freud first presented his ideas to the world in *The Interpretation of Dreams.* Fifteen years later he gave a series of lecture courses at the University of Vienna, covering his entire theory of neurosis, mental illness, and dreams, which were then put into book form as *A General Introduction to Psychoanalysis.* These amazingly clear discussions reveal the logical development of Freud's theories.

He began with the idea that our errors, our lapses of memory, and our slips of the tongue reveal a purpose within us that is contrary to our conscious goals and direction and often completely out of touch with our conscious thought. This was the same purpose he saw revealed in dreams. What errors betray in a small way, he realized, is continually being portrayed by dreams in a never-ending and inexhaustible panorama. Therefore, if people could come to a way of interpreting dreams, they would then be able to know those factors within themselves that were in conflict with their conscious attitudes and thus were causing their disruptive neuroses. The problem was that we had no way to understand dreams. So Freud set out to erect a theory that would enable people to understand their dreams, and by this method, the method of psychoanalysis, to deal with what troubled them from within themselves, and to find health.

In very general terms, Freud's theory went like this: The unconscious wishes to speak clearly in dreams and to express its desires and meaning, but it is impeded from this by the conscious attitudes of the dreamer. Much of the dream material is obnoxious to the conscious personality unless it is distorted, and so there exists within the personality a censoring capacity that is responsible for the form a dream takes. The "censor," according to Freud, supervises several interesting processes, all of them unconscious and helping to conceal the real meaning of the dream from the ego.

First, the original dream thoughts are condensed; then they are turned into images, and some of the objectionable ideas or wishes are replaced by associations for the dreamer. The unconscious may even produce an opposite meaning by making transpositions or substitutions before the original ideas are translated into images. Finally, when the dream does pass the censor, there are often very important gaps in the way it is seen or remembered.

Thus Freud made the important point that latent dream content may be quite different from the final, manifest dream. It is necessary, he believed, to distinguish carefully between the original dream thought and the actual dream that occurs after the distortions he described as censorship. He believed that it was because of this process that so few people had ever understood dreams. The original, sexual, wish-fulfilling nature of the unconscious was disguised so effectively that we did not realize the real, primitive roots of personality. It must be noted here that this theory was based upon Freud's own dreams and upon his listening to the dreams of the repressed people of Vienna who formed the greater part of his practice. Freud's method enabled him to get at the material that was bothering his patients, and many people found new life and new understanding of themselves through his method.

There was also a growing group of medical professionals who began to take Freud seriously, and among them were two groups.

Many, of course, became firm adherents to his theory, and the first group formed around Freud. But there were others who thoroughly appreciated his monumental genius, who saw the importance of the points he brought out, who could not totally go along with his theory of the unconscious or of dreams.

To them Freud's dream theory seemed artificial and contrived. It did not appear to them that human personality was actually contriving to deceive itself so artfully. These professionals also doubted the validity of reducing the unconscious primarily to sexuality or to the pleasure principle and the death wish. It seemed to them that out of the unconscious there arose other instinctive forces besides sex. Adler, for instance, broke away from Freud because he believed that the will to power was the basic human drive. These psychologists also believed that from dreams and other unconscious experiences people do receive guidance and wisdom that has something to offer the conscious mind, as well as unacceptable thoughts and incubuses that would keep consciousness constantly on guard. Jung particularly felt that Freud had dogmatized too much. His separation came because he felt that there was not as yet enough evidence upon which to erect a full system and, besides this, that Freud had left out certain important data in order to keep his system neat and simple.

The Development of Jung's Thinking

It is true that Jung could not accept Freud's systematic doctrine of sexuality, but there was a far more important and fundamental reason for the break. Freud was a rationalist, and rationalist he remained, while Jung was an empiricist through and through. Freud assumed that the unconscious thinks rationally and wishes to communicate in this way through dreams and that it is only impeded by a censorship working quietly in the rational mind to distort these essentially rational communications.

Jung, on the contrary, suggested that the unconscious does not think rationally to begin with, but rather symbolically, metaphorically, in images. And this, rather than purposeful distortion, accounts for the difficulty we have in understanding dreams. The difficulty is that we have either forgotten or have never known how to think symbolically. The task of dream interpretation, according to Jung, is that of learning a strange language with many nuances, of learning to understand the symbolic communications of the unconscious—the language of art, literature, mythology, and folklore. He saw no attempt on the part of the unconscious to deceive or distort. The unconscious is simply using the best method of communication available to it. And this we need to learn to understand.

About 1912 Jung set down his independent ideas in a book published in English as *The Psychology of the Unconscious*. In this work—

which he later rewrote and which is now published as *Symbols of Transformation*—Jung introduced his study with a discussion of our two ways of thinking, analytical thought and symbolic thought.[3] He showed that in one kind of thinking we are active, in the other passive. In one we lead; in the other we are led. One is the thinking of logic and science, the other is the thinking of imagination, of poetry, art, and religion, and also of dreams. In its analytical function the conscious mind uses known facts; it sorts and directs them toward a particular order. In symbolic thinking the function is quite different, for here the mind is flooded by new images, symbols of something that has been *un*known or has been laid aside and forgotten.

Jung went on in this work to demonstrate the importance of this latter kind of thinking in approaching the unconscious. Taking for his material the dreams and fantasies of a young woman whom he knew only from bits of writing (and much later from her doctors), he showed quite accurately how the unconscious was leading her to serious mental disorder. Yet at the same time it outlined for her a picture of new life and greater wholeness if she had only had the help to understand and act upon these directions. They were directions that Jung recognized because they had appeared over and over again in the myths and religious stories and works of art of every kind of people. It was clear how important such dream experiences were to the religions of humankind and how much attention had once been paid to them.

At the same time Jung was coming to know a similar realm of experience in himself. He saw that if he were to allow his patients' dream experiences to speak for themselves as facts, then he had to treat his own dreams in the same way. As he did, it became evident how little was actually known about the contents of the unconscious and the almost incredible realm that was opened. Dealing with these contents, Jung wrote, "brought home to me the crucial insight that there are things in the psyche which I do not produce, but which produce themselves and have their own life."[4] From this fact came the certainty that reality, and frequently the best of reality, is found in these depths. This is also reality that demands a religious attitude from people, and it is found only when we allow ourselves to be led by the thinking of the unconscious, symbolic thinking that can be found in fantasy and dream and in myth and story.

It is almost impossible to put too much stress on symbolic imagination, for this way of thinking has been almost entirely ignored in the development of modern Western culture. It is of primary importance to religious people; it puts into their hands a method through which they can come to know and understand the religious depths of themselves and perhaps get intimations of God speaking through these depths. This method of meditative, devotional, imaginative thinking is an approach to experience at which Christians ought to be adept.

For Jung this way of thinking was vital to an understanding of human personality. It offered a basic approach to the unconscious which allocated to the psyche all the complexity and the amazing depth that were often found in it. If offered the only view of human beings that satisfactorily reflected the empirical facts. Therefore Jung made it his business to listen to dreams and other productions of the unconscious in a way that practically no other psychologist has attempted. He also spent most of his life describing and integrating what he learned. His approach is one that has something constructive to offer Christianity, something that is hard to find elsewhere.

Listening to the Psyche

From the beginning Jung seemed to know that he was to listen to the psyche and hear what it had to tell him. Now and then he encountered some very strange experiences that made him know the different quality of the contents with which he was dealing. One of these, which occurred early in his career, was the vision that a paranoid schizophrenic patient in Zurich tried to show him. The man, who had been hospitalized for years, called Jung into the corridor one day to instruct him how to squint and move his head in order to see the phallus of the sun and how it moved from side to side; this, explained the patient, was the origin of the wind. Jung noted this experience in 1906; then in 1910 he was reading one of Albrecht Dieterich's works when he came across words from an ancient papyrus that had recently been published, to which his patient had had no possible access, and realized that he was reading almost exactly the same vision. It told how to see "hanging down from the disc of the sun something that looks like a tube," which is "the origin of the ministering wind."[5] It did not take many experiences of this kind to convince Jung of the need for a religious point of view in dealing with unconscious contents.

Indeed, he gave an essentially different value to the unconscious than other psychologists. About 1930 he wrote:

> In this respect I go several steps further than Freud. For me the unconscious is not just a receptacle for all unclean spirits and other odious legacies from the dead past. . . . It is in very truth the eternally living, creative, germinal layer in each of us, and though it may make use of age-old symbolical images it nevertheless intends them to be understood in a new way.[6]

But new understanding does not spring full-fledged like Minerva from the head of Zeus; "a living effect," he went on, "is achieved only when the products of the unconscious are brought into serious relationship with the conscious mind." Above all, the unconscious does not need to be further dissociated from consciousness; too many people are already suffering from inner incompatibility, from an inability to live with their unconscious drives and still get on with their conscious aims. The first thing needed was to hear what the unconscious really had to say, and so Jung listened to the dream as "one of the purest products of unconscious constellation."[7] For fifty years he studied and wrote about dreams.

Jung did not try to get around the fact that most dreams are attempting to say something that is *not* in accord with conscious wishes and intentions. Instead, he suggested, they are agents for an independent function in the psyche, and in this sense they act autonomously. In this way they also act very differently from daydreams, whose subject matter and direction is already present in consciousness, simply waiting to gather other elements around it. Daydreaming may be built around anything from wishful thinking about Hawaii or a new car to things of the spirit, and this has its place, but it is not the same as dreaming. The dream chooses its own time to speak, and we are not asked what topics will be brought up or what they will mean to us, or even what objects will be chosen to represent this meaning, for consciousness does not make the rules. Dreams operate autonomously in this realm, if not beyond it.

The Language of Dreams

Since this is the case, the language of dreams does present a real challenge to our understanding. In the first place, dreams are like cartoons or parables. They signify something beyond themselves. They attempt to tell a meaning, or many meanings, by means of images, in much the same way that cartoon artists express their meaning by the use of symbols. Cartoonists use an image because it is well enough known to readers to evoke the memories, feelings, and ideas that go with a whole situation. The dream does essentially the same thing, by switching on the picture of an experience that at least once was associated with a group of memories, feelings, and ideas.

Jung sometimes illustrated this to his American listeners by referring to our political cartoons. His favorite was a prize-winning depiction of the Democratic party in 1927 that showed a donkey being ridden by a Southern belle and stubbornly balking at the sight of a derby hat that lay in its path. Those who know this part of American history can see in this picture a meaningful representation of the political situation in that year—with the Southern states still in the saddle, the Democratic party was resisting being represented by Al Smith, the big-city politician who had tossed his celebrated brown derby into the ring. Basically this is the way most dreams speak. But just as a foreigner might have some trouble with the idea of someone leaving his hat in the road, or a girl in ruffles and pantaloons riding a donkey, so the language of dreams is very often puzzling to the conscious mind.

Except for the different level of meaning, however, this is very similar to the parable, the form in which Jesus so often spoke. He told the stories of the prodigal son, the good Samaritan, and the foolish virgins, not to conceal his meaning, but to express it. Furthermore, these same themes that Jesus brought out in the form of stories still come out in the dreams of people today. People dream of finding the great pearl, of coming across one beaten by thieves and caring for him, of seeing a person raised from the dead, or of watching a fire that does not go out. These are all dream images that have been described to me by people with whom I have counseled, and there are many other examples from psychological practice. This indeed is the greatness of Jesus' parables. They touch the deepest level in us, the substance of our lives; and it is interesting that this is how Jung described the level from which extremely significant dreams arise. He also called attention to the fact that, like Jesus' examples, these dreams do not always have to operate upon the conscious mind in order to bring about an effect upon the personality.[8]

Most dreams do tell a story, generally with definite dramatic form, although the plot may vary from the simplest to the most exceedingly complex. They are often just like plays, staged either before one's eyes or with the dreamer cast in an active role, and sometimes with a great variety of characters, both known and unknown. In what way, then, can the action and the people in these inner dramas be understood? If they are not to be taken concretely, but only symbolically, then what does a man do with a dream about his mother-in-law? Or what about a truly frightening nightmare in which someone sees a friend die in an automobile accident? I am well aware of the temptation to take such dreams all too concretely, but this brings us to the second major point about this mysterious language.

Primarily *my* dreams speak to *me*, to my own inner, psychic life, and each of the figures in them represents some part of *my being*. As Jung was careful to show, a dream is a way of self-reflection, and

> one should never forget that one dreams in the first place, and almost to the exclusion of all else, of oneself. . . . The "other" person we dream of is not our friend and neighbor, but the other in us, of whom we prefer to say: "I thank thee, Lord, that I am not as this publican and sinner."[9]

The fact that strange, unexplained phenomena are at times associated with dreams only reinforces this conclusion. Such psychic events as clairvoyant dreams and extrasensory perception are simply given, and they must be understood in this way in order to be valued in their religious meaning. They come to such persons and at such times, apparently, as are chosen by the same mysterious power that speaks to our own needs in our dreams. Jung suggested briefly how important it is to see oneself in the dream:

> No one who does not know himself can know others. And in each of us there is another whom we do not know. He speaks to us in dreams and

> tells us how differently he sees us from the way we see ourselves. When, therefore, we find ourselves in a difficult situation to which there is no solution, he can sometimes kindle a light that radically alters our attitude—the very attitude that led us into the difficult situation.[10]

Behind this is one of Jung's most basic ideas. Our unconscious life, he held, is made up of almost innumerable complexes, bundles of ideas and related thoughts and feelings that function with almost a life of their own. These complexes, then, are the parts of ourselves that are pictured in dreams, represented by the various characters and situations of the inner drama. For example, a man dreams of a religious figure, let us say of Paul. If the action that involves Paul is to have meaning for him, the dreamer must ask himself: What does this figure represent in my life? What part of me is actually like Paul? What stands out about Paul in my dream, and what does this mean to me? When the dreamer knows what this image represents to him, then the action of the dream can show how that part of himself is related to the other elements as they appeared. If the dream-figure is a familiar one, like a mother-in-law or friend, then the questions are the same; the only difference is that they may be more difficult and complicated to answer. In either case the problem is to understand the meaning that the unconscious has presented for one's knowledge and guidance, and this is anything but simple.

Dealing with dreams is not simple, because right away it involves the individual in a realm of experience beyond him or herself. Jung was one psychologist who realized that dreams could not be reduced only to personal factors. Symbols from mythology and from the history of religion continually appear in them so that it is difficult to ignore the presence of deeper, universal meanings. Very few dreams seem to be entirely free of these elements. But even more important is the fact that "big" or "meaningful" dreams do occur that seem to carry little or no personal significance for the dreamer but still produce a most powerful impression. As Jung pointed out, these dreams are generally difficult to interpret. Although they make a terrific impact, often with forms of poetic force and beauty, they do not produce many associations from the dreamer's own experience. One must turn to myth and parable and fairy tale to find the symbols and some illustration of their meaning.

Such dreams are no longer concerned with immediate, personal experience, but with the *ideae principales* of which Augustine spoke, "which are themselves not formed . . . but are contained in the divine understanding."[11] These dreams reveal powerful realities that have their being in the human unconscious, realities that a person needs to touch and know because they lead the human soul and through it often determine the person's whole approach to life. These are the realities that Jung called archetypes, which are probably at the core of all our dreaming. Certainly they account for the vast number and variety of figures that we dream about.

The *Dramatis Personae* of Dreams

Jung found these archetypal forms represented over and over again in the characters that people our dreams, and out of this vast *dramatis personae* he isolated several of the important images and carefully described them. The most significant of these are the images of the shadow, the anima, and the animus.

The first, the shadow, is one that appears at one time or another in the dreams of every person. As might be expected, it is a dark and threatening figure, usually someone unknown to the dreamer. In fairy tales the "trickster" shows the original nature of this figure, doing all sorts of mischief for which people must take the blame. What the shadow represents is that inferior or undeveloped side of human beings that has been left behind in our attempt to become as completely rational and moral as possible. It is the uncivilized part of us, the primitive, which is also an essential part. Jung never tired of reminding us that this figure is usually 90 percent pure gold when one no longer projects it out upon other people. But its real value or danger cannot be found until one looks at these elements objectively instead of seeing them in some other person who is hated, feared, or glorified. Jung also reminded us that the shadow can be 10 percent pure evil.

The other two principal figures, the anima and the animus, are counterparts in the dreams of men and women. In the psyche of every man there is an identifiable female figure, which Jung called by the ancient name of the "anima," and in a woman's psyche it is matched by the male figure, which he termed the "animus." In the same way that the shadow is a reality based on the instincts, these two dream-images come from something equally real and insistent in men and women. The unconscious feminine within a man and the masculine traits in women are rooted in our physical structure and are carried by our genes and chromosomes, as well as by our psychological structure and our culture. Generally this figure seems to carry all that is most foreign to the conscious personality—in a man his moods, his vanity, his touchiness, and also his belief in the good and beautiful, his knowledge of the divine, and his ability to love and make love work; and in a woman the worst of her opinionated, argumentative side and also her ability to relate the ideal, the perfect, the true (even unwanted truth), to the hard facts of being.

Unquestionably it is difficult for people to face and to come to terms with these realities within themselves. It seems far more agreeable to cloak the anima and animus in a cult of romantic love than to set these conflicting impulses loose within. Nor is the shadow a burden many of us want to bear. It is not pleasant to realize that our own lives contain primitive and destructive elements that cannot be escaped. We much prefer to see these things in other people. Unfortunately these images do not stay put when they are unconscious and only projected. The man who searches only for an appropriate woman to carry his psychic counterpart finds sooner or later that this kind of love turns sour. The shadow that is hidden from the outside world can burst forth and make the kindest of men into a tyrant within his own family, and we have seen what happens to the educated, hard-working people of a nation like Germany when these unconscious shadow elements break out and transform many people into demonic destroyers.

But these are the penalties of unconsciousness. Through dream experiences these elements can come into consciousness within people so that they find the very creative springs of life in them instead of conflict and turmoil. Of course, this is never automatic, never simple or easy. It is sure to cost whatever we have and to be worth it. As the shadow and the ego with its awareness come to form a harmonious team, we find that much of the zest and creativeness in ordinary daily living originate from these rejected parts of ourselves. The images of the shadow often change from dark, distasteful figures to pure gold. The man who comes to terms with his inner feminine qualities finds even deeper values; he finds his very soul and the peace of wholeness and detachment, along with a new level of creativity and relationship. Similarly, a woman, in finding her inner masculine function, will find her life inwardly fructified and made whole and satisfying.

The importance of dreams and of the proper understanding of dreams in these processes cannot be overemphasized. Through dreams these inner functions appear in images that come alive for us and can be dealt with. Otherwise they remain unconscious, and people fall into projection. When people do not deal inwardly with the shadow and the anima-animus, they are led by one into the cult of war, from the iron curtain within their own homes on up to global war, which our time has brought to such awful perfection; or by the other into the cult of love, the idolatry that destroys the very foundation of life and society—and this at the cost of their birthright of finding themselves, which has its beginning in the creative imagery of the dream.

The three figures we have discussed only begin to suggest the variety of forms that can appear. There are as many archetypes as there are typical situations in life, and these three happen to be the most common, the ones everyone must meet in one way or another. Jung went on to draw quite detailed pictures of others, such as the child archetype, the wise old man or woman, the maiden, the Self (or inner redeemer), and the holy marriage. He once remarked that it took so much research material to be sure what the symbols meant that he learned not to lecture about it. He risked putting some people to sleep if he offered enough explanation of such symbols to make valid comparisons with the way people react today.[12] Most of us, in fact, are a little afraid to imagine that we are connected with the great symbols we see moving in history, art, religion, and poetry.

In addition he outlined the meaning of many nonhuman images that are important in understanding dreams. For instance, the sea often symbolizes the vast unconscious out of which human conscious life emerged and from which much of its sustenance still comes. Many people dream of the house that is their personal dwelling or of the automobile in which they get around in life, representing their conscious life and their ego, as against images of hotels, or of trains and railway stations, which speak of group life and mores. These are fairly easy to comprehend, as is the realization that animals often stand as symbols for the instinctive life within us. But there are many, many images, like the rock, the fountain, the bird, vessels of many kinds, even the father, which leave the dreamer cold until their original, usually religious meaning can be found and brought to life. The journeys that are made in dreams frequently represent one's inner, spiritual quest, while earthquake or disaster may signify that a great, perhaps overwhelming change is taking place in the psychic structure of one's life. Going back to childhood experience, say to a school classroom, usually represents the process of psychological reorientation and learning again, of growth. Indeed, there are too many such figures and images to ignore the fact that dreams speak a basic general language that can be understood.

It must be made perfectly clear, however, that *these symbols can NEVER be studied from a book to give an easy, shorthand method of understanding dreams.* Like any living language, they must be read in context, in connection with the personal associations they hold for the dreamer. In fact, as Jung often pointed out, dream interpretation is never a static process, but always an evolving one. Before any attempt at interpretation can be made, one must know the dreamer and the general state of his or her psyche, as well as all the facts related to that dream. It was the failure to see dreams in this light that kept the ancient and modern dream interpreters from catching the full significance of the material that went into their dream books. They seemed to be seeking an eternal, dependable language rather than the parable of an inner life, and so they missed the meaning of many dreams. Yet, like Synesius, they did realize that no dream is meaningless.

The Ways of Expressing Meaning

There are several different ways in which dreams express meaning. Primarily because they picture what is *not* present in consciousness, they bring people memories, experiences, and images that can reveal the unconscious element in their relationships. Simply because they do not depend upon consciousness but bring up the images and associations as they occur, dreams often reveal dormant qualities in the personality. In fact, Jung observed that they very often stand in glaring opposition to conscious intentions, particularly if a person's attitude toward life is very one-sided.

In such cases there are sometimes striking examples of the compensatory behavior or function of dreams; a dream may speak directly to the person's situation, calling attention to qualities of life which he or she has forgotten or ignored. One dream like this that I will never forget was told me by a very sweet old woman who confessed with horror shortly before she died that she had a recurrent dream of strangling her mother. Yet nothing could have been further from possibility; and that was just the trouble. This woman would have had good reason for anger at her mother, who had ruined her life. But she was too nice to face such horrid thoughts, and so her dream reminded her that she was not being honest with herself. This same principle of compensation can also act with opposite force, as when criminals have been known to dream of acts of kindness and generosity which they would never think to do consciously.

This principle also accounts for many of the dreams that were seen by the early Christians as the work of the devil or demons. Since many of these people actually were one-sided, both in the way they lived and in the way they looked at life, they had dreams that simply seemed evil to them. It did not occur to them that these dreams represented a function of compensating for one's view of life. But when the hermit dreamed of his voluptuous women, something deep within him, whether we call it the devil or not, presented him with this fare. A part of his own deepest self was offering him a reminder of what he was denying and sacrificing. And if the sacrifice is not conscious, is it indeed a sacrifice? At the other extreme, there are dreams that simply emphasize the conscious attitude or only introduce variations in it, and these also suggest the process of compensation. These dreams suggest that an individual's conscious attitude is "adequate" toward the psychic forces within him or her; it takes in enough of the unconscious to be in balance with it, at least for the moment. These dreams are very often abstract; they deal with images and figures that symbolize the complex situation within the person, but they often stress form and relationship by putting the emphasis on geometric, numerical, or even color arrangements. One example of this is certainly found in Ezekiel's vision of the wheels (1:15-22), and in several places Jung discussed such dreams.[13]

Once in a while these dreams may take the form of clear, direct statements, although this does not happen very frequently. The unconscious, however, out of which consciousness has arisen, is quite capable of speaking consciously as well as symbolically. The dream we have described that came to Dr. A. J. Gordon in his Boston church was one of these. In it the setting, the people who were members of his church, and the words they spoke were all perfectly clear and familiar. Only the figure of Jesus, appearing as an ordinary churchgoer, had to be identified for him. It was dreams of this kind that were so highly valued in ancient times, undoubtedly because so many people hoped for specific guidance in this way.

Dreams of somewhat the same quality have also been reported by scientists at times when they were wholly engrossed in some problem. A story of this kind was told on a television program not long ago, of a physiologist who had been concentrating on a problem without reaching the solution. One night he was awakened by a dream that described the solution to a T, and he wrote it out and went back to sleep. In the morning his memory was not exact and his notes were undecipherable, but they were identified three nights later when he dreamed the same dream all over again.

Between these two extremes are all the "ordinary" dreams that take up bits of yesterday's experience and play them out as a strange new drama. These dreams are often profoundly symbolic, and it is my experience that they generally offer greater help and guidance than those that are clear and direct. Just because of their compensatory behavior, an understanding of them can disclose new ways of approaching the day's problems. But this is not all. Over a longer period something far more important can be observed.

Where attention is given to dreams over a long period of time, as in the analytical situation, a vital process of development appears in the personality itself. Age-old dream symbols appear that represent a new center of personality, a higher center. In the isolated dream this process remains hidden in the compensation of the moment. But "with deeper insight and experience, these apparently separate acts of compensation arrange themselves into a kind of plan. They seem to hang together and in the deepest sense to be subordinated to a common goal."[14] This is what Jung described as the process of *individuation,* by which a person becomes at one with his or her own individuality, and at the same time with humankind, with the humanity of which that person is a part. The process that Jung has described may well be the most important reason for paying attention to dreams. It is an inner way that is quite natural in human beings, but as is very obvious in today's world, it is by no means automatic. To bring together both the dream world within one and the outer world of real people and things is a living process that is demanding and difficult and can easily be sidetracked. Jung stressed the religious nature of this process in many ways, particularly in his discussions of the dream symbols that move people toward this goal.[15]

In addition, there is the precognitive, clairvoyant, or telepathic dream that sometimes brings spontaneous knowledge of something in the future or at a distance. This is abundantly clear from the numerous examples in the literature on dreams, although it is not understood. Jung has suggested that the constraining forces of time and space do not limit the unconscious as they do the conscious mind. It appears that, while the conscious mind is limited and circumscribed, the unconscious is not contained within the boundaries of either time or space. The controlled experiments at Maimonides Hospital in New York[16] leave no doubt about the ability of the unconscious mind to receive information in some way other than by sense experience and then to represent it in dreams.

We do not have any explanation of how these dreams occur, however, nor any real insight into the reason for them, even though there are many proven instances. For this reason it is probably wise, as we have already suggested, to value the occurrence of such dreams without making them an end in themselves. Jung suggested the basic nature of this problem in his excellent discussion "A Psychological View of Conscience."[17] There is no question that such dreams come from a wisdom beyond our own. But we will wait a long time for our consciousness to start catching up with the wisdom of God if we ignore the dream that has personal religious significance and sit around waiting for an ESP experience. Many of the people who come the closest to a real understanding of dreams and who have themselves experienced fruitful dream lives, have never once had a dream of a telepathic or prophetic nature.

Last of all, there are experiences of the numinous dream, the dream that is enlightened by a special light and power and quality. These dreams tell us that we stand in a holy place. There rises within us a holy fear and awe, the very foundations of life tremble, and we find ourselves in the very presence of God. It may be possible to understand certain attributes of these numinous contents, as Jung suggested in several places, but when it comes to the total effect one can only say as Jung did that a light has burst forth in the darkness which the dark cannot catch up with.[18] Something incomprehensible, which has all the quality of a religious experience, has taken over. Such dreams are as meaningful as a waking religious experience and, like any other divine encounter, are valuable in themselves. The symbols of the unconscious may even slip away, and we know the One who gives us our dreams, the One who has fashioned life, the One toward whom our lives turn as the lodestone toward the magnetic pole.

The Skill to Understand Dreams

It takes skill to understand and interpret dreams. There will probably not be much argument about this as a general proposition, but it is a subject on which Jung was quite specific and one that emphasizes the difference of his whole approach. It is also a subject he continued to write about. At least once he even recommended it to the Protestant clergy because of the great and unique opportunity he felt was given them in the world today.[19]

About the only hard and fast rule Jung made, however, was to listen to the unconscious, to approach it without deciding beforehand what it has to say. If we remind ourselves first of all, "I have no idea what this dream means," then we are forced to let the dream and the associations around it tell us what we want to know. Once the memories and experiences associated with the dream are known, then the exacting task of actual interpretation can begin. And this "needs psychological empathy, ability to coordinate, intuition, knowledge of the world and of men, and above all a special 'canniness' which depends on wide understanding as well as on a certain *'intelligence du coeur.'* "[20] One is reminded of the church's own words in the Renaissance, the recipe phrased by Pererius for an interpreter, "who, as it were, grasps the very pulse of man's social and individual activity . . . [who is] divinely inspired and instructed."

Where, then does one get the ability, let alone the courage, to attempt this? There are five ways, each of them indispensable. In the first place, there is no substitute for practice. By listening, by asking and offering explanations, we gain experience. We watch to see which thought clicks, both in the person's mind and in his or her life, and also which interpretations misfire, and gradually an instinct develops, a feeling for the meaning of one dream and also of many dreams. There is no other way but to try.

Second, we must come to know a great deal about the other person, about his or her conscious life and convictions. Dream images can only be truly understood as they are seen rising out of a total life; in this sense Jung calls them "true symbols . . . expressions of a content not yet consciously recognized or conceptually formulated."[21] They come into focus in the perspective of a person's life, and the more that is known of that life, the clearer these symbols become. Even during the hour that I am able to spend with most people I find that my understanding of the dreams they bring grows rapidly. Indeed, it is quite foolish to attempt more than very general interpretations of a person's dreams until we do know him or her fairly well. To interpret the dreams of those we do not know comes closer to magic than to a legitimate art.

The third requirement is even more important. We must listen to our own dreams if we are to help other people understand theirs. There is no easy way around this; it is the only way to reach the heights and depths, the far corners of the soul's life. Only by paying attention to the unconscious, by listening to the contents that are still unknown in ourselves, can we encourage these depths in ourselves and others to speak. In addition, we must know where these experiences lead; our dreams often bring us into dangerous and forbidden territory where there is conflict and struggle and pain, and we need the confidence of another person who knows the way. Besides this, it is amazing how much more someone else can tell me about the meaning of *my* dreams than I can ever figure out by myself. After all, they speak of what is not conscious in me, and it is simpler for me to see the meaning in others' dreams which *their* inner blindness hides from *their* eyes. Thus I doubt if we can help other people understand dreams unless we ourselves have been counseled, guided, and enlightened by someone wise in the ways of human beings and God.

Fourth, there is a requirement that is easy to put into words but is the most difficult to put into action. In order to understand dreams we must first of all seek wisdom; we must be conversant with life. According to Jung it takes a "special canniness," or in the medieval words of Pererius, "a complete and perfect knowledge, confirmed by many tests of human character, interests, customs, and persuasions." This is a large order. To understand dreams we must live *widely* and *well*.

Finally, we must know God if we are to recognize the divine significance in dreams. These meanings are not often discovered by people who are driven only by natural impulses and imprisoned in the commonplace. Yet there have always been expressions of the numinous or divine in dreams, and those who are open to the voice of God, whose consciousness and powers of reflection are developed, will recognize them. They must also know the religious and mythological traditions of humankind and know them well enough to bring life to the symbols in dreams and amplify their meaning. This is a truly religious task, as our own tradition certainly shows. From Paul on through the Middle Ages the church was never without people who used the gifts of wisdom and interpretation to understand dreams. Paul was only the first of many who made a conscientious effort to understand his dreams and, to a great extent, to govern his life by them.

The Importance of Jung

Indeed, Jung calls modern Christians back to the consideration of life from a point of view that was once the Christian way. For those who know what it is to be lost in the rationalism of this modern era, he has something to say that hardly anyone else is trying to express. Jung's approach to the psyche, to human experience, offers people a way by which they can find the lively religious meaning that once welled up in Christian life. Through the symbolic, the religious approach to human experience, they can know that God still speaks out of the depth of the human soul, and sometimes his voice will be heard clearly. Through this quite different view of life, Christians can reach once again a real understanding of their religious heritage, making it real and vital for themselves and others, and keeping in touch with the source of revelation that God is constantly providing through the depth of their being. Jung's theory of dream interpretation has significance far beyond the practice of psychotherapy.

If Jung is so important, then why is it that more clergy have not realized his significant contribution? Why has it not been more readily seized upon in religious circles? The answer is at the same time both simple and difficult. In the first place, Jung often wrote badly from the standpoint of most readers. It takes fortitude to wade through his writings unless one is already interested in Jung. For decades the only work by which he was generally known among English-speaking peoples was his first book, *The Psychology of the Unconscious,* which he himself referred to as one of the "sins of my youth." Even in the revised form as *Symbols of Transformation,* it took many years of acquaintance with Jung before I could get through it.

Jung's writings are based upon experience, and unless we have investigated such experiences in ourselves or in others, it is not too likely that we will be open to believing that such things happen. Jung's studies, which were based directly upon his own experiences and those of his patients, have appeared esoteric and farfetched to many people. The facts he presented are not generally accepted in our society, since they are derived from experiences to which few people have exposed themselves. This involves a major philosophical question which will be discussed in the next chapter.

The last reason is the most difficult and disturbing. Jung himself underwent a direct confrontation with God in his own life journey. Those who would understand or use the Jungian method must make a similar confrontation and journey. Jung's method must be lived. It cannot just be understood. Jung wrote in his autobiography: "These talks with the 'Other' were my profoundest experiences: on the one hand a bloody struggle, on the other supreme ecstasy" and "God alone was real—an annihilating fire and an indescribable grace."[22] Most of modern Christianity has forgotten the reality of such encounters, which are very painful, and it does not choose to be reminded.

Instead, the reminder that dream experience is very real is still coming from the scientific and medical world. In fact, there is much in the present medical work on dreaming that backs up the things we have been discussing.

A Third State of Existence

It is surprising how fast our ideas can change today. Thirty years ago most people held the idea that dreams were fleeting experiences that happened once in a while just by chance. Then the reports on new research began to be published. Using the electroencephalograph to study eye movements as well as brain waves in sleep, the investigators have discovered periods of dreaming so universal and so different from either waking or nondreaming sleep that these are considered by some a third state of existence. According to Dr. Charles Fisher, who has summarized this research for the American Psychoanalytic Association, the recent findings suggest that

> dreaming is a predictable, universal, and basic psycho-biological process, occurring in a special organismic *third* state, and associated with such distinctive physiological events that it has to be considered as very different from both non-dreaming sleep and waking, although it has some characteristics of both.[23]

A great deal has been learned about this state of dreaming, which takes up nearly 20 to 25 percent of the sleeping time of every one of us. At regular intervals it breaks "the monotonously impassive mask of sleep," and a whole set of physiological reactions begin that are tuned to a dream. The sleeper's eyelids begin to ripple, indicating that the eyes are moving rapidly and that the brain waves have changed from the random zigzag of sleep to a flattened, low-voltage pattern almost like attentive waking. At the same time metabolism rises; heart action, blood pressure, and breathing are all roused from the slow, even rhythms of sleep and suddenly speed up or slow down unaccountably. In men there is almost always full or partial penile erection. Although skin resistance and arousal thresholds are noticeably higher, the chemicals that normally prepare for arousal are released in abundance. Even the fine muscles of the ear respond as they do in waking attention, and in many regions of the brain spontaneous firing of nerve cells increases well beyond the waking level. This "uniquely intense condition of nervous excitation"[24] is called by the name *rapid eye movement*, or REM, which is one of several outward, muscular reactions.

Yet for all practical purposes the motor system is switched off; the elementary reflexes no longer function, and there is loss of muscle tone. Even things like sleepwalking and enuresis, which were always considered a part of dreaming, never occur during REM periods, or only rarely, as in the case of sleep talking. At the same time there is actually more body movement and movement of the fine muscles than there is in the rest of sleep, non-REM sleep, when muscle tone and reflexes are both in working order. In effect, the body is allowed certain expression and yet is protected from acting out its dream. It is no wonder that dreaming or REM sleep is sometimes called "paradoxical sleep."

Dreaming periods alternate with non-REM periods in regular cycles occurring on an average of four or five times per night. The

REM periods last from a few minutes to over an hour,[25] increasing successively in length during the night, while the non-REM periods become progressively shorter. The first rapid eye movements appear only after a prolonged period of non-REM sleep, although at sleep onset there is a brief period when hypnagogic images are appearing that is unique. It is the only time when the typical dreaming pattern of the electroencephalogram (EEG) occurs without the presence of REMs.

All people dream, whether this surprises them or not. Ninety percent of the time, persons wakened from REM sleep remember a dream. Besides this, some kind of mental activity seems to go on all of the time. When a sleeper is awakened in any period and asked what was going through his mind, there is almost always recall of something specific. Usually it is less distinct in non-REM sleep and is less visual, more connected with the events of the day and more like "thinking" than the vivid, spontaneous memory of a dream. Yet images and even full-length dreams have been reported from non-REM sleep, and it appears very difficult to confine dreaming to just one period of sleep or to one particular kind of mental activity.[26] Sometimes, in fact, a pattern seems to run through all the dreams of a night, as if these various periods were all working together to produce one final, very important product—our conscious being.

No one doubts the direct effect of the physical body in this process. REM periods are triggered in one of the most remote and primitive parts of the brain, the pontile limbic formation, which is probably tied to instinctual drives and emotions, including penile erection. They have also been studied in babies and in many different animals that cannot be questioned about a dream and yet show all the physical reactions that go with dreaming.[27] On the other hand, it appears equally certain that dreams have specific effect on the body, perhaps many of them. The best-known is the REM that reflects almost exactly what is happening in a dream. For instance, one of the experimenters who discovered this was watching some horizontal eye movements of a subject and predicted a dream about a tennis match; when the sleeper awoke, he reported that he had been watching two men throw tomatoes at each other across a fence. Sudden changes in heart rate, respiration, and blood pressure often dovetail so exactly with changes in eye movement that these functions, as well as other movements, appear to reflect the psychic experience of dreaming. Indeed, it is difficult to ignore the interplay of body and psyche that is being revealed by these studies. Some heart attacks might possibly be the direct result of psychic stimulation and excitement during dreaming.

The studies are also revealing a great deal about the need to dream. Subjects who were deprived of most of their REM sleep made inordinate attempts to dream during the experiments, as many as thirty by the fifth night, and then proceeded to make up for the deprivation on the first "recovery" nights. Various effects on the personality were observed, ranging from moderate anxiety and disturbance of motor control, memory, and concentration, to almost psychotic manifestations when deprivation was prolonged. In one case of a person who stayed awake for two hundred hours, psychotic episodes occurred that looked "for all the world like dream episodes during sleep"[28] and seemed to reflect the same basic rhythms. Alcohol and also certain drugs like Dexadrine and the barbiturates have been found to suppress dreaming, and it is suggested that dream deprivation may play a part in delirium tremens. On the other hand, certain drugs, notably LSD, have a striking effect of lengthening REM periods.

At any rate one thing is perfectly clear from these studies. The human organism has a need to dream. This need was originally based on certain physiological mechanisms. But sometime in early development, as Fisher puts it, "these physiological mechanisms are taken over by the psychological process of dreaming and a new function emerges, namely, the regulation of instinctual drive discharge processes through hallucinatory wish fulfillment, as opposed to physiological discharge through motor patterns."[29] In short, the human animal begins to dream its way to becoming a human being.

Thus the scientific world continues to pile up evidence that shows the importance of dreaming in people's lives. From the beginning of Freud's revealing discoveries, the medical interest in dreams has gradually grown. Jung's findings in particular offer support for the traditional religious view, and the most recent research suggests that dreams may be as important in the development of human beings as they have been in religious practice.

Chapter
9

A Return to the Christian Interpretation of Dreams

WE HAVE SEEN the importance of dream interpretation in Christian tradition and also in modern medical practice and research. In Christian theology the belief that God was able to speak to human beings through dreams and visions persisted until the one-sided view of Aquinas began to be almost universally accepted. In practice this belief in God's revelation still continues wherever people have not been brainwashed by a rationalistic materialism. Medically the importance of dreams has been appreciated since earliest times. Physicians have used them in various ways in practice; and now that practical methods of interpretation have been developed, dreams are interpreted by psychiatrists all over the world. The most recent research shows the extraordinary significance of REM sleep and dreaming to human life. It is even suggested that this function is necessary to human life and development.

In addition, one important group of psychiatrists, psychologists, counselors, and clergy, following the direction of Dr. C. G. Jung, has come full circle to a renewed and very deep appreciation of the dream from the religious point of view. Jung, in particular, came to the realization that dreams offer contact with a numinous realm that seems to be much the same as the spiritual realm described by the church, a realm of being with uncommon power for good as well as for evil in the lives of people.

In spite of all this, dreams are either ignored or strangely in disfavor in the modern church. At one point Jung was talking with Anglican archbishop William Temple and suggested that some of his clergy be sent to Jung for psychological training. The archbishop turned down the offer. What is the reason? Just what is the most common theology of the Christian church today?

Where Are We Today?

There have been several reasons for paying little attention to dreams. But today the Christian neglect comes from one main reason. There is no place for the dream in the materialistic and logical scientism that has almost completely replaced the original thinking and philosophy of Christianity. This Aristotelian view, as proposed by Aquinas, refined by Descartes (and taken as final truth by logical positivism), states quite simply that there are only two realities. There is material reality and there is rational consciousness, and beyond this there is nothing else for humankind to know. This is just about as far as one can get from traditional Hebrew and Christian thought.

Yet matter and reason are all that exist for most modern writers in the area of religious philosophy. This is the point of view of theologians from F. R. Tennant through Douglas Clyde Macintosh to John Baillie. It is also the point of view of existentialism and logical positivism. And these are the philosophies that seem to attract most modern theologians, Bultmann, Bonhoeffer, Robinson, and process theologians. When it is even admitted that patterns of reality can exist apart from their expression in physical matter, such "modes" or "forms" are considered unknowable, existing in some kind of metaphysical realm that cannot be experienced by human beings. I have discussed the history of this development at length in my book *Encounter with God, A Theology of Christian Experience.*

Much of this thinking today stems from the philosophy of Husserl (phenomenology), which limits the experience of phenomena to those consciously received. Husserl quite explicitly considered Freud and found his "notion" of the unconscious mind a contradiction of terms, thus rejecting any such dimension of personality or any consideration of dreams or of other forms of "divine madness." Jaspers, Heidegger, Marcel, and Sartre all followed suit. The European theologians who are the authorities for much religious thinking today have taken this same line, and Bultmann and Barth in particular have been closely associated with the leaders of this school of thought. Its thinking does not differ very much from that of Aristotle, except that reason as a means of knowledge has been dropped out. Indeed, existentialism is a last dying gasp of Aristotelianism. It was only with Merleau-Ponty that the unconscious has been reconsidered among existentialists, and his untimely death in 1962 kept him from working out the implications of his thought and seeing its effect upon theology.[1]

Thus the idea that any realm of nonphysical, nonrational reality makes contact with human beings is simply ruled out to begin with. There is no place for the dream to come from. Since dreams are certainly neither material nor rational, they must be merely the undigested bits of yesterday's physical sensations and thoughts, a rehash—and garbled at that. The fact that most dreams do not fit that description makes no difference. This is the only possible view of reality, and so the dream is rejected before it is allowed to speak. Henri Nouwen in his book *Behind the Mirror* describes his near-death experience. His theological discussion of this experience is a refreshing exception to the general tenor of much modern theology.[2]

This rejection of the religious and philosophic significance of dreams is stated very clearly by one of the editors of one symposium, *The Dream and Human Societies*. In his introductory article on the cultural function of the dream, based on examples from classical Islam, Dr. G. E. von Grunebaum begins by writing: "For our purpose, we designate Descartes as the first fully self-conscious spokesman of the recent West, and we term all civilization before his time Eastern or Western, 'medieval' or, more blandly, 'premodern.'"[3] He goes on to show that the theory of knowledge held by previous cultures and religions, the older theories of revelation in dreams, can no longer be taken seriously by modern men and women. The irony of all this is that Descartes, the first "modern" person, received the inspiration for his method and his point of view from a dream experience. It was a dream that gave Descartes the inspiration that would eventually put an end to the long tradition of valuing the dream.[4]

Not only Descartes but the whole of Western civilization has been given direction by Descartes' dream. It would seem logical to pay attention to the personal reality of Descartes as well as to his thinking. If we do so, we encourage a belief that a higher power expressed itself through a dream. The same kind of experience also happened to both Aquinas and John Baillie at the end of their lives, giving them a direct relationship with that higher purpose. To be logical, we need to consider the source from which the "modern" philosophical method has arisen, as well as the method itself. Otherwise we limit ourselves like the followers of Islam, who revere the dream-visions of the Prophet but find no truth in their own.

If Rudolf Bultmann is correct in holding that theology cannot challenge the prevailing worldview, but must adjust to it, then revelation and inspiration through dreams is a dead issue for Christians in our time. We would have to agree that Christianity must adjust itself, altering its traditional understanding and interpretation. If, however, it is possible to question the rational materialism of our time, it is then possible to consider a kind of worldview like the Platonism that made Christianity a world religion, a religion that worked. This requires us to find a view of the world very different from the prevailing one. We need to find a point of view that has a place for nonphysical reality and a method of knowing it.

Which View?

As we turn to this question, it is worth noting the direction that much scientific thinking is taking today, and how far, as Korzybski shows in *Science and Sanity*, the older thinking of Aristotle has been overthrown. Scientists who deal with relativity and quantum mechanics have to free themselves from Aristotelian rationalism and materialism in order to grasp a new conception of time and space, energy and matter. It is interesting how the great minds of modern science see the source of their inspiration. On one occasion when Einstein and Jung were together, Jung asked the scientist if it took a great deal of strict discipline and mental concentration to come to his conclusions. Einstein replied, "Oh no. I meditate and the numbers dance before me."

Those who have produced the revolutionary view of modern science have had to abandon the certainty of Aristotle and nineteenth-century science. The great physicist Werner Heisenburg has pointed out that modern science has become so skeptical that it has become skeptical of its own skepticism. He also pointed out that all the basic words of classical physics have changed their meaning (space, time, energy, and mass) and suggested that the words of natural language like spirit and God might well be closer to reality than the words of physics. In *God and the New Physics* Paul Davies shows how modern discoveries of subatomic physics have led us more into mystery than clarity. Robert Openheimer, invited to address the American Psychological Association, pleaded with his audience not to base their psychology on a theory of physics that physics has abandoned. Kurt Gödel demonstrated that even mathematics was not certain. In his ground-breaking book, *The Structure of Scientific Revolutions,* T. S. Kuhn shows how little certainty is provided in the physical sciences.

In *The New Biology,* Augros and Stanciu show that the most developed human organisms are possible only through *cooperation* and not through competition and survival of the fittest. They also suggest that the DNA may well contain a purposeful agency in evolution. Teilhard de Chardin has postulated the reality of nonphysical existence in accounting for the facts of evolution. Although Jung was first and foremost a medical doctor, he postulated the same reality in order to account for the facts that he uncovered in the empirical study of the human psyche—facts that he had to understand and deal with in order to bring health to his patients. It was Jung who opened my eyes to the reality of the worldview of Jesus. I myself have seen this same reality at work in the lives of many who have regained health and meaning as they learned to listen to the depth of themselves through meditation and contemplation and through their dreams, and then tried to live more in harmony with the depth and purpose that they encountered.

The reality of our experiences of the nonphysical is supported by a basic religious view of the universe and how we know it. In simplest terms, this theory sees human beings in touch with a spiritual world that is just as real as the physical world revealed by our five senses. Figure 1 provides a view of reality containing a real physical world, a real spiritual world, and a loving Divinity with whom we can have genuine communication, both from God to us and from us to God. I have sketched such a view in greater length in *Encounter with God, Companions on the Inner Way,* and *Reaching*.

Figure 1

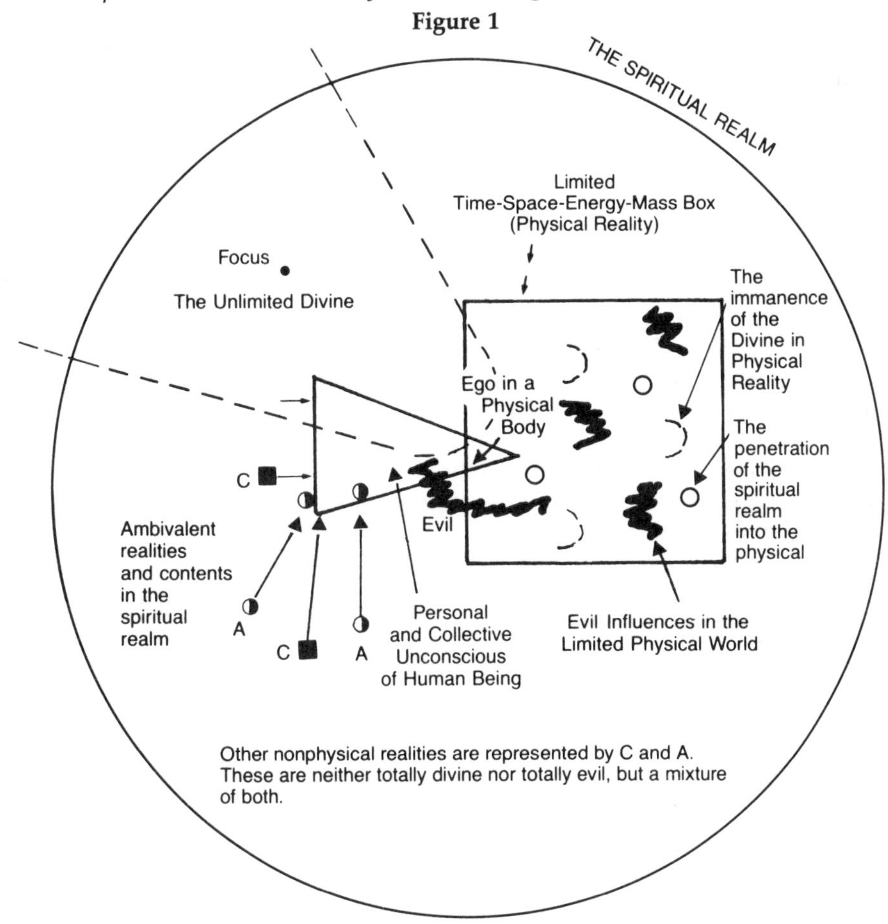

When we believe with Jesus and Plato that the Divine can and wishes to communicate with human beings, then our prayer life and meditations can bring us into real relationship with God. The dream can then become meaningful as well as a source of self-knowledge and revelation.

The actual fact of finding inspiration in dreams gives substance to the belief that such a level of reality does exist. We do not consciously create our dreams; their evidence of contact with the numinous is therefore very impressive. Once we accept the possibility of this world-view and then listen carefully to our dreams, we will find, as so many others have, that we are presented with a consistent body of impressive and powerful materials. We find a reality of many layers and levels apart from the physical world. We find that it contains everything from yesterday's memories and forgotten faces, to terrifying encounters with destructive and demonic darkness, to numinous experiences of the Divine. It may come as a single image, in the form of a poetic story, like an allegory, or directly as a command; or we may find endless tales and images that we must struggle to understand. Occasionally a dream breaks over the barriers of time and space and brings telepathic knowledge or some precognition. But unless we take time to record and consider our dreams, we usually remember only a few that were different enough to be startling or just goofy. Dreams move from one level to another of this inexhaustible reservoir of nonphysical reality but, in the long run, with a consistency and direction that is difficult to believe until we have experienced it.

Once we know this reality, it makes very little difference what name we give it. Call it the "unconscious," the "spiritual world," the "objective psyche," "psychoid reality," "heaven and hell," the "collective unconscious," the "realm of gods and demons," or even " *'ālam al-mithāl*"—these are all merely names to describe what we human beings find as we listen to the reality that comes *through* the depth of ourselves. In the last of Jung's writings, in which he spoke simply as an ordinary mortal rather than as a scientist, he suggested that what he had described as the objective psyche was similar to what had been called the spiritual world by religious people from the dawn of time. He wrote:

> I have, therefore, even hazarded the postulate that the phenomenon of archetypal configurations—which are psychic events *par excellence*—may be founded . . . upon an only partially psychic and possibly altogether different form of being. For lack of empirical data I have neither knowledge nor understanding of such forms of being, which are commonly called spiritual. From the point of view of science, it is immaterial what I may *believe* on that score, and I must accept my ignorance. . . . Nevertheless, we have good reason to suppose that behind this veil there exists the uncomprehended absolute object which affects and influences us—and to suppose it even, or particularly, in the case of psychic phenomena about which no verifiable statements can be made.[5]

In Jung's letter to me dated May 3, 1958, and in several other letters, he expresses the same point of view with emphasis and clarity.

What are modern Christians to make of dreams, then, when we have opened our minds in this way to the possibility that they may speak to us of something beyond or different from our conscious egos?

Possibilities of Meaning

Whatever else a dream is, once one has accepted the possibility of its having meaning, it at least mirrors what goes on in the human psyche or personality. About this there is growing agreement among medical professionals who work with dreams, psychologists who study them, and also other modern students of dreams. A great deal of literature expresses this same point of view.[6] In one way or another, then, dreams reveal the condition of our psychic being. They show many things that we have not wanted to look at, and sometimes they reveal what we really want. When either kind is properly understood, it can guide the direction of a person's life. Dreams can be precise guideposts through trouble and direction signs toward meaning and fulfillment. Thus they are the concern of those who would help people out of confusion and difficulty, who want to help women and men grow and mature psychologically and spiritually. In most cases the pastors who are interested in helping their flocks in this way can make good use of dreams. They offer a key to much that is going on in the personality that is hard to get at and understand in other ways. Counselors who listen to dreams can learn about people without being intrusive.

The history I have presented also makes it very clear that neither Freudian psychoanalysis nor Jungian analysis has any exclusive right to the use of dream material or its interpretation. In fact, it was a Jungian analyst who once suggested to me that the New Testament is undoubtedly the best guidebook known for anyone who is seeking maturity and integration of the personality. Christian dream interpretation is a legitimate individual Christian undertaking and an excellent Christian pastoral exercise. Indeed, learning how to interpret and understand this material, which so often reveals the human condition, has been helpful to many ministers in their pastoral work. Once pastors let it be known that they take dreams seriously, most people are eager to share them.

This brings us to a second and even more important point. From the Christian point of view and also that of other religions, God is in intimate relationship with the total human psyche or personality. In fact, from a religious point of view, nothing is more important to the health of the personality than its relation to God, to that center of nonphysical, creative meaning that is at the heart of things. Since dreams mirror and reveal the personality's innermost condition, they inevitably speak of the human-Divine relationship as well as of other relationships. Thus God is able to speak to us through them. Sometimes dreams that speak of the soul's religious health are shot through with a numinous quality mingled with the commonplace. Sometimes it even seems that God is directly present and with overpowering force, but these dreams are rare.

At other times dreams that tell us of our relationship with God replay the ancient symbols of myth or the stories of Jesus. When they speak symbolically, we have to track down the meaning of the symbols and relate them to our own lives in order to understand the deep significance of their content. For some people dreams of this kind are almost nightly occurrences, but for some people such dreams seldom occur. However, dreams that are sketchy or seem irrelevant also may mirror the dreamer's inner condition and can speak of God's relationship within, for God is deeply related to our total inner condition. If God is real at all, and if there is a nonphysical realm in which God can move the unlimited realities of the spirit, then dreams can have unquestionable importance for our psychological and spiritual growth.

Some Dreams that Were Important

Dreams that lead us to the depth of spiritual meaning are often heard by those who encourage others to share them. One of the most impressive dreams of this kind occurred to an acquaintance of mine just before he died; it is recorded in his son's book *God's Forgotten Language.* This dreamer was a priest of the Episcopal church, a fine pastor and the author of a book on healing, *God's Healing Power;* he had never been particularly interested in dreams. The last five years of his life were plagued by mounting physical illness and by increasing depression and anxiety about death. On several occasions he discussed this with his family. Then during the week before his death he had the following dream experience, which he described to his wife the morning after it occurred. She immediately wrote it down:

> In the dream [she wrote] he awakened in his living room. But then the room changed, and he was back in his room in the old house in Vermont as a child. Again the room changed: To Connecticut (where he had his first job), to China, to Pennsylvania (where he often visited), to New Jersey, and then back to the living room. In each scene after China, I . . . was present, in each instance being of a different age in accordance with the time represented. Finally he sees himself lying on the couch back in the living room. I am descending the stairs and the doctor is in the room. The doctor says, "Oh, he's gone." Then, as the others fade in the dream, he sees the clock on the mantelpiece: The hands have been moving, but now they stop! As they stop, a window opens behind the mantelpiece clock and a bright light shines through. The opening widens into a door, and the light becomes a brilliant path. He walks out on the path of light and disappears.

"My father knew, of course," the son's book goes on, "that this was a dream of his approaching death, but no longer did he have any anxiety. When he died a week later it was in complete peace; he fell asleep at home and 'forgot' to awaken. We had a special marker made for his grave, which has etched into it the 'path of light' down which he went."[7]

This dream is a telling example of those numinous experiences that can bring meaning and focus to a whole life. It gathered up the dreamer's life in retrospect, then pointed to the clock, which represents time and time that has run out. Behind the clock was light, a common symbol for divine life and radiance—"the light of the world." It appeared as a path on which he walked out. He had found his God in the last telling moment of life and saw his continued existence with the God of light.

Two other dreams came up in my counseling, each of which brought the dreamer to a new experience of the Holy One. The first of these came to a young man of nineteen who was overwhelmed by doubts and deep inner insecurity. He was potentially an excellent student, with a bent for philosophy, but he had lost his way and was not comfortable with his colleagues. He wrote that one night he dreamed that he was watching a movie that started

> with a whole group of children in a bicycle race. They are about nine years old and are riding like mad. There is a narrator off-scene who points out that the children are all racing, trying as hard as they can. He seems to be talking about running the race in life. One little redheaded child, who is racing furiously, has another child on his handle bar. The race goes over a hill and when they start down, the camera looks up, and there on a mountain side, like the rock of Gibraltar, is a diagram with the letters L O V E engraved in the stone. And the narrator continues: "If you can remember that love is not being loved or saved, but is more of a giving, then you will see how this diagram illustrates the concept of love's being—inside, outside, and all around."

The meaning of the dream was quite clear; he was in the race of life, but he had forgotten where he was racing and what was the object of his race. When we talked later, he brought up the words of the New Testament, Jesus' commandment "that you love one another as I have loved you." He also remembered Plato's belief that through love one came into relation with the spiritual dimension of reality, and he saw how this dream urged him on to an understanding of love that was necessary for his psychological and religious growth.

He realized that he had been trying to live his life only intellectually, and out of this dream experience he came to terms with his own capacity to love, which had been much repressed. As he overcame the fear of himself and of the world around him, his fear of meaninglessness and emptiness began to disappear. The experience of God became real for him once again, and he made significant human relationships.

Another young man told me how his religious life had come to a dead halt. Where it had once been very powerful and real, he found only an aching void. He had wanted to enter the ministry but decided that this was impossible without conviction. In the spring of 1967 he had heard a series of lectures on dreams, and now he decided in desperation to listen to his own dreams. In one of them he heard the instruction to make a long journey like Abraham and visit the person who suggested that dreams were a way to know God; and he followed through on it.

The night before he arrived at his destination, he had a dream in which he saw himself standing like the rich young ruler in the Bible, listening to be told the one thing that he lacked. During the days that followed he *was* told, through the depth of himself, the one thing that he lacked. And this young man, seizing it, found that his faith in God, his sense of meaning, the reality of God as a burning fire in his life all returned.

Again a close friend was warned in a startling, precognitive dream of the death of his newborn grandchild. The baby, born that day, a Friday, was in critical condition. In the night my friend dreamed of a woman's voice telling him that the child was dead. The next morning he shared the dream with his wife, and during the day he could not rid himself of the oppression it had caused. On Sunday morning the phone rang and he answered it; the same voice, using the same words he had heard in his dream, informed him that the child was dead. In this strange, inexplicable way, they had been prepared to accept the tragedy.

There are many, many such experiences today involving people of all ages, just as in the history we have just recorded. Dreams do still speak; how, then, do we understand them?

Understanding Symbols

Because most of us have forgotten how to think symbolically, the symbols of dreams have become a closed book. We forget that these images describe realities that influence the human psyche. Thinking in this way is very different from the rational, analytical thinking that Descartes helped to define for the modern world. Symbolic thinking is thinking through images, through imagination. It has its own meanings, its own direction and way, which cannot be understood by rational, conscious thinking. However, it is the basis of many great scientific discoveries, as well as being the language of literature and art. It is symbolic thinking that also produces religious writings and is used in the practice of Christian meditation and meditative reading. When we learn to think symbolically again, we not only understand the language of dreams, of art and literature, but we will also understand the Bible quite a bit better than most of us do now.

Each of these ways of using symbolic thinking is valuable to the individual who is trying to follow the Christian way of living. The life and teachings of Jesus, who lived and spoke symbolically, first of all require an understanding of this language. Then there are the great religious writers, from Augustine to Charles Williams and T. S. Elliot. These and other devotional writers offer the general instructions for Christian life, while the dream speaks specifically to the individual.

None of us can really afford to neglect these sources of God's direction or to be ignorant of the way in which they communicate it to us.

Beyond this, can we actually afford to neglect the theological foundations of our church? It never occurred to the early Christian leaders to doubt the validity and value of dream experiences as expressions of God's providence and as a way of communicating with the more-than-human world. In ignoring the value and significance of dreams, the church today is denying not only the biblical tradition and nineteen centuries of Orthodox tradition, but also fifteen centuries of Western Christianity. Christian leaders of all ages have recognized the deep and mysterious communication of God with humankind. Dreams and visions were an important part of that communication. Is it possible to believe that these Christians simply suffered from an illusion common to their age and not, in the same breath, cast doubts upon the entire theological formulation of Christianity?

Jesus, the Bible, the early church, and many influential Christians (saints) of every age—all speak from essentially the same point of view. They all say essentially the same thing. And what they say is not intelligible in the thinking of Aristotle or the rational materialism of the West. If Jesus speaks to the whole of life, as the church still says that he does, then it is worth trying his whole point of view, and dreams are an important part of that whole point of view. What concrete suggestions, then, can be offered for taking these experiences seriously?

How Can We Interpret Our Dreams?

The study of dream symbolism is vast and complicated. Volumes have been written on the subject. In the study of physics there are two levels. The first is theoretical, which has little or no immediate application. Then there is applied physics, which helps us light our houses and manage our plumbing. The theoretical study is necessary if there is going to be practical use of that knowledge. However, one need know very little physics to keep the drains flowing and the fuses changed. There is the same kind of difference in understanding one's dreams. The theoretical studies of dreams are very important and valuable, but all I wish to give at this juncture are some practical methods of trying to hear the essential messages of dreams.

Many people will want to know more about interpreting dreams than I can provide in this book. My book *Dreams, A Way to Listen to God* provides some concrete suggestions on dream interpretation for those who find the idea of dreams as divine messages an interesting possibility. However, it is not fair to the readers of this volume not to provide some simple and yet comprehensive suggestions on how to interpret their dreams.

I began a serious study of dreams in a time of confusion and turmoil. Jung has stated that most neuroses in people over age thirty-five are the result of being cut off from contact with that reality of which all the great religions of humankind speak. I was indeed cut off from an experiential knowledge of this reality, and this caused and created real anxiety. With the help of Max Zeller, a Jungian analyst, I began to understand messages coming through my dreams, and my inner confusion became less oppressive. Even more important, I came to know the dreamer within who had been sending me messages which I had ignored because I did not understand them. Within a short time my life had a new depth and direction, and I had new assurance of God's reality. During the years that have followed, I have learned that a wisdom and love speaks through dreams, a presence that seeks to guide me and bring the totality of me to reality itself. I now had an experiential knowledge of God as well as a rational belief.

I have learned that my dreams speak to me as an individual. They are tailored to me as a "well-made suit," to use John Sanford's phrase. At the same time dreams use symbols, language, and stories that may often have universal human meaning. Dreams have many levels of meaning. For most modern westerners they speak a language that is unintelligible. It is, however, a language that can be learned and that children understand more easily than the products of most Western educational systems.

Sometimes dreams speak with a clarity that can scarcely be missed, but most often they speak in the language of pictures, symbols, fairy tales, and myths. There is no easy way to understand them. One has to work in order to understand their meaning. God gives us dreams to help us manage our lives and to help to make the Holy One more real to us. The Divine does not run our lives for us as some religious enthusiasts fail to understand. Dreams and visions give us clues as to how to run our lives, but they require our cooperation and work. Learning to listen to dreams may well be learning to listen and work *actively* with God.

At a recent conference of people wishing to understand more about the religious significance of dreams, I was asked to summarize as simply as possible how ordinary people could interpret them. I reflected back over forty years of recording and trying to understand my dreams. I came up with the following suggestions.

A. *Be serious seekers.* If we wish to understand dreams, we must first be serious seekers for deeper meanings in life, searchers for a deeper contact with God than we already have. We must at least entertain the possibility, suggested by Alan McGlashan, that there is a dreamer within us who is separate from our ordinary ego and who has access to the wisdom and insight that the Holy One wants to share with us. This One speaks softly in an ancient language we can learn.

B. *Write dreams down.* The person who has already purchased a journal and a pencil to go with it has already responded to the first suggestion. If we are to keep a record of dreams, we need to have a notebook at our bedside and be ready to spend a few moments of reflection on the events of the night as we wake up. Most dreams are lost forever if we do not record them within five minutes of awakening. Dreams can be lost if we are wandering around looking for a pad and pencil. The radio alarm clock also brings us out of sleep with attention riveted on the outside world and thus also ruins much dream recall. Most people need seven hours of sleep if they are to recall a significant number of dreams. The most important dreams often come after seven hours of sleep. Dreams must be valued and seen as important if they are to be recalled. Dreams have to be remembered before they can be interpreted, as the Book of Daniel reminds us.

Writing dreams down preserves them from oblivion, and the very act of doing this sometimes unlocks their meaning. It also fixes dreams before us so they can be returned to again and again. They should be written down simply. If the recording of an ordinary dream takes more than ten to fifteen minutes, something is wrong.

Some years ago I visited a sleep laboratory at Point Loma, California. The U.S. Navy wanted to know how much sleep and dreaming was necessary for human beings so they could give and receive orders properly. I could quite easily identify the brainwave patterns indicating REM sleep. The researchers also discovered that 95 percent of dream content was forgotten after five to ten minutes of waking activity. Even impressive dreams that wake us up in the middle of the night are lost if they are not recorded.

Without these first two steps, there is little or no dream interpretation in our society and culture. In some societies dreams are discussed along with breakfast. The Senoi in Malaysia still carry on this tradition. When dreams are treated in this way, written records are not as essential as among westerners.

C. *Pretend the dream is someone else's.* When the dream appears meaningless to us, we can go back to the dream later and imagine it is the dream of a friend we know well. One reason dreams are difficult to understand is that they come from our unconscious, that of which we are not conscious. Therefore their meaning is often foreign to us. Sometimes a dream will reveal its meaning when we look at it as in no way related to us, as something totally outside of us. In other words, we pretend it is someone else's dream.

Once we come into this frame of reference, we can imagine that a dream is a play or a movie we have seen or a picture that has caught our attention in a magazine or at an art gallery. What message would the movie be giving if the dream were a movie? What would the photographer or artist have been trying to convey if the dream were such a picture?

We can imagine that we are talking to the one who has put on the dream production and ask the dreamer within what the dream is trying to tell us. What is the message? In order to have success in this process, we need to first quiet down, relax, and be still. We seldom can listen to the depth of ourselves until we come into silence.

D. *Ask for God's help.* After hearing me give a lecture on dreams, one person became convinced that dreaming was a way God could speak to her. She did not think that she ordinarily dreamed but found that, as soon as she expectantly put a pad and pencil by her bed, she could remember her dreams. Her first dream was a powerful one that changed her life. She interpreted it as far as she could and then brought it into the church before the reserved sacrament. She prayed for understanding, and understanding was given. The dream was telling her about her daughter who had been disabled by depression and how to help her toward health. When understood in prayer, the dream gave her hope for her daughter's recovery and then told her what she could do to facilitate the healing process.

As this woman continued to bring the dream before God in prayerful asking and listening, she realized that it also spoke of the sickness of her own inner "child" who had been imprisoned and unloved. The dream gave her many months of material to work on in prayer. Those who have found real meaning and answers in prayer will often find meaning in their dreams by bringing them before God with a prayerful attitude. When Joseph was asked in Egypt who there was who could interpret dreams, he replied, "Do not interpretations belong to God? Please tell them to me" (Gen. 40:8). This woman found that God has not changed. The Divine will still help us to understand our dreams when we ask for help.

E. *Read books about dream symbols.* We can also look at the dream symbols that seem to have no personal reference and ask, "Do the symbols have any particular or significant meaning in themselves?" There are volumes written on dream symbols. Sometimes it helps to look up the meaning of symbols that leave one completely in the dark. I have already mentioned Ad de Vries's *Dictionary of Symbols and Imagery.* This book can be most helpful if one uses the suggestions *only* as suggestions. In volume 20 of the *Collected Works,* we can find references to many helpful explanations of numerous dream symbols that Jung has interpreted. *It is of great importance to remember that one's personal associations with dreams take precedence over the meanings provided by another person or found in any book.* We also need to remember that a dream interpretation is only correct when the meaning of a symbol or dream "clicks" with the individual who dreamed it.

Some people find that they can dialogue with their dream symbols and ask them who they are or what they mean. When a symbol recurs again and again, it is usually telling us that we have not yet understood the message of the dream. It is surprising what insights come when we dialogue with a dream symbol like a gorilla, turtle, rug, tree, or a criminal who is pursuing us. It is almost as if the dream symbol is just waiting to be asked its meaning so it can reveal itself. We need to call on our imagination and intuition to help us in this dream world.

F. *See parts of yourself in the people you dream about.* It is important to realize that when we dream of other people, the meaning is usually not about them, but about a part of ourselves that is like that person. Most dreams are telling us about ourselves, the various parts of ourselves, and how we can be brought to wholeness and healing. Dreams seldom tell us about other people or outer events.

G. *Find out the level of experience your dream is presenting.* Dreams can refer to every level of human experience. We have far more capacities of knowing than we ordinarily realize. It is helpful to see which area of experience a dream is pointing to. Figure 2 gives us a map of the various areas to which a dream can refer.

Figure 2

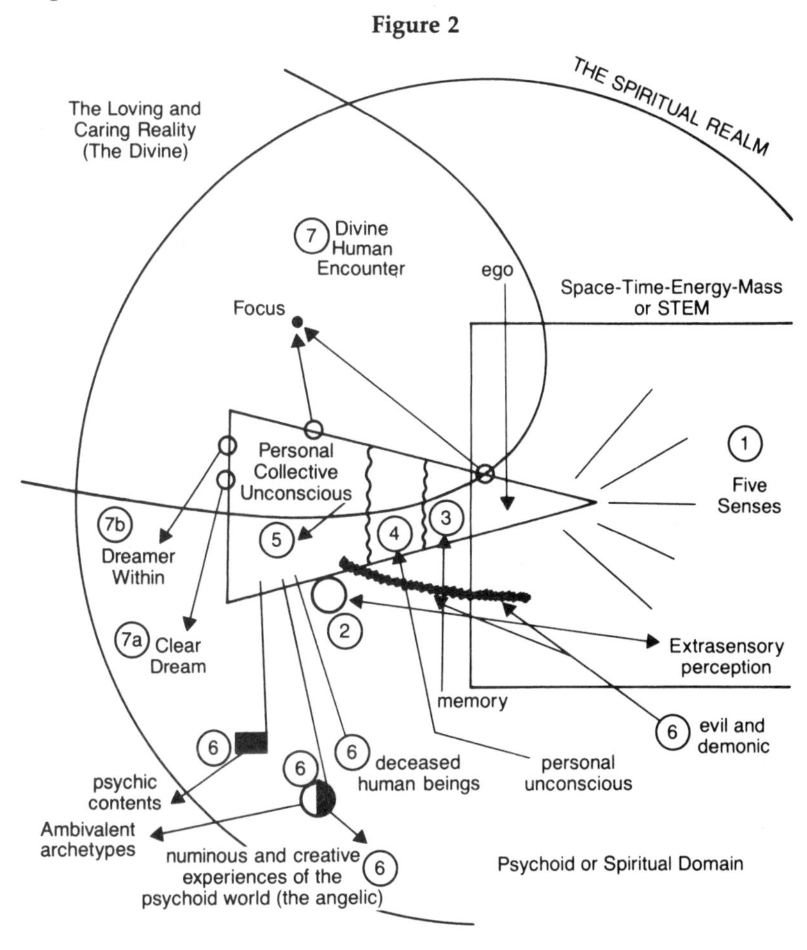

It is valuable to discern which part of the psyche or the physical or spiritual world is being expressed in a dream. What part of me is speaking most clearly? All nine levels may be present in a dream, but we need to decide which one is presenting the dominant message. Most people find these nine levels within them from time to time, although some are far rarer than others. The numbered paragraphs below refer to the numbered areas in the diagram.

1. Sometimes a dream refers mainly to yesterday's events and their significance but seldom without some alteration in the scene. We can always ask ourselves why this particular event from a former day has been seized upon and highlighted by the dreamer within. In forty years of listening to my own dreams and thirty-five of listening to others' dreams, I have found that dreams that merely repeat yesterday's events are really quite rare, in spite of the old wives' tale to the contrary.

2. We have already noted many examples of telepathy, clairvoyance, and precognition in dreams. Dreams can also spur scientific discovery as the Brown and Luckock article, "Dreams, Daydreaming and Discovery" (*The Journal of Chemical Education,* Nov. 1978) shows quite clearly. The dream can give knowledge that our ordinary five senses cannot give, and *very occasionally* we are given knowledge in dreams of the physical world that we do not get through ordinary sensory channels. This information can cross space and time and can even tell of the future. *One of the most dangerous uses of dreams is to expect that they are always or usually speaking of the future.* Less than 1 percent of our dreams have this meaning, and no one can tell which ones foretell the future until after an event has occurred. Most superstitious and silly uses of dreams involve using them for fortune-telling. Occasionally they do give this kind of information. However, people who do have this precognitive gift often find it a great burden. They do not know what to do with this information and feel anxious and alienated from other human beings. They need to be listened to and understood.

3. A dream can reproduce anything from memory, even a scene quite inaccessible to conscious recall, for instance a scene from second grade in school, in full color with names and faces. Nothing in one's life seems to be lost beyond remembrance to the dreamer within.

4. Sometimes a dream presents actions and thoughts of the past which we have repressed and forgotten because they cause us pain. The personal unconscious is not locked to the dreamer within. This kind of dream can bring up important material that can open us up and change our lives.

5. One of the great discoveries of both Freud and Jung was that there are universal symbols that bubble up out of the soul and tell us of its very nature and structure. This area of the soul has been named

the "collective unconscious" by Jung. Understanding this level requires much study and application, and here Jung's interpretations are very helpful.

6. Some dreams are charged with numinous or awe-inspiring power. When something beyond our soul touches us and is known, there is usually a sense of awe and holy fear. This can bring terror if it is some evil or demonic reality, amazement if it is some deceased person or an angelic or neutral spiritual reality, or ecstasy if God is the one who touches our soul. We call such visions of the night "numinous dreams."

7. Once or twice in a life, often near the end of it, we human beings are given a glimpse of life beyond us, a visionary overview of reality, of the divine center of love at the core of existence. These, of course, are the great revelatory experiences for which we all long. They seldom come or are appreciated, however, unless we have been working on and listening to our dreams. We have provided many examples of this kind of dream in the preceding chapters.

7a. Sometimes the message of a dream comes through clearly in a direct and understandable sentence or two. I have argued with God that divine messages should speak this way more often. The answer that has come to me is that God is more interested in relating to me than in giving me information. When I puzzle over a dream, I spend more time with the Holy One. We need to use discernment to decide whether our experience comes from the Divine or from some other source. Some people get clear messages to destroy; those do not come from God.

7b. From some deep center of reality the dreamer within speaks. This one knows everything about us, has a wisdom greater than ours, and provides these nightly dramas for our direction and transformation. The one who presents these night dramas knows who we are, where we are, how and why we got off our path, how we can find our way back on that path, where we need to be going, and how we can get there. I believe this dreamer within is none other than the Holy Spirit, who God gives as our inner guide, friend, and comforter.

H. *Ask yourself questions.* If we have not come to any clear meaning of the dream, we can meditate on our written dream. We can think back over the possibilities suggested by the map of human experiences that we have provided. We can mull over the dream, asking ourselves questions like these:

- Is the dream speaking of pains and guilts of the past or of the present?
- Could it be telling us that we have lost our way on our journey?
- Could the dream be giving us some hints how to get back on our journey and out of the dead-end street in which we find ourself?
- Could the dream simply be giving us guidance on our inner journey? (St. John Bosco, the great humanitarian priest-teacher, found

the voice of God speaking through his dreams, and his pope directed him to write down all his dream communications. *The Dreams and Visions of St. John Bosco* is a detailed account of how this great spiritual leader was led by his dreams—one of the most complete records of religious dreams available in any religion and culture and, as we have already noted, comparable with the dream record of Gregory of Nazianzen.)

- Do we find at a later time that a dream has given us a hint about the future? (We will never know this if we do not record even a dream that makes no sense at the time.)
- Is the dream warning us that we are on a dangerous course that could lead us into serious problems?
- Is the dream simply encouraging us on our present path, urging us on?
- Is the dreamer within providing a drama on the darkened and silent stage of the soul that can give insight into where we have come from, where we are, and where we may be called to go?
- Is the dream trying to show us a part of ourselves that we are not aware of, and that we do not *want* to be aware of? (Remember that most people in our dreams, along with the central action, represent a part of ourselves.)
- Does the dream open a door into a forgotten area of memory, something we are ashamed of?
- How are we to deal with the numinous evil we encounter in our dream? (In most instances, evil in dreams does not mask itself.)
- Do we find that the dream is presenting us with a symbol that seems to have no connection with our personal lives?
- Is the dream a revelation of the Holy One? Such a dream came to Martin Niemoller. He was confronted in a dream with the Light of God, and he heard the voice of Hitler behind him saying, "Martin, Martin, why didn't you even tell me?" He then awoke and realized that he had not been faithful to his God or church. He had been face to face with Hitler many times and never shared his conviction about Jesus with Hitler. He then spoke out on the faithlessness of his church in Nazi Germany, and he was instrumental in changing the attitude of the church's leaders about their responsibility for the rise of Hitler.

I. *Read the notes about your dreams aloud.* Sometimes when we have not been able to find any insight about a dream, we can read our notes about it out loud to a friend. Often hearing a dream read unlocks its meaning. Sometimes when I read one to my friend John Sanford, the dream reveals itself before he says a word in response. It is important to have a friend who is attuned to spiritual things and can at least take the idea of dreams and dream interpretation seriously.

Not everyone can find a person skilled in dream analysis. If, however, one prays for someone with whom one can discuss the reality of the spiritual world and one's dreams, God's hand will not be foreshortened. The Holy One can still give direction in finding someone to help. Jung once said that we receive the analyst we deserve.

We can ask these other people what they see in a dream. Sometimes they can show us something that was obvious but which we were blind to because we were so close to the dream. Remember, however, that no dream interpretation is to be taken seriously unless it fits, unless it clicks with meaning and relevance to the dreamer. Some people find a group helpful in which dreams are discussed as a part of a larger program.

J. *Consider seeking professional help.* If we are in deep trouble and turmoil and our dreams are chaotic, then it is important to find a professional person to whom we can turn. Again, God will direct us to individuals who can help. Whenever we think our souls are not worth the trouble of travel and money, we devalue the one who found us of enough value that he would have died for us even if we had been the only one. We usually must pay for professional help, and sometimes the fact we do pay can be of help to us. We take it more seriously.

K. *Use your imagination creatively.* We can also use the imagination in other ways than simply dialoguing with the dream symbols or the dreamer within. This requires some knowledge of the use of imagination in prayer such as I have outlined in *The Other Side of Silence.* Here are some suggestions of how this can be done.

1. We can go back into the dream in our waking imagination and allow a dream that was not completed to complete itself. Often this will give us great insight.
2. We can also return to a negative, painful, and destructive dream and imagine that, with Christ at our side, instead of coming out to the original tragic or destructive conclusion, the dream came out to quite another one. Sometimes reversing a negative dream can actually change the destructive aspects of one's inner life which led to the dream. Dr. Rosaline Cartwright, a University of Illinois psychology professor, has advocated just such a method of reshaping one's dreams in order to give relief to suffering patients.
3. Even with dreams that are not tragic but that leave us puzzled or frightened, we can return into those dreams with Christ as our companion. He can show us their meaning and bring us peace. The one who conquered death and evil can handle any situation that a dream presents.

L. *Write down some conclusions.* When we have finished our work with a dream, it is very helpful to write down what the dream has meant in a paragraph or two. This concludes the process of working on a dream and also sometimes adds some final insights about the dream and one's life. Every message that is given through dreams or the unconscious needs to be carefully discerned and weighed by our best rational and conscious abilities.

M. *Remember that dreams are not good or bad in themselves.* "Good" dreams show us the potentiality that lies ahead and into which we can step if we set our will to it. "Bad" dreams show us what needs to be avoided in our lives. Being as lazy as most of us are, bad dreams often have a more positive effect on us than good dreams, because they frighten us into action.

N. *Actualize the dream situation.* When I had a dream of driving a truck backwards downhill and being unable to control it, it was necessary that I first stop and see in what way I was going backwards and out of control. Then I needed to take steps to change that situation in my life. When I dreamed of a snakebite, I was told that I had been impregnated by the deep unconscious and that a positive potential lay ahead. However, unless I got up early and worked at my writing, that potential would not have been realized. When a great experience is given in a dream, it is our natural inclination to simply bask in it. In order to actualize an experience, we need at least to write poetry or a story about the experience. This activity may lead us to see what aspect of our lives needs to be emphasized and given freedom so that the positive experience can be fulfilled.

Most people in most places have viewed some dreams as divine gifts to increase understanding and provide direction for life both here and into eternity. Jung has suggested that only the people of Europe and their descendants have lost touch with the spiritual world to which dreams give access. They have also ignored dreams themselves, which are still a means of gaining access to that dimension of reality. However, for reasons I have set forth at length in my book, *Christianity as Psychology,* Jung did not treat the figure of the Risen Christ in his writings, nor did he find this historical event meaningful.

Creative Imagination Transforming a Dream

A long-time friend of mine has been working on her dreams for nearly two decades. She is a creative artist with great potential in many areas. She is married and has one child. Her actual situation is a happy one—a fine and loving husband, a capable child, and many accomplishments to her credit—yet she has a difficult time seeing her own self-worth. This devaluation came from her parents who have been part of a religious sect that allows salvation only for those within the sect. Others are damned. My friend has broken from the sect and is trying to establish her own identity and value.

She had the following dream:

I was with a group of women; it was some type of party but very boring to me. I decided to leave early, but before going I noticed a small baby lying on a couch. The poor child looked as if it hadn't been fed recently.

I decided to breast-feed the child, knowing full well that I wouldn't have any milk. Well, to my surprise, the milk began to flow. The baby became cheerful, laughing and happy.

The mother came; she looked like an irresponsible young thing. I thought that she was going to take the baby and go home, but she preferred to party. And in leaving, she told me that the baby was retarded anyway.

My friend realized that this dream spoke of her own vision of herself. It portrayed her inner idiot. A few days later she wrote the following fantasy, which lifted her mood and gave her a real sense of value once again. Seldom have I seen a better example of the process of turning a dream around in imaginative prayer.

I am sitting and cursing myself for being such a fool! "I am nothing," I tell myself. "Unintelligent, worthless—an idiot!" How I hate myself. Who would ever want and care for me?

The more I tell myself these things, of course, the gloomier I get. The world is horrible! No redemption, happiness, nothing!

The time passes, and I feel there's no hope. Hopelessness completely takes over. I am temporarily shaken from this mood, for a knock comes on the door—I open it, and there before me stands a most hideous-looking hag! She is holding a bundle. The bundle, of course, is a baby.

She tells me to take care of it for awhile. "No one else will," she said. She had been door-to-door, but each person had refused her.

The hag told me just to care for the child awhile.

Well, certainly I thought of refusing. I don't have time to care for any baby. And what right does the ugly creature standing in front of me have to tell me to take care of a brat!

The hag's eyes looked as if they were reaching to my very soul. I began to tremble. "Well," I said, "don't be too long." She said, "I won't be long, and I thank you." She handed me the baby and left.

It scarcely weighed anything, and I thought maybe the woman had fooled me and handed me nothing but blankets.

I began to take the blankets away from the child. I gave a scream of fright, for I was holding a most deformed-looking child. It was the most hideous of idiots. I put the child down and ran away from it! "What has this woman done to me?" I dared not enter into that room again.

After awhile, the child began to whimper. It was probably hungry, but I dared not feed it, let alone touch it. What was I to do?

The child then began to cry. A pathetic, desperate cry of complete helplessness. No one wanted it, no one loved or cared for it. One would rather have it rot than touch it.

The crying increased! What was I to do? I began wringing my hands in desperation. The child needed help, and I was the one left to do it.

I went into the room to the child. I looked into its face. How revolting! How horrible! I picked the baby up, and it quit crying. I could barely look into its face.

I had no bottle with which to feed it; it was too young to drink from a cup. What was I to do? My breasts began to throb. They felt hardened and full, as the breasts of a woman who nurses her child.

My blouse became soaked with milk that was pouring out of my breasts. How could this be? I have no baby myself.

I put the idiot to my breasts and he eagerly began drinking from my life. I looked down at the deformed head and little body, its twisted arms and legs. The color of its skin was not even normal.

"How pathetic," I said. "No one to care for the wretched creature. No one to love it."

I began to stroke its head and arms. Its claw-like hand grabbed one of my fingers. It had finally found someone.

I began to cry! Tears of compassion; tears of hope; tears of joy; tears of love; tears for this baby. I had reached out and touched someone who needed love. I quickly forgot my own helplessness, uselessness. I was looking down into the face of my own inner idiot who until this time I dared not look at and recognize—this inner idiot who needs love, nourishment, and care. If I don't care for this idiot, I will be thrown into despair and inner death.

My tears washed the child's head. He turned from my breast and looked into my face and smiled and laughed. His face no longer looked ugly and frightening. I was looking into the face of the Christ Child. The Christ Child in me.

I turned and looked at the open door. There standing in the doorway was a beautiful woman. She told me that she had come to take the child, and appreciated what I had done for this little one. I realized that this beautiful woman was the hag that first brought me the Child.

Conclusion: A Task for Christian Ministry

We come to the end of our study of the Christian interpretation of dreams. We have found that throughout the Old Testament, Apocrypha, and New Testament the dream is viewed as one important vehicle through which the Divine communicates with human beings. The same tradition still continues within Eastern Orthodox Christianity, and it continued in Western Christianity until the worldview of Aristotle and nineteenth-century science gradually took over the thinking of the Western world. This view of reality and how we know it has no place for a nonphysical world or an experience of it. In the nineteenth century most educated people accepted as inevitable the conclusion that only material reality and rational thought were significant and provided meaningful experience. There was no place for the dream or revelation, and so consideration of the dream as communication with a spiritual world or with the Divine simply disappeared. However, people still found their dreams fascinating, but without a critical view of the dream interpretation, this practice became silly and superstitious.

Most Christian theology accepted these conclusions. Christian ministry is *knowing* the love of God revealed in Jesus Christ, accepting that love for ourselves, and sharing that love with other human beings in concrete actions and attitudes. For most of us living in the last part of the twentieth century it is impossible to accept the reality of God without some experience of the Divine. Authority and rational thought are no longer convincing enough to us. We need a theological framework in which Divine-human communication is possible. Unless we can consider that possibility, consideration of dreams becomes absurd. Prayer and meditation also became absurd or superstitious or were left to New Age sects to explore. As I indicated earlier, modern science is much less dogmatic and more open to the possibility that we are in touch with more than a purely meaningless material world. We do not know enough to be dogmatically atheistic.

A careful and critical understanding of the dream gives us one evidence that such communication is possible. Baron von Hügel and A. E. Taylor gave me a theological framework in which Divine-human relationship was possible, but neither gave me a method by which I could be sure that a caring God was reaching out to me. However, as I listened to my dreams, I found a presence wiser than I trying to guide me through my difficulties to wholeness, a wholeness that was possible only when I continued to be in touch with the infinitely loving Holy One. As I have shared this path with others, first with the congregation at St. Luke's in Monrovia, then with the students at Notre Dame, and then in many years of lecturing, I found that many people who took these ideas seriously found a new vitality in their religious lives, a new meaning to prayer and a new incentive to actions of caring and social justice. Agnostic students at Notre Dame could no longer maintain their stance when they recorded the mystery and depth of their dream life and many returned to their Christian roots. Once they took the dream seriously from a religious point of view, they found a whole new realm of religious experience and interest opened to them through contact with something beyond the bounds of the ordinary church practice they had known.

A large part of mainline Christianity, particularly at the academic seminary level, is at present saddled with the prejudice of modern culture that only the material and the rational are real and significant. Large portions of our Christian tradition have been ignored. Little consideration is given to the healing ministry that was so central to the ministry of Jesus and the early church, and very few seminaries train people in this practice. I have shown the centrality of healing within the Christian community in *Psychology, Medicine and Christian Healing*. Few classes are offered in our seminaries on the practice of private prayer or on how we can listen to one another and care for one another. Listening to the dream can help to break us out of this prejudice and realize that God, the Holy Spirit, and the spiritual realm are very close to us. At the same time we find that the dreamer within is trying to guide us toward fulfillment.

Many will object, as they have about other matters: "But isn't this dangerous, this consideration of the murky, irrational, unconscious depths of human beings?" Most real living requires risks. Without risk our lives peter out in dead-end streets. But I would suggest that a religion that offers no experiential contact with the sacrificial love of the risen Christ is more dangerous. When religion is dead or merely conventional, the involuntary and unconscious forces may be either projected out upon others, invoking the cult of war and hate, or else they may break forth in the individual in depression and anxiety and psychosomatic illness. Some people should not delve in the unconscious; they can better profit from the sacramental life of the Christian community, and they should be guided by spiritual guides who know the dangers of plunging into the depth of ourselves and also the values of real relationship with God and the spiritual domain.

Probably the best place for the practice of dream study and interpretation is within the Christian community. This institution with all of its failings offers a stability and knowledge of historical values and practices that are most important when we deal with anything as potent as the dream and the deep powers of the spiritual world that it expresses. The very conservatism of the church is our safeguard when we deal with the dream and the realms of reality that it expresses. Christian leaders need training in this aspect of our lives.

We do not need to turn over the interest in dreams to the New Age counterculture or to professional psychology. The Christian community has a long and vital tradition concerning the way the Divine and the spiritual dimensions of reality touch human beings in their dreams and visions. On the whole this has been forgotten. We need to examine the evidence that we have collected over thirty years. We also need to incorporate the insights of depth psychology. We need to have men and women who are trained to teach others the religious values of dreams and to guide individuals on their journeys toward wholeness in this life and fulfillment in eternity.

Appendix A

Tertullian: *A Treatise on the Soul*—Chapters 44–49

Chapter 44: The story of Hermotimus, and the sleeplessness of the emperor Nero. No separation of the soul from the body until death.

With regard to the case of Hermotimus, they say that he used to be deprived of his soul in his sleep, as if it wandered away from his body like a person on a holiday trip. His wife betrayed the strange peculiarity. His enemies, finding him asleep, burnt his body, as if it were a corpse: when his soul returned too late, it appropriated (I suppose) to itself the guilt of the murder. However the good citizens of Clazomenae consoled poor Hermotimus with a temple, into which no woman ever enters, because of the infamy of this wife. Now why this story? In order that, since the vulgar belief so readily holds sleep to be the separation of the soul from the body, credulity should not be encouraged by this case of Hermotimus. It must certainly have been a much heavier sort of slumber: one would presume it was the nightmare, or perhaps that diseased languor which Soranus suggests in opposition to the nightmare, or else some such malady as that which the fable has fastened upon Epimenides, who slept on some fifty years or so. Suetonius, however, informs us that Nero never dreamt, and Theopompus says the same thing about Thrasymedes; but Nero at the close of his life did with some difficulty dream after some excessive alarm. What indeed would be said, if the case of Hermotimus were believed to be such that the repose of his soul was a state of actual idleness during sleep, and a positive separation from his body? You may conjecture it to be anything but such a licence of the soul as admits of flights away from the body without death, and that by continual recurrence, as if habitual to its state and constitution. If indeed such a thing were told me to have happened at any time to the soul—resembling a total eclipse of the sun or the moon—I should verily suppose that the occurrence had been caused by God's own inter-position, for it would not be unreasonable for a man to receive admonition from the Divine Being either in the way of warning or of alarm, as by a flash of lightning, or by a sudden stroke of death; only it would be much the more natural conclusion to believe that this process should be by a dream, because if it must be supposed to be, (as the hypothesis we are resisting assumes it to be) not a dream, the occurrence ought rather to happen to a man whilst he is wide awake.

Chapter 45: Dreams an incidental effect of the soul's activity. Ecstasy.

We are bound to expound at this point what is the opinion of Christians respecting dreams, as incidents of sleep, and as no slight or trifling excitements of the soul, which we have declared to be always occupied and active owing to its perpetual movement, which again is a proof and evidence of its divine quality and immortality. When, therefore, rest accrues to human bodies, it being their own especial comfort, the soul, disdaining a repose which is not natural to it, never rests; and since it receives no help from the limbs of the body, it uses its own. Imagine a gladiator without his instruments or arms, and a charioteer without his team, but still gesticulating the entire course and exertion of their respective employments: there is the fight, there is the struggle; but the effort is a vain one. Nevertheless the whole procedure seems to be gone through, although it evidently has not been really effected. There is the act, but not the effect. This power we call *ecstasy,* in which the sensuous soul stands out of itself, in a way which even resembles madness. [We had better give Tertullian's own succinct definition: *Excessus sensus et amentiae instar.*] Thus in the very beginning sleep was inaugurated by ecstasy: "And God sent an ecstasy upon Adam, and he slept" [Gen. 2:21]. The sleep came on his body to cause it to rest, but the ecstasy fell on his soul to remove rest: from that very circumstance it still happens ordinarily (and from the order results the nature of the case) that sleep is combined with ecstasy. In fact, with what real feeling, and anxiety, and suffering do we experience joy, and sorrow, and alarm in our dreams! Whereas we should not be moved by any such emotions, by what would be the merest fantasies of course, if when we dream we were masters of ourselves (unaffected by ecstasy). In these dreams, indeed, good actions are useless, and crimes harmless; for we shall no more be condemned for visionary acts of sin, than we shall be crowned for imaginary martyrdom. But how, you will ask, can the soul remember its dreams, when it is said to be without any mastery over its own operations? This memory must be an especial gift of the ecstatic condition of which we are treating, since it arises not from any failure of healthy action, but entirely from natural process; nor does it expel mental function—it withdraws it for a time. It is one thing to shake, it is another thing to move; one thing to destroy, another thing to agitate. That, therefore, which memory supplies betokens soundness of mind; and that which a sound mind ecstatically experiences whilst the memory remains unchecked, is a kind of madness. We are accordingly not said to be mad, but to dream, in that state; to be in the full possession also of our mental faculties [*prudentes*], if we are at any time. For although the power to exercise these faculties [*sapere*] may be dimmed in us, it is still not extinguished; except that it may seem to be itself absent at the very time that the ecstasy is energizing in us in its special manner, in such wise as to bring before us images of a sound mind and of wisdom, even as it does those of aberration.

Chapter 46: Diversity of dreams and visions. Epicurus thought lightly of them, though generally most highly valued. Instances of dreams.

We now find ourselves constrained to express an opinion about the character of the dreams by which the soul is excited. And when shall we arrive at the subject of death? And on such a question I would say, When God shall permit: that admits of no long delay which must needs happen at all events. Epicurus has given it as his opinion that dreams are altogether vain things; (but he says this) when liberating the Deity from all sort of care, and dissolving the entire order of the world, and giving to all things the aspect of merest chance, casual in their issues, fortuitous in their nature. Well, now, if such be the nature of things, there must be some chance even for truth, because it is impossible for it to be the only thing to be exempted from the fortune which is due to all things. Homer has assigned two gates to dreams,—the *horny* one of truth, the *ivory* one of error and delusion [*Odyssey,* 19.562ff.; *Aeneid,* 6.894]. For, they say, it is possible to see through horn, whereas ivory is untransparent. Aristotle, while expressing his opinion that dreams are in most cases untrue, yet acknowledges that there is some truth in them. The people of Telmessus will not admit that dreams are in any case unmeaning, but they blame their own weakness when unable to conjecture their signification. Now, who is such a stranger to human experience as not sometimes to have perceived some truth in dreams? I shall force a blush from Epicurus, if I only glance at some few of the more remarkable instances. Herodotus [1.107ff.] relates how that Astyages, king of the Medes, saw in a dream issuing from the womb of his virgin daughter a flood which inundated Asia; and again, in the year which followed her marriage, he saw a vine growing out from the same part of her person, which overspread the whole of Asia. The same story is told prior to Herodotus by Charon of Lampsacus. Now they who interpreted these visions did not deceive the mother when they destined her son for so great an enterprise, for Cyrus both inundated and overspread Asia. Philip of Macedon, before he became a father, had seen imprinted on the pudenda of his consort Olympias the form of a small ring, with a lion as a seal. He had concluded that an offspring from her was out of the question (I suppose because the lion only becomes once a father), when Aristodemus or Aristophon happened to conjecture that nothing of an unmeaning or empty import lay under that seal, but that a son of very illustrious character was portended. They who know anything of Alexander recognise in him the lion of that small ring. Ephorus writes to this effect. Again, Heraclides has told us, that a certain woman of Himera beheld in a dream Dionysius' tyranny over Sicily. Euphorion has publicly recorded as a fact, that, previous to giving birth to Seleucus, his mother Laodice foresaw that he was destined for the empire of Asia. I find again from Strabo, that it was owing to a dream that even Mithridates took possession of Pontus; and I further learn from Callisthenes that it was from the indication of a dream that Baraliris the Illyrian stretched his dominion from the Molossi to the frontiers of Macedon. The Romans, too, were acquainted with dreams of this kind. From a dream Marcus Tullius (Cicero) had learnt how that one, who was yet only a little boy, and in a private station, who was also plain Julius Octavius, and personally unknown to (Cicero) himself, was the destined Augustus, and the suppressor and destroyer of (Rome's) civil discords. This is recorded in the Commentaries of Vitellius. But visions of this prophetic kind were not confined to predictions of supreme power; for they indicated perils also, and catastrophes: as, for instance, when Caesar was absent from the battle of Philippi through illness, and thereby escaped the sword of Brutus and Cassius, and then although he expected to encounter greater danger still from the enemy in the field, he quitted his tent for it, in obedience to a vision of Artorius, and so escaped (the capture by the enemy, who shortly after took possession of the tent); as, again, when the daughter of Polycrates of Samos foresaw the crucifixion which awaited him from the anointing of the sun and the bath of Jupiter. [See an account of her vision and its interpretation in Herodotus 3.124.] So likewise in sleep revelations are made of high honours and eminent talents; remedies are also discovered,thefts brought to light, and treasures indicated. Thus Cicero's eminence, whilst he was still a little boy, was foreseen by his nurse. The swan from the breast of Socrates soothing men, is his disciple Plato. The boxer Leonymus is cured by Achilles in his dreams. Sophocles the tragic poet discovers, as he was dreaming, the golden crown, which had been lost from the citadel of Athens. Neoptolemus the tragic actor, through intimations in his sleep from Ajax himself, saves from destruction the hero's tomb on the Rhoetean shore before Troy; and as he removes the decayed stones, he returns enriched with gold. How many commentators and chroniclers vouch for this phenomenon? There are Artemon, Antiphon, Strato, Philochorus, Epicharmus Serapion, Cratippus, and Dionysius of Rhodes, and Hermippus—the entire literature of the age. I shall only laugh at all, if indeed I ought to laugh at the man who fancied that he was going to persuade us that Saturn dreamt before anybody else; which we can only believe if Aristotle, (who would fain help us to such an opinion) lived prior to any other person. Pray forgive me for laughing. Epicharmus, indeed, as well as Philochorus the Athenian, assigned the very highest place among divinations to dreams. The whole world is full of oracles of this description: there are the oracles of Amphiaraus at Oropus, of Amphilochus at Mallus, of Sarpedon in the Troad, of Trophonius in Boeotia, of Mopsus in Cilicia, of Hermione in Macedon, of Pasiphae in Laconia. Then, again, there are others, which with their original foundations, rites, and historians, together with the entire literature of dreams, Hermippus of Berytus in five portly volumes will give you all the account of, even to satiety. But the Stoics are very fond of saying that God, in his most watchful providence over every institution, gave us dreams amongst other preservatives of the arts and sciences of divination, as the especial support of the natural oracle. So much for the dreams to which credit has to be ascribed even by ourselves, although we must interpret them in another sense. As for all other oracles, at which no one ever dreams, what else must we declare concerning them, than that they are the diabolical contrivance of those spirits who even at that time dwelt in the eminent persons themselves, or aimed at reviving the memory of them as the mere stage of their evil purposes, going so far as to counterfeit a divine power under their shape and form, and, with equal persistence in evil, deceiving men by their very boons of remedies, warnings, and forecasts,—the only effect of which was to injure their victims the more they helped them; while the means whereby they rendered the help withdrew them from all search after the true God, by insinuating into their minds ideas of the false one? And of course so pernicious an influence as this is not shut up nor limited within the boundaries of shrines and temples: it roams abroad, it flies through the air, and all the while is free and unchecked. So that nobody can doubt that our very homes lie open to these diabolical spirits, who beset their human prey with their fantasies not only in their chapels but also in their chambers.

Chapter 47: Dreams variously classified. Some are God-sent, as the dreams of Nebuchadnezzar; others simply products of nature.

We declare, then, that dreams are inflicted on us mainly by demons, although they sometimes turn out true and favourable to us.

When, however, with the deliberate aim after evil, of which we have just spoken, they assume a flattering and captivating style, they show themselves proportionately vain, and deceitful, and obscure, and wanton, and impure. And no wonder that the images partake of the character of the realities. But from God—who has promised, indeed, "to pour out the grace of the Holy Spirit upon all flesh, and has ordained that His servants and His handmaids should see visions as well as utter prophecies" [Joel 2:28]—must all those visions be regarded as emanating, which may be compared to the actual grace of God, as being honest, holy, prophetic, inspired, instructive, inviting to virtue, the bountiful nature of which causes them to overflow even to the profane, since God, with grand impartiality, "sends His showers and sunshine on the just and on the unjust" [Matt. 5:45]. It was, indeed by an inspiration from God that Nebuchadnezzar dreamt his dreams [Dan. 2:1ff.]; and almost the greater part of mankind get their knowledge of God from dreams. Thus it is that, as the mercy of God superabounds to the heathen, so the temptation of the evil one encounters the saints, from whom he never withdraws his malignant efforts to steal over them as best he may in their very sleep, if unable to assault them when they are awake. The third class of dreams will consist of those which the soul itself apparently creates for itself from an intense application to special circumstances. Now, inasmuch as the soul cannot dream of its own accord (for even Epicharmus is of this opinion), how can it become to itself the cause of any vision? Then must this class of dreams be abandoned to the action of nature, reserving for the soul, even when in the ecstatic condition, the power of enduring whatever incidents befall it? Those, moreover, which evidently proceed neither from God, nor from diabolical inspiration, nor from the soul, being beyond the reach as well of ordinary expectation, usual interpretation, or the possibility of being intelligibly related, will have to be ascribed in a separate category to what is purely and simply the ecstatic state and its peculiar conditions.

Chapter 48: Causes and circumstances of dreams. What best contributed to efficient dreaming.

They say that dreams are more sure and clear when they happen towards the end of the night, because then the vigour of the soul emerges, and heavy sleep departs. As to the seasons of the year, dreams are calmer in spring, since summer relaxes, and winter somehow hardens, the soul; while autumn, which in other respects is trying to health, is apt to enervate the soul by the lusciousness of its fruits. Then, again, as regards the position of one's body during sleep, one ought not to lie on his back, nor on his right side, nor so as to wrench his intestines, as if their cavity were reversely stretched: a palpitation of the heart would ensue, or else a pressure on the liver would produce a painful disturbance of the mind. But however this be, I take it that it all amounts to ingenious conjecture rather than certain proof (although the author of the conjecture be no less a man than Plato [*Timaeus* 71]); and possibly all may be no other than the result of chance. But, generally speaking, dreams will be under control of a man's will, if they be capable of direction at all; for we must not examine what *opinion* on the one hand, and *superstition* on the other, have to prescribe for the treatment of dreams, in the matter of distinguishing and modifying different sorts of food. As for the *superstition,* we have an instance when fasting is prescribed for such persons as mean to submit to the sleep which is necessary for receiving the oracle, in order that such abstinence may produce the required purity; while we find an instance of the *opinion* when the disciples of Pythagoras, in order to attain the same end, reject the bean as an aliment which would load the stomach, and produce indigestion. But the three brethren, who were the companions of Daniel, being content with pulse alone, to escape the contamination of the royal dishes [Dan. 1:8-19], received from God, besides other wisdom, the gift especially of penetrating and explaining the sense of dreams. For my own part, I hardly know whether fasting would not simply make me dream so profoundly, that I should not be aware whether I had in fact dreamt at all. Well, then, you ask, has not sobriety something to do in this matter? Certainly it is as much concerned in this as it is in the entire subject: if it contributes some good service to superstition, much more does it to religion. For even demons require such discipline from their dreamers as a gratification to their divinity, because they know that it is acceptable to God, since Daniel (to quote him again) "ate no pleasant bread" for the space of three weeks [10:2ff.]. This abstinence, however, he used in order to please God by humiliation, and not for the purpose of producing a sensibility and wisdom for his soul previous to receiving communication by dreams and visions, as if it were not rather to effect such action in an ecstatic state. This *sobriety,* then, (in which our question arises,) will have nothing to do with exciting ecstasy, but will rather serve to recommend its being wrought by God.

Chapter 49: No soul naturally exempt from dreams.

As for those persons who suppose that infants do not dream, on the ground that all the functions of the soul throughout life are accomplished according to the capacity of age, they ought to observe attentively their tremors, and nods, and bright smiles as they sleep, and from such facts understand that they are the emotions of their soul as it dreams, which so readily escape to the surface through the delicate tenderness of their infantine body. The fact, however, that the African nation of the Atlantes are said to pass through the night in a deep lethargic sleep, brings down on them the censure that something is wrong in the constitution of their soul. Now either report, which is occasionally calumnious against barbarians, deceived Herodotus [4.184], or else a large force of demons of this sort domineers in those barbarous regions. Since, indeed, Aristotle remarks of a certain hero of Sardinia that he used to withhold the power of visions and dreams from such as resorted to his shrine for inspiration, it must lie at the will and caprice of the demons to take away as well as to confer the faculty of dreams; and from this circumstance may have arisen the remarkable fact (which we have mentioned) of Nero and Thrasymedes only dreaming so late in life. We, however, derive dreams from God. Why, then, did not the Atlantes receive the dreaming faculty from God, because there is really no nation which is now a stranger to God, since the gospel flashes its glorious light through the world to the ends of the earth? Could it then be that rumour deceived Aristotle, or is this caprice still the way of demons? (Let us take any view of the case), only do not let it be imagined that any soul is by its natural constitution exempt from dreams.

Appendix

B

Origen: *Against Celsus*— Book 1, Chapter 48

Chapter 48

Although the Jew, then, may offer no defence for himself in the instances of Ezekiel and Isaiah, when we compare the opening of the heavens to Jesus, and the voice that was heard by Him, to the similar cases which we find recorded in Ezekiel and Isaiah, or any other of the prophets, we nevertheless, so far as we can, shall support our position, maintaining that, as it is a matter of belief that in a dream impressions have been brought before the minds of many, some relating to divine things, and others to future events of this life, and this either with clearness or in an enigmatic manner,—a fact which is manifest to all who accept the doctrine of providence; so how is it absurd to say that the mind which could receive impressions in a dream should be impressed also in a waking vision, for the benefit either of him on whom the impressions are made, or of those who are to hear the account of them from him? And as in a dream we fancy that we hear, and that the organs of hearing are actually impressed, and that we see with our eyes—although neither the bodily organs of sight nor hearing are affected, but it is the mind alone which has these sensations—so there is no absurdity in believing that similar things occurred to the prophets, when it is recorded that they witnessed occurrences of a rather wonderful kind, as when they either heard the words of the Lord or beheld the heavens opened. For I do not suppose that the visible heaven was actually opened, and its physical structure divided, in order that Ezekiel might be able to record such an occurrence. Should not, therefore, the same be believed of the Saviour by every intelligent hearer of the Gospels?—although such an occurrence may be a stumbling-block to the simple, who in their simplicity would set the whole world in movement, and split in sunder the compact and mighty body of the whole heavens. But he who examines such matters more profoundly will say, that there being, as the Scripture calls it, a kind of general divine perception which the blessed man alone knows how to discover, according to the saying of Solomon, "Thou shalt find the knowledge of God;" and as there are various forms of this perceptive power, such as a faculty of vision which can naturally see things that are better than bodies, among which are ranked the cherubim and seraphim; and a faculty of hearing which can perceive voices which have not their being in the air; and a sense of taste which can make use of living bread that has come down from heaven, and that giveth life unto the world; and so also a sense of smelling, which scents such things as leads Paul to say that he is a sweet savour of Christ unto God; and a sense of touch by which John says that he "handled with his hands of the Word of life";—the blessed prophets having discovered this divine perception, and seeing and hearing in this divine manner, and tasting likewise, and smelling, so to speak, with no sensible organs of perception, and laying hold on the Logos by faith, so that a healing effluence from it comes upon them, saw in this manner what they record as having seen, and heard what they say they heard, and were affected in a similar manner to what they describe when eating the roll of a book that was given them. And so also Isaac smelled the savour of his son's divine garments, and added to the spiritual blessing these words: "See, the savour of my son is as the savour of a full field which the Lord blessed." And similarly to this, and more as a matter to be understood by the mind than to be perceived by the senses, Jesus touched the leper, to cleanse him, as I think, in a twofold sense,—freeing him not only, as the multitude heard, from the visible leprosy by visible contact, but also from that other leprosy, by His truly divine touch. It is in this way, accordingly, that John testifies when he says, "I beheld the Spirit descending from heaven like a dove, and it abode upon Him. And I knew Him not; but He that sent me to baptize with water, the same said to me, Upon whom you will see the Spirit descending, and abiding on Him, the same is He that baptizeth with the Holy Ghost. And I saw, and bear witness, that this is the Son of God." Now it was to Jesus that the heavens were opened; and on that occasion no one except John is recorded to have seen them opened. But with respect to this opening of the heavens, the Saviour, foretelling to His disciples that it would happen, and that they would see it, says, "Verily, verily, I say unto you, Ye shall see the heavens opened, and the angels of God ascending and descending upon the Son of man." And so Paul was carried away into the third heaven, having previously seen it opened, since he was a disciple of Jesus. It does not, however, belong to our present object to explain why Paul says, "Whether in the body, I know not; or whether out of the body, I know not: God knoweth." But I shall add to my argument even those very points which Celsus imagines, viz., that Jesus Himself related the account of the opening of the heavens, and the descent of the Holy Spirit upon Him at the Jordan in the form of a dove, although the Scripture does not assert that He said that He saw it. For this great man did not perceive that it was not in keeping with Him who commanded His disciples on the occasion of the vision on the mount, "Tell what ye have seen to no man, until the Son of man be risen from the dead," to have related to His disciples what was seen and heard by John at the Jordan. For it may be observed as a trait of the character of Jesus, that He on all occasions avoided unnecessary talk about Himself; and on that account said, "If I speak of Myself, My witness is not true." And since He avoided unnecessary talk about Himself, and preferred to show by acts rather than words that He was the Christ, the Jews for that reason said to Him, "If Thou art the Christ, tell us plainly." And as it is a Jew who, in the work of Celsus, uses the language to Jesus regarding the appearance of the Holy Spirit in the form of a dove, "This is your own testimony, unsupported save by one of those who were sharers of your punishment, whom you adduce," it is necessary for us to show him that such a statement is not appropriately placed in the mouth of a Jew. For the Jews do not connect John with Jesus, nor the punishment of John with that of Christ. And by this instance, this man who boasts of universal knowledge is convicted of not knowing what words he ought to ascribe to a Jew engaged in a disputation with Jesus.

[References: Prov. 2:5; 2 Cor. 2:15; 1 John 1:1; Ezek. 3:1ff.; Gen. 27:27; Matt. 8:3; John 1:32ff.; John 1:51; 2 Cor. 12:2; Matt. 17:9; John 5:31; and John 10:24.]

Appendix

C

Gregory of Nyssa: *On the Making of Man*— Chapter 13

Chapter 13: A rationale of sleep, of yawning, and of dreams.

1. This life of our bodies, material and subject to flux, always advancing by way of motion, finds the power of its being in this, that it never rests from its motion: and as some river, flowing on by its own impulse, keeps the channel in which it runs well filled, yet is not seen in the same water always at the same place, but part of it glides away while part comes flowing on, so, too, the material element of our life here suffers change in the continuity of its succession of opposites by way of motion and flux, so that it never can desist from change, but in its inability to rest keeps up unceasingly its motion alternating by like ways: and if it should ever cease moving it will assuredly have cessation also of its being.

2. For instance, emptying succeeds fulness, and on the other hand after emptiness comes in turn a process of filling: sleep relaxes the strain of waking, and, again, awakening braces up what had become slack: and neither of these abides continually, but both give way, each at the other's coming; nature thus by their inter-change so renewing herself as, while partaking of each in turn, to pass from the one to the other without break. For that the living creature should always be exerting itself in its operations produces a certain rupture and severance of the overstrained part; and continually quiescence of the body brings about a certain dissolution and laxity in its frame: but to be in touch with each of these at the proper times in a moderate degree is a staying-power of nature, which, by continual transference to the opposed states, gives herself in each of them rest from the other. Thus she finds the body on the strain through wakefulness, and devises relaxation for the strain by means of sleep, giving the perceptive faculties rest for the time from their operations, loosing them like horses from the chariots after the race.

3. Further, rest at proper times is necessary for the framework of the body, that the nutriment may be diffused over the whole body through the passages which it contains, without any strain to hinder its progress. For just as certain misty vapours are drawn up from the recesses of the earth when soaked with rain, whenever the sun heats it with rays of any considerable warmth, so a similar result happens in the earth that is in us, when the nutriment within is heated up by natural warmth; and the vapours, being naturally of upward tendency and airy nature, and aspiring to that which is above them, come to be in the region of the head like smoke penetrating the joints of a wall: then they are dispersed thence by exhalation to the passages of the organs of sense, and by them the senses are of course rendered inactive, giving way to the transit of these vapours. For the eyes are pressed upon by the eyelids when some leaden instrument, as it were (I mean such a weight as that I have spoken of), lets down the eyelid upon the eyes; and the hearing, being dulled by these same vapours, as though a door were placed upon the acoustic organs, rests from its natural operation: and such a condition is sleep, when the sense is at rest in the body, and altogether ceases from the operation of its natural motion, so that the digestive processes of nutriment may have free course for transmission by the vapours through each of the passages.

4. And for this reason, if the apparatus of the organs of sense should be closed and sleep hindered by some occupation, the nervous system, becoming filled with the vapours, is naturally and spontaneously extended so that the part which has had its density increased by the vapours is rarefied by the process of extension, just as those do who squeeze the water out of clothes by vehement wringing: and, seeing that the parts about the pharynx are somewhat circular, and nervous tissue abounds there, whenever there is need for the expulsion from that part of the density of the vapours—since it is impossible that the part which is circular in shape should be separated directly, but only by being distended in the outline of its circumference—for this reason, by checking the breath in a yawn the chin is moved downwards so as to leave a hollow to the uvula, and all the interior parts being arranged in the figure of a circle, that smoky denseness which had been detained in the neighbouring parts is emitted together with the exit of the breath. And often the like may happen even after sleep when any portion of those vapours remains in the region spoken of undigested and unexhaled.

5. Hence the mind of man clearly proves its claim to connection with his nature, itself also co-operating and moving with the nature in its sound and waking state, but remaining unmoved when it is abandoned to sleep, unless any one supposes that the imagery of dreams is a motion of the mind exercised in sleep. We for our part say that it is only the conscious and sound action of the intellect which

we ought to refer to mind; and as to the fantastic nonsense which occurs to us in sleep, we suppose that some appearances of the operations of the mind are accidentally moulded in the less rational part of the soul; for the soul, being by sleep dissociated from the senses, is also of necessity outside the range of the operations of the mind; for it is through the senses that the union of mind with man takes place; therefore when the senses are at rest, the intellect also must needs be inactive; and an evidence of this is the fact that the dreamer often seems to be in absurd and impossible situations, which would not happen if the soul were then guided by reason and intellect.

6. It seems to me, however, that when the soul is at rest so far as concerns its more excellent faculties (so far, I mean, as concerns the operations of mind and sense), the nutritive part of it alone is operative during sleep, and that some shadows and echoes of those things which happen in our waking moments—of the operations both of sense and of intellect—which are impressed upon it by that part of the soul which is capable of memory, that these, I say, are pictured as chance will have it, some echo of memory still lingering in this division of the soul.

7. With these, then, the man is beguiled, not led to acquaintance with the things that present themselves by any train of thought, but wandering among confused and inconsequent delusions. But just as in his bodily operations, while each of the parts individually acts in some way according to the power which naturally resides in it, there arises also in the limb that is at rest a state sympathetic with that which is in motion, similarly in the case of the soul, even if one part is at rest and another in motion, the whole is affected in sympathy with the part; for it is not possible that the natural unity should be in any way severed, though one of the faculties included in it is in turn supreme in virtue of its active operation. But as, when men are awake and busy, the mind is supreme, and sense ministers to it, yet the faculty which regulates the body is not dissociated from them (for the mind furnishes the food for its wants, the sense receives what is furnished, and the nutritive faculty of the body appropriates to itself that which is given to it), so in sleep the supremacy of these faculties is in some way reversed in us, and while the less rational becomes supreme, the operation of the other ceases indeed, yet is not absolutely extinguished; but while the nutritive faculty is then busied with digestion during sleep, and keeps all our nature occupied with itself, the faculty of sense is neither entirely severed from it (for that cannot be separated which has once been naturally joined), nor yet can its activity revive, as it is hindered by the inaction during sleep of the organs of sense; and by the same reasoning (the mind also being united to the sensitive part of the soul) it would follow that we should say that the mind moves with the latter when it is in motion, and rests with it when it is quiescent.

8. As naturally happens with fire when it is heaped over with chaff, and no breath fans the flame—it neither consumes what lies beside it, nor is entirely quenched, but instead of flame it rises to the air through the chaff in the form of smoke; yet if it should obtain any breath of air, it turns the smoke to flame—in the same way the mind when hidden by the inaction of the senses in sleep is neither able to shine out through them, nor yet is quite extinguished, but has, so to say, a smouldering activity, operating to a certain extent, but unable to operate farther.

9. Again, as a musician, when he touches with the plectrum the slackened strings of a lyre, brings out no orderly melody (for that which is not stretched will not sound), but his hand frequently moves skillfully, bringing the plectrum to the position of the notes so far as place is concerned, yet there is no sound, except that he produces by the vibration of the strings a sort of uncertain and indistinct hum; so in sleep the mechanism of the senses being relaxed, the artist is either quite inactive, if the instrument is completely relaxed by satiety or heaviness; or will act slackly and faintly, if the instrument of the senses does not fully admit of the exercise of its art.

10. For this cause memory is confused, and foreknowledge, though rendered doubtful by uncertain veils, is imaged in shadows of our waking pursuits, and often indicates to us something of what is going to happen: for by its subtlety of nature the mind has some advantage, in ability to behold things, over mere corporeal grossness; yet it cannot make its meaning clear by direct methods, so that the information of the matter in hand should be plain and evident, but its declaration of the future is ambiguous and doubtful—what those who interpret such things call an "enigma."

11. So the butler presses the cluster for Pharaoh's cup: so the baker seemed to carry his baskets; each supposing himself in sleep to be engaged in those services with which he was busied when awake: for the images of their customary occupations imprinted on the prescient element of their soul, gave them for a time the power of foretelling, by this sort of prophecy on the part of the mind, what should come to pass.

12. But if Daniel and Joseph and others like them were instructed by Divine power, without any confusion of perception, in the knowledge of things to come, this is nothing to the present statement; for no one would ascribe this to the power of dreams, since he will be constrained as a consequence to suppose that those Divine appearances also which took place in wakefulness were not a miraculous vision but a result of nature brought about spontaneously. As then, while all men are guided by their own minds, there are some few who are deemed worthy of evident Divine communication; so, while the imagination of sleep naturally occurs in a like and equivalent manner for all, some, not all, share by means of their dreams in some

more Divine manifestation: but to all the rest, even if a foreknowledge of anything does occur as a result of dreams, it occurs in the way we have spoken of.

13. And again, if the Egyptian and the Assyrian king were guided by God to the knowledge of the future, the dispensation wrought by their means is a different thing: for it was necessary that the hidden wisdom of the holy men should be made known, that each of them might not pass his life without profit to the state. For how could Daniel have been known for what he was, if the soothsayers and magicians had not been unequal to the task of discovering the dream? And how could Egypt have been preserved while Joseph was shut up in prison, if his interpretation of the dream had not brought him to notice? Thus we must reckon these cases as exceptional, and not class them with common dreams.

14. But this ordinary seeing of dreams is common to all men, and arises in our fancies in different modes and forms: for either there remain, as we have said, in the reminiscent part of the soul, the echoes of daily occupations; or, as often happens, the constitution of dreams is framed with regard to such and such a condition of the body: for thus the thirsty man seems to be among springs, the man who is in need of food to be at a feast, and the young man in the heat of youthful vigour is beset by fancies corresponding to his passion.

15. I also knew another cause of the fancies of sleep, when attending one of my relations attacked by frenzy; who being annoyed by food being given him in too great quantity for his strength, kept crying out and finding fault with those who were about him for filling intestines with dung and putting them upon him: and when his body was rapidly tending to perspire he blamed those who were with him for having water ready to wet him with as he lay: and he did not cease calling out till the result showed the meaning of these complaints: for all at once a copious sweat broke out over his body, and a relaxation of the bowels explained the weight in the intestines. The same condition then which, while his sober judgment was dulled by disease, his nature underwent, being sympathetically affected by the condition of the body—not being without perception of what was amiss, but being unable clearly to express its pain, by reason of the distraction resulting from the disease—this, probably, if the intelligent principle of the soul were lulled to rest, not from infirmity but by natural sleep, might appear as a dream to one similarly situated, the breaking out of perspiration being expressed by water, and the pain occasioned by the food, by the weight of intestines.

16. This view also is taken by those skilled in medicine, that according to the differences of complaints the visions of dreams appear differently to the patients: that the visions of those of weak stomach are of one kind, those of persons suffering from injury to the cerebral membrane of another, those of persons in fevers of yet another, that

those of patients suffering from bilious and from phlegmatic affections are diverse, and those again of plethoric patients, and of patients in wasting disease, are different; whence we may see that the nutritive and vegetative faculty of the soul has in it by commixture some seed of the intelligent element, which is in some sense brought into likeness to the particular state of the body, being adapted in its fancies according to the complaint which has seized upon it.

17. Moreover, most men's dreams are conformed to the state of their character: the brave man's fancies are of one kind, the coward's of another; the wanton man's dreams of one kind, the continent man's of another; the liberal man and the avaricious man are subject to different fancies; while these fancies are nowhere framed by the intellect, but by the less rational disposition of the soul, which forms even in dreams the semblances of those things to which each is accustomed by the practice of his waking hours.

Appendix

D

St. Augustine: *Letter 9*

Nebridius, who was a very close friend of Augustine, had written him asking: "When at any time it pleases higher (by which I mean heavenly) powers to reveal anything to us by dreams in our sleep, how is this done, my dear Augustin, or what is the method which they use? What, I say, is their method, i.e. by what art or magic, by what agency or enchantments, do they accomplish this?"

Augustine replied:

1. Although you know my mind well, you are perhaps not aware how much I long to enjoy your society. This great blessing, however, God will some day bestow on me. I have read your letter, so genuine in its utterances, in which you complain of your being in solitude, and, as it were, forsaken by your friends, in whose society you found the sweetest charm of life. But what else can I suggest to you than that which I am persuaded is already your exercise? Commune with your own soul, and raise it up, as far as you are able, unto God. For in Him you hold us also by a firmer bond, not by means of bodily images, which we must meanwhile be content to use in remembering each other, but by means of that faculty of thought through which we realize the fact of our separation from each other.

2. In considering your letters, in answering all of which I have certainly had to answer questions of no small difficulty and importance, I was not a little stunned by the one in which you ask me by what means certain thoughts and dreams are put into our minds by higher powers or by superhuman agents. The question is a great one, and, as your own prudence must convince you, would require, in order to its being satisfactorily answered, not a mere letter, but a full oral discussion or a whole treatise. I shall try, however, knowing as I do your talents, to throw out a few germs of thought which may shed light on this question, in order that you may either complete the exhaustive treatment of the subject by your own efforts, or at least

not despair of the possibility of this important matter being investigated with satisfactory results.

3. It is my opinion that every movement of the mind affects in some degree the body. We know that this is patent even to our senses, dull and sluggish though they are, when the movements of the mind are somewhat vehement, as when we are angry, or sad, or joyful. Whence we may conjecture that, in like manner, when thought is busy, although no bodily effect of the mental act is discernible by us, there may be some such effect discernible by beings of aerial or etherial essence whose perceptive faculty is in the highest degree acute,—so much so, that, in comparison with it, our faculties are scarcely worthy to be called perceptive. Therefore these footprints of its motion, so to speak, which the mind impresses on the body, may perchance not only remain, but remain as it were with the force of a habit; and it may be that when these are secretly stirred and played upon, they bear thoughts and dreams into our minds, according to the pleasure of the person moving or touching them: and this is done with marvellous facility. For if, as is manifest, the attainments of our earthborn and sluggish bodies in the department of exercise, e.g. in the playing of musical instruments, dancing on the tightrope, etc., are almost incredible, it is by no means unreasonable to suppose that beings which act with the powers of an aerial or etherial body upon our bodies, and are by the constitution of their natures able to pass unhindered through these bodies, should be capable of much greater quickness in moving whatever they wish, while we, though not perceiving what they do, are nevertheless affected by the results of their activity. We have a somewhat parallel instance in the fact that we do not perceive how it is that superfluity of bile impels us to more frequent outbursts of passionate feeling; and yet it does produce this effect, while this superfluity of bile is itself an effect of our yielding to such passionate feeling.

4. If, however, you hesitate to accept this example as a parallel one, when it is thus cursorily stated by me, turn it over in your thoughts as fully as you can. The mind, if it be continually obstructed by some difficulty in the way of doing and accomplishing what it desires, is thereby made continually angry. For anger, so far as I can judge of its nature, seems to me to be a tumultuous eagerness to take out of the way those things which restrict our freedom of action. Hence it is that usually we vent our anger not only on men, but on such a thing, for example, as the pen with which we write, bruising or breaking it in our passion; and so does the gambler with his dice, the artist with his pencil, and every man with the instrument which he may be using, if he thinks that he is in some way thwarted by it. Now medical men themselves tell us that by these frequent fits of anger bile is increased. But, on the other hand, when the bile is

increased, we are easily, and almost without any provocation whatever, made angry. Thus the effect which the mind has by its movement produced upon the body, is capable in its turn of moving the mind again.

5. These things might be treated at very great length, and our knowledge of the subject might be brought to greater certainty and fulness by a large induction from relevant facts. But take along with this letter the one which I sent you lately concerning images and memory, and study it somewhat more carefully; for it was manifest to me, from your reply, that it had not been fully understood. When to the statements now before you, you add the portion of that letter in which I spoke of a certain natural faculty whereby the mind does in thought add to or take from any object as it pleases, you will see that it is possible for us both in dreams and in waking thoughts to conceive the images of bodily forms which we have never seen.

Appendix
E

St. Augustine: *Letter 159*

The Bishop of Uzala, Evodius, was one of Augustine's early friends. In A.D. 414 he wrote to Augustine (Letter 158), describing certain dreams and visions which made him ask What are we after death? He went on to say:

9. These dreams suggest another question. I do not at this moment concern myself about the mere creations of fancy, which are formed by the emotions of the uneducated. I speak of visitations in sleep, such as the apparition to Joseph in a dream, in the manner experienced in most cases of the kind. In the same manner, therefore, our own friends also who have departed this life before us sometimes come and appear to us in dreams, and speak to us. For I myself remember that Profuturus, and Privatus, and Servilius, holy men who within my recollection were removed by death from our monastery, spoke to me, and that the events of which they spoke came to pass according to their words. Or if it be some other higher spirit that assumes their form and visits our minds, I leave this to the all-seeing eye of Him before whom everything from the highest to the lowest is uncovered. If, therefore, the Lord be pleased to speak through reason to your Holiness on all these questions, I beg you to be so kind as make me partaker of the knowledge which you have received. There is another thing which I have resolved not to omit mentioning, for perhaps it bears upon the matter now under investigation:

10. This same youth, in connection with whom these questions are brought forward, departed this life after having received what may be called a summons at the time when he was dying. For one who had been a companion of his as a student, and reader, and shorthand writer to my dictation, who had died eight months before, was seen by a person in a dream coming towards him. When he was asked by the person who then distinctly saw him why he had come, he said, "I have come to take this friend away"; and so it proved. For

in the house itself, also, there appeared to a certain old man, who was almost awake, a man bearing in his hand a laurel branch on which something was written. Nay, more, when this one was seen, it is further reported that after the death of the young man, his father the presbyter had begun to reside along with the aged Theasius in the monastery, in order to find consolation there, but lo! on the third day after his death, the young man is seen entering the monastery, and is asked by one of the brethren in a dream of some kind whether he knew himself to be dead. He replied that he knew he was. The other asked whether he had been welcomed by God. This also he answered with great expressions of joy. And when questioned as to the reason why he had come, he answered, "I have been sent to summon my father." The person to whom these things were shown awakes, and relates what had passed. It comes to the ear of Bishop Theasius. He, being alarmed, sharply admonished the person who told him, lest the matter should come, as it might easily do, to the ear of the presbyter himself, and he should be disturbed by such tidings. But why prolong the narration? Within about four days from this visitation he was saying (for he had suffered from a moderate feverishness) that he was now out of danger, and that the physician had given up attending him, having assured him that there was no cause whatever for anxiety; but that very day this presbyter expired after he had lain down on his couch. Nor should I forbear mentioning, that on the same day on which the youth died, he asked his father three times to forgive him anything in which he might have offended, and every time that he kissed his father he said to him, "Let us give thanks to God, father," and insisted upon his father saying the words along with him, as if he were exhorting one who was to be his companion in going forth from this world. And in fact only seven days elapsed between the two deaths. What shall we say of things so wonderful? Who shall be a thoroughly reliable teacher as to these mysterious dispensations? To you in the hour of perplexity my agitated heart unburdens itself. . . .

[Evodius went on to tell one of his own dreams and ask urgently about the soul's existence after death and what is meant by wisdom, such as the gift given to Solomon. In answer Augustine wrote:]

Letter 159

To Evodius, my lord most blessed, my venerable and beloved brother and partner in the priestly office, and to the brethren who are with him, Augustin and the brethren who are with him send greeting in the Lord.

1. Our brother Barbarus, the bearer of this letter, is a servant of God, who has now for a long time been settled at Hippo, and has been an eager and diligent hearer of the word of God. He requested

from us this letter to your Holiness, whereby we commend him to you in the Lord, and convey to you through him the salutations which it is our duty to offer. To reply to those letters of your Holiness, in which you have interwoven questions of great difficulty, would be a most laborious task, even for men who are at leisure, and who are endowed with much greater ability in discussing and acuteness in apprehending any subject than we possess. One, indeed, of the two letters in which you ask many great questions has gone amissing, I know not how, and though long sought for cannot be found; the other, which has been found, contains a very pleasing account of a servant of God, a good and chaste young man, stating how he departed from this life, and by what testimonies, communicated through visions of the brethren, his merits were, as you state, made known to you. Taking occasion from this young man's case, you propose and discuss an extremely obscure question concerning the soul,—whether it is associated when it goes forth from this body with some other kind of body, by means of which it can be carried to or confined in places having material boundaries? The investigation of this question, if indeed it admits of satisfactory investigation by beings such as we are, demands the most diligent care and labour, and therefore a mind absolutely at leisure from such occupations as engross my time. My opinion, however, if you are willing to hear it, summed up in a sentence, is, that I by no means believe that the soul in departing from the body is accompanied by another body of any kind.

2. As to the question how these visions and predictions of future events are produced, let him attempt to explain them who understands by what power we are to account for the great wonders which are wrought in the mind of every man when his thoughts are busy. For we see, and we plainly perceive, that within the mind innumerable images of many objects discernible by the eye or by our other senses are produced,—whether they are produced in regular order or in confusion matters not to us at present: all that we say is, that since such images are beyond all dispute produced, the man who is found able to state by what power and in what way these phenomena of daily and perpetual experience are to be accounted for is the only man who may warrantably venture to conjecture or propound any explanation of these visions, which are of exceedingly rare occurrence. For my part, as I discover more plainly my inability to account for the ordinary facts of our experience, when awake or asleep, throughout the whole course of our lives, the more do I shrink from venturing to explain what is extraordinary. For while I have been dictating this epistle to you, I have been contemplating your person in my mind,—you being, of course, absent all the while, and knowing nothing of my thoughts,—and I have been imagining from my knowledge of what is in you how you will be affected by my words; and I have been unable to apprehend, either by observation or by inquiry, how

this process was accomplished in my mind. Of one thing, however, I am certain, that although the mental image was very like something material, it was not produced either by masses of matter or by qualities of matter. Accept this in the meantime from one writing under pressure of other duties, and in haste. In the twelfth of the books which I have written on Genesis this question is discussed with great care, and that dissertation is enriched with a forest of examples from actual experience or from trustworthy report. How far I have been competent to handle the question, and what I have accomplished in it, you will judge when you have read that work; if indeed the Lord shall be pleased in His kindness to permit me now to publish those books systematically corrected to the best of my ability, and thus to meet the expectation of many brethren, instead of deferring their hope by continuing further the discussion of a subject which has already engaged me for a long time.

3. I will narrate briefly, however, one fact which I commend to your meditation. You know our brother Gennadius, a physician, known to almost every one, and very dear to us, who now lives at Carthage, and was in other years eminent as a medical practitioner at Rome. You know him as a man of religious character and of very great benevolence, actively compassionate and promptly liberal in his care of the poor. Nevertheless, even he, when still a young man, and most zealous in these charitable acts, had sometimes, as he himself told me, doubts as to whether there was any life after death. Forasmuch, therefore, as God would in no wise forsake a man so merciful in his disposition and conduct, there appeared to him in sleep a youth of remarkable appearance and commanding presence, who said to him: "Follow me." Following him, he came to a city where he began to hear on the right hand sounds of a melody so exquisitely sweet as to surpass anything he had ever heard. When he inquired what it was, his guide said: "It is the hymn of the blessed and the holy." What he reported himself to have seen on the left hand escapes my remembrance. He awoke; the dream vanished, and he thought of it as only a dream.

4. On a second night, however, the same youth appeared to Gennadius, and asked whether he recognised him, to which he replied that he knew him well, without the slightest uncertainty. Thereupon he asked Gennadius where he had become acquainted with him. There also his memory failed him not as to the proper reply: he narrated the whole vision, and the hymns of the saints which, under his guidance, he had been taken to hear, with all the readiness natural to recollection of some very recent experience. On this the youth inquired whether it was in sleep or when awake that he had seen what he had just narrated. Gennadius answered: "In sleep." The youth then said: "You remember it well; it is true that you saw these things in sleep, but I would have you know that even now you are seeing in sleep."

Hearing this, Gennadius was persuaded of its truth, and in his reply declared that he believed it. Then his teacher went on to say: "Where is your body now?" He answered: "In my bed." "Do you know," said the youth, "that the eyes in this body of yours are now bound and closed, and at rest, and that with these eyes you are seeing nothing?" He answered: "I know it." "What, then," said the youth, "are the eyes with which you see me?" He, unable to discover what to answer to this, was silent. While he hesitated, the youth unfolded to him what he was endeavoring to teach him by these questions, and forthwith said: "As while you are asleep and lying on your bed these eyes of your body are now unemployed and doing nothing, and yet you have eyes with which you behold me, and enjoy this vision, so, after your death, while your bodily eyes shall be wholly inactive, there shall be in you a life by which you shall still live, and a faculty of perception by which you shall still perceive. Beware, therefore, after this of harbouring doubts as to whether the life of man shall continue after death." This believer says that by this means all doubts as to this matter were removed from him. By whom was he taught this but by the merciful, providential care of God?

5. Some one may say that by this narrative I have not solved but complicated the question. Nevertheless, while it is free to every one to believe or disbelieve these statements, every man has his own consciousness at hand as a teacher by whose help he may apply himself to this most profound question. Every day man wakes, and sleeps, and thinks; let any man, therefore, answer whence proceed these things which, while not material bodies, do nevertheless resemble the forms, properties, and motions of material bodies: let him, I say, answer this if he can. But if he cannot do this, why is he in such haste to pronounce a definite opinion on things which occur very rarely, or are beyond the range of his experience, when he is unable to explain matters of daily and perpetual observation? For my part, although I am wholly unable to explain in words how those semblances of material bodies, without any real body, are produced, I may say that I wish that, with the same certainty with which I know that these things are not produced by the body, I could know by what means those things are perceived which are occasionally seen by the spirit, and are supposed to be seen by the bodily senses; or by what distinctive marks we may know the visions of men who have been misguided by delusion, or, most commonly, by impiety, since the examples of such visions closely resembling the visions of pious and holy men are so numerous, that if I wished to quote them, time, rather than abundance of examples, would fail me.

May you, through the mercy of the Lord, grow in grace, most blessed lord and venerable and beloved brother!

Appendix

F

Synesius of Cyrene: Excerpts from *Concerning Dreams*

Commentary by Augustine Fitzgerald, translator

1. If dreams are prophets, and if the visions seen in dreams are riddles of their future fortunes to anxious men, they would in that case be full of wisdom, though certainly not clear. In sooth their lack of clearness is their wisdom. "For the gods keep man's life concealed."

To obtain the greatest things without labour is a divine prerogative, whereas for men, not merely "in front of virtue" but of all fair things, "The gods have set sweat."

Now divination must be the greatest of all good things, for it is in knowledge and, in a word, in the cognitional part of his faculties that God differs from man, as does man from the brute. But whereas the nature of God is sufficient unto Himself for knowledge, man through divination attains to much more than belongs to our human nature. For the mass of mankind can know only the present . . .

[but not the affairs of the gods, which the common language of poetry shows are ruled by Zeus, the oldest in time and in knowledge. Philosophy confirms that the gods are nothing else but minds, intelligences, and one who is worthy to rule over gods does so because of the superior force of wisdom. For this reason also the wise man is akin to God.]

2. Let the foregoing be proof that divinations are amongst the best of the vocations of man; and if all things are signs appearing through all things, inasmuch as they are brothers in a single living creature, the cosmos, so also they are written characters of every kind, just as of those in a book some are Phoenician, some Egyptian, and others Assyrian. . . .

[Just as men learn to read books—each in his own way, some only a phrase, others the whole story—so they learn to read signs in the universe, signals of the relationship between the parts of a great whole. What is called magic is actually the attraction of one thing through the agency of another. The wise man knows that he has present with him the pledges of things which are for the most part far away.

Men learn to use this magic, and to find what binds the parts together, just as the musicians learn which notes come next in a particular harmonic series, or as the mathematician manipulates the parts of a problem from outside of it. But there is also discord in the cosmos, parts of the universe which agree and yet battle with other parts, and this struggle contributes to the unity of the whole. The unity resulting from opposites is the harmony of the cosmos. The man who places himself outside of it can no longer make any use of his wisdom, but uses the universe against itself.

The diversity of things in the universe and their relationship furnish the bulk of the subject-matter in the initiations and prophecies. And while it is not lawful to discuss initiations, there is no offense in explaining divination.]

3. The whole of this art has already been praised as much as possible, but now it is time to appropriate the best part that is in it, and to linger over its speculative side. . . .

[Obscurity is common to all forms of divination. Dreams should not be dismissed for this reason. Rather we should seek this branch of knowledge which is within us and is the special possession of the soul of each of us. For the soul holds the forms of things that come into being, only producing what is befitting, and reflecting as in a mirror the image by which a person grasps those things that remain there.]

Therefore, as we do not understand the activities of the mind before the controlling force has announced them to the multitude, and whatever has not come to that controlling force is hidden from the living being; so then we shall not have a perception even of the forms in the first soul, before the impress of them comes to the imagination. And this very imagination seems to be a sort of life in itself, a little lower down in the scale, and have its basis in a peculiar property of nature. It has even its own sense-perceptions, for we see colours and we hear sounds, and we have an overpowering sense of touch, at times when the organic parts of the body are at rest. Perhaps this form of sense-perception is the more hallowed. In this way we constantly enter into relationship with gods who give us counsel and answer us in oracles, and take care of us in other ways. So then, if any one, in his dreams, received the present of a treasure, I shall not be at all surprised; or if a man quite uncultured should fall asleep and, meeting the Muses in his dream and exchanging question and answer with them, should become a cunning bard. This has happened in our own time and does not seem to me very astounding. I pass over plots that have been revealed, and the number of people whom the dream in the guise of a physician has cured of illness. But whenever a dream opens up to the soul a path conducting it to the most perfect points from which to view existing things, a soul that has never yet aspired, nor has given its mind to the ascent, it would be indeed the climax of the occult force in existing things that this dream should override nature and unite to the realm of mind the man who has wandered so far from it that he knows not whence he has come.

And if any one deems the way upward a great undertaking, but disbelieves in the imagination, for that even by its means the happy union may ne'er be gained, let him listen to the sacred oracles which tell of the diverging paths, after hearing, of course, the whole list of the available resources for the ascent, in virtue of which it is possible to make the seed within us grow: " 'To some,' it is written, 'he gave the revelation of the light to be a lesson, Others even in their dreams, he made fruitful with his courage.' "

Do you see? He makes a distinction between the happy possession of knowledge and its acquirement. One man learns, he means, while awake, another while asleep. But in the waking state man is the teacher, whereas it is God who makes the dreamer fruitful with His own courage, so that learning and attaining are one and the same. Now to make fruitful is even more than to teach.

[Synesius then turns to the relation of man's psyche to the total universe, depicting in great depth and detail the role of the imagination, of spirit in the life of the soul. Aside from the studies of Augustine, this is about the most sophisticated discussion of human psychology which has come down to us from antiquity. It goes beyond our present study, and we summarize only the necessary points.

Some men despise dreams and seek an art of divination above the common herd. But is not a man wise, precisely because he gains a greater share out of things common to all? It is the greatest good to look upon God by the imagination, for the imaginative spirit is the most widely shared organ of sensation, the first body of the soul. About it nature has constructed all of the functions of the brain. Sense-perception through the outer organs remains only animal in character, no perception at all, until it comes into contact with the imagination. This is the divine faculty which sees with its whole spirit and has power over all the remaining senses.

The man who thinks he knows best what he has seen with his own eyes has no way of knowing which images he sees are distorted. Then the imaginative spirit becomes diseased, and the extraneous bodies which have entered in must be purged and purified if the man is to see clearly again.

The imagination comprehends our spiritual nature, because it moves on the border between reason and unreason, between matter and that which has no body, between the divine and the demonic. It borrows from each extreme, thus imaging in one nature things that dwell far apart. This is difficult for philosophy to comprehend.

The imaginings of dreams, however, are similar to the other life for which our soul prepares. The envelope of soul-matter is in turn god, demon of every sort, and phantom. Within it the soul enters a struggle to fulfill its own contract with the life of the universe, to descend to the regions ruled by the elements of matter, and to bring back up to the spheres what it has snatched from the extremes of fire and air. The imaginative spirit lives in all this enormous interval of space, and is able to accompany the soul as it rises, even until it reaches the highest point.

Thus, man's imaginative spirit obtains true impressions of the life of the soul. It also influences that life, and can even draw the soul towards God; or, if the imagination is empty and inactive, it leaves a vacuum into which an evil spirit enters. To investigate the state of the soul and the spirit around it, we must pay attention to the visions which the imaginative spirit emits, particularly in sleep.]

7. We, therefore, have set ourselves to speak of divination through dreams, that men should not despise it, but rather cultivate it, seeing that it fulfils a service to life; and it is to this end that we have so much occupied ourselves with the imaginative nature. The immediate need of it here below has been perhaps less clearly shown by our discourse, but a better fruit of a sane spirit is the uplifting of the soul, a really sacred gain; so that it becomes a sort of cult of piety to endeavour that this form of divination should be ours. Nay, some men already through some such motive, enticed by their passion for knowledge of the future, have had set before them, instead of a groaning board a sacred and modest one, and have hailed the joys of a couch pure and undefiled. For as to the man who would consult his bed as he does the tripod of the Pythian deity, far be it from him to make the nights spent in it witnesses of unbridled passion. Rather does he bow before God and pray to Him. What is collected little by little becomes much in the end, and that which happens through quite another cause terminates in a greater one. Thus those who did not set out at first with this object have come, in their advance, to love God and one day to be united to Him. We must not therefore disregard a prophetic art which journeys to divine things, and has, dependent on it, the most precious of all things which are in the power of man. Nor indeed has the soul that is united with God less need here because of the fact that it has been deemed worthy to handle better things. Nor is it heedless of the animal in us.

Nay, from its vantage ground it has a steady and much more distinct view of things below than when it is with them and is mingled with the inferior elements. Remaining unmoved, it will give to the animal in us the appearances of things that come into existence. This is, according to the proverb, "to descend without descending," where the better takes unchallenged mastery of the worse. This art of divination I resolve to possess for myself and to bequeath to my children. In order to enter upon this no man need pack up for a long journey or voyage beyond the frontiers, as to Pytho or to Hammon. It is enough to wash one's hands, to keep a holy silence, and to sleep. "Then did she make all ablutions, and dressing in purified raiment prayed she long time to Athene. . . ."

8. We shall pray for a dream, even as Homer, perchance, prayed. And if you are worthy, the god far away is present with you. Nay, even what time the god sets little store on these matters, he comes to your side if only you are asleep; and this is the whole system of the initiation. In it no one has ever yet lamented his poverty, on the ground that thus he had less possessions than the rich. On the other hand, some of the ceremonies which deal with foreknowledge choose their priests from the most heavily assessed as the Athenians chose their trierarchs. And great expense there must needs be, and, no less, happy opportunity, if we are to obtain a Cretan herb, an Egyptian feather, an Iberian bone, and, by Zeus, some prodigy begotten and nourished in a hidden corner of earth or sea, "Where that the sun god sinks neath the earth and where he arises."

For surely this and much like it is said of those who practise external divination, and what ordinary person would be rich enough for this out of his own resources? But the dream is visible to the man who is worth five hundred *medimni,* and equally to the possessor of three hundred, to the teamster no less than to the peasant who tills the boundary land for a livelihood, to the galleyslave and the common labourer alike, to the exempted and to the payer of taxes.

It makes no difference to the god whether a man is an *eteoboutades* or a newly bought slave. And this accessibility to all makes divination very humane; for its simple and artless character is worthy of a philosopher, and its freedom from violence gives it sanctity. . . .

[Almost with tongue in cheek, Synesius discusses the fantastic complications of other forms of divination or foreknowledge, compared with the great simplicity of the really divine work. If we give ourselves up to these other things, we not only need trunk-loads of equipment, but we have to be content if they make some concession to the remaining needs of life. And, seriously, these other practices are base, and hateful to God. For not to await voluntarily any one's coming, but to set him moving by pressure and leverage, is even punished by law when it happens among men.]

Of divination by dreams, each one of us is perforce his own instrument, so much so that it is not possible to desert our oracle there even if we so desired. Nay, even if we remain at home, she dwells with us; if we go abroad she accompanies us; she is with us on the field of battle, she is at our side in the life of the city; she labours with us in the fields and barters with us in the market place. The laws of a malicious government do not forbid her, nor would they have the power to do so, even if they wished it, for they have no proof against those who invoke her. For how then? Should we be violating the law by sleeping? A tyrant could never enjoin us not to gaze into dreams, at least not unless he actually banished sleep from his kingdom; and it would be the act of a fool to wish for that which is impossible of fulfilment, and of an impious man to make laws which should be contrary to nature and to God. To her then we must go, woman and man of us, young and old, poor and rich alike, the private citizen and the ruler, the town dweller and the rustic, the artisan and the orator. She repudiates neither race, nor age, nor condition, nor calling. She is present to every one, everywhere, this zealous prophetess, this wise counsellor, who holdeth her peace. She herself is like initiator and initiated, to announce to us good tidings; in such wise as to prolong our pleasure by seizing joy beforehand; to inform against the worst so as to guard against and to repel it beforehand. . . .

[For whatever use and sweetness there is in hope, and whatever reality fear controls, all are found in dreams. In fact, there is nothing else that so entices men towards hope. This element is so abundant and so healing in dreams that men who have been bound by fear, when they awaken to dreams of hope, find themselves straightway unbound. Furthermore, it is not well to despair of dreams, when so often one is only confusing the weakness of the interpreter with the nature of the visions themselves. And since we have a pledge from the divinity in the promise of our dreams, we profit twice if we prepare to enjoy these greater things which the dream state can hold out to us. Not only do we have the pleasure of anticipation, but we can profit from the chance to examine them beforehand and prepare wisely for what we shall do.]

9. Yet I have narrowly missed incurring a charge of ingratitude; for while I explained just now that it (i.e., divination by dreams) is a good thing wherewith to journey or stay at home, to trade or command troops, and that it helps all men and all things, yet I have never made public what it has done for me personally. Certainly no other thing is so well calculated to join in man's pursuit of wisdom; and of many of the things which present difficulties to us awake, some of these it makes completely clear while we are asleep, and others it helps us to explain. And something of this sort happens. At one moment one seems like a man asking questions, at another the same man discovering and in process of thought. It has frequently helped me to write books, for it has prepared the mind and made the diction appropriate to the thought. Here it cuts out something, there it brings in new

matter instead. It has befallen me already to be admonished by it also in respect of the whole style of my language, when it runs riot and flames up with novel forms of diction, in emulation of the archaic Attic, which is foreign to us, and this by the agency of a god who, at one moment tells me something, and again what something means, and at another shows me how to smooth down the excrescences growing out of my language. Thus it has restored my diction to a state of sobriety, and has castigated my inflated style. Moreover when I am engaged in the chase, it has suggested to me stratagems of the hunter's art against those wild beasts who show skill alike in running and hiding; and when in weariness I have been on the point of abandoning the quest, the dream has enjoined upon me a blockade of the quarry, and has promised me fortune on an appointed day, so that we have slept in the open more happily and with confidence. And when the day appointed has come and fortune is with us at last, it has shown us swarms of netted game and of wild beasts that have fallen to our spears.

My life has been one of books and of the chase, except what time I spent as an ambassador. Would that I had not been compelled to see three unspeakable years lost to my life! But even in them I derived the greatest profit from divination, and that on many occasions. For plots directed against me it made ineffective, plots of ghost-raising sorcerers. It exposed these to me, saved me from them all, and helped me in the management of public office in the best interest of the cities, and it finally placed me, more undaunted than was ever any Greek, on terms of intimacy with the emperor.

One man may prefer one, another man another (system of divination), but dream divination is present to all, the good genius to every man, and one that contrives something for the minds of the awakened also. In this way is a soul a wise possession, that it is free from a whole flood of vulgar sensations which attract to it extraneous matter of every sort. Whatever ideas it has, and however many things it receives from the mind, all these, when left to itself, it makes over to those who are inclined towards that which is within, and it ferries across to them whatsoe'er comes from the godhead. For as it is itself of such a character, a cosmic god is also associated with it, from the fact that its nature comes from the same source.

10. Such categories of dreams, then, are more divine, and are either quite clear and obvious, or nearly so, and in no wise stand in need of the diviner's science. But they may come to the help only of such men as live according to virtue, whether that be acquired by wisdom or engrained by habit, and if at a given moment they should come to any other, it would be with difficulty, though they might so come.

It is not for some trifling purpose that a dream of this higher order will come to the chance recipient. Further, a frequent and a very widely shared class will be the enigmatic. To this the science of divination must be applied, for its genesis was, so to speak, strange and portentous, and it has sprung from such sources, its development is most obscure. Now its character is as follows. From all that nature possesses, all things that are, that have come into being and that shall be (since this too is a phase of existence), from all these things, I say, images flow and rebound from their substance. For if each perceptible thing is form coupled with matter, and if we discover an escape of matter in the combination, reasoning shows that the nature of the images also is canalized, so that in both cases perceptible things renounce the dignity of real being. Now the imaginative *pneuma* is a powerful reflecting mirror of all the images that flow off in this way. For, wandering in vain and slipping from their base, on account of the indefiniteness of their nature, and because they are recognized by no being of real existence, whenever these fall in with psychical *pneumata*, the which are images indeed, and have a seat fixed in nature, then they lean upon them and take their rest as though at their own hearthstone. Of those things, therefore, which have come into being, inasmuch as they have already passed into the activity of existence, the images sent forth are distinct, until in the fullness of time they become faint and evanescent. Of existing things, inasmuch as they are still standing, the images are more tenacious of life and more distinct, but those of future events are more indefinite and indistinguishable. For they are the advanced waves of things not yet present, efflorescences of unfulfilled nature, as it were, riddles of closely stored seeds, skipping away and darting out.

Thus also art is needed with a view to coming events, for the images which proceed from them are only shadowed, and the symbols are not as clear as in the case of already existing things. Nevertheless they are of a wonderful nature, even as they stand, wonderful in that they have come into existence from things that have not yet existed.

11. But it is high time that we should say of this art how it may help us. The best way is to prepare the divine *pneuma* in such wise that it may be worthy of the direction of mind and of God, and not be a recipient of obscure energies. And the best culture is the one leading through philosophy, which brings a calm from passions, for when once disturbed by these the *pneuma* is occupied, as it were a territory; and through a wise and temperate life, one that least maddens the animal nature and that has least tendency to bring it into the last body. For turmoil would reach even to the first body, but this ought to be kept unperturbed and unmoved. But since this is an easy prayer for every one to join in, but is of all things the most difficult to co-operate in attaining, then as we wish sleep to be unprofitable to none, come now, let us seek a definition even for indefinable things; in a word, let us put together an art of divining dream-images. Now it is something in this wise. When mariners sailing the sea come

suddenly upon a rock, and presently disembarking see a city of men, as often as they see the same rock, they will take it as a sign of the city. And just as when, in the case of generals, we know from the scouts that they themselves will appear, though we do not see them (for that from the same indication they have always in the past appeared on the scene); so on each occasion we obtain from the dream-images a signal of the activity of coming events.

For these are forerunners of those same things, and like things are forerunners of like. Therefore it is the skipper's fault if, when the same rock becomes visible, he fails to recognize it, or is unable to say to what land the ship is moving. . . .

[But understanding dreams is not this simple. Aristotle and reason have asserted that in every case sense-perception creates memory, memory experience, experience in turn science. And there are many dream books which follow exactly this reasoning. But these are to be laughed at, because they are little use. This standard conforms to the nature of bodies, but it is not the case with the imaginative spirit. The imagination does not act like matter, putting together one body after another out of elements which one logically expects to find associated together. Instead the imaginative spirit associates the most dissimilar things.

How then can completely dissimilar things be revealed by the same images? Obviously this is impossible. Some difference must exist, and if it does, let us ask first if we should naturally expect a plane mirror, a concave one, and a distorted one to reflect exactly the same images. It is even more difficult in an individual character to capture that which is like a general image.]

12. For this reason we must dismiss the idea that all men are under the same laws; rather must each man hold himself as material for the art. Let him inscribe on his memory the affairs in which he has been involved, and the nature of the visions which have preceded them. . . .

It would be a wise proceeding even to publish our waking and sleeping visions and their attendant circumstances; the wise thing to do, I say, unless the culture of the city is like to be too rustic for so novel an enterprise. We shall therefore see fit to add to what are called "day books" what we term "night books," so as to have records to remind us of the character of each of the two lives concerned; for our argument already laid it down that a certain life exists in imagination, at one moment better, at another worse than the intermediate, according to the relation of the *pneuma* to health and disease. If in this way, therefore, we make profitable the observation by which the art is developed, and if nothing slips our memory, in other respects also the result will be a refined pastime; it will be paying oneself the compliment of a history of one's waking and sleeping moments. . . .

Any one can see how great the work is, on attempting to fit language to visions, visions in which those things which are united in nature are separated, and things separated in nature are united, and he is obliged to show in speech what has not been revealed. It is no mean achievement to pass on to another something of a strange nature that has shirred in one's own soul, for whenever by this phantasy (of dreaming) things which are expelled from the order of being, and things which never in any possible way existed, are brought instead into being—nay, even things which have not a nature capable of existence, what contrivance is there for presenting a nameless nature to things which are *per se* inconceivable? Again, it (the phantasy) neither makes these forms appear numerous and all present at the same moment, nor yet does it present them after an interval, but exactly as the dream itself might have them and pass them on to us; for we believe whatever it wills us to believe. To survive at all and without cutting a sorry figure amidst all this, would be proof of a masterly rhetoric. It conducts itself wantonly even against our understanding itself, becoming the cause of something more than thought. For we are not indeed insensible to the visions; rather are our approbations and partialities strong, and not least our detestations. And the many trickeries that are bound up with this, attack us in our sleep. Pleasure is at that moment most of all a thing full of charm, such as to impart to our souls loves or hatreds even in the waking state. If any one were to utter no lifeless words, but rather to accomplish that for the sake of which the discourse was seriously undertaken, he would need stirring language to put his auditor into the same condition and amidst the same thoughts as himself.

Now in dreams one conquers, walks, or flies simultaneously, and the imagination has room for it all; but how shall mere speech find room for it? So a man sleeps and dreams; he sees a dream, and arises from it still sleeping, as he thinks, and shakes off his dream while still recumbent. He philosophizes a little on the vision that has appeared to him, according to his knowledge; and this is a dream, but the other is a double dream. Accordingly he believes it not, and thinks that now he is awake and that what appears to him is really alive. Forthwith a fierce struggle ensues, and a man dreams that an attack is made on himself, then that he has left all behind and is waking up, again that he has made trial of himself and has discovered the deception. In some such way must the sons of Aloeus be suffering punishment for piling up the mountains of Thessaly against the gods. [Otus and Ephialtes, who attempted to pile Ossa on Olympus and Pelion on Ossa. *Odyssey*, 11.315.] But there is no law of Adrastea in the way of the sleeper, to forbid him from rising from earth more happily than Icarus, from soaring above the eagles, or reaching a point above the loftiest spheres themselves. So one looks steadily upon the earth from afar, and discovers a land not visible even to the moon.

It is also in his power to hold converse with the stars and to meet the unseen gods of the universe. That which is difficult to describe then takes place easily, namely that the gods are visibly manifest, nor do the gods feel even a particle of jealousy. The dreamer has not even descended to the earth after a short interval; he is already there. Nothing is so characteristic of dreams as to steal space and to create without time. Then the sleeper converses with sheep and fancies their bleating to be speech, and he understands their talk. So new and so extensive a wealth of subjects is there for one who has the courage to let loose his language upon them.

13. I even think that myths take their authority from dreams, as those in which peacock, fox, and sea hold converse. But these are small things compared with the independence of dreams. And although myths are a very small part of dreams, nevertheless they were approved by the sophists as a preparation for the work of eloquence. And for these men to whom the myth is the beginning of their art, the dream ought to be its appropriate end. And there is this in addition, that one has not worked the tongue in vain, as in the case of myths, but that he has become wiser in judgment. Let every man, then, with leisure and ease proceed to write a narrative of whatsoe'er happens in his waking and sleeping states. Let him spend some of his time on this. Of the time so spent the greatest help will be found in his knowledge of letters. Let him put together the art of divination which we have extolled, than which nothing could be of more varied service to him.

[Nicephorus Gregoras, in the early part of the fourteenth century in Constantinople, wrote a Commentary on this treatise of Synesius. In a letter to Joannes Cantacuzenus (Ep. 23), the substance of which is repeated in one addressed to Demetrios Cavasilas many years later (Ep. 155), he extols this work in the following terms: "You know, I think, that I wrote a book long ago inspired by my profound gratitude towards the great Synesius. He wrote, as you are aware, a most remarkable work on dreams. Just as nature made every effort, and with great success, to show in him a man of the highest order among the Greeks, in like manner this work is the best of all that he has written, and he made every effort that it should appear so. . . . He gives us his own personal evidence in the matter. God inspired him, and he had no recourse to his forces as a man, he tells us, in this work. He simply lent his pen to it. God did all. Thus the work is the production, so he writes, of a man possessed by a prophetic inspiration, and full of the Divinity. For this reason the greater part of the book has been composed in an obscure style, as were the oracles that the Delphic Tripod gave forth, and that were, as you know, full of prophetic phrases sedulously concealed and unintelligible to the ignorant, phrases which screened them as if behind a curtain of heavy obscurity. Yielding to numerous requests, we have sought to elucidate this work, to what extent it was possible, by the help of a varied Commentary" (Nic. Greg. *Ep.*, ed. Guilland, Paris, 1927).

There is nothing in this passage from the Letters of Nicephorus that is not contained in the text of *De Insomniis,* and a Letter to Hypatia (Ep. 154), concerning the manner in which it was written. But it is interesting as showing to what an extent the works of Synesius were admired by the erudite of the fourteenth century, and also as indicating that at this time the work on dreams, which has been regarded by modern commentators with less favour than the other essays, was esteemed as the most important. One of the friends who urged Nicephorus to write a commentary on it was Theodorus Metochites, the prime minister of the Emperor Andronicus II, who was the most learned man of the fourteenth century, and had instructed Nicephorus in Greek philosophy as well as astronomy, and had become his patron at the court. Nicephorus, like Synesius, was an astronomer as well as a rhetorician, and wrote a work on the construction of an astrolabe, which, he tells his correspondent Cavasilas (Ep. 155), he laboured over with the same ardour that he put into his study of Synesius. It seems that Byzantium in the fourteenth century was not so far off in point of culture from Athens and Alexandria of the fourth and fifth centuries.].

Appendix

G

Benedict Pererius: *De Magia—Concerning the Investigation of Dreams and Concerning Astrological Divinations. Three books. Against the false and superstitious arts.*

Book 2: Concerning the investigation of dreams

There is no one class of dreams nor one explanation for them. Therefore, the cause of all of them is not the same, so that they should not all be either confirmed or rejected on the same grounds. Indeed, sacred works deride many dreams and even condemn them; but certain dreams they praise and highly respect. For the majority of them are groundless; but more than a few are natural, arising from definite causes in nature. Others, moreover, are thrust upon mortals by the cunning and malice of the devil. Finally, some are given to men by divine inspiration. Further diligent examination of dreams produces a most felicitous knowledge of them, very fine in itself, and serves immensely to illuminate several obscure passages in the Holy Scripture. It can, in truth, be most useful in regulating and tempering the lives of men. But first, it is of great assistance to refute the ignorance (more accurately, I should say, the foolishness and stupidity) of certain men who examine dreams too carefully, anxiously and superstitiously. Thus encouraged by these considerations about the nature, variety and validity of dreams, I have engaged in several useful inquiries exacting the utmost skill, and have attempted to explain them in this book.

Index of Inquiries of Book 2. Concerning dreams.

1. Can one have any faith in dreams?
2. Concerning the causes of true dreams.
3. By what signs may it be known whether a dream has been sent by God or not?
4. Why should God convey his secrets to men in sleep?
5. Why should dreams be given by God to obscure and uneducated men but not to the learned?

6. Why are divinely inspired dreams sometimes obscure and perplexing?
7. Is a Christian permitted to examine dreams?
8. What man may rightfully interpret dreams?
9. Can there be free use of reason and will in sleep?
10. On the dream of Solomon in which God promised and granted to him the gift of wisdom.

First Inquiry: Can one have any faith in dreams?

The opinions of the vulgar and the wise on this matter are drawn in various directions. However, this inquiry may in one sentence be able to sort out the facts through the classification of dreams. For without doubt, a few dreams are to be trusted, though most should be entirely discredited. To be sure, it is equally foolish to believe either in all dreams or in none, and either belief seems to be a mark of extreme stupidity or stubbornness. But assuredly, that adage of Cicero is both clever and true: nothing can be said which is so absurd that it might not be said by some philosopher. For what can be more *irrational* (ἄλογον) and *impossible* (ἀδύνατον) than to think that all dreams are true and must be believed? For yourself see how Protagoras, clearly one of that group of ancient and venerable philosophers, claims faith in all dreams and, examining them with great authority, claims to establish their veracity or fallaciousness not by the very nature of things but only by the opinion of men. Man is the measure of all things, and each and every thing is such as it seems to man, be he sober or drunk, in good or poor health, awake or sleeping. Close to this type of error are certain Stoics, far too superstitious and almost fanatical philosophers, who rejected no dreams and maintained that in all there is power to indicate and signify something. Nevertheless they say that certain dreams are thought to be meaningless and misleading (1) in so far as they are tenuously expressed and for this reason obscure and difficult to understand; (2) because, on account of their ambiguity, they seem to be applicable to various subjects and therefore able to confirm nothing certain for us through observation of them; but (3) especially since cleverness and wisdom equal to discerning the force of these dreams will not easily be found among men. In contrast, Xenophanes of Colophon—a memorable philosopher even by virtue of his very age, for he was nearly contemporary with the birth of philosophy in Greece—and also the advocates of the gentle and attractive Epicurean discipline held views contrary to these and denied the authority and the validity of all dreams. "Moreover, one must not believe in any dreams," so they would argue. Nature is the one and the same force behind all dreams; thus, there ought to be a constant criterion for believing either in all dreams or in none. But in most dreams it is not possible to believe; therefore, there is no reason why, when most dreams have been discredited, we ought to believe in any in particular. In addition, if certain dreams are trustworthy and definite, it is necessary that there be some definite efficient cause of them. But what are the causes? Nature, people say, and God. Yet nature, indeed, is a friend of order and constancy; and in dreams there is no order, but inconstancy full of accident. Moreover, it seems beneath God and foreign to his majesty, that He should approach the couches of sleeping men, rush to their bedsides and interrupt their snoring with dreams which they would not remember, not understand, or even contemn upon awakening. Or, should they think the dreams were important to them, they would be filled with foolish superstition; for days and nights their minds would hang either paralyzed with inane fear of impending evils or elated with the false expectation of future blessings. Yet how much more suitable it would have been to the purpose of God, how much more worthy of his superiority and advantageous to the interest of men, to give visions not to the base and uneducated, but to the excellent and wise, not to the sleeping but to those awake, in truth, to those more fitted to understand; and that God give signs—not through riddles and devious, intricate ways—but directly, openly, clearly because he would wish to be understood by man.

In this fashion those philosophers ramble on about dreams, in sum either accrediting or condemning them, but wandering manifestly very far astray from the paths of truth. But the proper attitude, standing as a middle road so to speak, distinguishes different classes of dreams. Of these dreams it flatly denounces and rejects most as being groundless, empty of all rational basis and meriting no confidence. It is superfluous to argue this, since it is clearer than the light of the sun. For everyday experience, as each day we dream the whole night through, teaches how many and what dreams we have. Out of so many dreams does truth emerge? Indeed occasionally some truth does emerge, but since this is extremely rare and occurs without any logical pattern, nothing can be adduced as to why it should not be thought to have happened by chance and fortuitously. Reason herself also compels that the same thing be admitted. For what other cause of such dreams—those meriting no confidence—is there unless it be spirits, servants of the conscious, sensing mind, and more especially of fantasy which characteristically fashions dreams in which fragments and traces of impressions received in the waking hours—fragments which in the schools we call "species," and thus I term "spirits"—settle and entrench themselves and are agitated during sleep by vapors of food and drink stealing into the head. And tossed about from here to there, these spirits give rise to various dreams and visions, but on account of the disorderly tossing of these spirits the dreams are exceedingly confused, frequently even turbulent and distorted, and ultimately such that they can have no power to signify anything. So then are dreams as they variously take shape in cloudy forms; images and likenesses of living things or of other objects which for a very brief moment we watch changing into other images and again into others; and soon all are dispersed and vanish into the deep. He who would think that these images bear a definite meaning of anything should be regarded as dull and fatuous. But it seems no less a sign of ignorance to attribute to dreams definite indications and signs of symbolic meaning (*significandarum rerum*). If we ignore the visions of the drunk, the crazed and the insane and do not take them into consideration, assuredly dreams must be equally ridiculed and contested—rather even more so, because generally they are themselves more jumbled, confused and bizarre. Wittily indeed, but nevertheless truthfully, people have said that if it had been arranged by nature that sleeping men should do what they dream, it would be absolutely necessary that all men who went to bed should be bound, on the ground that they were about to do things more ridiculous, absurd and incredible than the insane do. The Holy Scriptures also confirm this opinion in declaiming the levity and superficiality of those who by believing in dreams—that is, in most vain and deceptive things—show themselves worthy to be jibed at by the mockery of all. Thus in Ecclesiastes, Chapter V, it is written. "Where there are many dreams, there are a maximum of vanities and countless words." Similarly, in Ecclesiasticus, Chapter XXXIV, we read this: "The imprudent extol dreams; just as he who catches a shadow and runs after the wind, so is he who heeds dreams; dreams have made many men stray and have ruined those who have hope in them." Finally, whenever the Scriptures wish to point out something vain, tenuous, elusive and fallacious, they express it most frequently through comparison and similarity to dreams.

On the other hand, as it must not be denied that truth and validity are absent in most dreams, so it must be admitted that certain dreams are true and sure. For if there were nothing truthful and sure in any dreams, the most renowned of physicians would be acting quite naïvely and superstitiously when with such painstaking care they study the dreams which often come over the sick in order to diagnose their ills and to cure them. The natural philosophers (*physiologi*), likewise, would spend themselves in futile labor, hunting down and investigating with so great zeal into the causes, powers and significance of dreams. Besides, so many of the stories of former times, attested to by well-known men, confirmed and substantiated by records and by examples of truthful dreams which amazingly conformed to the very word with the actual outcome of the situation, would be false. How many dreams are mentioned in sacred writings, dreams not only valid and truthful, but also very full of divine mysteries. Let the reader recall to his memory the dreams of Abraham, Abimelech, Jacob, Laban, Joseph, Pharaoh, Solomon, King Nebuchadnessar, Daniel, Mordecae (*Mardochaeus*), and Judas Maccabaeus; and in addition to these the dreams in the New Testament of blessed Joseph, the Magi and the wife of Pilate; and finally the dream of St. Paul, which is told by Luke in the Acts of the Apostles. Even Homer noted this distinction among dreams, though it was veiled, in the poetic tradition, in the garments of fable, when he fashioned two gates, one of horn through which truthful dreams are sent out to men and the other of ivory through which false dreams are released. Vergil, imitating Homer, as indeed he was accustomed to do, expressed the same sentiment in the Aeneid, Book VI, with these words: "There are twin gates of sleep: one of them is wrought of horn, through which easy exit is given to true visions; the other is made of gleaming ivory and shines brightly but through it the shades send false dreams toward heaven." But why did the poet assign the gate of horn to truthful dreams and the gate of ivory to false ones? Macrobius in that commentary in which he explains the dream of Scipio sets forth the reason for this.

Second inquiry: Concerning the causes of true dreams

It has been said that some dreams are false and others true. Since we have rejected the false ones, therefore, let us consider the true ones. But since what dreams are true and by what sign and peculiar mark they are recognized from the false cannot be clearly understood unless we investigate and discover all the causes of truthful dreams, it is quite fitting at this time to discuss what has been believed and advanced by others concerning causes of this sort. Hippocrates in his book on dreams (*de insomniis*) established two types of truthful dreams: one he calls divine, the other natural. Divine dreams, he says, are sent by God and always presage memorable occurrences and events marked by joy or sorrow, good fortune or misery, be they private or public affairs. Moreover, he says that the explanation of these dreams must be sought from soothsayers and interpreters of divine meanings. The dream of Cyrus the Great who founded the monarchy of the Persians is said to have been of this nature. The sun was seen at his feet while he was sleeping, and three times he reached out for it with his hands, and three times turning it slipped away. The wise, learned magi of the Persians answered that this dream signified that he would hold imperial power for thirty years, and so indeed it happened. Hippocrates thinks that natural dreams arise nearly always out of causes latent within the body of the person sleeping and that they indicate good or bad states of the body itself, i.e., abundance and excess or, on the other hand, insufficiency and absence of those humors which exist in the body, or the presence of any one of them that may be spoiled by motion in its own place or wildly and turbulently agitated. Indeed, the observation and conjectural interpretation of these dreams for medical purposes to devise and establish cures is thought to be of very great value. Plato in the Symposium thinks that truthful dreams and portents of the future originate with demons; for demons are the medium between God, who is immortal and incorporeal, and man who is both corporeal and mortal, especially since they themselves are also corporeal like us and immortal like God. (The word Plato used for *demon* would be better translated *spiritual entity*.) For Plato thinks that God does not meddle in human affairs nor have any intimate association or intercourse with men, but rather that contacts and colloquies between God and men, either awake or sleeping, are initiated and accomplished by means of demons. Doubtless, he says, it is the function and duty of demons to convey the prayers and offerings of men to God and to bear God's assistance and blessings down to men. Through them, prophecies, sorcery, magic, every method of divination and the practice of interpreting omens reach men. Thus demons are the heralds, mediators and agents of God; but they act also as the patrons of men, their defenders and masters and, as I should say using the word coined by Apuleius, their "guardian angels" (*salutigerulos,* literally "greeting carriers"). These are the opinions not only of Plato but of Empedocles and Pythagoras before him. Augustine discusses and argues learnedly and incisively against them in Book VIII, Chapters 20–21 and Book IX of the *City of God*. Aristotle in the tract which he wrote *On Divination through Dreams* denies that any dreams are given to men by God. On the contrary truthful dreams are either certain natural signs that have proceeded from natural causes, which skillful philosophers and physicians actually examine to good advantage, or else they are in a certain measure the origins of those things which one will do later upon awakening. For sometimes during sleep certain things occur which seem able to lead us toward some action and which afterward when awakened we appropriately utilize and in taking proper action we are pleased. The Stoics have established three causes of dreams. The first is God Who, since He is supremely omniscient and provident of all things and the benevolent patron of mankind, by Whom man becomes the more discrete (*cautior*), gives him dreams which are tokens of the future and warnings of those things which he must act upon and guard against. The second cause which they establish is fate, by which things are linked in a kind of eternal chain and fixed in a knot, since the Stoics think that antecedent causes and forewarning signs of all future occurrences are sent ahead both through other media and also through dreams themselves. They make the third cause the nature of our soul which is divine. For the soul of man, when his outward senses have been numbed by sleep and are void of all activity and the soul is itself free and delivered of all cares and preoccupations, becomes more vigorous and apt to understand, since at that time it more vividly remembers the past, is alert to the present and foresees the future. Porphyry traces the validity of dreams in part to the innate conceptions in the souls of men, which he takes as meaningful hints of all things that the soul has retained from another life as it enters this body. But the soul, forcibly overcome and suppressed here, cannot apprehend them when the senses are awake; in sleep, however, they manifest themselves to it more clearly and become known. In part he traces dreams to demons: the good and true dreams to good demons, and to evil demons, the perverse, deceptive and false dreams. Synesius discourses at length on the "phantastical spirit" (*phantasticus spiritus*), which is the vehicle of the life-giving principle (*animae*). For by this medium which acts as a chain that principle is attached and linked to this earthly body. Likewise the soul when released from the body moves from one place to another through it, and through it the souls of evil-doers suffer the punishments of hell; without its presence in the body no one is able to perceive or understand. Furthermore, reflections of all things which are, were and will be are impressed upon this spirit, and on it they shine as in a mirror, those of the present clearer than those of the past—for the older they are the less brilliant—and still less clear, reflections of future things which obviously are not, nor ever have been, in existence. But since future events are constrained within the power of causes, they have certain antecedents and forerunners which are the less distinct as the signs are far away and it is in this class that he thinks dreams must be placed. Thus through dreams things are indicated in almost imperceptible images and likenesses—not evenly, however, but according to the varying makeup and plan of that phantastical spirit, as with the action in mirrors and because of the differentiation in matter and form, images are reflected as varied and unlike one another. Synesius further advises us sufficiently to condition and well prepare this phantastical spirit to receive calm and veracious visions in sleep by moderate nourishment, upright actions and pursuits, and by settling the anxieties of the mind. So it was that Pythagoras, when he was about to go to bed, would make himself sleepy by the song and verses of the lyre and this way prepare himself to have good and happy dreams; for the same reason he forbade his servants to eat beans because this food undergoes a great inflation aggravating to the tranquility of a mind seeking truth. But these notions concerning a phantastical spirit which have been handed down by Synesius are nonsense as are the fancies of Pythagoreans and Platonists more void of truth and more incredible even than the tales of the poets.

But so that we may also enjoy something from the ecclesiastical authorities, St. Gregory in the *Dialogues*, Book IV, Chapter 48, lists six causes of dreams. For dreams exist, he says, either (1) from the plenitude or emptiness of the body, or (2) from preceding daily thoughts and cares, or (3) from illusion created by the devil, or (4) out of thought of man together with illusion of the devil, or (5) out of the revelation of God, or (6) finally out of the thought of man together with the revelation of God. When Gregory has recalled the same six causes of dreams in his *Moralia*, Book 8, Chapter 13, he then illustrates them with pertinent opinions in the Holy Scriptures and confirms them with examples.

> The first two types which we have advanced we all know from experience. Four, however, we find in sacred literature. For if dreams did not very often take shape through illusions created by a concealed enemy, the Scriptures, Ecclesiasticus 34, would never have said: "Dreams and empty illusions lead many men astray" and certainly it would not have been written in Leviticus 19, "You shall not practice augury nor shall you analyze dreams." With these words, which form part of an execration, it is clearly demonstrated what attitudes are associated with augurs. Again, if at times dreams did not arise from reflection together with illusion, Solomon would not declare in Ecclesiastes, Chapter 5: "Dreams follow upon many cares." And if dreams did not sometimes originate in the mystery of a revelation, why would Joseph have seen himself in a dream appointed to be advanced above his brethren, or the espoused of Mary have been warned by the Angel in a dream to take the Child and fly into Egypt? Again unless dreams did not upon occasion proceed from reflections combined with revelation, Daniel in explaining the vision of Nebuchadnezzar would not have begun his interpretation by saying, "O king, the thoughts which came into your head upon the bed are those which will come to pass hereafter."

This is what Gregory wrote in the *Moralia,* and the foregoing is what others have advanced on the causes of dreams.

I have personally diligently scrutinized the causes of dreams which are of value for signifying something and worthy of observation and I have noted four causes in particular that can be recalled.

The first cause concerns any effect upon the body which is dominant and overpowering within the body itself—that is, if, for example, yellow or black bile, the phlegmatic humor, or the blood should be in excess, or if any other vitiating and noxious substance should be lying inordinately within the body. Galen in *On Prophecies Drawn from Dreams,* Book 5, relates that a certain man dreamed that a second shinbone was made for him out of stone; soon, however, he began to become paralyzed in that very part of his body. Furthermore, those who are about to sweat profusely in an incipient crisis often dream that they are sweating, being sprinkled with hot water in a bath or swimming in a lake or river. It also comes to pass not infrequently that we toss about while sleeping or that we suffer even though only dreaming, like those who sweat in their sleep or are seized by fever and dream that they are so affected. It has been related by Pliny in the *Natural Histories,* Book VII, Chapter 50, that Publius Cornelius Ruffinus [*sic*] lost his sight while he was sleeping and that he himself dreamed it as it was happening.

The second cause of dreams attests to any strong disturbance or aroused state of mind. I mean love, hope, fear, or hate. For those who love ardently often dream of their amours; those who are afraid are frequently troubled in sleep by threatening and fearful visions.

Here also the ingrained habits and experiences of the life we lead are pertinent. For a fisherman nearly always dreams of seas, lakes, rivers, nets, fish; a hunter, of forests, ravines, mountains, and wild animals; a soldier, of the calls of the trumpet, the clashing of armor, wounds, blood, slaughter. A certain fisherman in Theocritus drolely says, "Every dog dreams of bread and I dream of fish." This same cause includes the cares and anxieties of our preceding waking hours and whatever preys upon our minds and preoccupies us; very often visions similar to those anxieties come to us in sleep. Thus in the Book of Ecclesiastes, Chapter V, it is written "Dreams follow upon cares." I would certainly place Hannibal's dream, which has been transmitted and believed by many, in this class of dreams. Hannibal was burning with an insatiable hate of the Roman name, aflame with utter passion to exterminate Roman rule. In order that this might be accomplished more easily he was anxious to transfer the war from Spain to Italy so that he might seek out the Roman seat of power. Since, therefore, he was extremely perturbed by various thoughts and considerations about this matter, he had a vision in his sleep which miraculously answered his question and prayer. He saw a youth of super-human nature, who said that he had been sent to him by Jove as a leader of his invasion into Italy and bade him not glance around at what would take place behind his back. At first Hannibal was terrified and did not dare divert his eyes in any direction from that boy. But as human nature is inclined toward the forbidden, he was unable to constrain his eyes, and looking back, he saw a portent awful not only to see but even to describe, a huge monster with many serpents coiled about him, which trampled down and crashed through everything whichever way he charged. At the same time he saw heaven darken with deep black clouds everywhere he looked, and dense clouds shot through with lightning rushing over. Hannibal was stunned and asked his guardian what was the significance of this monster and portent. He answered that it was the devastation of Italy, that he (Hannibal) should continue to push forward toward whatever place he intended and that he should not inquire anything further, but rather allow the fates to remain veiled. And certainly, this dream did take shape out of Hannibal's previous reflections and concerns while he was awake. But nevertheless, the outcome of the situation well enough confirmed the verity of his dream, for Hannibal brought even more evil into Italy than had been foretold by that vision.

The third cause of dreams I attribute to the power and cunning of the devil. For he breathes many things into the sleeping and suggests dreams, always in an insidious and malicious way, obviously so that by whatever method he can, he may be troublesome and do injury to many. The devil, then, is the architect and agent of certain dreams, and here is apparent what is clearly understood in sacred writings: the analysis (*observationem*) of dreams is so despised by God that when practised by magicians and augurs, it, together with other evil works of the sorcerers is condemned to dire punishments. This is not at all surprising for any other reason, as blessed Gregory explains in the *Dialogues*, Book IV, Chapter 48, since the devil is most always implicated in dreams, filling the minds of men with poisonous superstition and not only uselessly deluding but perniciously deceiving them. The stories about Aesculapius, Serapis, and Amphiaraus confirm the fact that the devil at one time was wont in many instances to sport with the mortal races, blinded by impiety, with this kind of dreams. For it is written in Philostratus, Pausanias and Strabo that the three former men, highly esteemed by the people, were accustomed, like God, to prescribe cures for individual diseases through the medium of dreams to those who entered their temples afflicted by various diseases. In this classification, I think, belongs that noble dream of Alexander the Great, according to the authority of the writings which have passed on the affairs of his life and merit confidence among many people. For when, in a certain battle, Ptolemy, who was the first king of Egypt after Alexander, had been struck by a poison spear and lay dying in extreme agony from this wound, Alexander, sitting next to him, fell asleep and saw in his sleep a dragon carrying a small root in his mouth at the same time indicating where that root would grow which would assuredly have immediate power to cure Ptolemy and many soldiers wounded by the same weapon. The herbs were sought, found and put to use, and soon followed the promised effect. There are, however, two particular types of dreams initiated by the devil, one of which pertains to the disclosure and manifestation of occult secrets. For the devil can know and indicate to men through dreams the natural effects which will necessarily arise at any moment from certain causes, whatever he himself is about to do, and what things, both present and past, are hidden from men. The second type of dream has the power of exciting confusion in the mind so that when the humors and vapors which are in the body have been agitated and thrown off balance, men are excessively aroused, either to sensual pleasure, or to hate and vindictiveness, or to other perverse states of mind.

Furthermore, it can be conjectured in two ways quite probably enough which are the dreams sent by the devil. First, indeed, if dreams take place frequently which are significant of future events or occult matters, knowledge of which does not contribute to a constructive end, either for oneself or for others, but to a wrong or idle display of curious knowledge, it will be considered, and not rashly, that the initiator of these dreams is the devil, that it is he who by this method attempts to infuse the minds of men with vain superstition, if not even ensnare them in criminal impiety. Second, if dreams that are obscene, repulsive and full of cruelty and impiety come so very often to sober, upright and religious men, it is not unjustly held that these dreams proceed from the devil. For the devil tries to pollute the bodies of sleeping men with impure dreams and defile them so that he may make their minds, when they awaken, somehow partners in his foulness. But if he cannot accomplish this, he at least attends to one thing, that by grieving, disturbing, and afflicting pious men with such sights, he may render them slower and more indolent for prayer, for the offices of charity, and for the taking of the holy sacraments. Cassian in his twenty-second *Collation,* Chapter 6, gives a most enlightening example of diabolic cunning and maliciousness. Indeed, Justin Martyr in response to the twenty-first question of the Orthodox, lucidly and skillfully expresses his position on this matter. For when these questions were put to him, he replied to the interrogation in the manner we have here indicated. There remains the fourth and last cause of dreams which we can rightly call divine. This entire discussion of ours was instituted above all for the sake of stating and elucidating this cause. What has been said up to now serves this end. However, examples of dreams which have been sent by God are encountered at random in the divine books; above we have lifted some examples from sacred books and more can be added if anyone wishes to assemble all of them. For the rest, so that the force and nature of divine dreams may be fully and clearly understood, I shall, in the scholastic tradition, take up several questions, lucidly to be sure, but briefly and concisely, and still observing brevity, I shall also refer to many examples, complete and undiminished for the consideration of the reader.

Third inquiry: By what signs may it be known whether a dream has been sent by God or not?

As it now occurs to me, one can determine whether a dream has been sent by God in two ways. First, certainly, the excellence of the thing signified in the dream: if things, of which certain knowledge can only reach man by the will and grant of God, become known to a man through a dream, they are of such kinds as are called "future contingencies" (*futura contingentia*) in the schools of theologians. Indeed, they are the heart's secrets which, enclosed within the soul's deepest recesses, completely conceal themselves from all intellectual perception of mortals; and, finally, they are the principal mysteries of our faith, made manifest to no one except by the instruction of God. A dream, therefore, which contains this sort of knowledge and revelation may be considered divine. Second, the divinely inspired dream is powerfully conveyed by a certain interior illumination and stirring of souls whereby God thus enlightens the mind, influences the will, and convinces man of the trustworthiness and validity of this dream in order that he may clearly recognize that God is its author and freely decide that without any doubt he both wants to and ought to believe in it. On this point that memorable opinion of Gregory in the *Dialogues,* Book IV, Chapter 48, is, as Gregory says,

> Saints at times distinguish between illusions and revelations, the real voices and images of visions, with penetrating delicacy, so that they know what they may receive from good inspiration and what they may suffer from illusion. For if the mind of man, which does occasionally utter many truths that it might serve in the end to free the soul from some misconception, were not alerted against these things, it would plunge itself through the agency of the deceiving spirit into many futile pursuits.

This is as far as Gregory goes here. In his works, the reader will find this same position more extensively and lucidly treated in the *Moralia,* Book VIII, Chapter 13. Thus, just as the natural light of the mind makes us clearly perceive the truth of first principles and embrace it with our approval immediately before the introduction of any proof, so indeed, when dreams have been given by God, the divine light flooding into our souls has effect with the result that we recognize these dreams as being both true and divine and are confirmed in our faith. Correctly, therefore, it is told in Ecclesiasticus 34 that "If the visitation were not sent by the Lord, you would not open your heart to dreams," which means that a few dreams are given to men by God, through his miraculous visitation of their souls.

However, according to sacred writings, this visitation of God through dreams often comes about in many different ways. For sometimes God troubles and frightens men through dreams, as it is related of Abimelech and Laban in Genesis. In Job 4 and 7 it says: "You will make me afraid by dreams and visions and you will strike me with terror." Sometimes during sleep God arouses man and incites him to undertake some great and difficult task by disclosing the definite prospect of a favorable outcome, just as it happened in the dreams of Gideon and Judas Maccabaeus. Often He warns and advises what a man ought to do or whether he ought to flee: such were the dreams of blessed Joseph and the Magi. The words which are written in Job 33 attest to this: "When men are sleeping in bed, He opens their ears and, enlightening them, provides them with knowledge." And it was also at one time the practice of God to bestow prophetic inspiration upon some men. For in Numbers 12 God says: "If there be a prophet of the Lord among you, I shall appear to him in a vision or I shall speak to him in a dream." And in Joel 2 dreams are included among other gifts of the Holy Spirit. We also read in I Kings 3 that the gift of wisdom and knowledge was promised by God to Solomon during his sleep. The future brilliance of some men's honor and glory is also revealed from time to time through a dream, as we read in the Scriptures happened to the young Joseph and to Mordecai. To certain ones, moreover, divine mysteries were disclosed in sleep: Jacob's dream of the mystic ladder and Daniel's concerning the kingdom of Christ were of this nature. Finally, at times God has prefigured and revealed beforehand the future event of human affairs: such were the dreams of Abraham in Genesis 15, of Pharaoh in Genesis 41 and of Nebuchadnezzar in Daniel 2 and 4.

Divine dreams reach men in different ways, sometimes accompanied by terror and a great upheaval of body and soul, as happened to Abraham and Nebuchadnezzar. Occasionally a dream has been given to someone who has not been permitted to apprehend the meaning, as in the dreams of Pharaoh and Nebuchadnezzar. To Daniel, however, and to other prophets, comprehension was divinely conveyed at the same time as the dreams themselves. On the other hand, understanding of the two dreams through which Joseph's future dignity and power over his brothers was foretold to him was given to no one at the time; but, later, the truth of these dreams was made known and understood by the very outcome of the situation. That variety too is seen in divine dreams; for some dreams are clear and lucid, obviously denoting the actual things themselves, as were the dreams of blessed Joseph, the three Magi, and St. Paul, whereas others are obscure and involved, actually making implications through metaphors (*similtudines*). Of this kind were the dreams of Pharaoh about the seven ears of corn and the seven oxen, of Nebuchadnezzar about the statue and the tree, and not least those of Pharaoh's butler and baker. In addition, it seems that upon occasion either God himself speaks with men in sleep, as in the dreams of Jacob and Solomon; or an angel, as in the dreams of blessed Joseph; or some man, as in the dream of St. Paul. Moreover, when He has been repeatedly asked, God often sends dreams as an interpretation of a dream: thus He entrusted Daniel in sleep, who had so fervently prayed to Him while awake, the interpretation of the dreams which Nebuchadnezzar had had. Indeed, it is seen in I Samuel, Chapter 28, that there was once among the Hebrews a certain admirable procedure and custom of taking counsel with God in extremely uncertain, critical matters, so that He would indicate through dreams what was true or what needed to be done. Last, certain divinely inspired dreams answer to the preceding reflections and cares of men's waking hours. Among this kind ought to be included the first dream of Nebuchadnezzar, told in Daniel 2, and similarly the first dream of blessed Joseph which St. Matthew relates in his first chapter, the above mentioned dream of Hannibal, and also that of Scipio Aemilianus, concisely composed and most eloquently narrated by Cicero.

Fourth inquiry: Why should God convey his secrets to men in sleep?

Since the soul of a man in sleep would seem to be the least receptive and the least capable of understanding divine matters, it definitely seems fitting to inquire why God has wished not infrequently to instruct men both in the secrets of His providence and in the mysteries of heavenly affairs through dreams. But actually, we can bring forth varied reasons for this occurrence. Hippocrates touches upon the first reason at the beginning of his book on dreams: the soul is cut off by men while awake in various preoccupations. It is held apart by serious business, and distracted by cares; moreover, it is called toward things outside itself by those matters which are exterior to it, and because of the different impressions of the senses, it is led astray and hindered by the multiplicity of noises of human activity; it is drawn away from contemplation of itself and of things celestial. In addition, it vacillates in uncertain deliberations; it is aroused by different interests and emotions which do not allow it to see clearly or judge impartially that which is true and valid. On the other hand, in rest and sleep the mind is free and delivered of all disturbances and hindrances of this kind; it is entirely present and conscious of its own being; it attends to itself, and all of its own powers are with it; it holds its faculties collected together and joined; keen, prepared to understand, it is fully and utterly capable of all things which should be placed before it from without. One may set down the second reason for the same thing. What we receive when awake we are accustomed to discuss and examine with subtle analysis and to recall to calculation and to weighing upon the balance of human reason, for we demand that all things conform to the rule of reason. If what has been presented to us meets this standard, we approve; if there is discrepancy, it is renounced and rejected. In sleep, however, the mind of man accepts without examination things which have been cast before it; it is more prepared and conditioned to trust and follow divinely inspired visions. Moreover, all men who have written on divine matters agree that it is more conducive to understanding these things—not only intellectually but also emotionally, so to speak, and with a sort of spiritual sensitivity and with taste—for a man to be directed and ruled from without rather than governing himself, for him to be a listener rather than an arbitrator and judge, and, last, for him to have a simple faith rather than to investigate and ponder the reasons for believing. The third reason, which lies in dreams itself, has been treated in Aristotle's tract *On Divination*. He says:

> Whatever impulse by which the mind of a sleeping person is kept activated and stirring from without, however slight and nominal, has nevertheless a great power to motivate the mind, is firmly grounded in it and cleaves to it tenaciously. This occurs, moreover, because of the stillness of the night, the calm and idleness of the sense organs and the absence of all things to which minds normally direct their attention. For at that time when the senses have been lulled to sleep and the body languishes, what is exterior is not perceived.

For at that propitious moment, God instructs man without any disturbance, without the observation of other men, finally without the interruption of anything. Particularly, moreover, since the further our mind is drawn away from association with the senses and contact with the body, the more readily it seems to be influenced and the keener it is for understanding the divine messages. Too, during sleep, which is a kind of likeness or imitation of death, the mind somehow seems to be separated from participation in the body and the body's chains, and to a certain extent unquestionably relaxes. The fourth reason is, in my opinion, how much more influential is God than any man in teaching and enlightening man. Certainly man can teach man, but not unless he is awake, listening, and attentive. God, however, can even instruct him very effectively when he is sleeping and dreaming. Thus he rightfully proclaims that he holds supreme power and influence over all the forces and faculties of the human mind. And then I shall suggest a fifth reason, evidently so that no one may think that death takes away from man all knowledge and that there is no other method of organizing knowledge except through consciousness, discursive reasoning, and preliminary understanding of other things. Averroes in his own commentary on Aristotle, *On Divination through Dreams,* does not dare to deny that prophecy can come to man either through sleep or through revelation. Yet, he denies that the arts or speculative sciences are available to anyone by this process. He says:

> The nature of man is one: just one, therefore, will be the mode of learning and teaching, namely, through the intermediary senses, so through the various experiences received and careful rational analysis of them. For if, in addition to the common and usual means of learning, there were yet this other one through dreams or revelation, which would be much easier and far superior, the former method would be the more difficult and trying, thus the more superfluous, and therefore would not be given to man. For God and nature do not act fruitlessly, and God would not act on things of which I am capable of doing very well and securely.

And so he writes, Indeed, this argument would not be obviously groundless if anyone should say (though no one among us does) that this way of learning through dreams or revelations were either natural to man or frequent and customary. But that these comments of Averroes, like others of his on the knowledge, power and providence of God and the nature of the human soul are unscholarly, dull and fallacious and arise from an overflowing fountain of impiety and ignorance of things divine, is clear enough alone from the examples noted in the Scriptures of Adam, Solomon, Daniel and many of the prophets, to whom knowledge of numerous things was suddenly given by God; but in addition from those of Bezaleel and Aholiab who, it is narrated in the Book of Exodus, were suddenly informed by divine inspiration that Moses had completed the tabernacle together with all its appurtenances and adornments with perfect skill.

Fifth inquiry: Why should dreams be given by God to obscure and uneducated men but not to the learned?

Aristotle and Cicero thought that by just this one reckoning of all dreams which are believed to be divine, their trustworthiness and validity could be disparaged and disregarded. For if these dreams, they say, were given to men by God, it is reasonable that they would not be given to humble and uneducated men, but to those individuals excelling in knowledge and wisdom. In this they erred because they obviously ignored the distinction between divine dreams, those which I say are truly divine, and those which are not divine but erroneously regarded as such. Witness the gods of the pagans who, there is absolutely no doubt, were demons as far as we Christians are concerned. They were somehow unable to foresee with certainty and to know the future occurrences and the consequences of human affairs, for this is the province of God alone, and so they could not predict or reveal in advance these events with definite words or signs. This is why they did not give dreams through which the future was unveiled to educated and wise men clearly so that these men, recognizing the vanity and fallaciousness of those dreams, would not shatter the authority of the very gods in the eyes of others and publicly expose their oracles which were void of supposed divinity and the inanities of their "truth" to the derision and contempt of the masses. Therefore, they gave such dreams to the uneducated and to those unskilled at differentiating between truth and deception, but most particularly to the superstitious who for this reason are within themselves quite prepared and inclined to believe anything whatsoever. On the other hand, dreams which are sent by the true God of which we read are generally given to men of piety preeminent in their wisdom, such as Abraham, Jacob, Solomon and Daniel. Nevertheless, a few dreams are also given to men not so learned in this way but still of strong faith and renowned for their exceptional purity. Outstanding virtue and piety, moreover, render the soul of a man more docile and more fit for the comprehension of things divine than do either human wisdom or knowledge. For those who excel in worldly capacities or learning are nearly always either impious or proud or twisted by the iniquitous sins, and these qualities completely cut off the souls of men from spiritual doctrines or divine enlightenment. It does not escape me that certain divinely inspired dreams have come to wicked and impious men such as Pharaoh and Nebuchadnezzar. But these dreams were not given to them primarily for their own sakes nor were they bestowed along with understanding of them. As a result, when those men could not find an interpretation of those dreams among their own seers, they were compelled to seek it from worshippers of the true God and by this way came to now the true God and to venerate Him and hold His servants in admiration and respect. This is what the dreams of Pharaoh and Nebuchadnezzar, which were interpreted by Joseph and Daniel, manifestly illustrate.

Sixth inquiry: Why are divinely inspired dreams sometimes obscure and perplexing?

But let us investigate and discover the reason why divinely inspired dreams are not always clear and open but rather perplexing, shadowed and obscured by images and likenesses of other things and not only hidden in meaning to others but least perceptible even to those to whom they are given. Although the gods of the pagans, i.e., the demons, could not have certain knowledge of future events, they quite often gave dreams to indicate the future, but obscure and ambiguous ones which could easily be distorted and applied to different, even conflicting consequences; this way the dream would seem to conform to whatever happened. But if the dreams did not correspond to the outcome, this was attributed not to their falsity but to the ignorance of the interpreters who, because of the dreams' obscurity and ambiguity, had not correctly interpreted them. However, dreams whose origin we know from the Scriptures to have been God's are most often given distinctly and explicitly; such, we read, were the dreams of Abimelech, Laban, Judas Maccabaeus, Solomon, blessed Joseph and the three Magi. Nevertheless, it must not be denied that certain dreams have been sent in a covered, obscure manner to refined men also and clearly for this end: that they acquire an understanding of these dreams which they could get from no others but holy men, and that they should honor those servants of God and seek after God with the highest reverence and veneration. Indeed, if these obscure dreams have also been given to the servants of God, it is for that purpose that in entreating God in extreme earnestness with many tears and ardent prayers, they should at last gain insight and understanding of these dreams and, on account of the difficulty in gaining this, have more esteem for Him and hold Him dearer. Besides the vagueness of the dreams themselves, that of the things they signify is also clarified. In addition, most of the more sublime mysteries are conveyed more quickly through images and representations than if they had been expressed in words clear and exact. For many and varied and profound as the mysteries are, one statue seen by Nebuchadnezzar in his sleep was able to foreshadow them, whereas had it been necessary to impart them through words proper, they could hardly have been declared in the longest discourse. Finally, God sometimes intends that dreams be hidden and incomprehensible for a while so that their truth may be the more firmly recognized and acknowledged through the consequences itself and the succession of events. This is clearly seen in Joseph's two dreams which prefigured his ascent to supreme rank and power.

Seventh inquiry: Is a Christian permitted to examine dreams?

Two difficulties are touched upon in these words, the first of which is whether divine law permits Christians to examine dreams inquisitively. The answer to this is easy and immediate, for they are permitted to examine certain dreams but not others. First, dreams which indicate good or bad states of the body and the maladies of both body and soul are observed and exploited to full advantage by physicians of the soul and body. Second, it is allowed to take note of the causes from which arise the dreams which infect our brain, frighten, confuse and unnerve us so that either we may by observing effects study the causes unknown to us and grasp them, or we may discover some way of repelling this nuisance from us. And this privilege has often been utilized by holy men. Indeed, we read in Cassian's twenty-second *Collation* that the ancient masters and tutors of the monks were carefully versed in investigating and ferreting out the causes of certain dreams. Third, the observation of dreams, in so far as some truth pertaining to the speculative sciences or giving counsel as to what should be done is thus made known to man, ought not to be condemned either as superstitious or vain. Finally, dreams which often arouse us and provoke us to crime are forced upon us for consideration by the devil just as, conversely, those by which we are moved and encouraged toward good acts, such as celibacy, generosity, compassion, and espousal of religion, are sent by God to be pondered, not by the superstitious of spirit, but by the religious man, wise, cautious and mindful of his own well-being.

However, it is characteristic of the foolish—that I may not say stupid—to think that an account must be made and concern taken for any dream whatsoever, regardless of how it reaches us, be it rarely, without purpose and by accident. For as has been illustrated above, the majority of dreams possess nothing true or certain but are pervaded by deception and chance. Moreover, it has not only been permitted to regard dreams as though there were invariably something divine in them as the pagans evidently believed there to be in the chatter, flight and feeding of birds and in the entrails of animals so that they thought to derive foreknowledge from them and divined the future. But this practice has been utterly censured, condemned and forbidden in the Scriptures, as even no less than the sins of magic and spells. This is clearly understood in Leviticus 19 and Deuteronomy 18, and the last book of the Paralipomenon, ("leftovers," 2 Chronicles), Chapter 33 [The three places in which Jerome translated *soothsaying* as *to observe dreams*. See note, p. 291, n.69.], and in other passages of the Holy Scriptures. And actually, to wish to know the future, which God has placed in His power alone, is arrogant, impious curiosity. To think, moreover, that sure signs of the future are contained in dreams which have no connection or relationship with future things is foolish. Too little have I stressed that this is plainly impious and stupid, for the following proves that those who regard dreams in such a way have been infected and depraved by foolish, profane and absurd opinions. Either those people think that all future happenings depend upon natural causes, and this is false; or they think that these things can be indicated by any dreams whatsoever, which is obviously ridiculous; or they think that all future events are accurately foreseen and known by the devil, which is blatant impiety; or else they think that the future is revealed by God at random and indifferently through any dreams to any men, which is absurd. There is no one who does not see it. And in the end, to place so much importance on dreams and to depend upon them to such an extent that one directs the whole rationale of his life toward their standard, as it were, and either undertakes or declines action and personal affairs out of habitual consideration of dreams, is not only beneath the excellence of man, but also smells of that fatal necessity of the Stoics, which has been so many times damned in the Church and exploded and rejected by better philosophers. So if the astrologers, who think that human affairs hang upon the stars, suspended so to speak and entirely removed, are deservedly censured and refuted by scholars, then assuredly so much the more ought the superstitious observers of dreams to be reprehended, especially since the stars are superior to dreams in their stature in nature, stability of motion, constancy of order, amplitude of power and superior efficacy.

Eighth inquiry: What man may rightfully interpret dreams?

We answer the foregoing question which is asked as to which man may rightfully interpret dreams in the following manner. Not just any man may interpret those dreams which have the power to indicate something and which merit examination and interpretation. Three classes of dreams of this nature can be distinguished: many are natural, certain ones human and still a few are divine. There is no doubt that interpretation of the natural dreams should be properly left to skilled and learned natural philosophers (*physici*) and physicians, especially to those who know how to compare the images presented in dreams with one another and discern what they represent and from what causes they customarily arise; similar to him who, taking in hand any fragmented patterns and images and successfully fitting together their scattered parts, accurately perceives that the likenesses concern, be it men, horses, or other things, and he correctly evaluates them. However, the shrewdest appraiser of human dreams, the most apt and accurate interpreter, will be naturally he who is most thoroughly versed in human affairs and likewise one who, as an extremely experienced man, has attained to a complete and perfect knowledge, confirmed by many tests of human character, interests, customs and persuasions, which also assume great variety in different men; one who, as it were, grasps the very pulse of man's social and individual activity. Yet again, it is up to him to explicate divine dreams who stands in readiness to apprehend them, since it is clear that no one can interpret them unless he be divinely inspired and instructed. "For no one has known what is of God," says Paul in Chapter 2 of the First Epistle to the Corinthians, "except the Spirit of God." But this is especially so since the symbols of divine dreams are ordained through the plan and will of God alone and for this reason can be made known to men only through the revelation of God. Wherefore Daniel thus addressed King Nebuchadnezzar who was anxious and distraught about his dream by which he had been utterly terrified because he could learn its meaning from none of his wise men: "Neither magicians nor seers, nor augurs nor wise men can explain to the King the mystery about which he asks; but it is God in heaven revealing his mysteries."

Iamblichus thinks that divine dreams almost never come to men, except at the beginning or end of sleep, clearly because at the former time the mind of man is not yet possessed and stultified by vapors of food and drink and at the latter time when, with sleep fleeting, the fog of the vapors has been dispersed and the mind has emerged from those baser considerations, it is purer and more keyed to receiving divine messages. Therefore, it was the custom of seers and interpreters of dreams to inquire of those referring dreams to them at what time they occurred. For if they happened in deep sleep, the seers flatly rejected them since it was not consistent with any logic that dreams should be divinely bestowed upon a mind sunk in heavy sleep. But, if, however, the dreams occurred at the end of sleep when the mind was now almost awakened to its proper functions, then the seers, deciding that these dreams were divinely inspired and worthy of God as their author, accepted their obligation to consider and interpret them. Philostratus' *Life of Apollonius,* Book 2, Chapter 24, should also be read. Yet actually Iamblichus' teachings of which this one is the most scholarly were chronicled from the superstitious observations, or more accurately, I should say, figments of Egyptian priests. In truth, God has not been bound in that way to the laws of time nor does He need the moment of time to act. For wherever, whenever and whomever He wishes He inspires with His dreams. He can at any time, and indeed even without time, suddenly calm the nervous agitation of human beings, still the tumult of their animal souls, purge them of phantasy, enlighten their minds and properly ready their spirits to receive divine dreams.

Ninth inquiry: Can there be free use of reason and will in sleep?

Very often in dreams, especially in those which come to the learned, wise and saintly, the soul of man, because it is related to the use of reason and the activity of the mind, is unfettered, extricated and free. For sometimes the reasoning power of a sleeping person lucidly understands simple things and either places them in proper context or distinguishes them, analyzes, evaluates, and marvels at them, and often it makes new discoveries. The very soul also turns inward upon itself to review its own actions and appraise its keenness. It reflects upon its strength, waits, hangs back, hesitates, debates within itself whether or not the man is sleeping at that time. These things moreover, clearly demonstrate the free exercise of reason during this period. Nevertheless, it must not therefore be concluded that, since the power of reason is sometimes liberated in sleep, the exercise of free will is likewise implemented. For perfect liberty of a man is necessary for complete and perfect exercise of free will: that is, it is imperative that there be liberation of all the senses and powers so that it is the man himself who then acts and is in no way acted upon, that he is the master of himself and of all his own actions, and that during that time it is in his power either to act in a particular way or not to act at all. This never occurs in sleep.

Tenth inquiry: On the dream of Solomon in which God promised and granted to him the gift of wisdom

There remains a slight problem which is found in I Kings Chapter 3. While sleeping, Solomon saw God and He bade him request whatever of all things Solomon longed for most. Solomon, thereupon, asked for wisdom and understanding to rule over his people for whom he was responsible and had sacrificed all of his other possessions, riches which still seem to be sought after and coveted above all things by the princes of this world. Solomon's request so pleased God that He promised to give Solomon supreme wisdom, in addition to the wealth which he had not asked for, and to bestow them both in overflowing abundance. From this account in the very Scriptures it seems to be well enough established that in this dream Solomon was exercising freely and without impediment not only reason but also volition: for that entreaty made in sleep would not have been able to please God so much and to elicit such a great gift of wisdom had it not been made by his own free will. This difficulty can be handled and solved in three ways. First certainly, it can be replied that Solomon's petition during sleep pleased God not in itself, but on account of a certain similar request made previously in waking hours and from which the one in sleep unquestionably derived. For Solomon had most ardently entreated and beseeched of God the gift of knowledge and wisdom. God expressed through that dream that this request had been most gratifying to Him and that it would have the desired effect. But perhaps this answer will seem more than slightly awkward and contrived to some. Therefore, let me submit another solution; for it could be said that this was a dream in the beginning but then by the miraculous working of God was converted into an ecstatic or rapturous experience, such as actually often occurred to St. Paul or the prophets. In this state the spirit of Solomon, as permitted by the body, was deflected from consciousness of external things like the spirit of sleeping people; though here it was done through the power of God so that, delivered and free then to exercise the functions of both reason and free will, Solomon voluntarily sought of God what he wished, and by asking things which were pleasing to God, was all worthy to receive them from him. But this answer is not satisfactory. Now I submit for consideration whether a perfect use of free will can exist in rapture and ecstacy. I firmly maintain that the Holy Scriptures do not support the foregoing explanation. At least in the above mentioned passages where they are about to describe that vision of Solomon, they declare that God appeared to Solomon in a dream; and then, having related the vision, they add "Thereupon Solomon awoke and understood that it was a dream," whereby it is specifically indicated that this vision was in no way a rapturous transport or ecstacy, but entirely a dream, albeit a divine dream, obviously given by God to enlighten and to instruct Solomon. St. Thomas gives these two solutions to the proposed question in I, 2. Question 113, article 3, to 2.

Therefore, unless I am mistaken, there will yet be a third more likely and suitable answer, which has been highly praised even by Tostadus in his twelfth inquiry concerning the First Book of Kings, Chapter 3. We maintain that since Solomon was then truly sleeping and his vision was a dream just as the Scriptures attest, anything that is said to have been accomplished thereupon, as a consequence enacted at that time, was done not in reality, but rather through the imaginary vision of the sleeping person. Thus Solomon at that moment seemed to himself to be seeking knowledge from God and God also seemed to him to assent to his request, while in reality, however, there was no petition, no desire on Solomon's part and likewise no response and no promise from God. Why therefore, you ask, was that dream given to Solomon by God? Evidently, unless my conjecture is wrong, He did it for three reasons: first, that it might be recognized that the author and bestower of all blessings is God and that all benefits must be sought and requested from Him. Second, that it might be made clear which choice and petition of blessings is pleasing and welcome to God: those which are spiritual are far preferred to the corporeal, the celestial blessings to the terrestrial, and finally those concerning the coming interest and well-being of others to those which are vain and fruitless. And last, so that it might be open and manifest from the example of Solomon how great is the benignity and munificence of God toward his servants, whose prayers and entreaties He not only answers but far surpasses and over abundantly fulfills. Consider, then, Solomon: he sought only knowledge from God, having renounced all other goods beyond this, which are the most precious and dear to men. But God generously granted both knowledge above Solomon's hope and other blessings beyond Solomon's prayer.

Now let our discussion on dreams terminate here, as I fear it would become painful and boring to the reader should it be protracted. For even as sleep sweetly revives the limbs and restores strength because it is quiet and peaceful, if dreams which are too long, serious and oppressive occur in sleep, they will tire and weaken the body and soul alike. Thus we have had to be extremely cautious that this discussion of ours on dreams not become long beyond usefulness, lose the appreciation of the readers and turn the pleasure which they have perhaps derived into criticism and hostility.

Notes

Preface

1. I have described the development of the rational-materialistic view of reality and its inadequacy in *Encounter With God* and *Reaching: The Journey to Fulfillment*.
2. A fine summary of Hobson's work is presented by Edward Dolnick in his article "What Dreams Are (Really) Made Of," *The Atlantic* 266, no. 1 (July 1990): 41–61. Dr. Hobson's theory of dream interpretation is much closer to Jung than Freud. He believes, like Jung, that the dream is not trying to deceive us, but to lead us to meaning.
3. R. A. Brown and R. G. Luckcock, "Dreams, Daydreams and Discovery," *Journal of Chemical Education* 55, no. 11 (November 1978).

Chapter 1

1. A comprehensive survey of the material on experimental study of sleep was compiled by Charles Fisher in his article "Psychoanalytic Implications of Recent Research on Sleep and Dreaming," *Journal of the American Psychoanalytic Association* 13, no. 2 (April 1965): 197–303. A more popular treatment of the work of William Dement was given in the feature article in *The New Yorker* of September 18, 1965. *MD Medical Newsmagazine* for December 1965 also featured dreams, dealing with several aspects, including the interesting cover story, "Dreams and History" (vol. 9, no. 12). There is also an excellent and very readable summary of the subject published by the U.S. Department of Health, Education and Welfare, called *Current Research on Sleep and Dreams,* Public Health Service Publication, No. 1389, Washington, D.C., U.S. Government Printing Office.
2. One of these volumes was the hardback edition of *Zolar's Encyclopedia and Dictionary of Dreams,* brought out by Doubleday in 1963. One of the most popular little handbooks is the Dell paperback *Dreams,* which has gone through at least one revision. Although, as I shall indicate later, dream symbols cannot be handled in the arbitrary way these books employ, they at least make a stab at understanding dreams, and the great amount of interest in them is a token of the popular attitude.
3. Quoted in *MD* (December 1965), 180.
4. Lawrence S. Kubie, "Blocks to Creativity," *International Science and Technology* 42 (June 1965): 74ff.
5. Visions, however, are still fairly common today. Two studies made by the Society for Psychical Research in England show that about 10 percent of the normal adult population have had such an experience. *Proceedings* 10 (1894): 25ff.; *Journal* 34 (1948): 187ff.
6. This is rather different from the attitude of science and the arts. Many scientists show something of pride, almost reverence, for the visionary experiences that have been known to produce basic scientific discoveries. The story is repeated of how one of Poincaré's famous mathematical solutions came to him while he was half-dreaming on a bus ride. Even more famous was Kekulé's discovery of the structure of the benzene ring from a vision in which he suddenly saw six snakes in a ring, each swallowing the tail of the one ahead.

In the manuscript "Inner Music," being prepared by Francis Leach, a friend of mine, there are several references to well-known composers who told of music coming to them in auditory visions or even in actual dreams. Among them were Beethoven; Schumann; the American composer Roy Harris; Tartini, whose great work "The Devil's Trill" came as a whole in sleep; and also Wagner, whose remarkable creation of the prelude to *Das Rheingold* took form in a visionary state. Others like Tschaikovsky, Mozart, and Brahms have described how close they often were to a dream state during the work of composing. Some of these references are included in the bibliography.

7. For the sake of simplicity, when I refer to dreams generically from this point on, all four of these related activities will be signified.
8. There were excellent surveys of the "God is dead" movement in *Time* for October 22, 1965 (in the Religion section), and in the main feature article by Ved Mehta in *The New Yorker* for November 13, 20, and 27, 1965.
9. This fact has kept psychologists as sophisticated as O. Hobart Mowrer and Seward Hiltner, on their own admission, from reading Jung.

Chapter 2

1. First published in 1909.
2. E. A. Speiser, *Genesis, The Anchor Bible,* vol. 1 (Garden City, N.Y.: Doubleday, 1964), 162ff.
3. Incubation was the practice of sleeping in a temple or holy place specifically to receive a divine dream. I will say more about this later.
4. Prophets individually or as a group are referred to as "seers" in 1 Samuel 9:9; 2 Samuel 24:11; 2 Kings 17:13; 1 Chronicles 21:9; 25:5; 29:29; and 2 Chronicles 9:29; 12:15; 19:2; 29:30; 33:18-19; and 35:15. There are also many experiences of precognition or extrasensory perception described of various prophets, as in 1 Samuel 9:20 and 2 Kings 5:26.
5. Sources Orientales, *Les Songes et Leur Interprétation* (Paris: Editions du Seuil, 1959), 116ff. This study presents an excellent bibliography on the biblical study of dreams and incubation.
6. The problem of interpreting any passage in Ecclesiastes is complicated by the nature of the book. There is a strange interweaving of passages that express the skeptical point of view with those that express the traditional faith. One of the most interesting of the several attempts to solve this critical problem is Morris Jastrow's *A Gentle Cynic: Being a Translation of the Book of Koheleth, Commonly Known as Ecclesiastes* (Philadelphia: Lippincott, 1919).
7. The chapter and verse numbers are those of the King James Version, which places all the parts of the Greek story that do not appear in the Hebrew version into a supplement at the end of the book.
8. *The Jewish Encyclopedia* (New York: Funk and Wagnalls, 1925), 4:654ff.
9. Moses Maimonides, *The Guide for the Perplexed,* trans. M. Friedlander (London: Routledge & Kegan Paul, 1951), 225.
10. Berthold Strauss, *The Rosenbaums of Zell: A Study of a Family* (London: Hamakrik, 1962).
11. Ibid., 38.
12. Alexander Heidel, *The Gilgamesh Epic and Old Testament Parallels* (Chicago: University of Chicago Press, 1949).
13. The current interest in such beliefs is shown by the number of eminent scholars from Europe and the Orient who have contributed to *Les Songes et Leur Interprétation* (vol. 2 of the Sources Orientales series). Not only is the ancient religious interpretation of dreams discussed, represented by the Egyptians, Babylonians, Persians, Hittites, Canaanites, and Jews, but also the belief in dreams found among the shamanistic people, the Cambodians, the Chinese, Japanese, and Indians, as well as the attitude of Islam. It is interesting to note that, although Christianity was for a large portion of its history one of the significant religions of the very part of the world under discussion, not a word is included about the Christian belief. In spite of this omission, this is one of the best such studies available, indeed the only one that covers some of the material.

Chapter 3

1. The last Jewish Christian church, in Pella, existed until about A.D. 350.
2. Yet it was at this very point that Greek culture broke down. A principal reason for the rapid conquest of the Greek world by Christianity was that Christianity offered a method

of dealing with and relating to these nonrational depths, whereas the later Greek thinking failed to integrate them. Between the philosopher and the common person a great gulf became fixed. The people's irrational desires and impulses, their sudden whims and fears, became separated from their rational understanding of life. There came to be such a wide chasm between the rational and the irrational that popular thought broke down and disintegrated into a hodgepodge of superstition and necromancy. The early Christian church, undergirding itself with Greek thinking, stepped into the breach to offer an integration of the rational and the irrational. Ironically, Christianity did not have as much to offer to the Hebrews. They had forged out of their travails a religion of adversity that gave its adherents a tool for dealing with the most pressing irrational problems of life. Greek philosophy gave no such tool.

3. E. R. Dodds, *The Greeks and the Irrational* (Boston: Beacon, 1957), 104–5. Dodds has written a masterful study of dreams among the Greek people in his fourth chapter, which he calls "Dream-Pattern and Culture-Pattern."
4. George Herbert Palmer, trans., *The Odyssey of Homer* (Boston: Houghton Mifflin, 1921), 19:559ff.
5. Two works that consider this subject from different points of view are C. Kerényi, *Asklepios: Archetypal Image of the Physician's Existence* (New York: Pantheon, for the Bollingen Foundation, 1959); and Mary Hamilton, *Incubation (or the Cure of Disease in Pagan Temples and Christian Churches)* (London: Simpkin, Marshall, Hamilton, Kent & Co., 1906).
6. Dodds, *Greeks,* 193, 203, nn. 85–86.
7. Dodds, *Greeks,* 117, 135.
8. See particularly 1:34ff., 107ff., 209ff.; 2.139; 3.64ff., 124–25; 4.172; 5.56; 6.105ff., 118, 131; 7.12ff.

   It is interesting to find, as Kenneth Rexroth detailed in a 1967 issue of the *Saturday Review* (December 2), that modern scholars have had to change their idea of Herodotus as a superstitious romancer. Instead, his facts check out, and he has come to be regarded as a truly scientific historian of the cultures of his time.
9. Very few of us are aware of these passages; although there are several, they have seldom been discussed by scholars. The graduate course on Plato that I took in one of the leading universities in the East called no attention to this aspect of Plato's philosophy.
10. B. Jowett, *The Dialogues of Plato,* 4th rev. ed. (London: Clarendon, 1953), 44.
11. Ibid., 60–61.
12. Ibid., 571–72.
13. Hackforth's translation, as quoted by Josef Pieper; see n. 14 below.
14. Josef Pieper, *Love and Inspiration: A Study of Plato's Phaedrus* (London: Faber & Faber, 1965), 61.
15. This explanation tallies closely with the understanding that Euripides expressed in *Iphigenia Among the Tauri* that Apollo's oracle at Delphi had originally been a dream oracle, but once the great serpent (the bitter side) had been vanquished, dreams sent by the gods had to be closed off. Farnell, in *Encyclopedia Britannica,* shows that incubation was originally practiced at Delphi (11th ed., 20:143).
16. In this study Pieper comes to much the same conclusions as I have reached.
17. Even when he was concerned more strictly with formal or rational matters, Plato did not deny this deeper side of human life. In the *Laws* (909–10) he recognized the reality of dreams and visions that led or drove people to worship, but he denied people the right to establish private temples or shrines whenever they had such visitations or found remedy for sickness or difficulty before an altar. As he had already shown (738), the traditional gods and temples were originally established because of visions (apparitions) or some other inspiration of heaven, but intellect was needed to decide rightly about establishing further shrines.

    Plato was also well aware of the illusory quality of dreams and visions. This is particularly clear in the *Theaetetus* where Socrates is beginning to demonstrate the impossibility of "knowing" knowledge (155ff.). The discussion is introduced with the telling preface that only the initiated are to be listening:

    SOCRATES: Take a look round, then, and see that none of the uninitiated are listening. Now by the uninitiated I mean people who think that nothing *is* save what they can grasp in their

hands, and who will not allow that action or generation or anything invisible can have real existence.
THEAETETUS: Indeed, Socrates, they are themselves a very hard and metallic sort of men.
SOCRATES: Yes, my boy, outer barbarians.

Far from proving, then, that dreams are illusions while the world of sense experience is entirely real, Socrates sees something quite different. Dreams are true to the dreamer, and they even cast doubt upon the reality of sense experience, since it is impossible to be sure that one who relates a fact is not awake and telling a dream or even dreaming and telling a dream.

18. Pedro Meseguer, in the work I have mentioned, *The Secret of Dreams,* centers his discussion around a very appreciative account of Aristotle's theory of dreams (London: Burns & Oates, 1960).
19. Or, compared with the "strange dream" and the extensive medical results reported in detail in *Life,* September 29, 1967. This was the dream of Jack Dreyfus, Jr., founder of the Dreyfus Fund, which led to the diagnosis of his own medical problem and then to the initiation of new research at Johns Hopkins and Harvard that offers great hope for certain kinds of mental illness. Dreyfus's dream was simply that he had somehow been *electrically* frozen into immobility. From this fact the connections established themselves one after another until, one day, he spoke to his physician about the possibility of abnormal electrical activity in his brain, and the doctor surprisingly agreed with his idea and the suggestion he made for medication. This led to the establishment of the Dreyfus Foundation and research into the idea that came from a dream.
20. Descriptions of dreams are scattered all through Galen's works, which were the first textbooks of modern medicine. These references are discussed in detail by Joseph Walsh, M.D., "Galen's Writings and Influences Inspiring Them," *Annals of Medical History* 6, no. 1 (January 1934): 2ff.
21. *De Divinatione,* 2.72, as quoted by Meseguer, *Secret,* who presents an appreciative treatment of Cicero's dream theory (pp. 26ff.).
22. *Plutarch's Lives,* "Cicero," rev. by A. H. Clough (Boston: Little, Brown & Co., 1872), 44.2ff.
23. For instance, in the *Anabasis* 3.1.11 and 4.3.8, Xenophon recorded dreams that occurred at times when decisions had to be made. In Plutarch's *Lives* the following references to crucial dreams are found: Agesilaus 6.4–5; Agis and Cleomenes 7.2ff.; Alcibiades 39.1ff.; Alexander 2.2–3; 18.3; 24.2ff.; 26.2–3; Antony 16.3–4; Aristides 11.5–6; Marcus Brutus 20.5–6; 36.1ff.; 41.4; 48.1; Caesar 42.1–2; 63.3ff.; 69.4–5; Caius Gracchus 1.6; Cicero 2.2; 44.2ff.; Cimon 13.2–3; Coriolanus 24.1ff.; Crassus 12.3; Demetrius 4.2ff.; 29.1–2; Demosthenes 29.2ff.; Dion 2.1ff.; 55.1–2; Eumenes 6.5–6; Lucullus 10.2–3; 12.1–2; 23.3ff.; Lysander 20.5–6; Pelopidas 21.1ff.; Pericles 3.2; 13.8; Pompey 23.1–2; 32.4–5; 68.2ff.; 73.3ff.; Pyrrhus 11.2–3; 29.1ff.; Sulla 9.4; 28.4ff.; 37.1–2; Themistocles 26.2–3; Timoleon 8.1–2.

    Typical references in Josephus are found in *The Life* 208–9; *Against Apion* 1.207ff.; *Antiquities of the Jews* 11.8.4–5, 16.6.4, and 19.8.2; and in Suetonius's *Lives of the Caesars* 2.94.4-5 (Catalus) and 6.46 (Nero). One of Philo's longest treatises was his work *On Dreams.* Books 2 and 3, which are extant, are interesting examples of Philo's symbolic interpretation, first, of dreams partly due to divine agency, and then of those of a human level. The first category is represented by the dreams of Jacob, and the second by those of Joseph. Three other books on dreams by Philo are mentioned which are wholly lost.

Chapter 4

1. Quoted from Lloyd Lewis, *Myths after Lincoln* (New York: Grosset & Dunlap, 1957), 294–95. This story comes from Ward Hill Lamon, the biographer who did the least to romanticize Lincoln. In fact, Lamon's biography was so down to earth and factual that it did not sell well. The public wanted a more perfect figure than this friend and bodyguard

of Lincoln told about. He had planned a second volume, but it was never finished. Even so, Lamon's work is one of the best historical sources we have for the life of Lincoln.

2. *Eidolon,* meaning phantasm and also idol, is derived from *eido.*
3. These references occur in Matthew 4:24; 7:22; 8:16, 28ff.; 9:32ff.; 10:1, 8; 12:22ff.; 15:22; 17:18; Mark 1:23ff., 32, 34, 39; 3:11, 15, 22ff.; 5:2ff.; 6:7, 13; 7:25ff.; 9:17ff., 38; 16:9, 17; Luke 4:33ff.; 6:18; 7:21; 8:2, 27ff.; 9:1, 39ff., 49; 10:17ff.; 11:14ff.; 13:11ff., 32.
4. In Galatians Paul told how it pleased God by his grace (*charitos*) "to reveal [*apokalupsai*] his Son in me" (1:16); and in Ephesians he spoke of how the mystery of Christ was made known to him by revelation "as it has now been revealed [*apokalupsthe*] to his holy apostles and prophets by the Spirit [*en pneumati*]" (3:5). When Paul told the tribune in Jerusalem about his experience, he also mentioned the trance (*ekstasei*) in which the Lord had again appeared to him as he was praying in the temple (Acts 22:17).
5. *Antiquities* 19.8.2, where the symbolism is slightly different.
6. See W. F. Arndt and F. W. Gingrich, *A Greek-English Lexicon of the New Testament* (Chicago: University of Chicago Press, 1952), 683ff.
7. R. H. Charles, *A Critical History of the Doctrine of a Future Life* (New York, A. & C. Black, 1913), 174, quoted in *The Interpreter's Bible,* 12:350.

Chapter 5

1. The excellent translations of the Fathers brought out by the Roman Catholic foundation, Fathers of the Church, Inc., have also been helpful.
2. C. G. Jung, *Psychological Types* (London: Routledge & Kegan Paul, 1953), 275ff. The Jungian medical doctor M. Esther Harding has written an interesting analysis of *Pilgrim's Progress,* entitled *Journey Into Self* (New York: David McKay, 1956), which shows the depth and significance expressed by the imagery in this kind of work.
3. These materials are found in *The Ante-Nicene Fathers,* ed. Alexander Roberts and James Donaldson (Grand Rapids: Eerdmans, 1951): *The Pastor of Hermas,* 2:9ff.; *Epistle Concerning the Martyrdom of the Holy Polycarp* 5, 1:40.
4. Ibid.: *Acts of the Holy Apostle Thomas,* 8:542; *Consummation of Thomas, the Apostle,* 8:550; *Apocalypse of Moses,* 8:565; *Testament of Abraham* 4 and 7, 10:187, 189; *Acts of Xantippe and Polyxena* 15ff. and 22ff., 10:209ff., 212ff.; *Clementine Homilies* 14ff., 8:322ff.; *Clementine Recognitions,* 4.15ff., 10:136ff.
5. Only a few attempts were made in the ancient world to relate the church to Aristotelian thinking, and these ended in heresy. Most Arianism had an Aristotelian base. See Adolf Harnack, *History of Dogma* (London: Williams & Norgate, 1912), 3:46; 4:48, 65, 74ff.
6. E. R. Dodds demonstrates this graphically in the story of Aelius Aristides and his interpretations of his dreams. He also offers excellent detail of the Hellenistic worldview in the early Christian era, particularly as seen by Plotinus and Porphyry. Dodds, *Pagan and Christian in an Age of Anxiety* (Cambridge: University Press, 1965), 39ff., 72ff.
7. The references above are found in *Ante-Nicene Fathers,* ed. Roberts and Donaldson: Justin Martyr, *The First Apology* 14 and 18, 1:167, 169; Irenaeus, *Against Heresies* 3.12.7, 15; 3.14.1; 4.23.1; 3.9.2; 2.33.1–4; 4.20.8–12, 1:432, 436, 437, 494, 409–10, 490ff.; Tatian, *Address to the Greeks* 18, 2:73.
8. The passages from Clement and Origen come from ibid., 2:258–59, 458, 435; 4:416–17, 583, 389–90, 415, 546, 426, and 429, as follows: Clement of Alexandria, *The Instructor* 2.9; *The Stromata, or Miscellanies* 5.9 and 4.22; Origen, *Against Celsus* 1.48 (This chapter is included in Appendix B), 6.21–23; *A Letter from Origen to Africanus* 10; *Against Celsus* 1.46, 5.9, 1.66, and 2.1.
9. The principal references to dreams in Tertullian's works are found in ibid., 3:37, 558, 343, 609–10, 699ff., and 221ff., as follows: *The Apology* 23; *On the Resurrection of the Flesh* 18; *The Five Books Against Marcion* 3.25; *Against Praxeas* 14; *The Passion of the Holy Martyrs Perpetua and Felicitas;* and *A Treatise on the Soul* 42–49 (These chapters are included in Appendix A).
10. Ibid., 5:266.
11. S. Gregorii Nysseni, *De Vita S. Gregorii Thaumaturgi,* J. P. Migne, *Patrologiae Graecae* (Paris, 1862), vol. 46, cols. 911–13.
12. The material in this section comes from *Ante-Nicene Fathers,* ed. Roberts and Donaldson, 5:375, 290, 338, 312, 473–74, 271–72; 6:79, 128–29, 263, and 291, as follows: Cyprian,

Epistles 68.10, 9.4, 53.5, 33.1; *Treatise VII On Mortality* 19–20; Pontius, the Deacon, *The Life and Passion of Cyprian, Bishop and Martyr* 12–13; Introductory Notice to Dionysius, Bishop of Alexandria; Julius Africanus, *Events in Persia; The Genuine Acts of Peter* (Bishop of Alexandria); Alexander, Bishop of Alexandria, *Epistle on the Arian Heresy* 1.1.

13. These materials are found in ibid., 5:204ff., 177ff., 242ff.; 6:406ff., 418, 436, 426; 7:51–52, 73, 240–41, 318ff., as follows: Hippolytus, *Treatise on Christ and Anti-Christ* 2ff.; Fragment from the *Commentary on Daniel* 1–3; *A Discourse by the Most Blessed Hippolytus, Bishop and Martyr, on the End of the World, and on Anti-Christ, and on the Second Coming of Our Lord Jesus Christ* 1ff.; Introductory Notice to Arnobius; Arnobius, *Against the Heathen* 1.24, 2.7, 1.46; Lactantius, *The Divine Institutes* 2.8, 3.6; *The Epitome of the Divine Institutes* 45ff.; and *Of the Manner in Which the Persecutors Died,* 44ff.

Chapter 6

1. Hans Lietzmann, *A History of the Early Church* (Cleveland: World, 1961), 3:75.
2. *Lactantius, Of the Manner in Which the Persecutors Died,* 44, *The Ante-Nicene Fathers,* ed. Alexander Roberts and James Donaldson (Grand Rapids: Eerdmans, 1951), 7:318. Unless otherwise noted, further references to the fathers are found in *A Select Library of the Nicene and Post-Nicene Fathers* (Grand Rapids: Eerdmans, various dates).
3. Eusebius, *Church History* 9.9.
4. Eusebius, *The Life of Constantine* 1:28-30.
5. Louis Duchesne, *Early History of the Christian Church* (London: John Murray, 1931), 2:47–48.
6. Socrates, *Ecclesiastical History* 1.2, 17; Sozomen, *Ecclesiastical History* 1.3; 2.1.
7. Eusebius, *Church History* 4.7; 7.7; 5.28.
8. Socrates, *Ecclesiastical History* 4.26, 30; 6.8.
9. Theodoret, *Ecclesiastical History* 5.35; 6.
10. Sozomen, *Ecclesiastical History* 2.3; 7.5.
11. Lietzmann, *History,* 3:80ff.
12. Ladislas Farago, *Patton: Ordeal and Triumph* (New York: Dell, 1965), 254.
13. Lietzmann, *History,* 234, 286–87.
14. Athanasius, *Festal Letter* 13.7; *History of the Arians* 8.75.
15. Athanasius, *Against the Heathen* 2.31.5, 33.3.
16. Athanasius, *Life of St. Antony* 34.
17. Gregory of Nyssa, *On the Making of Man* 13; quotations from pars. 10, 12, and 17. (This chapter is included in the appendix.)
18. Gregorii Nysseni, *In Quadraginta Martyres,* J.-P. Migne, *Patrologiae Graecae* (Paris, 1862), vol. 46, cols. 783–86.
19. S. Gregorii Nysseni, *De Vita S. Gregorii Thaumaturgi;* J.-P. Migne, *Patrologiae Graecae,* vol. 46 (Paris, 1862), cols. 911–13. Also told in *Ante-Nicene Fathers,* ed. Roberts and Alexander, 6:7.
20. Basilii Magni, *Commentarium in Isaiam Prophetam,* Prooemium 6–7, J.-P. Migne, *Patrologiae Graecae,* vol. 30 (Paris, 1888), cols. 127–30.
21. Saint Basil the Great, Letter 283, To a widow; *The Hexaemeron,* Homily 1.1; *On the Spirit* 5.12; 26.62.
22. Saint Basil the Great, Letter 2, Basil to Gregory, 6; Letter 210, To the notables of Neo-Caesarea, 6.
23. Gregorii Theologi, *Carminum,* Liber 2, 994–95, 98; J.-P.Migne, *Patrologiae Graecae,* vol. 37 (Paris, 1862), cols. 1449–50.
24. Ibid., 930–33, lines 229–84 (cols. 1367–74).
25. Ibid., 92, lines 5–6 (cols. 1445–46).
26. Ibid., 844–45, lines 7–29 (cols. 1255–56).
27. Ibid., 992–93, lines 4–5 (cols. 1447–48).
28. Ibid., 822–23, lines 805–10 (cols. 1225–26).
29. Ibid., Liber 1, 608–9, lines 209–12 (cols. 943–44).
30. Gregory Nazianzen, Oration 43, *The Panegyric on S. Basil* 71–72.
31. *Nicene and Post-Nicene Fathers* (Grand Rapids: Eerdmans, n.d.), 2d ser., 7:iv–v.
32. Chrysostom, *Commentary on Acts* 5.1.
33. Ibid., 34.6; *Homilies on Matthew* 4.10–11, 18; 5.5.

34. Ibid., 4.18; 86.1; 53.6; 8.4; 9.5; 12.3.
35. Chrysostom, *Commentary on Acts* 39.2; 49.1–2.
36. *Homilies on Romans* 24 (v. 14); 12 (v. 13); *Homilies on Matthew* 53.6.
37. Joannis Chrysostomi, *Homiliae in Genesin*, 36 and 63, J.-P. Migne, *Patrologiae Graecae* (Paris, 1863), vol. 53, cols. 332–35; vol. 54, cols. 541–49.
38. Chrysostom, *Commentary on Acts* 22; *Homilies on Second Corinthians* 26.1ff.
39. Chrysostom, *Homilies on Matthew* 12.3.
40. *The Works of Sir Thomas Browne*, ed. Charles Sayle (Edinburgh: John Grant, 1912), 3:553.
41. Duchesne, *Early History*, vol. 3 (1938), 203.
42. Augustine Fitzgerald, "Concerning Dreams," *The Essays and Hymns of Synesius of Cyrene* (London: Oxford University Press, 1930), 332.
43. Ibid., pp. 345–46.
44. Ambrose, Letter 51, 14.
45. Ambrose, *On the Decease of Satyrus*, Book 1, 72–73.
46. Ambrose, Letter 22; Augustine, *The Confessions* 9 (7).16; *The City of God* 22.8.
47. Ambrose, *On the Holy Spirit* 2.5.37; 2.10.101–6; *Letter 16*.
48. Ambrose, *Duties of the Clergy* 2.10.54–55; 2.16.82ff.; *De Joseph Patriarcha* 2.7–8; 3.9ff., 485–88; J.-P. Migne, *Patrologiae Latinae*, vol. 14 (Paris, 1882), cols. 675–78.
49. Ambrose, *On the Decease of Satyrus*, Book 2 (*On Belief in the Resurrection*), 100.
50. Augustine, *On the Trinity* 11.4.7.
51. The references to Augustine's psychology of perception and parapsychological experiences are scattered throughout his writings. Most important theoretically are his discussions on the nature of human beings in his book *On the Trinity*, where he sees in a human being's inner diversity and unity an archetype of the nature of God. Discussions are found in this work in Book 2, 5.9, 6.11, 13.23, and 18.34; Book 3, 1.4–11.26; Book 4, 17.22, 21.30ff.; Book 8, 7.11; Book 11, 4.7, 5.8–9, 8.13–11.18; Book 12, 15.24; Book 15, 12.21–22, 13.22. In addition, in Book 3 of Augustine's *Literal Commentary on Genesis*, he presents a complete discussion of his psychology, together with his theory of angels, and in Book 12 he discusses ideas about different kinds of visions in relation to modes of revelation (*De Genesi ad Litteram*, J.-P. Migne, *Patrologiae Latinae*, vol. 34 [Paris, 1887]). Shorter discussions are found in Letter 9, To Nebridius, and Letter 159, To Evodius. There is even one reference to the relation between dreams and providence in his earliest Christian work, *The Soliloquies* 2.10ff. This belief is found from the earliest to the latest of his works, and it is essential to his teaching.
52. *On Care to Be Had for the Dead* 12.
53. *The Divination of Demons* 5.9 (New York: Fathers of the Church, 1955), 27:430.
54. Letter 159, To Evodius, 2ff.; *The City of God* 11.2.
55. *The Confessions* 3.19, 5.17, 6.23, 8.30.
56. Letters 9 and 159; Letter 227; *The City of God* 4.26 and 22.23.
57. Jerome, Letter 22, To Eustochium, 30.
58. Eusebii Hieronymi, *Commentariorum in Jeremiam Prophetam* 4.23; J.-P. Migne, *Patrologiae Latinae*, vol. 24 (Paris, 1863), cols. 858–61.
59. Eusebii Hieronymi, *Commentariorum in Isaiam Prophetam* 65; J.-P. Migne, *Patrologiae Latinae*, vol. 24 (Paris, 1863), cols. 656–57.
60. Eusebii Hieronymi, *Commentariorum in Epistolam ad Galatos* 1; J.-P. Migne, *Patrologiae Latinae*, vol. 26 (Paris, 1884), col. 353.
61. Jerome, Letter 57, To Pammachius, 6; *The Perpetual Virginity of Blessed Mary* 4, 5, 7; Letter 125, To Rusticus, 2; Letter 41, To Marcella, 1. Also, Eusebii Hieronymi, *Commentariorum in Ezechielem Prophetam* 3, 8.2ff.; *Commentariorum in Danielem Prophetam* 2.1ff.; J.-P. Migne, *Patrologiae Latinae* vol. 25 (Paris, 1884), cols. 77ff., 498ff.
62. *The Life of St. Hilarion* 6ff.
63. *The Apology Against the Books of Rufinus* 1.30–31, 3.32; Rufinus, *Apology* 1.11.
64. William Harris Stahl, *Macrobius: Commentary on the Dream of Scipio* (New York: Columbia University Press, 1952), 9ff., 60ff.
65. Ibid., 87ff.
66. Sulpicius Severus, *The Life of Saint Martin* 3, 5–6.
67. Letter 2, To the Deacon Aurelius.

68. Joannis Cassiani, *Collatio* 22, *De Nocturnis Illusionibus,* J.-P. Migne, *Patrologiae Latinae* vol. 49 (Paris, 1874), cols. 1217–42.
69. Not in the Confraternity-Douay Version or the new Jerusalem translation. The Bible Gregory read was the Latin translation by Jerome, the Vulgate, on which the scholarly, long-used, and often-consulted Douay Version was based. In it, as we have noted, the Hebrew word for soothsaying was given two very different meanings by Jerome. In three places he mistranslated the Hebrew. In 2 Chronicles 33:6 his incorrect rendition is still in use in the Confraternity-Douay Version of the Bible.

    This word (*anan*) occurs ten times in the Old Testament. In most cases in the current versions it is simply translated "soothsayer or soothsaying," although the words *witch, sorcerer, magic,* and *diviner* are also variously used, as well as "observer of times" in the King James Version.

    In Deuteronomy 18:14; 2 Kings 21:6; Isaiah 2:6; 57:3; and Jeremiah 27:9 where the word is used alongside of "prophet," "diviner," "dreamer" and "sorcerer," Jerome translated it quite correctly as augur or augury (*auguror, augur*) which included the ideas of interpreting the hum of insects, the whisper of leaves, the flight of birds, and of divining by lightning and by the entrails of sacred birds and animals. In Micah 5:11 he translated it as "evil-doing" (*maleficium*). And in Judges 9:37, where it designates one of the places from which Abimelech's soldiers are approaching, generally called the "Diviners' Oak" in current translations, he rendered the Hebrew compound by the phrase "the oak which looks backward" (*quae respicit quercuum*).

    But when Jerome came to the statement of the Law in Leviticus 19:26 and Deuteronomy 18:10, and the direct negative valuation of these practices in 2 Chronicles 33:6, he changed the meaning of the word *anan*. He replaced the verb meaning "to practice augury or soothsaying" (*auguror*) with the phrase "to observe dreams" (*observo somnia*). This direct mistranslation was in authoritative use throughout the Middle Ages, and it has not yet been completely eliminated (Eusebius Hieronymus, *Divinae Bibliothecae: Pars Prima,* J.-P. Migne, *Patrologiae Latinae,* vol. 28 [Paris, 1889], cols. 361, 479, 567, 815, 830, 890, 944, 1105, 1466).
70. St. Gregory the Great, *Dialogues* 4.50 (New York: Fathers of the Church, 1959), 261–62. Also, *Morals: On the Book of Job* 8, 42-43 (Oxford: John Henry Parker, 1844), 448ff.
71. *Dialogues* 1.4, 2.22ff., 4.47ff., in ibid., 16–17, 89ff., 258ff., 262–63.
72. Gregory the Great, *Register of the Epistles* 1.5, 11.45, 9.65; *The Book of Pastoral Rule* 2.5, 3.12.
73. Surahs 96 and 97; also, introduction to *The Meaning of the Glorious Koran,* M. M. Pickthall (New York: Mentor, 1960), x.
74. We do not attempt to do justice to this whole subject, which has been treated intensively by the several authors in *The Dream and Human Societies,* G. E. von Grunebaum and Roger Caillois, eds. (Berkeley: University of California Press, 1966), and in their prior publications.

Chapter 7

1. These experiences were a part of the lives of practically every one of the Orthodox spiritual leaders and were described with wonder and excitement. This is shown by G. P. Fedotov in *A Treasury of Russian Spirituality* (New York: Sheed & Ward, 1948), and it is also discussed in *Writings from the Philokalia on Prayer of the Heart* (London: Faber & Faber, 1954), and other works, as well as finding a place in Russian literature right down to the twentieth century, as in the brilliant stories of Nikolai Leskov, for instance in *Selected Tales* (New York: Farrar, Straus & Cudahy, 1961).
2. C. G. Jung, *Collected Works,* vol. 11 (New York: Random House [Pantheon Books], 1958), 19ff.
3. The general significance of these words is obvious, except for *somme,* which means a nap, a brief sleep, or in this context a dream content that does not persist but vanishes because it simply represents some irritation or condition of the day which has popped up to disturb one's sleep briefly; and *songe,* a dream as we know it, or more particularly, a dream content expressed in symbolic language.
4. Baedae, *Opera Historica* (The Venerable Bede, *Ecclesiastical History of the English Nation*), Book 4.24.

5. Philip Mason Palmer and Robert Pattison More, *The Sources of the Faust Tradition* (New York: Oxford University Press, 1936), 58ff.
6. Pseudo-Augustine, *De spiritu et anima,* published in Migne, *Patrologiae Latinae,* vol. 40 (Paris, 1887), among the works of Augustine.
7. Moses Maimonides, *The Guide for the Perplexed,* trans. M. Friedlander (London: Routledge & Kegan Paul, 1951), 225ff., 234ff.
8. Two of the most interesting works that touch on the medieval thinking about dreams are by Walter Clyde Curry, *Chaucer and the Mediaeval Sciences* (New York: Barnes & Noble, 1960), and by William Harris Stahl, *Macrobius: Commentary on the Dream of Scipio* (New York: Columbia University Press, 1952).
9. St. Thomas Aquinas, *Summa Theologica,* trans. The Fathers of the English Dominican Province (New York: Benzinger Bros., Inc., various dates).
10. In *Science and Sanity* Alfred Korzybski has shown the inadequacy of dealing with this matter simply as black and white. This book is integral to the whole movement in general semantics, which sees that people must be freed from Aristotle's categories. In fact, today's science has been possible only as this release has been accomplished. Korzybski's approach was not a completely intellectual one but arose directly from the facts that modern science was developing. Anyone who wishes to understand the point of view of today's science must understand this idea, which Korzybski developed so fully (*Science and Sanity: An Introduction to Non-Aristotelian Systems and General Semantics* [Lakeville, Conn.: The International Non-Aristotelian Library Publishing Co., 1958.])
11. *Great Books of the Western World,* vol. 19 (*Thomas Aquinas*) (Chicago: *Encyclopaedia Britannica,* 1952), vi.
12. According to Raissa Maritain, the wife of Jacques Maritain, this was far from being the only such experience connected with Aquinas. Knowledge of his death was given in a vision to his old teacher, Albert, who was in Ratisbon at the time and told those around him that he had seen his beloved disciple go.

    The monk who wrote Aquinas's biography was also given a vision of his marvelous gifts in a dream, while Aquinas himself was once instructed in the night by the apostles Peter and Paul and dictated a passage that had been troubling him as if he were reading it from a book. Raissa Maritain, *St. Thomas Aquinas: The Angel of the Schools* (New York: Sheed & Ward, 1955), 76–77, 85–86, 115.
13. This was made official by Pope Leo XIII in 1879. In *Aquinas* (Baltimore: Penguin Books, 1961), 235ff. F. C. Copleston traces the story of the adoption of his ideas, and in my book *Tongue Speaking* (New York: Crossroad,1982), 186ff., I have outlined the position of the Protestant churches.
14. Ralph L. Woods, ed., *The World of Dreams* (New York: Random House, 1947), 149ff.
15. Ibid., 152ff.
16. *The Works of Sir Thomas Browne,* ed. Charles Sayle (Edinburgh: John Grant, 1912), 3:552–53.
17. Woods, *World of Dreams,* 157ff.
18. Quoted by Lancelot Law Whyte in *The Unconscious before Freud* (New York: Basic Books, 1960), 115.
19. Burnett Hillman Streeter, *Reality* (New York: Macmillan, 1927), 331.
20. John Baillie, *Christian Devotion* (New York: Scribner, 1962), 106. Baillie's standard work on the knowledge of God (*Our Knowledge of God* [New York: Scribner, 1939]) is fully consistent with this point of view.
21. Pedro Meseguer, *The Secret of Dreams* (London: Burns & Oates, 1960), 203.
22. Hugh Lynn Cayce, son of the famous psychic Edgar Cayce, has written two appreciative accounts of the place of dreams in the religious life. One is his *Venture Inward* (New York: Harper & Row, 1964), and the other is *Dreams: The Language of the Unconscious,* written with Shane Miller and Tom Clark (Virginia Beach: A.R.E. Press, 1966). The insights on dreams are excellent, but they are not developed in relation to historical Christianity or the ministry today.
23. John A. Sanford, *Gottes Vergessene Sprache* (Zurich: Fascher Verlag, 1966).
24. *The Life of the Rev. John Newton* (Oradell, N.J.: American Tract Society, n.d.), 28ff.
25. A. J. Gordon, *How Christ Came to Church: A Spiritual Autobiography* (New York: Revell, 1895), 63.

26. Ibid., 4ff.
27. Therese of Lisieux, *Autobiography of a Saint,* trans. Ronald Knox (London: Fontana, 1960), 182–83.

Chapter 8

1. In the century or so before Freud there was wide medical interest in dreaming; among the doctors writing on the subject were David Hartley, John Abercrombie, Wilhelm Griesinger, Robert MacNish, A. J. B. de Boismont, S. Weir Mitchell, and August Forel, to name only a few. In France the purely scientific interest in dreams began particularly early and has continued to grow, as also happened later in the rest of Europe and in America. See Ralph L. Woods, *The World of Dreams* (New York: Random House, 1947), 397ff.; also Pedro Meseguer, *The Secret of Dreams* (London: Burns & Oates, 1960), 39ff.
2. The great philosophers from Descartes on added little to the understanding of dreams. They were almost totally absorbed in the study of consciousness, and while most of them had opinions about dreams that were mentioned in passing, none of them treated the subject on its own merits. Their opinions were divided between those who saw the dream as meaningless or merely a reflection of the organic state of the body, and those who saw it as signifying more. Among the followers of Aristotle and Cicero there were Hobbes, Bayle, Leibnitz, Kant, Nietzsche, and Santayana. On the other hand, Locke, Voltaire, Goethe, Schopenhauer, Schelling, Emerson, and Bergson could not dismiss the dream so lightly. In 1901 Bergson wrote:

   > If telepathy influences our dreams, it probably has the best opportunity to manifest itself during very deep sleep. But, I repeat, I can make no pronouncement on this point. I have gone forward with you as far as possible. I stop at the threshold of the mystery. To explore the innermost depths of the unconscious, to work in what I have called earlier the substratum of consciousness, that will be the main task of psychology in the century that is dawning. I do not doubt that wonderful discoveries await it there, as important perhaps as were in the preceding centuries the discoveries in the physical and natural sciences. (Henri Bergson, *The World of Dreams* [New York: Philosophical Library, 1958], 57)

   This was the period in which interest in psychic research and the occult began to grow, as Henry Holt, Frederick Van Eeden, and F. W. H. Myers, to mention but a few of the best-known, pursued the subject which most philosophers had come to ignore. Long forgotten were the significant insights of the previous century, developed by scientists and literary people like Lichtenberg, Herder, G. H. von Schubert, C. Nodier, and Henri Amiel, which often anticipated the investigations of Freud.
3. C. G. Jung, *Collected Works,* vol. 5 (New York: Random House [Pantheon Books], 1956), 16ff.
4. C. G. Jung, *Memories, Dreams, Reflections* (New York: Pantheon Books, 1963), 183.
5. C. G. Jung, *Collected Works,* vol. 8 (1960), 150–51.
6. Ibid., vol. 4 (1961), 330.
7. Ibid., 4:148.
8. Ibid., 8:294.
9. Ibid., vol. 10 (1964), 151–52.
10. Ibid., 10:153.
11. Quoted by Jung, in ibid., vol. 9 (1959), pt. 1, p. 4; from J.-P. Migne, *Patrologiae Latinae,* vol. 40 (Paris, 1882), col. 30.
12. Ibid., 9.1.50. Jung wrote two entire books, *Aion Researches into the Phenomenology of the Self* (Princeton: Princeton University Press, 1979) and *Mysterium Coniunctionis (Collected Works,* vol. 14 [1963]), on the last two of these symbols, the self and the holy marriage. These are among his most complex and interesting works.
13. Particularly 11:65ff. and 9.2.290ff.
14. Jung, *Collected Works,* 8:289.
15. Some of the most fascinating of this material was presented in the seminars on dream analysis given by Jung in 1928, 1929, and 1930, in which he turned for comparative material to many experiences and stories described by Christians, often

from old and neglected sources. The printed reports of these seminars are available in the library of the Jung Institute in Zurich for study by qualified persons.
16. Montague Ullman, Stanley Krippner, and Sol Feldstein, "Experimentally-induced Telepathic Dreams: Two Studies Using EEG-REM Monitoring Technique," *International Journal of Neuropsychiatry* 2, no. 5 (October 1966): 420ff.
17. C. G. Jung, *Collected Works,* 10:450ff.
18. Ibid., 14:255.
19. Ibid., vol. 11 (1958), 348ff.
20. Ibid., 8:286.
21. Ibid., vol. 16 (1954), 156.
22. *Memories, Dreams, Reflections,* 48, 56.
23. Charles Fisher, "Psychoanalytic Implications of Recent Research on Sleep and Dreaming," *Journal of the American Psychoanalytic Association* 13, no. 2 (April 1965): 198. A visit to a sleep laboratory is invaluable in understanding the fascinating discoveries that keep coming from this new science. Here—where we can see the sleepers, the wires taped about their heads, and the electronic machines tracing out the individual rhythms of brain waves and various muscular movements in coordinated patterns—we begin to comprehend the possibilities of dream research. Even the inexperienced eye can quickly detect the distinctive difference between the waking tracing and the various stages of sleep. My own initiation was under the skillful direction of Dr. Paul Naitoh at the Naval Medical Research facility at Point Loma, California, where sleep deprivation is studied. In most aspects, however, the apparatus and methods here are essentially the same as those used in many other laboratories where the content and varied significance of dreams are being studied.
24. Frederick Snyder, "Toward an Evolutionary Theory of Dreaming," *The American Journal of Psychiatry* 123, no. 2 (August 1966): 122–23.
25. The original study by Dement and Kleitman showed that, for persons dreaming four times a night, the mean duration of the first REM period was nine minutes, the second nineteen, the third twenty-four, and the fourth twenty-eight minutes (Fisher, "Implications," 201).
26. Ibid., 213ff. Also, W. David Foulkes, "Dream Reports from Different Stages of Sleep," *Journal of Abnormal and Social Psychology* 65, no. 1 (January 1962): 15, 21ff.
27. REM periods seem to be present at birth in all mammals, and there is good reason to suspect that they go on before birth (Snyder, "Evolutionary Theory," 125). Perhaps Lovejoy is right in his ideas, and the brain of the newborn infant already houses images that are active and ready to be worked on. Arthur O. Lovejoy, *The Revolt Against Dualism* (New York: Norton, 1930).
28. Fisher, "Implications," 247.
29. Ibid., 280.

Chapter 9

1. *Existential Philosophers: Kierkegaard to Merleau-Ponty,* ed. George Alfred Schrader, Jr. (New York: McGraw-Hill, 1967), 423ff.
2. Henri Nouwen, *Beyond the Mirror* (New York: Crossroad, 1990).
3. *The Dream and Human Societies,* ed. G. E. von Grunebaum and Roger Caillois (Berkeley: University of California Press, 1966), 5.
4. The very idea that rational consciousness provides the only method to understand life was given birth in a triple dream experience that occupied Descartes as he slept during the night of November 10, 1619, and brought him from chaos to clarity. L. L. Whyte notes that Descartes as a thinker considered that dreams "expressed a movement of the organs of the sleeper, that they constituted a language translating a desire. But to Descartes as a person the dreams were, as he said, a divine command to devote his inner life to the search for truth."

   This experience, which Whyte describes in some detail,

> marked out the path for the rest of his life. After a few days Descartes regained his normal composure and began to write. Descartes tells us that the triple dream was associated with the supreme question, "What way of life shall I follow?" and that the dream brought him the answer as a compelling command from Heaven or Olympus: Search for the truth, by applying the mathematical method (analytical geometry, in the main) to all other studies. This twin experience, the dream and the discovery of his method, did in fact put an end to his emotional and intellectual confusions and gave a decisive direction to his subsequent life. Olympus had spoken through his unconscious, and Descartes had been lifted out of his past self to acquire a new vision of truth. (Lancelot Law Whyte, *The Unconscious Before Freud* [New York: Basic Books, 1960], 87, 89–90)

Jungian analyst, Marie Louise von Franz had discussed Descartes' dream in depth in *Timeless Documents of the Soul* (Evanston, Ill.: Northwestern University Press, 1968), 55–147.

5. C. G. Jung, *Memories, Dreams, Reflections* (New York: Pantheon Books, 1963), 351–52.
6. Literature from the Renaissance to the present abounds in dreams, which are seen as either a reflection of the state of one's personality or as an intrusion from beyond or from a deeper level of one's being. Dante, Chaucer, Shakespeare, Rabelais, Milton, Tolstoy, Goethe, and Dickens are but a few who based incidents or whole stories on dreams. *Dr. Jekyll and Mr. Hyde* came from a dream of Stevenson's; Mary Shelley wrote *Frankenstein* on the inspiration of a dream. The influence of dreams and the unconscious in the theater today is the subject of an interesting work by W. David Sievers, *Freud on Broadway.* In *Demian* Hermann Hesse wrote of dreams as a profound and integral part of his own life story. This subject alone deserves an entire book.
7. John A Sanford, ed., *Fritz Kunkel: Selected Writings* (New York: Paulist, 1984), 42ff.

Bibliography

Abell, Arthur M. *Talks with Great Composers*. New York: Philosophical Library, 1955.

Adler, Gerhard, and Aniela Jaffe. *C. G. Jung: Letters*. Princeton: Princeton University Press, 1979.

Aeschylus (Plays). Translated by Lewis Campbell. London: Oxford University Press (Humphrey Milford), 1912.

Alex, William. "Dreams—The Unconscious and Analytical Therapy." Paper presented December 4–6, 1970, at the C. G. Jung Institute, San Francisco.

The Anchor Bible. Garden City, N.Y.: Doubleday, various dates.

The Ante-Nicene Fathers. "Tertullian" (vol. 3, pp. 223–27), "Origen" (vol. 4, pp. 416–17). Grand Rapids: Eerdmans, various dates.

Apuleius. *The Golden Ass*. Translated by Robert Graves. New York: Pocket Books, 1958.

Aquinas, St. Thomas. *The "Summa Theologica."* Translated by The Fathers of the English Dominican Province. New York: Benziger Brothers, various dates.

Aristotle. *The Basic Works of Aristotle*. Edited by Richard McKeon. New York: Random House, 1941.

———. *On the Soul, Parva Naturalia, and On Breath*. Translated by W. S. Hett. Cambridge: Harvard University Press, 1957.

Arndt, W. F., and F. W. Gingrich. *A Greek-English Lexicon of the New Testament*. Chicago: University of Chicago Press, 1952.

Artemidorus (Artemidorus Daldianus). *The Interpretation of Dreams*. Translated by Robert Wood. 10th ed. London, 1690.

Augros, Robert, and George Stanciu. *The New Biology*. Boston: Shambala, 1988.

Augustine. *Treatises on Marriage and Other Subjects*. Translated by Ruth Wentworth Brown. New York: Fathers of the Church, 1955.

Aumuller, Anneliese. "Dreams in Nazi Germany." *Psychological Perspectives*, Spring 1978, 13.

Avens, Robert. *Imagination Is Reality*. Irving, Tex.: Spring Publications, 1980.

Babylonian Talmud. Translated by Michael L. Rodkinson. 2d ed. New York: New Talmud Publishing Co., 1901.

Baedae. *Opera Historica* (The Venerable Bede, *Ecclesiastical History of the English Nation*). Translated by J. E. King. Cambridge: Harvard University Press, 1954.

Baillie, John. *Christian Devotion*. New York: Scribner, 1962.

———. *Our Knowledge of God*. New York: Scribner, 1939.

Bakan, David. *Sigmund Freud and the Jewish Mystical Tradition*. Princeton: D. Van Nostrand Co., 1958.

Baldwin, Christina. *Life's Companion: Journal Writing as a Spiritual Quest.* New York: Bantam, Doubleday, Dell, 1990.
Bass, Virginia, ed. *An Anthology: Dreams Can Point the Way.* Sugar Land, Tex.: Miracle House Books, 1984.
Begley, Sharon. "The Stuff That Dreams Are Made of." *Newsweek,* August 14, 1989, 41.
Bennet, E. A. *C. J. Jung.* New York: Dutton, 1962.
Bergson, Henri. *The World of Dreams.* New York: Philosophical Library, 1958.
Berne, Eric. *Games People Play.* New York: Grove, 1964.
Bingham, John P. *Inner Treasure.* Pecos, N.M.: Dove, 1989.
Birkhauser, Peter. *Light from Darkness: The Paintings of Peter Birkhauser.* Basel, Boston, and Stuttgart: Birkhauser Verlag, 1980.
Bosnak, Robert. *Dreaming of an AIDS Patient.* Boston: Shambala, 1989.
Breuer, Joseph, and Sigmund Freud. *Studies in Hysteria.* Boston: Beacon, 1961.
Bro, Harmon H. *Dreams in the Life of Prayer.* New York: Harper & Row, 1970.
Brown, Eugene M. *Dreams, Visions and Prophecies of Don Bosco.* New Rochelle, N.Y.: Don Bosco Publications, 1986.
Brown, Francis, S. R. Driver, and Charles A. Briggs. *A Hebrew and English Lexicon of the Old Testament.* Oxford: Clarendon Press, 1907.
Brown, R. A., and R. G. Luckcock. "Dreams, Daydreams, and Discovery." *Journal of Chemical Education* 55, no. 11 (November 1978).
Burhmann, M. Vera. *Living in Two Worlds.* Cape Town, South Africa: Human & Rousseau, 1984.
Burtt, Edwin A. *Types of Religious Philosophy.* New York: Harper & Brothers, 1951.
Campbell, Joseph. *The Hero with a Thousand Faces.* New York: Meridian Books, 1949.
Canale, Andres. *Masters of the Heart.* New York: Paulist Press, 1978.
———. *Understanding the Human Jesus.* New York: Paulist Press, 1985.
Caprio, Betsy, and Thomas Hedberg. *At a Dream Workshop.* New York: Paulist Press, 1987.
Cartwright, Rosalind D. *Night Life—Explorations in Dreaming.* Englewood Cliffs, N.J.: Prentiss-Hall, 1977.
Carus, Karl Gustav. *Psyche: zur Entwicklungsgeschichte der Seele.* Pforzheim: Flammer and Hoffman, 1846.
Cayce, Edgar. *On Dreams.* New York: Warner Paperback Library, 1968.
Cayce, Hugh Lynn. *Venture Inward.* New York: Harper & Row, 1964.
Cayce, Hugh Lynn, Tom C. Clark, and Shane Miller. *Dreams: The Language of the Unconscious.* Virginia Beach: A.R.E. Press, 1966.
Cherry, Lawrence. "A New Vision of Dreams," *New York Times Magazine,* July 3, 1977.
Cicero. *De Senectute, De Amicitia, De Divinatione.* Translated by William Armistead Falconer. Cambridge: Harvard University Press, 1964.
Cirlot, J. E. *A Dictionary of Symbols.* New York: Philosophical Library, 1962.
Clift, Jean Dalby, and Wallace B. Clift. *The Hero Journey in Dreams.* New York: Crossroad, 1988.
Clift, Wallace B. *Jung and Christianity.* New York: Crossroad, 1982.
Copleston, F. C. *Aquinas.* Baltimore: Penguin, 1961.
Corriere, Richard, and Joseph Hart. *The Dream Makers.* New York: Funk & Wagnalls, 1977.
Coukoulis, Peter. *Guru, Psychotherapist, and Self.* Marina del Ray, Calif.: Devorss, 1976.

Covitz, Joel. *Visions of the Night: A Study of Jewish Dream Interpretation.* Boston: Shambala, 1990.

Cruden, Alexander. *Cruden's Complete Concordance to the Old and New Testaments.* New York: Holt, Rinehart & Winston, 1949.

Curry, Walter Clyde. *Chaucer and the Mediaeval Sciences.* New York: Barnes & Noble, 1960.

Cutten, George Barton. *The Psychological Phenomena of Christianity.* New York: Scribner, 1908.

Davies, Paul. *God and the New Physics.* New York: Simon and Schuster, 1983.

de Becker, Raymond. *The Understanding of Dreams.* New York: Hawthorne, 1968.

Delitzsch, Franz. *A System of Biblical Theology.* Edinburgh: T.& T. Clark, 1867.

Dermenghem, Emile. *Muhammad and the Islamic Tradition.* Translated by Jean M. Watt. New York: Harper & Brothers, 1958.

de Vries, Ad. *Dictionary of Symbols and Imagery.* Amsterdam: North Holland Publishing Co., 1984.

The Dialogues of Plato. Translated by B. Jowett. 4th ed., rev. London: Clarendon Press, 1953.

Diamond, Edwin. "The Most Terrifying Psychic Experience Known to Man." *New York Times Magazine,* December 7, 1969, 54.

Dodds, E. R. *The Greeks and the Irrational.* Boston: Beacon, 1957.

———. *Pagan and Christian in an Age of Anxiety.* Cambridge: Cambridge University Press, 1965.

Doldnick, Edward. "What Dreams Are (Really) Made Of." *The Atlantic* 266, no. 1 (July 1990).

Donington, Robert. *Wagner's "Ring" and Its Symbols.* New York: St. Martin's Press, 1963.

Dourley, John P. *The Illness That We Are.* Toronto: Inner City Books, 1984.

Dreams: A Key to Your Secret Self. New York: Dell, 1965.

Dreamworks—An Interdisciplinary Quarterly 1, no. 1 (Spring 1980).

"Dreams and History," *MD Medical Newsmagazine,* 9, no. 12 (December 1965), 167ff.

Duchesne, Louis. *Early History of the Christian Church.* London: John Murray, vol. 2 (1931), vol. 3 (1938).

Dunne, J. W. *An Experiment with Time.* New York: Macmillan, 1938.

Edinger, Edward. *Ego and Archetype.* New York: Putnam, 1972.

Eliade, Mircea. *Images & Symbols.* New York: Sheed & Ward, 1969.

———. *Myths, Dreams and Mysteries.* New York: Harper & Brothers, 1960.

Ellis, Havelock. *The World of Dreams.* London: Constable, 1915.

Existential Philosophers: Kierkegaard to Merleau-Ponty. Edited by George Alfred Schrader, Jr. New York: McGraw-Hill, 1967.

Faraday, Ann. *The Dream Game.* New York: Harper & Row, 1974.

———. *Dream Power.* New York: Berkeley Medallion Books, 1972.

Farago, Ladislas. *Patton: Ordeal and Triumph.* New York: Dell, 1965.

Fedotov, G. P. *A Treasury of Russian Spirituality.* New York: Sheed & Ward, 1948.

Fisher, Charles, M.D. "Psychoanalytic Implications of Recent Research on Sleep and Dreaming," *Journal of the American Psychoanalytic Association* 13, no. 2 (April 1965), 197–303.

Fitzgerald, Augustine. *The Essays and Hymns of Synesius of Cyrene.* London: Oxford University Press (H. Milford), 1930.

Five Comedies of Aristophanes. Translated by Benjamin Bickley Rogers. Garden City, N.Y.: Doubleday, 1955.

Foulkes, David. *The Psychology of Sleep.* New York: Scribner, 1966.

Foulkes, W. David. "Dream Reports from Different Stages of Sleep." *Journal of Abnormal and Social Psychology* 65, no. 1 (January 1962), 14–25.
Fox, Robin Lane. *Pagans and Christians.* San Francisco: Harper & Row, 1986.
Franz, Marie-Louise von. *Apuleius' Golden Ass.* Zurich: Spring Publications, 1970.
———. *C. G. Jung—The Myth in Our Time.* New York: Putnam, 1975.
———. *On Dreams and Death.* Boston: Shambala, 1986.
Franz, Marie Louise von, and Fraser Boa. *The Way of the Dream.* Toronto: Weindrose Films, 1988.
Freud, Sigmund. *Beyond the Pleasure Principle.* New York: Bantam, 1959.
———. *Civilization and Its Discontents.* Garden City: Doubleday, 1930.
———. *Collected Papers.* New York: Basic Books, 1959.
———. *The Future of an Illusion.* Garden City: Doubleday, 1953.
———. *A General Introduction to Psychoanalysis.* New York: Washington Square Press, 1960.
———. *The Interpretation of Dreams.* New York: Basic Books, 1955.
———. *Moses and Monotheism.* New York: Vintage Books, 1959.
———. *Totum and Taboo.* New York: Random House, 1946.
Friedlander, Paul. *Plato: An Introduction.* Translated by Hans Meyerhoff. New York: Harper & Row, for the Bollingen Foundation, 1964.
Gackenbach, Jayne. Lucidity Letter 1982–84. Department of Psychology, University of Northern Iowa, Cedar Falls, Iowa.
Gay, Peter. *Freud: A Life for Our Time.* New York: Norton, 1988.
Ghiselin, Brewster, ed. *The Creative Process: A Symposium.* Berkeley: University of California Press, 1952.
Gillespie, George. "From Lucid Dream to Dreamless Sleep." Paper presented at the international conference of the Association for the Study of Dreams. Charlottesville, Va.: June 20, 1985.
———. "The Language of Mysticism," *The Indian Journal of Theology* 32, nos. 3, 4 (July–December 1983).
———. "Ordinary Dreams, Lucid Dreams and Mystical Experience," a talk given to the Association for the Study of Dreams, Charlottesville, Va., June 19, 1985.
Gordon, A. J. *How Christ Came to Church: A Spiritual Autobiography.* New York: Revell, 1895.
Great Books of the Western World. Chicago: *Encyclopaedia Britannica,* 1952.
Gregory the Great. *Dialogues.* Translated by Odo John Zimmerman. New York: Fathers of the Church, 1959.
———. *Morals: On the Book of Job.* Oxford: John Henry Parker, 1844.
Grenshaw, James. *Telephone Between Worlds.* Los Angeles: DeVorss, 1950.
Grunebaum, G. E. von, and Roger Caillois, eds. *The Dream and Human Societies.* Berkeley: University of California Press, 1966.
Hamilton, Mary. *Incubation (or the Cure of Disease in Pagan Temples and Christian Churches).* London: Simpkin, Marshall, Hamilton, Kent & Company, 1906.
Hannah, Barbara. *Jung—His Life and Work.* New York: Putnam, 1976.
Harding, M. Esther. *Journey Into Self.* New York: David McKay, 1956.
———. *The Way of All Women.* New York: Longmans, Green and Co., 1933.
———. *Woman's Mysteries, Ancient and Modern.* New York: Putnam, 1971.
Harnack, Adolf. *History of Dogma.* Translated by James Miller. London: Williams & Norgate, 1912.
Harrison, Jane. *Prolegomena to the Study of Greek Religion.* New York: Meridian Books, 1960.
Hartmann, Eduard von. *Philosophy of the Unconscious.* New York: Harcourt, Brace & Co., 1931.

Hastings, James, ed. *Dictionary of the Bible*. New York: Scribner, 1943.
———. *Encyclopedia of Religion and Ethics*. Vols. 1–13. New York: Scribner, n.d.
Hatch, Edwin. *The Influence of Greek Ideas on Christianity*. New York: Harper & Brothers, 1957.
Heaney, John J. *The Sacred and the Psychic*. New York: Paulist Press, 1984.
Heidel, Alexander. *The Gilgamesh Epic and Old Testament Parallels*. Chicago: University of Chicago Press, 1949.
Heisenberg, Werner. *Physics and Philosophy: The Revolution in Modern Science*. New York: Harper & Row, 1958.
Heisig, James W. *Imago Dei*. London: Associated University Presses, 1979.
Hendricks, Lois Lindsey. *Discovering My Biblical Dream Heritage*. San Jose, Calif.: Resource Publications, 1989.
Herodotus. *Histories*. Translated by A. D. Godley. London: William Heinemann, 1921–28.
Hesiod. *Works*. Translated by Hugh G. Evelyn-White. Cambridge: Harvard University Press, 1950.
Hippocrates (Works). Translated by W. H. S. Jones. Cambridge: Harvard University Press, 1957.
Hill, Brian, ed. *Gates of Horn and Ivory*. New York: Taplinger, 1967.
Hillman, James. *Emotion*. Evanston, Ill.: Northwestern University Press, 1964.
———. *Insearch*. New York: Scribner, 1967.
Hobson, J. Allan. *The Dreaming Brain*. New York: Basic Books, 1988.
Hostie, Raymond. *Religion and the Psychology of Jung*. New York: Sheed & Ward, 1957.
Huyghe, Patrick. "Mind-Group Dreaming." *Omni*, December 1983, 24.
Iliad of Homer. Translated by Theodore Alois Buckley. Philadelphia: David McKay, 1896.
The Interlinear Greek New Testament. Chicago: Follett, 1960.
The Interpreter's Bible. New York: Abingdon, 1951–57.
The Interpreter's Dictionary of the Bible. New York: Abingdon, 1962.
Jacobi, Jolande, ed. *C. G. Jung: Psychological Reflections: A New Anthology of His Writings*. Princeton: Princeton University Press, 1979.
Jacobsohn, Helmut, Marie-Louise von Franz, and Siegmund Hurwitz. *Timeless Documents of the Soul*. Evanston, Ill.: Northwestern University Press, 1968.
Jaffe, Aniela. *Apparitions: An Archetypal Approach to Death, Dreams and Ghosts*. Irving, Tex.: Spring Publications, 1979.
———. *From the Life and Work of C. G. Jung*. New York: Harper & Row, 1971.
James, William. *The Varieties of Religious Experience*. New York: Longmans, Green & Company, 1925.
Jastrow, Morris. *A Gentle Cynic: Being a Translation of the Book of Koheleth, Commonly Known as Ecclesiastes*. Philadelphia: Lippincott, 1919.
Jerome. *Dogmatic and Polemical Works*. Translated by John N. Hritzu. Washington, D.C.: Catholic University of America Press, 1965.
The Jewish Encyclopedia. New York: Funk and Wagnalls, 1925.
Joannis Saresberiensis (John of Salisbury). *Opera Omnia* (vol. 3, *Polycratici Libri*). Oxonii: Apud J. H. Parker, 1848.
Johnson, Robert. *He!* King of Prussia, Pa.: Religious Publishing Co., 1974.
———. *She!* King of Prussia, Pa.: Religious Publishing Co., 1976.
Josephus (Works). Vol. 1, *The Life, Against Apion*. Translated by H. St. J. Thackeray. Cambridge: Harvard University Press, 1956.
Jung, C. G. *Aion: Researches into the Phenomenology of the Self*. Princeton: Princeton University Press, 1979.

———. *Collected Works.* Princeton: Princeton University Press.
Vol. 1, *Psychiatric Studies,* 1979.
Vol. 2, *Experimental Researches,* 1979.
Vol. 3, *The Psychogenesis of Mental Disease,* 1979.
Vol. 4, *Freud and Psychoanalysis,* 1979.
Vol. 5, *Symbols of Transformation,* 1979.
Vol. 6, *Psychological Types,* 1979.
Vol. 7, *Two Essays on Analytical Psychology,* 1979.
Vol. 8, *The Structure and Dynamics of the Psyche,* 1979.
Vol. 9, pt. 1, *The Archetypes and the Collective Unconscious,* 1979.
Vol. 10, *Civilization in Transition,* 1979.
Vol. 11, *Psychology and Religion: West and East,* 1979.
Vol. 12, *Psychology and Alchemy,* 1979.
Vol. 13, *Alchemical Studies,* 1979.
Vol. 14, *Mysterium Coniunctionis,* 1979.
Vol. 15, *The Spirit in Man, Art, and Literature,* 1979.
Vol. 16, *The Practice of Psychotherapy,* 1979.
Vol. 17, *The Development of Personality,* 1979.
Vol. 18, *The Symbolic Life: Miscellaneous Writings,* 1979.
Vol. 19, *General Bibliography of Jung's Writings,* 1979.
Vol. 20, *General Index,* 1979.

———. *Dreams.* Princeton: Princeton University Press, 1974.

———. *Memories, Dreams, Reflections.* Recorded and edited by Aniela Jaffe. New York: Pantheon Books, 1963. Princeton: Princeton University Press, 1963.

Kaestner, Erhart. *Mount Athos: The Call from Sleep.* London: Faber & Faber, 1961.

Kelsey, Morton T. *Afterlife: The Other Side of Dying.* New York: Paulist Press, 1979.

———. *Can Christians Be Educated?* Birmingham, Ala.: Religious Education Press, 1977.

———. *Caring: How Do We Love One Another?* New York: Paulist Press, 1982.

———. *The Christian and the Supernatural.* Minneapolis, Minn.: Augsburg, 1976.

———. *Christianity as Psychology: The Healing Power of the Christian Message.* Minneapolis, Minn.: Augsburg, 1986.

———. *Christo-Psychology.* New York: Paulist Press, 1982.

———. *Companions on the Inner Way.* New York: Crossroad, 1983.

———. *Discernment: A Study in Ecstasy and Evil.* New York: Paulist Press, 1978.

———. *Dreams: A Way to Listen to God.* New York: Paulist Press, 1978.

———. *Encounter with God.* New York: Paulist Press, 1987.

———. *Myth, History and Faith.* New York: Paulist Press, 1974.

———. *The Other Side of Silence: A Guide to Christian Meditation.* New York: Paulist Press, 1976.

———. *Prophetic Ministry.* New York: Crossroad, 1982.

———. *Psychology, Medicine & Christian Healing.* San Francisco: Harper & Row, 1988.

———. *Reaching: The Journey to Fulfillment.* San Francisco: Harper & Row, 1989.

———. *Resurrection.* New York: Paulist Press, 1985.

———. *Sacrament of Sexuality.* Warwick, N.Y.: Amity House, 1986.

———. *Tales To Tell.* Pecos, N.M.: Dove, 1981.

———. *Tongue Speaking: The History and Meaning of Charismatic Experience.* New York: Crossroad, 1982.

———. *Transcend.* New York: Crossroad, 1981.

Kerenyi, C. *Asklepios: Archetypal Image of the Physician's Existence.* New York: Pantheon Books, for the Bollingen Foundation, 1959.

Kirsch, Hilde, ed. *The Well-Tended Tree.* New York: Putnam, 1971.

Kirsch, James. *The Reluctant Prophet.* Los Angeles: Sherbourne, 1973.

———. *Shakespeare's Royal Self.* New York: Putnam, 1966.

Kitto, H. D. F. *The Greeks.* Baltimore: Penguin, 1958.

Kleitman, Nathaniel. *Sleep and Wakefulness.* Chicago: University of Chicago Press, 1963.

Kockelmans, Joseph J., ed. *Phenomenology: The Philosophy of Edmund Husserl and Its Interpretation.* Garden City, N.Y.: Doubleday, 1967.

The Koran (commonly called the Alkoran of Mohammed). London: Frederick Warne, n.d.

Korzybski, Alfred. *Science and Sanity: An Introduction to Non-Aristotelian Systems and General Semantics.* Lakeville, Conn.: The International Non-Aristotelian Library Publishing Co., 1958.

Kubie, Lawrence S. "Blocks to Creativity," *International Science and Technology* 42 (June 1965), 74ff.

Kuhn, Thomas S. *The Structure of Scientific Revolutions.* Chicago: University of Chicago Press, 1970.

Kunkel, Fritz. *Creation Continues.* New York: Scribner, 1947.

———. *In Search of Maturity.* New York: Scribner, 1943.

Langland, William. *Piers the Ploughman.* Translated by J. F. Goodridge. Harmondsworth, Middlesex, Eng.: Penguin, 1959.

Laughlin, Tom. *Jungian Psychology.* Vol. 2. Los Angeles: Panarion, 1982.

Lee, Frank. *Do Dreams Mean Anything?* Liguori, Mo.: Liguori Publications, May 22, 1977.

Leskov, Nikolai. *Selected Tales.* New York: Farrar, Straus & Cudahy, 1961.

Lewis, Lloyd. *Myths after Lincoln.* New York: Grosset & Dunlap, 1957.

Lietzmann, Hans. *A History of the Early Church.* Cleveland: World, 1961.

The Life of the Rev. John Newton. Oradell, N.J.: American Tract Society, n.d.

Lindblom, J. *Prophecy in Ancient Israel.* Philadelphia: Fortress, 1962.

Lorris, William, and J. Clopinel (Jean de Meun). *Roman de la Rose.* Translated by J. S. Ellis. London: Dent, 1890.

Lovejoy, Arthur O. *The Revolt Against Dualism.* New York: Norton & Co., 1930.

McGlashan, Alan. *The Savage & Beautiful Country.* Boston: Houghton Mifflin, 1967.

McGuire, William, ed. *The Freud/Jung Letters.* Princeton: Princeton University Press, 1979.

McGuire, William, and R. F. C. Hull. *C. G. Jung Speaking.* Princeton: Princeton University Press, 1977.

Mack, John E. *Nightmares and Human Conflict.* Boston: Little, Brown and Co., 1970.

MacKenzie, Norman. *Dreams and Dreaming.* London: Aldus, 1965.

Mahoney, Maria F. *The Meaning in Dreams and Dreaming.* New York: Citadel, 1970.

Maimonides, Moses. *The Guide for the Perplexed.* Translated by M. Friedlander. London: Routledge & Kegan Paul, 1951.

Maritain, Raissa. *St. Thomas Aquinas: The Angel of the Schools.* New York: Sheed & Ward, 1955.

Melnechuk, Theodore. "The Dream Machine," *Psychology Today,* November 1983, 22.

Meseguer, Pedro, *The Secret of Dreams.* London: Burns & Oates, 1960.

"Mind and Supermind," *Saturday Review,* February 22, 1975, special section, 10–23.

Mitchel, Edgar D. "Consciousness: The Ultimate Enigma." Address given at Notre Dame University, November 16, 1972.

Monick, Eugene. *Phallos: Sacred Image of the Masculine*. Toronto: Inner City Books, 1987.

"The Mystery of Sleep," *Newsweek*, July 13, 1981, 48.

Nouwen, Henri. *Beyond the Mirror*. New York: Crossroad, 1990.

O'Connor, Peter. *Dreams and the Search for Meaning*. New York: Paulist Press, 1986.

O'Donohue, Noel D. *Aristocracy of the Soul: Patrick of Ireland*. Wilmington, Del.: Michael Glazier, 1984.

The Odyssey of Homer. Translated by George Herbert Palmer. Boston: Houghton Mifflin, 1921.

O'Nell, Carl W. *Dreams, Culture, and the Individual*. San Francisco: Chandler & Sharp, 1976.

Ornstein, Robert E. *The Mind Field*. New York: Pocket Books, 1976.

Palmer, Philip Mason, and Robert Pattison More. *The Sources of the Faust Tradition: From Simon Magus to Lessing*. New York: Oxford University Press, 1936.

Panati, Charles. *Supersenses: Our Potential for Parasensory Experience*. New York: New York Times Book Co., 1974.

Patrologiae: Cursus Completus (Latinae et Graecae). Parisiis, Apud Garnier Fratres, Editores, et J.-P. Migne, Successores, various dates (translations by Gerald F. Penny).

Pererius, Benedictus. *De Magia: Concerning the Investigation of Dreams and Concerning Astrological Divinations. Three Books. Against the False and Superstitious Arts*. 1598. (Translation by Elizabeth Shedd.)

Peucer, Gaspar. *Les Devins, ou commentaire des principales sortes de divination*. Anvers, 1584.

Philo (Works). Vol. 5 (*On Dreams: That They are God-Sent*). Translated by F. H. Colson and G. H. Whitaker. Cambridge: Harvard University Press, 1949.

Pickthall, Mohammed Marmaduke. *The Meaning of the Glorious Koran*. New York: New American Library of World Literature, 1960.

Pieper, Josef. *Love and Inspiration: A Study of Plato's Phaedrus*. London: Faber & Faber, 1965.

The Plays of Euripides. Translated from the text of Paley by Edward P. Coleridge. London: G. Bell & Sons, 1913.

Plutarch's Lives (the translation commonly called Dryden's). Revised by A. H. Clough. Boston: Little, Brown & Co., 1872.

Post, Laurens van der. *The Heart of the Hunter*. New York: Wm. Morrow, 1961.

———. *Jung and the Story of Our Time*. New York: Pantheon Books, 1975.

Poulain, A. *The Graces of Interior Prayer: A Treatise on Mystical Theology*. Translated by Leonora L. Yorke Smith. London: Routledge & Kegan Paul, 1957.

Progoff, Ira. *Jung, Synchronicity, and Human Destiny*. New York: Dell, 1973.

Puner, Helen Walker. *Freud: His Life and His Mind*. New York: Dell, 1959.

Ratcliff, A. J. J. *A History of Dreams*. London: Grant Richards, 1923.

Reed, Henry. "Dream Incubation." Unpublished paper, Department of Psychology, Princeton University.

Regush, June V., and Nicholas M. Regush. *Dream Worlds*. New York: New American Library, 1977.

———. *Mind Search*. New York: Berkeley Publishing, 1977.

Reid, Clyde H. *Dreams—Discovering Your Inner Teacher*. Minneapolis: Winston, 1983.

Rexroth, Kenneth. "Classics Revisited—LV: The Works of Herodotus," *Saturday Review* 50, no. 48 (December 2, 1967), 23.

Rhodes, Richard. "You Can Direct Your Dreams." *Parade Magazine*, February 19, 1981, 10.

Rice, Howard. *Reformed Spirituality.* Louisville, Ky.: Westminster/John Knox Press, 1991.
Riffel, Herman H. *Voice of God.* Wheaton, Ill.: Tyndale, 1978.
———. *Your Dreams: God's Neglected Gift.* Lincoln, Va.: A Chosen Book, 1981.
Rohde, Erwin. *Psyche: The Cult of Souls and Belief in Immortality Among the Greeks.* London: Kegan Paul, Trench, Truebner & Co., 1925.
Roheim, Geza. *The Gates of the Dream.* New York: International Universities Press, 1952.
Rosenfeld, Albert. "10,000-to-1 Payoff." *Life* 63, no. 13 (September 29, 1967), 121–28.
Ross, David. *Aristotle.* New York: Barnes & Noble, 1966.
Sacks, Oliver. *Awakenings.* New York: Dutton, 1983.
———. *A Leg to Stand On.* New York: Harper & Row, 1987.
———. *A Man Who Mistook His Wife for a Hat.* New York: Harper & Row, 1987.
Sanford, Agnes. *Dreams Are for Tomorrow.* New York: Lippincott, 1963.
Sanford, John A. *Dreams and Healing.* New York: Paulist Press, 1978.
———. *Evil—The Shadow Side of Reality.* New York: Crossroad, 1981.
———. *God's Forgotten Language.* San Francisco: Harper & Row, 1988.
———. *Gottes Vergessene Sprache.* Zurich, Rascher Verlag, 1966.
———. *The Invisible Partners.* New York: Paulist Press, 1980.
———. *King Saul, The Tragic Hero.* New York: Paulist Press, 1985.
———. *The Kingdom Within.* New York: Harper & Row, 1988.
———. *The Man Who Wrestled with God.* King of Prussia, Pa.: Religious Publishing Co., 1974.
———. *The Strange Trial of Mr. Hyde.* San Francisco: Harper & Row, 1987.
Sanford, John A., ed. *Fritz Kunkel: Selected Writings.* New York: Paulist Press, 1984.
Savary, Louis M., Patricia H. Berne, and Strephon Kaplan Williams. *Dreams and Spiritual Growth.* New York: Paulist Press, 1984.
Sayle, Charles, ed. *The Works of Sir Thomas Browne.* Edinburgh: John Grant, 1912.
Schaer, Hans. *Religion and the Cure of Souls.* New York: Pantheon Books, 1950.
Schary, Jill. *The Cosmo Girl's Dream Book.* The Heart Corporation, 1972.
Schauffler, Robert Haven. *Florestan: The Life and Work of Robert Schumann.* New York: Henry Holt & Co., 1945.
Schwenck, Robert L. *Digging Deep.* Pecos, N.M.: Dove 1979.
Sechrist, Elsie. *Dreams—Your Magic Mirror.* New York: Cowles Education Corp., 1968.
A Select Library of the Nicene and Post-Nicene Fathers of the Christian Church. "Eusebius" (vol. 1), "Athanasius" (vol. 4), "Gregory of Nyssa" (vol. 5, pp. 399–402), "Ambrose" (vol. 10). 1st and 2d ser. Grand Rapids: Eerdmans, various dates.
Serrano, Miguel. *C. G. Jung and Hermann Hesse: A Record of Two Friendships.* New York: Schocken Books, 1966.
Sharp, Daryl. *The Survival Papers: Anatomy of a Midlife Crisis.* Toronto: Inner City Books, 1988.
Sievers, W. David. *Freud on Broadway.* New York: Hermitage House, 1955.
Simpson, David. *A Discourse on Dreams and Night-Visions.* Macclesfield, Eng.: Edw. Bayley, 1791.
Singer, June K. *Boundaries of the Soul.* Garden City: Doubleday, 1972.
———. *The Unholy Bible.* New York: Putnam, 1970.
Slusser, Gerald H. *From Jung to Jesus.* Atlanta: John Knox, 1986.
Snyder, Frederick, M.D. "Toward an Evolutionary Theory of Dreaming." Discussion by William C. Dement, M.D., *The American Journal of Psychiatry* 123, no. 2 (August 1966), 122–42.
Society for Psychical Research, *Proceedings* 10, 1894; *Journal* 34, 1948.

Soth, Connie. *Insomnia—God's Night School.* Old Tappan, N.J.: Power Books, 1989.
Sources Orientales, *Les Songes et Leur Interpretation.* Paris: Editions du Seuil, 1959.
Stahl, William Harris. *Macrobius: Commentary on the Dream of Scipio.* New York: Columbia University Press, 1952.
Stein, Murray. *Jung's Treatment of Christianity.* Wilmette, Ill.: Chiron, 1986.
Strachey, James, ed. *Sigmund Freud, Collected Papers.* New York: Basic Books, 1959.
Strauss, Berthold. *The Rosenbaums of Zell: A Study of a Family.* London: Hamakrik, 1962.
Streeter, Burnett Hillman. *Reality.* New York: Macmillan, 1927.
Suetonius. *Lives of the Caesars.* Translated by J. C. Rolfe. Cambridge: Harvard University Press, 1928.
Sundance Community Dream Journal. Virginia Beach: Atlantic University, Fall 1976—Spring 1977.
Tart, Charles, ed. *Altered States of Awareness: Readings from Scientific American.* San Francisco: Freeman, 1972.
Taylor, Jeremy. *Dream Work.* New York: Paulist Press, 1983.
Tchaikovsky, Modeste. *The Life and Letters of Peter Illich Tchaikovsky.* New York: John Lane, 1906.
Therese of Lisieux. *Autobiography of a Saint.* Translated by Ronald Knox. London: Fontana, 1960.
Thurston, Mark A. *How to Interpret Your Dreams.* Virginia Beach: A.R.E. Press, 1978.
Toben, Bob, and Fred A. Wolfe. *Space-Time and Beyond.* New York: Bantam, 1975.
The Tragedies of Sophocles. Translated by Richard C. Jebb. Cambridge: Cambridge University Press, 1917.
Trillin, Calvin. "A Third State of Existence." *The New Yorker* 41, no. 31 (September 18, 1965), 58–125.
Trombitas, Dezso. *God and Our Dreams.* Los Angeles: Privately printed pamphlet, 1964.
Ullman, Montague, Stanley Krippner, and Sol Feldstein, "Experimentally-induced Telepathic Dreams: Two Studies Using EEG-REM Monitoring Technique," *International Journal of Neuropsychiatry* 2, no. 5 (October 1966), 420–37.
U.S. Public Health Service. *Current Research on Sleep and Dreams* (Pub. no. 1389). Washington, D.C.: U.S. Government Printing Office, 1966.
Walsh, Joseph, M.D. "Galen's Writings and Influences Inspiring Them," *Annals of Medical History* 6 (new Ser.), no. 1 (January 1934), 1-30.
Weaver, Rix. *Spinning on a Dream Thread.* Perth: Wyvern Publications, 1977.
West, Katherine Lee. *Crystallizing Children's Dreams.* Lake Oswego, Ore.: Amata Graphics, 1978.
White, John W. "The Consciousness Revolution," *Saturday Review,* February 22, 1975, 15.
White, Victor. *God and the Unconscious.* Cleveland: World, 1961.
Whittaker, Thomas. *Macrobius: or Philosophy, Science and Letters in the Year 400.* Cambridge: Cambridge University Press, 1923.
Whyte, Lancelot Law. *The Unconscious Before Freud.* New York: Basic Books, 1960.
Wickes, Frances G. *The Inner World of Childhood.* New York: New American Library, 1966.
Wild, John. *Plato's Theory of Man: An Introduction to the Realistic Philosophy of Culture.* New York: Octagon Books, 1964.
Williams, Strephon Kaplan. *Jungian-Senoi Dreamwork Manual.* Berkeley: Journey Press, 1980.

Willis, John R., ed. *The Teachings of the Church Fathers*. New York: Herder & Herder, 1966.
Wolff, Werner. *The Dream—Mirror of Conscience*. New York: Grune & Stratton, 1952.
Works of Flavius Josephus, The. Translated by William Whiston. Philadelphia: Porter & Coates, n.d.
Woods, Ralph L., ed. *The World of Dreams*. New York: Random House, 1947.
Writings from the Philokalia on Prayer of the Heart. Translated by E. Kadloubovsky and G. E. H. Palmer. London: Faber & Faber, 1954.
Xenophon. *The Anabasis*. Translated by J. S. Watson. New York: Harper & Brothers, 1894.
Zeller, Max. *The Dream: The Vision of the Night*. Los Angeles: Analytical Psychology Club, 1975.
Zimmer, Heinrich. *The King and The Corpse*. Princeton: Princeton University Press, 1957.
Zolar's Encyclopedia and Dictionary of Dreams. Garden City, N.Y.: Doubleday, 1963.

Index